STUDENTS' SOLUTIONS MANUAL

for use with

SIXTH CANADIAN

Management Accounting

Hansen Mowen Senkow Pollanen

PREPARED BY
David W. Senkow, University of Regina

THOMSON

™

NELSON

THOMSON

™

NELSON

Contents

MANAGEMENT ACCOUNTING
CANADIAN SIXTH EDITION
SOLUTIONS MANUAL

CHAPTER 1
INTRODUCTION: THE ROLE, HISTORY, AND
DIRECTION OF MANAGEMENT ACCOUNTING

ANSWERS TO ODD-NUMBERED QUESTIONS FOR WRITING AND DISCUSSION

1. A management accounting information system is an information system that uses inputs and processes to produce the outputs needed to satisfy specific management objectives. Inputs are economic events. Processes include the accounting activities of collecting, measuring, storing, analyzing, reporting, and managing information. Outputs include reports on product costs, customer costs, budgets, and performance reports.

3. The three objectives of a management accounting information system are to (1) provide information for costing services, products, and other objects of interest to managers – to assign costs to cost objects; (2) to provide information for planning, controlling, evaluation, and continuous improvement; and (3) to provide information for decision making.

5. This statement is incorrect. The potential benefit to managers from management accounting information is not limited to manufacturing operations. Organizations involved in other types of operations – merchandising or service – also benefit from management accounting information. Management accounting information is essential for effective management of business, not-for-profit, and government organizations. Managers in all of these organizations require information for planning, controlling, and decision-making.

7. Managers and other decision makers use management accounting information for planning, controlling, evaluation, continuous improvement, and other decisions.

9. Continuous improvement is searching for ways to increase the overall efficiency and productivity of activities by reducing waste, increasing quality, and reducing costs.

11. Operational (nonmanagement) workers need management accounting information to make effective operating decisions and to monitor and evaluate the outcomes of their decisions.

13. Performance reports are formal reports that compare actual financial and nonfinancial data with planned data or benchmarks (internal, external, or historical). Performance reports provide managers with signals of the need to take corrective action as part of their controlling activity.

15. Management accounting and financial accounting are usually part of a common accounting system and share many activities and processes. Management accounting reports are often derived from the accounting systems established to support financial accounting reporting requirements – in particular inventory costing for inventory valuation and income measurement. Managers and companies relied on aggregated average cost information about individual products as the basis for most management decisions and management reports followed the financial reporting structure. Often the benefit of more accurate product costs for decision-making didn't offset the incremental cost of producing the information. This was particularly true for companies that had relatively homogeneous products that consumed resources at about the same rate – the average cost information required for financial reporting was good enough.

In recent years, the size of the benefits lost by making decisions on average cost information has increased – products have become more heterogeneous and more detailed information was needed to allow managers to improve quality, productivity, and to reduce costs. Also information technology has decreased the cost of processing information. With increased benefits and reduced costs, more organizations are developing accounting systems that satisfy the needs or financial accounting but also provide better information to managers.

17. Customer value is the difference between what a customer receives (customer realization) and what the customer gives up (customer sacrifice). Focusing on customer value forces managers to consider the entire set of value-chain activities, including what happens after a product is sold. Managers need a broader set of management accounting information than is found in a traditional system (focused on product costing and only a portion of the value-chain activities).

19. The industrial value chain is the linked set of value-creating activities from basic raw materials to the disposal of the final product by end-use customers. Understanding the industrial value chain is critical to understanding a company's strategically important activities. Managers strive to identify the important internal and external linkages and use these linkages to create a competitive advantage.

21. Supply chain management is the management of materials flows beginning with suppliers and their upstream suppliers, moving to production and finishing with the distribution of finished goods to customers and their downstream customers. Supply chain management focuses on the entire industrial value chain because going beyond immediate suppliers and customers may reveal potential beneficial relationships that can be developed for a "win-win" outcome.

23. Time-based competition involves reducing the time to market by compressing design, implementation, and production cycles. A common strategy is to eliminate time spent on nonvalue-added activities. The management accounting system should be able to provide information about the relationship between time reductions and such things as quality and cost on both a projected and realized basis. This information enhances planning, controlling, and decision-making.

25. The controller is a member of the top management group in many organizations. The controller is responsible for the management accounting information system and plays a key role in managing the information used for planning, controlling, and decision-making. The controller is a financial expert and can provide critical advice and insights.

27. Ethical behaviour is choosing actions that are right, proper, and just. Ethical behaviour often requires a sacrifice of some individual self-interest for the well being of others. It is possible to teach ethical behaviour in virtually any course. By considering ethical issues in management accounting, students can become aware of the behaviour that is expected in professional and business settings.

29. The three accounting designations in Canada are the Certified Management Accountant (CMA), the Chartered Accountant (CA), and the Certified General Accountant (CGA). Individuals with any of these designations may practice management accounting with business, not-for-profit, and government organizations. The growing importance of management accounting in today's economic environment is evident by the increased emphasis on management issues and management accounting in the preparation of candidates trying to obtain these accounting designations.

SOLUTIONS TO ODD-NUMBERED EXERCISES, PROBLEMS, AND CASES

EXERCISES

1-1

Item	Category
a.	Surveying customers to assess postpurchase costs	process
b.	Incurrence of postpurchase costs	input
c.	Costing out products	system objective
d.	Assigning the cost of labour to a product	process
e.	Report showing the cost of a product	output
f.	Measuring the cost of quality	process
g.	Repairing a defective part	input
h.	Providing information for planning and control	system objective
i.	Designing a product	input
j.	Measuring the cost of design	process
k.	A budget that shows how much should be spent on design activity	output
l.	Using output information to make a decision	system objective
m.	Usage of materials	input
n.	A report comparing the actual costs of quality with the expected costs of quality	output

1-3

1. b

2. c

3. f

1-5

1.	Continuous reduction in cost	k.	Efficiency
2.	Linked set of value-creating activities	g.	Industrial value chain
3.	Using cost data to identify superior strategies	a.	Strategic cost management
4.	Selling over the Internet	f.	E-business
5.	A product's total tangible and intangible benefits	i.	Total product
6.	Suppliers and customers	h.	External linkages
7.	Flow of materials from upstream to downstream	j.	Supply chain management
8.	Internal value chain	c.	Internal linkages
9.	Zero defects	b.	Total quality management
10.	Realization of less sacrifice	e.	Customer value
11.	Activity-based costing and process value analysis	d.	Activity-based management

1-7

The right choice for the manager is to retain the three salespeople.

A manager has a responsibility to the company as well as to society. If the manager decides to lay off the employees he/she ignores both of these responsibilities to further his/her self-interest (in order to receive the bonus). The manager would be placing his/her self-interest before the interests of the company and the interests of the other employees. While pursuit of self-interest is not necessarily unethical, it can be if it harms others. In this case, the manager's action could harm the company. The company's profits may be lower if sales decrease as a result of the decision to lay off the salespeople and the company would incur unnecessary training costs when the sales positions are refilled at the beginning of the next year. The manager would receive a $10,000 bonus (an additional cost for the company) that he/she has not earned. It is unjust to penalize productive salespeople simply to earn a bonus for the manager.

The ethical dilemma faced by the manager was, in part, caused by the reward system. It seems that the manager is paid a bonus if profits exceed 10 percent of planned profits. With rewards based on a short-term measure such as profit, a manager has the incentive to manipulate profits in the short-term. One way to increase short-term profits is to reduce discretionary expenditures.

1-7 continued

Expanding the performance measures to include longer-term factors such as market share, productivity, and personnel development can discourage this type of behaviour. The accounting system can track trends such as training costs over time. Managers can be required to provide explanations for significant changes in discretionary expenses. The effect is to more closely align the manager's self-interest with the interests of the company and others.

PROBLEMS

1-9

1. Excellence teams and minicompanies both have the objective of involving production line personnel more fully in the management process so that the company can take advantage of the direct contact and knowledge that operating workers have about production and their work environment. This is expected to translate into continuous improvement of processes and improved operating performance. The objective seems to be realized in these two cases. Duffy Tool and Stamping has reduced costs and increased profits, attributing much of the change to the contributions of the excellence teams. Grand Rapids Spring and Wire Products has been recognized as a competitive, world-class manufacturer – much of the success in quality improvement appears to be grounded in the organizational change to minicompanies.

2. Employee empowerment is often a good idea. Employee empowerment is viewed as a key element of continuous improvement. Operating workers have tremendous skills, knowledge, and first-hand contact with the operating environment, all of which can be exploited to discover more efficient ways of producing. When employees are allowed more input, their self-esteem grows and their commitment to the company's objectives increases. Morale also increases, making for a more pleasant and productive environment.

   There are potential disadvantages. Too much latitude in employee empowerment might sidetrack employees to the point where they begin to attack personalities and argue about wage and other grievances or become involved in hiring, firing, and disciplinary matters. Many of these decisions are best left centralized. Skilful management is needed to ensure that operating employees are primarily involved in improving efficiency.

3. Management accounting information is used to inform empowered employees so that they can identify problems and monitor and evaluate the effect of their decisions.

4. Quality culture means that employees have a commitment producing high-quality products and services. A learning organization means that employees are always seeking better ways of doing things – they have a commitment to continuous improvement.

1-11

1. The total product purchased by Nadria is the product (a personal computer), its features (processing speed, disk drives, software packages, and so on), service, the operating and maintenance requirements, and delivery time.

2. Drantex is emphasizing low operating and maintenance costs. Confiar is attempting to differentiate its product by offering faster delivery and higher quality service.

3. The source of greater value for the Confiar machine is the better service level and quicker delivery time. The realization of these features appears to outweigh the additional sacrifice (the higher operating and maintenance costs) associated with the Confiar PC.

   The implications for the management accounting information systems are that information about customer realization and sacrifice should be collected and reported. Much of this information is external to the supplying company but clearly needed by management.

4. Better quality and shorter delivery time increase customer realization. Lowering the selling price decreases customer sacrifice. Customer value increases in total and this should make the Drantex PC more competitive with the Confiar PC. This example illustrates how quality, time, and costs are essential competitive tools. It also illustrates how critical it is that the management accounting information system collects and reports information concerning these three dimensions.

1-13

Maureen Hughes has violated the standards of ethical behaviour required of a management accountant by discussing the potential purchase of Webson's stock with her team. She has disclosed confidential information that she had obtained in the course of her work and was not authorized to share with her team. This is a clear violation of the general standard of confidentiality. She may also have violated the standard of professional confidence (including the obligation to perform her duties in accordance with relevant laws, regulations, and technical standards). Discussion of a potential stock purchase may be illegal under laws regulating the use of inside information. The information she revealed has become widespread in the company and could be used improperly by others. She has also violated the standard of integrity – her actions are unprofessional and may discredit the accounting profession.

MANAGEMENT ACCOUNTING
CANADIAN SIXTH EDITION
SOLUTIONS MANUAL

CHAPTER 2
BASIC MANAGEMENT ACCOUNTING CONCEPTS

ANSWERS TO ODD-NUMBERED QUESTIONS FOR WRITING AND DISCUSSION

1. Product-costing accuracy means assigning the cost of the resources consumed by a cost object as well as possible to the cost object. Accuracy is a relative concept and has to do with the reasonableness and logic of the cost assignment methods used. Some cost assignments are more accurate than others.

3. An activity is a basic unit of work performed within an organization. Activities are aggregations of actions taken to perform some task or produce some output. We can use an action verb and an object that receives the action to describe an activity. Examples include moving materials, paying bills, designing a product, serving a customer, purchasing materials, and so on.

5. Traceability is the ability to assign a cost to a cost object in an economically feasible way using a causal relationship.

   Tracing is the assignment of costs to a cost object using an observable measure of the cost object's resource consumption or factors that capture a causal relationship.

7. Drivers are observable causal factors that measure a cost object's resource consumption. Drivers cause changes in resource usage and thus have a cause-and-effect relationship with the costs associated with a cost object. The time spent on a product may be the driver for the cost of production labour. The number of items shipped could be the driver for the cost of the shipping activity.

9. Driver tracing is the use of drivers to trace activity costs to cost objects. Often this means that costs are first traced to activities (using direct or driver tracing) and then activity costs are traced to cost objects using a driver to capture the relationship between the activity cost and the cost objects consuming the activity.

11. A service is a task or activity performed for a customer or an activity performed by a customer using an organization's products or facilities.

13. Three examples of different product cost definitions are traditional, operating and value chain definitions. The different definitions are needed because they satisfy different management objectives and purposes.

    The traditional product cost definition includes only production costs (materials, labour, and overhead). This definition is related to the needs of financial reporting (inventory valuation) and production management decisions.

    The operating product cost definition includes production costs and other operating activities required to supply the product to a customer – marketing, distribution, and customer service. This definition is related to management decisions involving product pricing and customer relation management.

    The value-chain product cost definition includes the costs of all value-chain activities associated with a product – design, development, production, marketing, distribution, and customer service activities. This definition is related to strategic product decisions and strategic profitability analysis.

15. A manufacturing company's income statement will usually require a supporting statement of cost of goods manufactured. The cost of goods sold for a manufacturing company will depend on the cost of goods manufactured and the amount of beginning and ending finished goods inventory. A service organization will

normally not have any finished goods inventory (service is normally intangible and perishable) and the cost of services sold will correspond to the cost of service produced.

17. A company can receive many benefits from adopting an activity-based cost management system – improved product costing accuracy, improved decision making, enhanced strategic planning, and better ability to manage activities. These benefits become more valuable when the costs of making bad decisions increases – because of more intense and global competition, deregulation, and other factors. At the same time, with advances in information technology, the cost of implementing an activity-based approach is decreasing. For many companies an activity-based approach is attractive and often necessary.

SOLUTIONS TO ODD-NUMBERED EXERCISES, PROBLEMS, AND CASES

EXERCISES

2-1

1. Calculation of cost per page:

	Mary	Natalie
Paper (a)	$4.00	$8.00
Ink (b)	10.00	20.00
Total	$14.00	$28.00
Number of pages	500	1,000
Cost per page	$0.028	$0.028

(a) $1 \times \$4; 2 \times \$4$

(b) $\$80 \div 4,000 = \$0.02$ per page; $500 \times \$0.02; 1,000 \times \$0.02$

2. The cost of paper is assigned using direct tracing (each person supplies the paper she uses). Ink is assigned using driver tracing – the driver is the number of pages printed.

3. When we selected pages printed as the driver for the cost of ink, we assumed that each page used a similar amount of ink. Graphs may increase the amount of ink consumption per page. Thus Natalie is assigned too little cost.

    To improve the cost assignment, one solution would be to determine the amount of ink a page with graphs uses relative to a normal page and use the equivalent to a normal page as the driver to trace the cost of the ink. Suppose each page with graphs uses twice as much ink as a normal page and Natalie had 200 pages with graphs (and 800 normal pages). Natalie would be assigned the cost of 1,200 normal pages $(2 \times 200 + 800)$ or $24.00.

2-3

Other answers are possible.

	Cost	Cost Object	Cost Driver
a.	Processing cheques in a bank	Customer accounts	Number of cheques processed
b.	Unloading shipments of raw materials	Products	Number of receiving orders
c.	Shipping goods	Customers	Number of sales orders
d.	Ordering supplies	Departments	Number of purchase orders
e.	Reworking products	Products	Number of rework hours
f.	Moving materials	Products	Number of material moves
g.	Nursing care	Patients	Number of nursing hours
h.	Processing insurance claims	Claims	Number of processing hours
i.	Special product testing	Products	Number of testing hours
j.	Physical therapy in a hospital	Patients	Number of hours of therapy

2-5

	Activity	Value-Chain Category
a.	Advertising products	marketing
b.	Repairing goods under warranty	supporting
c.	Designing a new process	designing
d.	Assembling parts	producing
e.	Shipping goods to a wholesaler	distributing
f.	Inspecting incoming raw materials and parts	producing
g.	Storing finished goods in a warehouse	marketing and distributing
h.	Creating a new computer chip	designing and developing
i.	Answering product-use questions using a customer "hot line"	supporting
j.	Moving partly finished goods from one department to another	producing
k.	Building a prototype of a new product	developing
l.	Creating plans for a new model of an automobile	designing
m.	Conducting a sales campaign by phone	marketing
n.	Picking goods from a warehouse	distributing
o.	Setting up equipment	producing

2-7

1.

LAWTON COMPANY
STATEMENT OF COST OF GOODS MANUFACTURED
For the month ended September 30, 200x

Direct Materials:		
Beginning Inventory	$ 37,000	
Add: Purchases	61,500	
Materials Available	$98,500	
Less: Ending Inventory	16,800	
Direct Materials Used		$81,700
Direct Labour		40,500
Total Overhead Costs		105,750
Manufacturing Costs Added		$227,950
Add: Beginning Work in Process		18,000
Total Manufacturing Costs		$245,950
Less: Ending Work in Process		29,500
Cost of Goods Manufactured		$216,450

2.

LAWTON COMPANY
STATEMENT OF COST OF GOODS SOLD
For the month ended September 30, 200x

Beginning Finished Goods Inventory	$ 20,200
Add: Cost of Goods Manufactured	216,450
Goods Available for Sale	$236,650
Less Ending Finished Goods Inventory	19,100
Cost of Goods Sold	$217,550

2-9

1. Iquitos Manufacturing appears to be using a functional-based management accounting system. Production costs are used to determine product costs – the product cost definition follows the requirements of financial accounting rather than an operating or value-chain approach. Iquitos uses a single unit-level driver – direct labour hours – to assign overhead costs. Many of the overhead costs are assigned using allocation because many of the overhead costs are related to nonunit-level drivers. Iquitos controls costs by evaluating each departmental manager rather than system wide performance. An activity-based system uses unit and nonunit drivers to assign costs, controls costs by managing activities and their causes, and makes use of nonfinancial measures.

2. Iquitos assigns setup costs based on direct labour hours at a rate of $1.00 per DL hour [$100,000 ÷ 100,000]. The assigned setup cost is as follows:

	Automatic	Manual
Setup costs:[$1 × 30,000]; [$1 × 70,000]	$30,000	$70,000
Units	60,000	40,000
Setup cost per unit	$0.50	$1.75

By using direct labour hours to assign the setup costs Iquitos is using allocation. The assignment of setup costs is not direct tracing because a product does not exclusively use the assigned cost. If direct labour hours is a causal factor that measures the consumption of the setup activity the cost assignment would be driver tracing but the use of the setup activity is not related to the direct labour hours for a product. The automatic model uses more setup activity but less direct labour hours than the manual model.

3. A better way to assign the setup activity costs is to identify a driver that measures the use of the setup activity by each product and use driver tracing. A more likely cause-and-effect measure of the use of the setup activity is setup hours. Setup costs will be assigned at a rate of $10 per setup hour [$100,000 ÷ 10,000]. The assigned setup cost is as follows:

	Automatic	Manual
Setup costs:[$10 × 7,000]; [$10 × 3,000]	$70,000	$30,000
Units	60,000	40,000
Setup cost per unit	$1.17	$0.75

This method is more compatible with an activity-based approach – it uses driver tracing rather than allocation and uses a nonunit-level driver rather than a unit-level driver to assign the setup costs.

2-11

1. Cost of materials used for the muffler-changing service during April is $212,050:

Beginning inventory of material	$26,300
Purchases of material in April	200,000
Materials available in April	$226,300
Ending inventory of material	14,250
Materials used in April	$212,050

2. Prime cost for April is $265,050:

Direct materials used in April	$212,050
Direct labour for April	53,000
Prime cost for April	$265,050

2-11 continued

3. Conversion cost for April is $173,000:

Direct labour for April	$53,000
Overhead cost for April	120,000
Conversion cost for April	$173,000

4. Total service cost for April is $385,050:

Direct materials used in April	$212,050
Direct labour for April	53,000
Overhead cost for April	120,000
Total service cost for April	$385,050

5. Income Statement for April:

CONFIABLE MUFFLER
INCOME STATEMENT
For the month ended April 30, 200x

Sales Revenue		$500,000
Cost of sevices sold		385,050
Gross margin		$114,950
Less operating expenses		
Advertising	15,000	
Franchise fees [$3,000 × 3]	9,000	24,000
Operating income		$ 90,950

6. Confiable produces and sells a service (replacing mufflers – a job performed for a customer) that uses mufflers as a raw material. Remington produces and sells a tangible product (mufflers). Services differ from tangible products on four dimensions: intangibility, perishability, inseparability, and heterogeneity.

   Intangibility means that buyers of services cannot see, feel, hear, or taste a service before it is bought. Perishability means that a service cannot be stored for later sale or use. Inseparability means that producers of services must usually be in direct contact with the customer for an exchange to take place. Heterogeneity means that there is a greater chance of variation in the performance of services than in the production of products.

2-13

1. d

2. e

3. a

4. c

5. e

PROBLEMS

2-15

1. Nursing cost per patient day (costs assigned using patient days):

   Annual nursing cost (cost to be assigned):

Nursing hours required	34,944	[4 nurses × 3 shifts × 8 hours × 7 days × 52 weeks]
Hours per full time nurse	2,000	[40 hours per week × 50 weeks]
Nurses required	17.472	[34,944 ÷ 2,000]

   The hospital will need 17 full time nurses and one part time nurse. The annual cost of the nurses is $700,000 [17 × $40,000 + 1 × $20,000].

   Annual activity (patient days):

   10,000 patient days [8,000 normal care patient days + 2,000 intensive care patient days]

   Cost per patient day: $70.00 [$700,000 ÷ 10,000]

2. Nursing cost per patient day (costs assigned using nursing hours):

   Nursing costs are assigned using nursing hours to each type of patient care. Normal care patients use 50% of the nursing hours and intensive care patients use 50% of the nursing hours. Each type of care is assigned $350,000 [$700,000 × 50%] of the nursing cost. The cost per patient day is calculated as follows:

	Assigned Cost	Patient Days	Cost per Patient Day
Normal Care	$350,000	8,000	$43.75
Intensive Care	$350,000	2,000	$175.00

   This cost assignment is more accurate than the cost assignment based on patient days. Intensive care patients use more nursing care (as measured by nursing hours) than normal care patients. Using nursing hours instead of patient days to assign nursing costs better reflects the actual use of the nursing resource by the different types of patients.

3. The cost of the nurse assigned to the intensive care unit (and providing care exclusively to intensive care patients) is directly traceable to intensive care patients. The cost of the other three nurses (working with both normal care and intensive care patients) is assigned based on the hours spent with each type. We need to collect information about the nursing hours (for these three nurses) worked in the intensive care unit and for normal care patients to assign these costs. Note: in the question we are given that the hours are used 50% and 50% but this relationship could vary depending upon the patient load in intensive care.

2-17

	Classification	Explanation
a.	functional	focus on individual unit performance rather than a system-wide perspective; focus on managing costs rather than activity.
b.	functional	reward for individual unit performance rather than system-wide performance.
c.	activity	focus on activity resource use for assigning activity costs
d.	functional	focus on individual unit performance rather than a system-wide perspective
e.	activity	emphasis on activity analysis
f.	activity	emphasis on managing activities and activity analysis
g.	functional	emphasis on managing and controlling costs
h.	activity	emphasis on managing and evaluating activities
i.	activity	focus on driver and activity analysis
j.	functional	reward for controlling cost and individual unit performance
k.	activity	focus on driver analysis and managing activities
l.	functional	emphasis on controlling cost
m.	activity	use of a nonfinancial measure of performance
n.	activity	focus on managing activity, activity analysis, and nonfinancial measures of performance
o.	functional	emphasis on controlling costs and individual unit performance

2-19

1.

W. W. PHILLIPS COMPANY
STATEMENT OF COST OF GOODS MANUFACTURED
FOR THE YEAR ENDED DECEMBER 31, 2004

Direct materials:		
Beginning inventory	$ 46,800	
Add: Purchases	320,000	
Materials available	$366,800	
Less: Ending inventory	66,800	
Direct materials used		$300,000
Direct labour		200,000
Manufacturing overhead:		
Indirect labour	$40,000	
Rent, factory building	42,000	
Amortization, factory equipment	60,000	
Utilities, factory	11,956	
Total overhead costs		153,956
Total Manufacturing Costs Added		$653,956
Add: Beginning Work in Process		13,040
Total Manufacturing Costs		$666,996
Less: Ending Work in Process		14,996
Cost of Goods Manufactured		$652,000

2. Average cost of producing one unit during 2004 = $652,000/4,000 = $163

3.

W. W. PHILLIPS COMPANY
INCOME STATEMENT
FOR THE YEAR ENDED DECEMBER 31, 2004

Sales (3,800* × $400)		$1,520,000
Cost of Goods Sold:		
Beginning Finished Goods Inventory	$ 80,000	
Add: Cost of Goods Manufactured	652,000	
Goods Available for Sale	$732,000	
Less Ending Finished Goods Inventory	114,100	617,900
Gross Margin		$ 902,100
Less Operating Expenses		
Salary, sales supervisor	$ 90,000	
Commissions, salespersons	180,000	
Administrative expenses	300,000	570,000
Operating Income		$ 332,100

  * FGBI + Produced – FGEI = 500 + 4,000 – 700 = 3,800 units sold

2-21

1.

STATEMENT OF COST OF GOODS MANUFACTURED
For the period January 1 to 30, 2004

Direct materials		
Direct materials inventory, January 1, 2004	$32,000	
Direct materials purchases	320,000	
Direct materials available	$352,000	
Direct materials inventory, January 30, 2004 [3]	152,000	$200,000
Direct labour		360,000
Overhead [1]		240,000
Total manufacturing costs added [2]		$800,000
Work in process inventory, January 1, 2004		68,000
Total manufacturing costs		$868,000
Work in process inventory, January 30, 2004 [4]		80,000
Cost of goods manufactured		$788,000

[1] Overhead is 40% of conversion cost (which is direct labour plus overhead). When direct labour cost is $360,000, overhead cost is OH = 40% × ($360,000 + OH)
or OH = $240,000.

[2] Prime costs (direct materials and direct labour) are 70% of manufacturing costs – thus overhead is 30% of manufacturing costs. If overhead is $240,000 the total manufacturing costs added must be $800,000 ($240,000 ÷ 0.3).

[3] The direct materials used is $200,000 (or $800,000 − 360,000 − 240,000) and the direct materials inventory at January 30, 2004 is $152,000 ($352,000 − 200,000).

[4] Ending work in process is 10% of the monthly manufacturing costs or $80,000 (10% × $800,000).

2-21 continued

2. The cost of goods sold is estimated from the sales ($900,000) and the normal gross profit (20% of sales). Cost of goods sold is $720,000 ($900,000 × (1 − 0.2)). Finished goods inventory on January 30, 2004 is calculated as:

Finished goods inventory, January 1, 2004	$30,000
Cost of goods manufactured	788,000
Cost of goods available for sale	$818,000
Cost of goods sold	720,000
Finished goods inventory, January 30, 2004	$98,000

The total cost of inventory lost on January 30, 2004 is:

Direct materials inventory	$152,000
Work in process inventory	80,000
Finished goods inventory	98,000
Total cost of lost inventory	$330,000

MANAGERIAL DECISION CASES

2-23

1. Classification of expenses:

Expense Item	Classification
Utilities	General administration
Machine operators	Production – direct labour
Rent (office building)	General administration
Accounting fees	General administration
Other direct labour	Production – direct labour
Administrative salaries	50 % selling; 50% general administration
Supervisor salaries	Production – overhead
Pipe	Production – direct materials
Tires and fuel	Production – overhead
Amortization, equipment	Production – overhead
Salaries of mechanics	Production – overhead
Advertising	Selling

2-23 continued

2.

GATEWAY CONSTRUCTION COMPANY
INCOME STATEMENT
For the year ended December 31, 2004

Sales (18,200 equipment hours at $165)			$3,003,000
Cost of services sold			
Pipe		$1,401,340	
Machine operators		218,000	
Other direct labour		265,700	
Tires and fuel		418,600	
Supervisor salaries		70,000	
Amortization, equipment		198,000	
Salaries of mechanics		50,000	2,621,640
Gross margin			$ 381,360
Administration expenses			
Administrative salaries	$57,000		
Accounting fees	20,000		
Utilities	24,000		
Rent (office building)	24,000	$125,000	
Selling expenses			
Sales salaries	$57,000		
Advertising	15,000	72,000	197,000
Net income			$ 184,360

The average cost per equipment hour for laying pipe is $144.05 [$2,621,640 ÷ 18,200].

3. The cost of machine operators is directly related to the equipment hours. Equipment hours are related to the activity of laying pipe, therefore other direct labour (related to the quantity of pipe laid) also can be traced using equipment hours. The cost of pipe could also be traced using equipment hours but is more likely to be assigned by direct tracing (as direct material).

The cost of fuel and tires and maintenance (salaries of mechanics) is related to equipment usage and may be reasonably assigned using equipment hours as the driver. Amortization of equipment, if based on equipment usage, could also be traced using equipment hours.

Costs of supervision are not affected by the amount of activity and would not be traced using equipment hours. Gateway might allocate these costs based on equipment hours as a convenient way of assigning the costs to individual jobs.

The cost traced per equipment hour is $63.20.

Machine operators	$ 218,000
Other direct labour	265,700
Tires and fuel	418,600
Salaries of mechanics	50,000
Amortization, equipment	198,000
Total costs traced by equipment hours	$1,150,300
Equipment hours	18,200
Cost per equipment hour	$ 63.20

2-23 continued

In addition Gateway may allocate $3.85 per equipment hour.

Supervision	$70,000
Equipment hours	18,200
Cost per equipment hour	$ 3.85

CHAPTER 3
ACTIVITY COST BEHAVIOUR

ANSWERS TO ODD-NUMBERED QUESTIONS FOR WRITING AND DISCUSSION

1. Knowledge of cost behaviour is important for managerial decision making because it allows managers to assess changes in cost that result from changes in activity. Managers can evaluate the cost effects of choices that change activity. For example, if excess capacity exists, bids that at least cover variable cost may be appropriate. Knowing whether costs are variable or fixed can help a manager make better bids.

3. Resource spending is the cost of acquiring capacity to perform an activity. Resource usage is the activity capacity actually used. Resource spending and resource usage are the same for flexible resources. Resource spending is often greater than resource usage for committed resources.

5. Committed resources are supplied in advance of use through either explicit or implicit contracts to obtain a certain quantity of resource, regardless of whether the quantity of available resource is fully used or not. The cost of a committed resource doesn't change as the amount used changes. For multiperiod commitments, the cost of the resource corresponds to a committed fixed cost. Other resources acquired in advance are more short term in nature and correspond to discretionary fixed costs.

7. A variable cost changes in direct proportion to changes in the amount of an activity. A one-unit increase in the activity produces a uniform increase in cost. A step-cost with narrow steps increases only as activity changes in small amounts. A one-unit increase in the activity may not result in an increase in cost. Cost will increase only if activity increases by several units. A step-cost with narrow steps will appear to change in a manner similar to a variable cost for larger changes in activity.

9. A step-cost with narrow steps is often treated as a variable cost; small changes in activity will cause small changes in cost. A step-cost with wide steps is often treated as a fixed cost; small changes in activity do not usually cause changes in cost as long as the activity remains within a step.

11. Mixed costs are usually reported in total in the accounting records. The total cost is recorded with no attempt to segregate the fixed and variable components. Formal analysis is required to identify each portion.

13. When we use the scatterplot method to break out the fixed and variable costs of a mixed cost, we fit a line that represents the relationship between cost and activity that we see on the scattergraph. We calculate a linear cost formula from any two points on the scatterplot line. When we use the high-low method, we calculate a linear cost equation using two prescribed points – the point for the lowest activity and the point for the highest activity. The difference between the methods is how the two points used to calculate the linear cost formula are selected. The points are specified for the high-low method while the scatterplot method relies on judgment to fit the scatterplot line.

15. The method of least squares will find the best-fitting line for a set of activity and cost data points. The least squares line is "closer" to the data points than any other line. The least squares approach is based on the solution to the minimization of the sum of the squared deviations from a line to the data points. The least squares line is better than either the high-low line or a scatterplot line.

The least squares method uses more information than the high-low method and is more objective than the scatterplot method. Goodness of fit measures, such as R^2 and other statistics (measures of reliability and quality of the linear relationship between cost and activity), are readily available from the least squares analysis.

17. A best-fitting line is not necessarily a good-fitting line. A good fitting line is a linear function that explains the relationship between changes in activity and changes in cost. A good-fitting line will explain most of the total cost variability. The "best fitting" line may not explain the relationship very well if there isn't a strong linear relationship between the activity measure and the cost. In other words, there may be a large amount of unexplained variability in the cost data.

19. The coefficient of determination (or R^2) is the percentage of the total variability explained by the activity measure. It is a relative measure of "goodness of fit" and measures the strength of the relationship between cost and activity. R^2 will have a value between 0 (no relationship between the cost and activity) to 1 (a perfect linear relationship or 100 percent of the cost variability explained by the activity measure).

    The correlation coefficient (the square root of R^2) is a measure of the correlation between the cost and activity variables. The correlation coefficient measures the strength of the relationship and shows the direction of the relationship. A correlation coefficient will have a value between –1 (perfect negative correlation) and +1 (perfect positive correlation). A correlation coefficient of 0 indicates no relationship between the cost and the activity measure.

21. If the amount of mixed cost is insignificant compared to costs that can be readily classified as fixed or variable, a company may not be concerned with further analyzing mixed costs.

SOLUTIONS TO ODD-NUMBERED EXERCISES, PROBLEMS, AND CASES

EXERCISES

3-1

1. Cost behaviour of the cost of plant supervision:

Number of kilograms	Total cost	Per-kilogram cost
0	$80,000	na
20,000	80,000	$4.00
40,000	80,000	2.00
60,000	80,000	1.33
80,000	80,000	1.00

2. The supervision cost is fixed over the range of 0 to 80,000 kilograms because it is constant as the number of kilograms produced varies. Note that the per-unit or average cost decreases as the activity increases.

3-3

1. Cost behaviour of cost of renting machines:

Number of units	Total machine rent cost*	Per-unit cost
0	$15,000	na
10,000	15,000	$1.50
20,000	15,000	0.75
30,000	30,000	1.00
40,000	30,000	0.75
50,000	30,000	0.60

* One machine (at a cost of $15,000) can produce from 0 to 25,000 units; a second machine (at an additional cost of $15,000) is required to produce from 25,001 to 50,000 units.

2. The rental cost of forming machines is a step-cost – each step is $15,000 with a step width of 25,000 units. In the range of 0 to 50,000 units, we see two steps.

3-5

1. Classification by type of resource and cost behaviour:

Resource	Type of Resource	Cost Behaviour
plastic	flexible	variable
mould	committed	step
direct labour	flexible	variable
variable overhead	flexible	variable
other facility	committed	fixed

3-5 continued

2. Note: Action Figures produces 100,000 units from each set of moulds. Each set of moulds lasts three months four sets of moulds are used each year. Total annual production is 400,000 units.

Total and per unit cost is:

Resource	Total Cost		Unit Cost*
plastic	$6,000	[(400,000 × 25 ÷ 1,000) × $0.60]	$0.015
mould	16,000	[4 × $4,000]	0.040
direct labour and variable overhead	4,000	[400,000 × $0.10]	0.100
other facility	10,000	[given]	0.025
Total	$36,000		$0.090

* unit cost is total cost divided by 400,000 units

3-7

Activity	Activity Driver	Type of Resource	Cost Behaviour Type
Maintenance	maintenance hours	equipment – committed labour – committed parts – flexible	committed fixed discretionary fixed variable
Inspection	number of batches	test equipment – committed inspectors – committed units inspected – flexible	committed fixed discretionary fixed variable
Packing	number of boxes	materials – flexible labour – committed conveyor belt – committed	variable discretionary fixed committed fixed
Processing payables	number of payments	clerks – committed materials – flexible equipment – committed facility – committed	discretionary fixed variable committed fixed committed fixed
Assembly	units produced	conveyor belt – committed supervision – committed direct labour – committed materials – flexible	committed fixed discretionary fixed discretionary fixed variable

3-9

1. Resource classification:

Plan Charge	Resource Category
Monthly fee	committed
Airtime	flexible
Long distance	flexible
Activation fee	committed
Cancellation fee	committed (if triggered by early termination)

2. Average use: 45 local minutes per month:

	Minutes available	Minutes used	Unused minutes
Plan 1	60	45	15
Plan 2	120	45	75

   Plan 1 is more cost effective. Both plans have unused minutes and Plan 1 costs $10 less than Plan 2.

3. Average use: 60 local minutes and 30 long distance minutes per month:

	Minutes available	Local minutes used	Long distance minutes used	Unused minutes	Extra minutes used
Plan 1	60	60	30	0	30
Plan 2	120	60	30	30	0

   Plan 2 is more cost effective. Although there are unused minutes with Plan 2, the cost is $30 per month (there is no additional charge for long distance usage). Plan 1 would cost Jana $32 per month. This is made up of the basic plan cost of $20, the cost of additional airtime of $7.50 [30 × $0.25] and the cost of long distance of $4.50 [30 × $0.15]. With Plan 2 she could increase her use by 30 minutes without increasing her cost. With Plan 1, this additional activity would cost between $7.50 (30 minutes of local calls) and $12.00 (30 minutes of long distance calls).

3-11

1.   The scattergraph of the cost of oil changes and the number of oil changes shows a linear relationship.

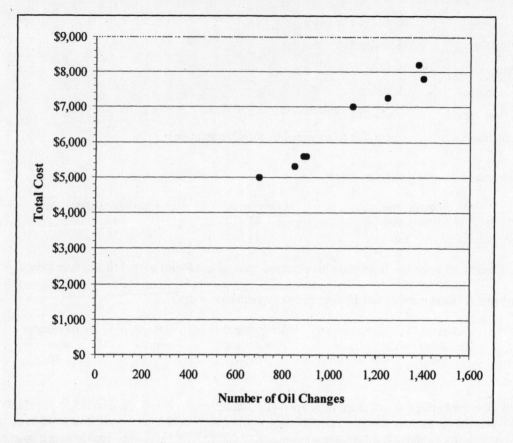

2.   The high point is [1,400, $7,800]. The low point is [700, $5,000]. The high-low cost formula is Y = $2,200 + $4X calculated as follows:

	X	Y
High	1,400	$7,800
Low	700	5,000
Difference	700	$1,800

V = $1,800 ÷ 700 = $4 per oil change
F = $7,800 – $4 × 1,400 = $2,200 per month

The predicted cost for 800 oil changes in January is $5,400 [$2,200 + $4 × 800].

3. The least squares formula (calculated using a spreadsheet) is $Y = \$1,547 + \$4.65X$ as shown in the regression output below:

Regression Statistics

Adjusted R Square	0.961530061
Standard Error	243.6783917
Observations	8

	Coefficients	Standard Error	t Stat	P-value
Intercept	1547.096691	380.7590143	4.06319124	0.00662657
Number of Oil Changes	4.646779985	0.350303775	13.2650012	1.1345E-05

The predicted cost for 800 oil changes in January is $5,267 [$1,547 + $4.65 × 800].

The coefficient of determination (R^2) is 0.96. R^2 indicates that 96 percent of the variability in the cost of providing oil changes is explained by the number of oil changes done. The least squares line is an excellent fit to the oil change activity cost data.

4. The least squares method is better – it uses all of the data and finds the best fitting line. In this case, the high point is a bit of an outlier (take a look at the scattergraph) and the high-low line is "pulled down" from the pattern of the other data points.

3-13

1. The independent variable is inspection hours and the dependent variable is inspection costs. The high point is 50 inspection hours and an inspection cost of $500. The low point is 10 inspection hours and an inspection cost of $120.

2. The High-Low cost formula is $Y = \$25 + \$9.50X$, calculated as:

	Hours	Cost
High	50	$500
Low	10	120
Difference	40	$380

Variable cost = $V = \$380 \div 40 = \$9.50$

Fixed cost = $F = \$500 - \$9.50 \times 50 = \$25$

The estimated inspection cost for 26 inspection hours is $272 [calculation: $25 + $9.50 × 26].

The High-Low line for the inspection cost is shown on the scattergraph below (not required).

3-13 continued

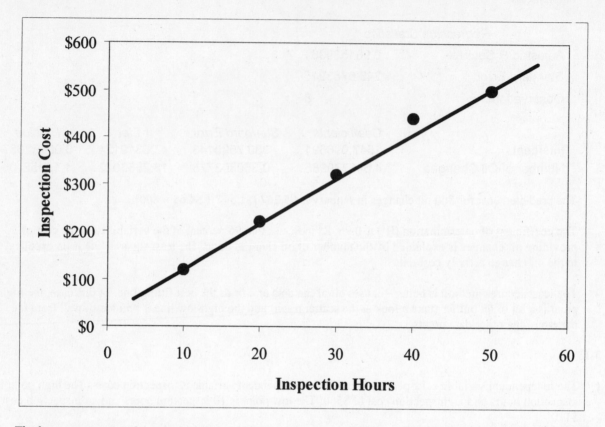

3. The least squares cost formula for inspection costs is Y = $26 + $9.80X, found using the regression tool in Excel. The regression output is shown below:

SUMMARY OUTPUT			
Regression Statistics			
Multiple R	0.996066645		
R Square	0.99214876		
Adjusted R Square	0.98953168		
Standard Error	15.91644852		
Observations	5		
ANOVA			
	df	*SS*	*MS*
Regression	1	96040	96040
Residual	3	760	253.3333333
Total	4	96800	
	Coefficients	*Standard Error*	*t Stat*
Intercept	26	16.69331203	1.557509974
Inspection Hours	9.8	0.503322296	19.47062565

The estimated inspection cost for 26 inspection hours is $281 [calculation: $26 + $9.80 × 26].

3-13 continued

4. The coefficient of determination (or R^2) indicates the percentage of the variability in the dependent variable (inspection cost) that is explained by the independent variable (inspection hours). In this case $R^2 = 0.99$ or 99%. This indicates a strong relationship between inspection hours and inspection cost. Only 1% of the inspection cost variability is unexplained by the number of inspection hours.

3-15

1. Scattergraph of Total Costs with Machine Hours as the independent variable:

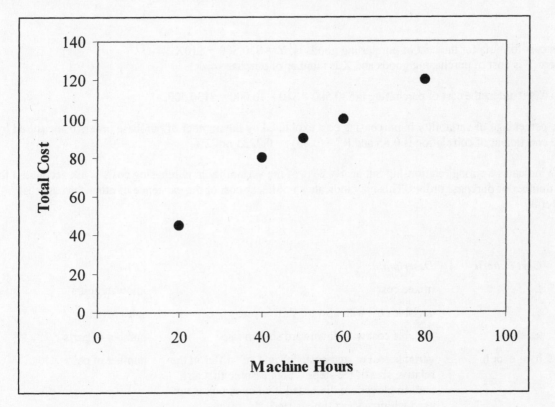

The scattergraph appears to support the assumption of linear cost behaviour.

2. Using a spreadsheet the least squares analysis gives the following:

	Coefficients	Standard Error	t Stat	P-value
Intercept	25.75	6.169481	4.173771	0.025044
X Variable 1	1.225	0.114564	10.69268	0.001749

The cost equation is: $Y = \$25.75 + \$1.225X$

Within the relevant range, the y-intercept represents fixed costs, which are independent of machine hours. The slope is the variable cost per machine hour.

3. From the results of the spreadsheet least squares analysis, $R^2 = 0.9744$

R^2 gives the proportion of variability explained by the equation developed by the least squares regression. That is, 97.44% of the variability in total costs can be explained by variability in machine hours.

3-15 continued

4. For 75 machine hours, the predicted total cost is $117.63 using the least squares cost formula [calculation: $25.75 + $1.225 × 75]. We would have confidence in this estimate because the least squares formula is a good fit to the cost data and 75 machine hours is within the range of activity used to develop the formula.

5. For 200 machine hours, the predicted total cost is $270.75 using the least squares cost formula [calculation: $25.75 + $1.225 × 200]. We would have less confidence in this prediction because, although the least squares formula is a good fit to the cost data, 200 machine hours is not within the range of activity used to develop the formula – we are looking at an activity that is outside the relevant range for the cost behaviour model.

3-17

1. The cost formula for the cost of purchasing goods is: $Y = \$30,500 + \$10X$
   where Y is cost of purchasing goods and X is number of purchase orders.

2. At 10,000 orders the cost of purchasing is $30,500 + $10 × 10,000 = $130,500.

3. The percentage of variability in purchasing cost explained by the number of purchase orders is measured by R^2. The coefficient of correlation is 0.85 and $R^2 = (0.85)^2 = 0.7225$ or 72%.

   This indicates a strong relationship but nearly 28% of the variability in purchasing costs is not accounted for by the number of purchase orders. This may indicate a nonlinear cost or the existence of other factors (cost drivers).

3-19

	Cost Pattern	Description	Driver
1.	f.	mixed cost	kilowatt hours
2.	a.	variable cost with upward shift in rate	sales revenue
3.	k.	variable cost with downward shift in rate	number of parts
4.	b. or e. or h.	variable cost or step-cost; "b" and "e" differ in the relative size of the steps – both assume that any unused gloves are discarded if an open box is not used within a short time period. "h" is the appropriate answer if gloves can be saved for later use if not used immediately.	number of pairs
5.	g.	variable cost with maximum	number of credit hours
6.	c.	variable segment; fixed segment; variable segment	number of credit hours
7.	b. or e. or h.	same as (4)	number of nails
8.	d.	fixed cost	number of orders
9.	h.	variable cost	number of gowns (or patients)
10.	i.	fixed segment; variable segment	number of customers
11.	l.	nonlinear with increasing rate	age of equipment

PROBLEMS

3-21

1. Our first step is to identify the cost items that are part of overhead. Our second step is to determine the 2003 cost behaviour for each of the overhead cost items. The cost driver for the overhead cost items will be the number of units produced. We can then prepare a cost formula for overhead cost.

    The following cost items would be part of overhead:

    Amortization of factory equipment
    Factory rent
    Heat, light, and power
    Indirect labour
    Insurance on factory
    Supplies used

    We can use the property that fixed costs don't change when the amount of the cost driver changes to identify the following fixed costs:

Amortization of factory equipment	$5,000
Factory rent	12,000
Insurance on factory	2,500

    We can use the property that variable costs change in proportion to the change in the cost driver (or constant average cost) to identify the following variable costs:

    Supplies used $2.00 per unit   ($40,000 ÷ 20,000)

    The other overhead cost items (Heat, light, and power and Indirect labour) have both a variable and fixed component and are mixed costs. We will use the high-low method to identify the fixed and variable parts of each mixed cost.

    Heat, light, and power:
      Variable: $0.80 per unit   [($17,000 − 11,400) ÷ (20,000 − 13,000)]
      Fixed: $1,000   [$17,000 − (20,000 × $0.80)]

    Indirect labour:
      Variable: $1.50 per unit   [($60,000 − 49,500) ÷ (20,000 − 13,000)]
      Fixed: $30,000   [$60,000 − (20,000 × $1.50)]

3-21 continued

2003 fixed costs are:

Amortization of factory equipment	$ 5,000
Factory rent	12,000
Insurance on factory	2,500
Heat, light, and power	1,000
Indirect labour	30,000
Total fixed cost	$50,500

2003 variable costs per unit are:

Supplies used	$2.00
Heat, light, and power	0.80
Indirect labour	1.50
Total variable cost	$4.30

The 2003 overhead cost formula is $50,500 + $4.30 × units produced.

2. The budget for overhead costs in June 2004 if 17,000 units are produced is

Overhead Budget – June 2004:

Variable Overhead		
Supplies used	$ 36,040	[$2.12 × 17,000]
Heat, light, and power	14,416	[$0.848 × 17,000]
Indirect labour	27,030	[$1.59 × 17,000]
Total Variable Overhead	$ 77,486	
Fixed Overhead		
Amortization of factory equipment	$5,200	[$5,000 × 1.04]
Factory rent	12,480	[12,000 × 1.04]
Insurance on factory	2,600	[2,500 × 1.04]
Heat, light, and power	1,040	[1,000 × 1.04]
Indirect labour	31,200	[30,000 × 1.04]
Total Fixed Overhead	$ 52,520	
Total Overhead	$130,006	

Notes:

Variable costs in 2004 will be 6% higher than in 2003:

Supplies used	$2.120	[$2.00 × 1.06]
Heat, light, and power	0.848	[0.80 × 1.06]
Indirect labour	1.590	[1.50 × 1.06]

Fixed costs in 2004 will be 4% higher than in 2003.

3-23

1. Resource classification:

   Flexible resources:
     Machine operating costs; Direct materials; Direct labour

   Committed resources – short term:
     Purchasing; Inspection; Material handling

   Committed resources – long term:
     Equipment

   Both the types of committed resources would be considered as fixed costs – discretionary fixed costs for the short term committed resources and committed fixed costs for the long term committed resource.

2. Total annual resource spending with production of 100,000 sets of rollers:

Activity	Fixed Cost	Variable Cost	Total Cost	
Direct materials	$0	$75,000	$75,000	[$0.75 × 100,000]
Direct labour	0	25,000	25,000	[$0.25 × 100,000]
Machine operating	0	25,000	25,000	[$0.50 × 50,000]
Equipment	30,000	0	30,000	[annual lease]
Purchasing	100,000	0	100,000	[see below]
Inspection	150,000	0	150,000	[see below]
Material handling	30,000	0	30,000	[see below]
Total	$310,000	$125,000	$435,000	

The demand for purchasing will be 19,000 orders (22,000 – 5,000 + 2,000). The supply required is 20,000 with a cost of $100,000 [(20,000 ÷ 5,000) × $25,000].

The demand for inspection will be 9,750 hours (9,000 + 750). The supply required is 10,000 with a cost of $150,000 [(10,000 ÷ 2,000) × $30,000].

The demand for material handling will be 4,600 moves (4,300 – 200 + 500). The supply required is 5,000 with a cost of $30,000 [(5,000 ÷ 2,500) × $15,000].

Effect on resource spending caused by production of rollers:

Activity	Added Cost	Cost Savings	
Direct materials	$75,000	$ 0	
Direct labour	25,000	0	
Machine operating	25,000	0	
Equipment	30,000	0	
Purchasing	0	25,000	[see below]
Inspection	0	0	[see below]
Material handling	0	0	[see below]
Purchase of rollers	0	190,000	[100,000 × $1.90]
Total	$155,000	$215,000	

Spending for the purchasing activity decreases because the demand for purchase orders is reduced. Increasing the use of inspection and material handling activities does not require any additional resources because sufficient excess capacity exists.

Resource spending decreases by $60,000 by producing rather than purchasing the rollers.

3-23 continued

3. Flexible resources (direct materials, direct labour, and machine operating costs) will not have unused capacity and the cost of activity used is equal to the cost of activity supplied. For the committed resources the cost of activity usage and unused capacity is:

Activity	Cost of Activity Supplied	Activity Supplied	Activity Rate	Cost of Activity Used	Cost of Unused Activity
Equipment (hours)	$30,000	60,000	$0.50	50,000 $25,000	10,000 $5,000
Purchasing (orders)	$100,000	20,000	$5.00	19,000 $95,000	1,000 $5,000
Inspection (hours)	$150,000	10,000	$15.00	9,750 $146,250	250 $3,750
Material handling (moves)	$30,000	5,000	$6.00	4,600 $27,600	400 $2,400

3-25

Scattergraph – Receiving Orders as Driver (not required):

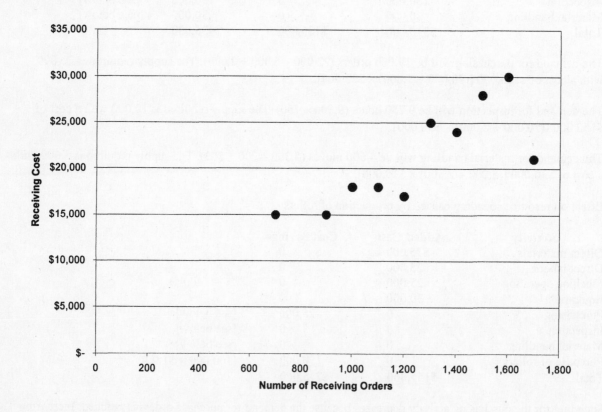

3-25 continued

1. The high-low cost formula for the receiving activity cost (based on receiving orders) is $Y = \$10,800 + \$6.00X$, calculated as follows:

	Receiving Orders	Receiving Cost
High	1,700	$21,000
Low	700	15,000
Difference	1,000	$6,000

Variable cost = $V = \$6,000 \div 1,000 = \$6.00$
Fixed cost = $F = \$21,000 - \$6.00 \times 1,700 = \$10,800$

Note: from the scattergraph we can see that the high-low line doesn't fit the data very well. The high point is a clear outlier and has pulled the cost line downwards.

2. The least squares cost formula for the receiving activity cost (based on receiving orders) is $Y = \$4,513 + \$13.38X$ (calculated using a spreadsheet program):

	Coefficients	Standard Error	t Stat	P-value
Intercept	4512.987	4590.522	0.98311	0.354347
X Variable 1	13.37662	3.595575	3.720302	0.005869

Regression Statistics	
R Square	0.63371

The coefficient of determination or R^2 is 0.63. R^2 indicates that the number of receiving orders accounts for approximately 63% of the variability in receiving cost. Receiving orders is a reasonable choice as a cost driver but other cost drivers should be considered.

3-25 continued

Scattergraph – Kilograms of Material Received as Driver (not required):

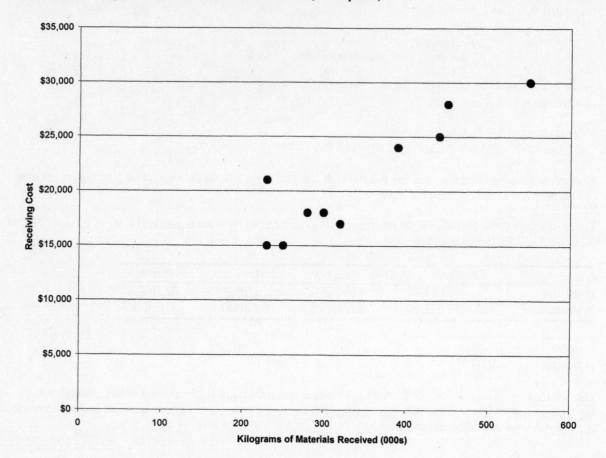

3-25 continued

3. The least squares cost formula for the receiving activity cost (based on kilograms of material received) is
Y = $5,632 + $0.045X, (calculated using a spreadsheet program):

	Coefficients	Standard Error	t Stat	P-value
Intercept	5632.281	2631.031	2.140713	0.064705
X Variable 1	0.044964	0.007326	6.137663	0.000278

Regression Statistics	
R Square	0.824834

The coefficient of determination or $R^2 = 0.82$. This represents a stronger relationship between receiving costs and kilograms of materials used.

4. The least squares cost formula for the receiving activity cost (based on both the number of receiving orders and the kilograms of material received) is Y = $752 + 7.15X_1$ + 0.033X_2$, where X_1 is number of receiving orders and X_2 is the kilograms received (calculated using a spreadsheet program):

	Coefficients	Standard Error	t Stat	P-value
Intercept	752.1041	1878.501	0.400375	0.700818
X Variable 1	7.147029	1.681829	4.249557	0.003795
X Variable 2	0.033388	0.004955	6.73797	0.000268

Regression Statistics	
R Square	0.951068

The coefficient of determination or $R^2 = 0.95$. This is the best of the three regression equations. 95% of the variability in receiving costs is explained by the independent variables of the number of orders received and the kilograms of material received.

3-27

1. The high-low cost formula for the nursing-care activity is Y = –$50,000 + $85.00X, calculated as follows:

	Hours	Cost
High	2,000	$120,000
Low	1,200	52,000
	800	$ 68,000

Variable rate per hour = $68,000 ÷ 800 = $85.00
Fixed cost = $120,000 – $85.00 × 2,000 = –$50,000

Note: Fixed cost is a negative number. What does this mean? Think about the idea of a "relevant range."

3-27 continued

2. The scatterplot for the nursing-care activity is:

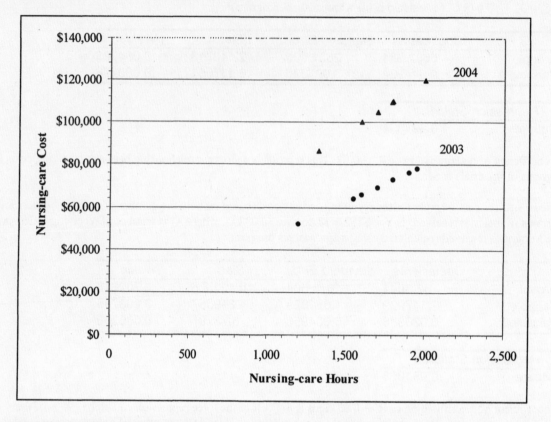

Note that the high point used in the high-low analysis is from 2004 and the low point is from 2003. This explains the negative intercept calculated in part 1. We would investigate to discover why costs appear to be different in 2003 from 2004.

3. This problem illustrates how the high-low method can provide misleading results when the cost behaviour pattern for an activity changes from one year to the next. The new equipment introduced in 2004 has changed the activity and the cost behaviour pattern. The analysis in part 1 uses one observation from 2003 (the old cost behaviour pattern) and one observation from 2004 (the new cost behaviour pattern).

a. The least squares cost formula with all data (2003 and 2004) based on nursing hours is
$Y = \$2,678 + \$48.43X$ with $R^2 = 0.264$:

	Coefficients	Standard Error	t Stat	P-value
Intercept	2678.016	39507.4	0.067785	0.947073
X Variable 1	48.42877	23.32396	2.076353	0.060009

Regression Statistics	
R Square	0.264311

3-27 continued

b. The least squares cost formula with 2003 data based on nursing hours is $Y = \$10,081 + \$34.95X$ with $R^2 = 0.999$:

	Coefficients	Standard Error	t Stat	P-value
Intercept	10081.33	253.41	39.78269	1.69E-08
X Variable 1	34.95333	0.151088	231.3446	4.4E-13

Regression Statistics	
R Square	0.999888

c. The least squares cost formula with 2004 data based on nursing hours is $Y = \$19,964 + \$50.02X$ with $R^2 = 0.999$:

	Coefficients	Standard Error	t Stat	P-value
Intercept	19964.24	40.95523	487.465	1.06E-10
X Variable 1	50.02168	0.02387	2095.586	3.11E-13

Regression Statistics	
R Square	0.999999

d. The least squares cost formula with all data based on nursing hours [X_1] and a dummy variable [X_2: 0, 2003; 1, 2004] is $Y = \$236 + \$40.88\ X_1 + \$35,308\ X_2$ with $R^2 = 0.994$:

	Coefficients	Standard Error	t Stat	P-value
Intercept	236.2112	3745.736	0.063061	0.950849
X Variable 1	40.87521	2.220735	18.40616	1.3E-09
X Variable 2	35307.51	970.2011	36.39195	8.12E-13

Regression Statistics	
R Square	0.99394

4. The 2004 cost equation should be used to budget the cost of the nursing-care activity for the remainder of 2004 because it reflects the cost behaviour after the recent changes (equipment, supervisor, cost increases). It has a high R^2 and is an excellent fit to the 2004 cost data. The other three least squares equations include costs from 2003 that are not representative of current activity cost behaviour.

MANAGERIAL DECISION CASES

3-29

1. The scattergraph of overhead costs and the number of administrative staff is:

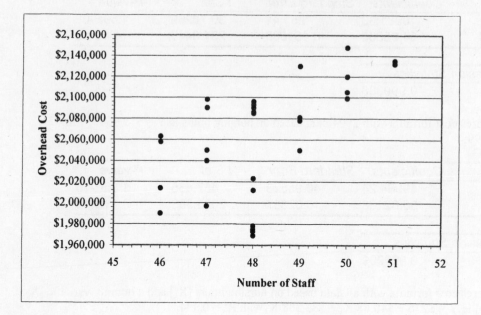

Note that the intersection of the X-axis and Y-axis is not at zero.

2. The scattergraph of overhead costs and the number of patient admissions is:

Note that the intersection of the X-axis and Y-axis is not at zero.

3-29 continued

3. Although we don't see a strong relationship with overhead costs and either activity measure, the number of patient admissions is our better choice. The data in the scatterplot of overhead costs and patient admissions is less dispersed than the scattergraph of overhead costs and administrative staff. As well, the number of staff has not changed very much (a range from 46 to 51 over the last 30 months). It is unlikely that an independent variable with low variability will be useful in explaining the cost behaviour of overhead costs. The number of patient admissions has varied between 414 and 516. An independent variable with greater variability is more useful for analyzing the overhead cost behaviour.

4. The least squares overhead cost equation based on the number of staff is $Y = \$1,027,385 + \$21,479X$, calculated using a spreadsheet program:

Regression Statistics

Adjusted R Square	0.2981			
Standard Error	44887.9749			
Observations	30			
	Coefficients	*Standard Error*	*t Stat*	*P-value*
Intercept	1027385	283609.59	3.62	0.00
Administrative Staff	21479	5885.63	3.65	0.00

5. The least squares overhead cost equation based on the number of patient admissions is $Y = \$1,275,743 + \$1,674X$, calculated using a spreadsheet program:

Regression Statistics

Adjusted R Square	0.7682			
Standard Error	25793.9416			
Observations	30			
	Coefficients	*Standard Error*	*t Stat*	*P-value*
Intercept	1275743	79911.2902	15.9645	0.0000
Patient Admissions	1674	169.8490	9.8554	0.0000

6. R^2 is a measure of goodness of fit for the least squares cost equations. R^2 is 0.30 for the cost equation based on the number of staff – this means that 30 percent of the variability in overhead cost is explained by the staff variable. R^2 is 0.77 for the cost equation based on the number of patient admissions – this means that 77 percent of the variability in overhead cost is explained by the patient variable. The equation based on patient admissions is a much better fit to the overhead cost data.

7. It is possible that the hospital has changed how it operates over the last 30 months. If so, the relationship between the activity measure – patient admissions – and the overhead costs may not be stable. This might account for some of the 23 percent of the variability in overhead cost not related to changes in the number of patients admitted. New equipment and technology, with different costs, may have been introduced. Staffing policies may have changed. New contracts may have been negotiated with staff. If costs have changed over the 30-month period, the fit of the least squares equation will be reduced.

MANAGEMENT ACCOUNTING
CANADIAN SIXTH EDITION
SOLUTIONS MANUAL

CHAPTER 4 – ACTIVITY-BASED COSTING

ANSWERS TO ODD-NUMBERED QUESTIONS FOR WRITING AND DISCUSSION

1. Unit costs are important information for inventory valuation and income measurement (cost of goods sold). Unit costs are used by managers in making many decisions – pricing, production scheduling, accepting a special order, etc.

3. Actual overhead rates are rarely used for product costing because unit cost information is not available on a timely basis when an actual costing approach is used. Managers are not willing to wait until the end of a period to know an accurate unit cost. Managers need information during the period when they are making decisions. Using a shorter time period provides more timely information but this solution often causes overhead rates to be volatile because activity volume fluctuates and seasonal cost variations are present. Normal costing with predetermined overhead rates is a better solution.

5. For departmental rates, the first stage is to assign overhead costs to individual production departments (using a combination of direct tracing, driver tracing, and allocation). A separate overhead rate is calculated for each departmental cost pool using an appropriate (unit-level) activity driver for each department. The second stage is to assign each department's overhead cost to products, multiplying the departmental rates by the actual amount of the activity driver used by each product in the respective departments.

7. A plantwide rate, using a unit-level activity driver, can produce distorted product costs when (1) nonunit-level costs represent a significant proportion of total overhead costs, and (2) products use some overhead activities in different proportions than assigned by a unit-based activity driver (or product diversity). The overhead costs assigned to a product by a plantwide rate will not accurately reflect the amount of overhead activities used by the product.

9. Cost information that undercosts low-volume products and overcosts high-volume products will cause managers to incorrectly assess the profitability of different products. Managers may favour low-volume (undercosted) products and under-price these products. High-volume products may appear to be less profitable or may be priced too high to be competitive.

11. "Product diversity" exists when products consume overhead activities in different proportions.

13. Departmental rates normally use unit-based activity drivers. If products consume nonunit-level overhead activities in different proportions than those of unit-level activity measures, then it is possible for departmental rates to be further away from the true consumption of overhead costs than if costs were assigned on a plantwide basis, because of the additional variation introduced by the departmental rates.

15. Activity-based product costing is an overhead cost assignment approach that, at the first stage, assigns overhead costs to activities and then, at the second stage, assigns activity costs to products. An ABC system emphasizes direct and driver tracing at both stages and uses a combination of unit-level and nonunit-level activity drivers.

17. A primary activity is an activity used by a product or customer (final cost object). A secondary activity is an activity that is used by primary activities and other secondary activities.

19. We form homogeneous sets of activities by combining individual activities that have similar characteristics – logically related by activity-level classification and consumed in the same proportion by each product.

Homogeneous sets of activities are used to reduce the number of overhead rates required to assign overhead costs in an ABC system.

21. A unit-level activity is an activity performed each time a unit is produced. The cost of a unit-level activity varies with the number of units produced.

    A batch-level activity is an activity performed each time a batch of a product is produced. The cost of a batch-level activity varies with the number of batches but not with the number of units of a product in a batch.

    A product-level activity is an activity performed as needed to support the variety of products produced by a company. The cost of product-level activities varies with the number of different products a company manufactures.

    A facility-level activity is an activity that sustains a company's manufacturing capacity but is independent of any particular product or production activity.

23. Managers can use activity-based customer costing to identify the costs of serving different customers. A company can adopt strategies to focus on more profitable customers and convert unprofitable customers into profitable ones.

SOLUTIONS TO ODD-NUMBERED EXERCISES, PROBLEMS, AND CASES

EXERCISES

4-1

1. Unit actual cost per quarter and annually:

	Quarter 1	Quarter 2	Quarter 3	Quarter 4	Year
Units produced	100,000	40,000	20,000	140,000	300,000
Total prime cost	$2,000,000	$800,000	$400,000	$2,800,000	$6,000,000
Total overhead cost	$800,000	$600,000	$900,000	$700,000	$3,000,000
Unit prime cost (a)	$20	$20	$20	$20	$20
Unit overhead costs (b)	8	15	45	5	10
Unit cost (c)	$28	$35	$65	$25	$30

2. Actual costing can produce great changes in the average overhead cost assigned to a unit. This may be caused by variations in the volume of production in the presence of large amount of fixed overhead costs. Average actual costs are also affected by the presence of seasonal costs (may be the cause of the high costs in Quarter 3).

3. Normal costing would involve predetermined overhead rates calculated based on estimates of the expected production and expected overhead costs. The predetermined overhead rate is $9.70 per unit [$2,910,000 ÷ 300,000] for a total unit cost of $29.70 [$20.00 + $9.70].

    Overhead costs are assigned during the year using the predetermined overhead rate. Normal costing produces a smoother pattern of unit product costs and is close to the actual annual average cost of $10.00 per unit [$3,000,000 ÷ 300,000].

4-3

1. The predetermined overhead rate is $7.50 per direct labour hour.

    Estimated overhead ÷ Estimated activity = Predetermined overhead rate
    $600,000 ÷ 80,000 = $7.50

2. Applied overhead for 2004 is $585,000 [$7.50 × 78,000 actual direct labour hours].

3. Overhead is underapplied by $10,500:

Actual overhead cost	$595,500
Applied overhead cost	585,000
Underapplied overhead	$ 10,500

4. Unit cost for 2004 is $14.85.

Prime cost	$ 900,000
Applied overhead cost	585,000
Total product cost	$1,485,000
÷ units produced	100,000
Unit cost	$ 14.85

4-5

1. The overhead rates are $2.14 per machine hour for the drilling department and $1.96 per labour hour for the assembly department.

	Drilling	Assembly
Overhead cost	$300,000	$196,000
Activity	140,000	100,000
Overhead rate	$2.14	$1.96

2. The applied overhead for 2004 is $308,160 for the drilling department, $192,080 for the assembly department, and $500,240 for the company. Overhead is overapplied by $7,160 for the drilling department, underapplied by $13,920 for the assembly department, and underapplied by $6,760 for the company.

	Drilling	Assembly	Company
Overhead rate	$2.14	$1.96	
Actual activity	144,000	98,000	
Applied overhead	$308,160	$192,080	$500,240
Actual overhead	301,000	206,000	507,000
Overhead variance	$ 7,160	$ 13,920	$ 6,760
	(overapplied)	(underapplied)	(underapplied)

3. The overhead cost per unit for the order is $1.462.

	Drilling	Assembly	Total
Overhead rate	$2.14	$1.96	
Actual activity used	2,000	800	
Applied overhead	$4,280	$1,568	$5,848
Units			4,000
Overhead per unit			$1.462

4-7

1. Yes. Direct materials and direct labour are directly traceable to each product and their cost assignment should be accurate. Each product is an exclusive consumer of particular material and labour inputs

2. Overhead applied using a plantwide rate based on direct labour costs:

Setup	$3,000	
Amortization	10,000	
Operating	8,000	
Total	$21000	
÷ Direct labour costs	$12,000	[$9,000 + $3,000]
Overhead rate	$1.75	per direct labour dollar
	or 175%	of direct labour cost

Overhead costs assigned:
Elegant: ($1.75 × $9,000) ÷ 3,000 = $5.25 per purse
Eminent: ($1.75 × $3,000) ÷ 3,000 = $1.75 per purse

4-7 continued

More machine costs are assigned to the Elegant line than the Eminent line. This is clearly a distortion since the production of the Eminent line is automated and uses more of the machine resources than used by the handcrafted Elegant purses. The consumption ratio for the machine activity is 10% for Elegant and 90% for Eminent (based on machine hours as the activity driver). The consumption ratio for direct labour is 75% for Elegant and 25% for Eminent. Allocating machine activity using direct labour cost distorts the costing of the two products. The assignment of setup costs (consumption ratio of 50% for Elegant and 50% for Eminent, based on setup hours) is similarly distorted.

3. Overhead applied using a plantwide rate based on machine hours:
   Overhead costs ÷ machine hour = $21,000 ÷ (500 + 4,500) = $4.20 per machine hour

   Elegant: ($4.20 × 500) ÷ 3,000 = $0.70 per purse
   Eminent: ($4.20 × 4,500) ÷ 3,000 = $6.30 per purse

   This cost assignment appears more reasonable given the relative demands each product places on machine resources. However, once a company moves to a multiple product setting, using only one activity driver to assign costs will likely produce product cost distortions. Products tend to make different demands on overhead activities and this should be reflected in overhead cost assignments. Usually this means the use of both unit and nonunit activity drivers. The consumption ratios for the setup activity and machine activity are quite different and the setup costs are not assigned properly. A better approach is to create two homogeneous cost pools and assign machine costs using machine hours and setup costs using setup hours.

   The overhead rates would be:

   Machine activity: $18,000 ÷ 5,000 = $3.60 per machine hour
   Setup activity: $3,000 ÷ 200 = $15.00 per setup hour

   The assigned overhead is:

	Elegant	Eminent	
Machine costs	$1,800	$16,200	[$3.60 × 500; $3.60 × 4,500]
Setup costs	1,500	1,500	[$15 × 100; $15 × 100]
Total	$3,300	$17,700	
Units	3,000	3,000	
Cost per unit	$1.10	$5.90	

4-9

1. d. (calculation below)

Labour cost	$30,000	[75% × $40,000]
Forklift cost	6,000	[100% × $6,000]
Total receiving cost	$36,000	

2. b. (calculation below)

   Activity rate for receiving: $36,000 ÷ 50,000 = $0.72 per part

3. a. (calculation below)

   Activity rate for setting up equipment: $60,000 ÷ 300 = $200 per setup

4-9 continued

4. c. (calculation below)

Activity rate for grinding: $90,000 ÷ 18,000 = $5.00 per machine hour

5. d. (calculation below)

Activity rate for inspecting: $45,000 ÷ 4,500 = $10.00 per inspection hour

6. a. (calculation below)

Setting up	$ 60,000
Inspecting	45,000
Grinding	90,000
Receiving	36,000
Total	$231,000
÷ direct labour hours	20,000
Overhead rate	$11.55

Unit cost of subassembly A:

Direct materials	$ 850.00	
Direct labour	600.00	
Overhead	577.50	[50 × $11.55]
Total	$2,027.50	
÷ Units completed	100	
Cost per unit	$20.28	

7. b. (calculation below)

Unit cost of subassembly A:

Direct materials	$850.00	
Direct labour	600.00	
Overhead:		
Setting up	200.00	[$200 × 1]
Inspecting	40.00	[$10 × 4]
Grinding	100.00	[$5 × 20]
Receiving	14.40	[$0.72 × 20]
Total	$1,804.40	
÷ Units completed	100	
Cost per unit	$18.04	

4-11

1. Classification of overhead activities. (Note: other classifications are also correct.)

Activity	Level
Machining	unit
Setups	batch
Receiving	product
Packing	batch

2. Creation of homogeneous cost pools:

Activity	Activity Driver	Consumption Ratio
Machining	machine hours	50:50
Setups	number of setups	67:33
Receiving	number of receiving orders	33:67
Packing	number of packing orders	67:33

Cost pools:
Unit-level cost pool:
   Machining activity   only unit-level activity

Batch-level cost pool:
   Setup activity   same activity level and same consumption ratios
   Packing activity

Product-level cost pool:
   Receiving activity   only product-level activity

3. Cost pools rates:

Unit-level cost pool:

Machining activity cost	$80,000	
Activity driver (machine hours)	40,000	[20,000 + 20,000]
Unit-level pool rate	$2.00	

Batch-level cost pool:

Setup activity cost	$24,000	
Packing activity cost	30,000	
Total pool cost	$54,000	
Activity driver (packing orders)*	2,400	[1,600 + 800]
Batch-level pool rate	$22.50	

* could also use number of setups

Product-level cost pool:

Receiving activity cost	$18,000	
Activity driver (receiving orders)	600	[200 + 400]
Product-level pool rate	$30.00	

4-11 continued

4. Overhead cost assignment:

	Sports	Police
Unit-level pool [$2 × 20,000; $2 × 20,000]	$40,000	$40,000
Batch-level pool [$22.50 × 1,600; $22.50 × 800]	36,000	18,000
Product-level pool [$30 × 200; $30 × 400]	6,000	12,000
Total	$82,000	$70,000

4-13

Note: The following answers are common responses but in some cases alternative answers are reasonable and supported by the characteristics of a particular example.

	Activity	Classification	Activity Driver
1.	Setting up equipment	Batch-level	Setup hours
2.	Receiving materials	Product-level	Number of receiving orders
3.	Inspecting goods	Batch-level	Inspection hours
4.	Shipping goods	Product-level	Number of shipments
5.	Ordering supplies	Product-level	Number of purchase orders
6.	Scheduling production	Batch-level	Number of production orders
7.	Administering parts	Product-level	Number of parts
8.	Moving materials	Batch-level	Number of moves
9.	Processing customer orders	Product-level	Number of customer orders
10.	Supervising plant	Facility-level	*
11.	Welding subassemblies	Unit-level	Machine hours
12.	Assembling components	Unit-level	Direct labour hours
13.	Testing special products	Product-level	Testing hours
14.	Providing heat and air conditioning in the plant	Facility-level	*
15.	Expediting goods	Product-level	Number of expedited orders
16.	Providing plant space	Facility-level	*

* Identifying an activity driver for facility-level costs is usually not practical. These costs are necessary to sustain a factory's general manufacturing processes. It is not possible to identify how individual products consume these activities. In effect, these costs are fixed in relation to changes in the manufacturing activity. The application of these costs is often done with drivers like square metres, direct labour or similar measures.

4-15

Supplier cost comparison:

Activity rates:

Activity	Inspecting Components	Reworking Products	Warranty Work
Cost	$240,000	$760,500	$4,800,000
Activity driver	Sampling hours	Rework hours	Warranty hours
Activity amount			
Vance	40	90	400
Foy	1,960	1,410	7,600
Total	2,000	1,500	8,000
Activity rate	$120	$507	$600

Supplier costs:

	Vance	Foy
Inspection activity		
Sampling hours	40	1,960
Inspection cost (@$120)	$4,800	$235,200
Rework activity		
Rework hours	90	1,410
Rework cost (@$507)	$45,630	$714,870
Warranty activity		
Warranty hours	400	7,600
Warranty cost(@$600)	$240,000	$4,560,000
Total	$290,430	$5,510,070
Units purchased	400,000	1,600,000
Unit supplier cost	$0.726	$3.443
Unit purchase cost	$23.500	$21.500
Total unit cost	$24.226	$24.943

This ABC analysis shows that Vance is the low-cost supplier when other supplier related costs are considered. The offer of a lower purchase price adds to Vance's cost advantage. As long as Jill is confident that Vance will continue to deliver a high-quality component, Lumus should accept Vance's request for a long-term supply contract and reduce its purchases from Foy. Jill could also approach Foy to negotiate for lower process or better quality.

PROBLEMS

4-17

1. Activity classifications:
    Note: other classifications could also be correct.

Activity	Activity Level	Cost driver	Consumption Ratio Small	Large
Material handling	Batch	number of moves	0.33	0.67
Maintaining equipment	Product	maintenance hours	0.67	0.33
Producing power	Unit	KW hours	0.50	0.50
Amortization (machines)	Unit	machine hours	0.50	0.50
Engineering	Product	engineering hours	0.67	0.33
Receiving	Product	number of orders	0.33	0.67
Setups	Batch	number	0.75	0.25
Inspecting	Batch	inspection hours	0.75	0.25

2. Cost pools and pool rate calculations:

Cost Pools:	Defining Activities
Machining	Producing power and Amortization (machines)
Batch processing	Setups and Inspecting
Batch handling	Material handling
Technical support	Engineering and Maintaining equipment
Material support	Receiving

Each cost pool is made up of activities that have the same activity level and the same consumption ratio. The names of the pools describe the logical relationships of the defining activities. Each set of activities is made up of several activities. This reduces the total number of cost pools needed for product costing. In our example, the number is reduced from 8 to 5, but in a real setting the reduction is often more dramatic.

Note: Even though material handling and receiving have the same consumption ratios (the same driver classification), they have different activity-level classifications and are in different activity sets. Similarly, even though engineering and maintaining have the same activity-level classification as receiving, they have a different driver classification and so are in a different activity set.

Pool rate calculations:

Machining: Pool 1, consumption ratios (0.5, 0.5)

Producing power	$30,000
Amortization	60,000
Total	$90,000
Activity Driver*	100,000 machine hours
Pool rate	$0.90 per machine hour

* Direct labour hours or kilowatt hours could be used as well. The key thing to note is that power and amortization can use the *same* activity driver to assign costs to products.

4-17 continued

Batch-processing: Pool 2, consumption ratios: (0.75,0 .25):

Setups	$ 96,000
Inspecting	60,000
Total	$156,000
Activity driver*	80 setups
Pool rate	$1,950 per setup

* Inspection hours could also be used.

Batch handling: Pool 3, consumption ratios: (0.33, 0.67):

Material handling	$120,000
Activity driver	6,000 material moves
Pool rate	$20 per move

Technical support: Pool 4, consumption ratios: (0.67, 0.33):

Engineering	$100,000
Maintaining	80,000
Total	$180,000
Activity driver*	6,000 maintenance hours
Pool rate	$30 per hour

*Number of engineering hours could also be used

Material support: Pool 5, consumption ratios: (0.33, 0.67)

Receiving	$30,000
Activity driver	750 orders
Pool rate	$40 per order

3. Computation of unit overhead costs:*

		Small Clock	Large Clock
Unit-level activities:	Machining	$ 45,000	$ 45,000
Batch-level activities:	Batch Processing	117,000	39,000
	Batch Handling	40,000	80,000
Product-level activities:	Technical support	120,000	60,000
	Material Support	10,000	20,000
Total overhead costs		$332,000	$244,000
Units produced		100,000	200,000
Overhead cost per unit		$3.32	$1.22

* for each activity, overhead cost is Activity Pool Rate × Amount of Activity Driver

4-19

1. Cheetah should use departmental rates because the Skins Department's activity is labour intensive while the Stuffing Department's activity is machine intensive. If products use a varying amount of each activity, a plant-wide rate based on a single activity measure will fail to reflect the difference in product cost.

2. The way Cheetah assigns the cost of its purchasing activity and cleaning and maintenance activity to its production activities could be improved by identifying better activity drivers for these activities. The amount of materials ordered may not be the best activity measure for the purchasing activity. The Skins Department requires special orders for materials while the Stuffing Department requires a standard material. The amount of materials ordered may not reflect the different requirements. A measure based on the amount of time purchasing spends on processing an order may be better related to the activity used. If different products have different material ordering needs, the purchasing activity should be identified as a separate activity and traced to the individual products using an activity measure such as number of purchase orders or hours to process a purchase request. Total space occupied may not be the best activity measure for the cleaning and maintenance activity. The Stuffing Department is more machine intensive than the Skins Department and may require more of the cleaning activity than is indicated by the space occupied. An activity measure such as hours of maintenance activity could improve the assignment of this cost.

4-21

1. Cost of material handling activity:

Input	Cost		Cost Assignment Method
Forklifts	$12,000	$6,000 × 2	direct tracing
Propane	18,000	$3 × 6,000	driver tracing; number of moves
Labour	90,000	$40,000 × 3 × 75%	driver tracing; time
Total	$120,000		

2. The plantwide overhead rate (based on direct labour hours) is $30 per direct labour hour:

    $600,000 ÷ (10,000 + 10,000) = $30 per direct labour hour

Unit cost calculation:	Basic Model	Deluxe Model
Prime cost per unit	$80.00	$160
Overhead cost per unit*	7.50	15
Cost per unit	$87.50	$175

    * [$30 × 10,000 direct labour hours] ÷ 40,000 units; [$30 × 10,000 direct labour hours] ÷ 20,000 units

3. We form homogeneous cost pools by classifying the activities by activity level and then grouping activities (at each level) by activity driver. These pools are formed in order to reduce the total number of cost pools needed for product costing.

    Unit-level activities: none

    Batch-level activities: Material handling (number of moves: 0.33, 0.67)
                                Setting up equipment (number of setups: 0.25, 0.75)

    Because these activities have different consumption ratios we will form two pools with separate rates.

    Pool 1 – Material handling pool: $20 per material move [$120,000 ÷ (2,000 + 4,000)]

    Pool 2 – Setup pool: $1,200 per setup [$96,000 ÷ (20 + 60)]

4-21 continued

Product-level activities: Maintaining equipment (maintenance hours: 0.25, 0.75)
Engineering support (engineering hours: 0.25, 0.75)
Purchasing materials (number of requisitions: 0.33, 0.67)
Receiving goods (orders processed: 0.33, 0.67)
Paying suppliers (invoices processed: 0.33, 0.67)

Maintenance and engineering are grouped in a pool (with the same consumption ratios) and purchasing, receiving, and paying are grouped in a pool (with the same consumption ratios).

Pool 3 – Product support pool: $58.50 per maintenance hour [($114,000 + 120,000) ÷ (1,000 + 3,000)]

Pool 4 – Material acquisition pool: $433.33 per requisition [($60,000 + 40,000 + 30,000) ÷ (100 + 200)]

Facility-level activities: Providing space

As stated in the question, facility level costs are allocated in proportion to machine hours.

Pool 5 – Facility pool: $2.00 per machine hour [$20,000 ÷ (5,000 + 5,000)]

4. Unit cost calculation:

	Basic Model	Deluxe Model	
Prime costs:	$3,200,000	$3,200,000	[40,000 × $80; 20,000 × $160]
Overhead:			
Pool 1	40,000	80,000	[2,000 × $20; 4,000 × $20]
Pool 2	24,000	72,000	[20 × $1,200; 60 × $1,200]
Pool 3	58,500	175,500	[1,000 × $58.50; 3,000 × $58.50]
Pool 4	43,333	86,666	[100 × $433.33; 200 × $433.33]
Pool 5	10,000	10,000	[5,000 × $2.00; 5,000 × $2.00]
Total Cost	$3,375,833	$3,624,166	
÷ Units produced	40,000	20,000	
Unit cost	$84.40	$181.21	

The ABC costs are more accurate because driver tracing more closely represents the actual resource consumption of overhead items. The basic model was "overcosted" using the plant-wide approach and the deluxe model was "undercosted."

4-23

1. Cost per patient day using a functional-based approach is $200. This is the total cost of patient care divided by the patient day capacity:

Activity	Annual Cost	
Occupancy and feeding	$1,000,000	
Nursing care	950,000	
Nursing supervision	50,000	[see calculation below]
Total cost	$2,000,000	
Patient days	10,000	
Cost per patient day	$200	

Cost of nursing supervision:

Activity	Annual Cost	
Supervisor salary	$ 70,000	
Secretary salary	22,000	
Assistants' salaries	108,000	[3 × $48,000 × 75%]]
Other traceable costs	100,000	
Total cost	$300,000	
Number of nurses supervised	150	
Cost per nurse supervised	$2,000	
Maternity care share	$50,000	[25 × $2,000]

2. The cost per patient day using an activity-based approach is $150 for a normal patient, $225 for a caesarean patient, and $500 for a patient with complications.

    The first step is to assign the costs of nursing supervision (a secondary activity) to the cost of maternity nursing care (a primary activity). In part 1, $50,000 of the nursing supervision Activity cost is traceable to the maternity nursing care (using the number of nurses as the activity driver). The cost of maternity nursing care is $1,000,000 [$950,000 + $50,000] with an activity rate of $20 per nursing hour [$1,000,000 ÷ 50,000 nursing hours]. The activity rate for occupancy and feeding is $100 per patient day [$1,000,000 ÷ 10,000 patient days].

    The next step is to calculate the cost per patient day using these activity rates:

		Type of Patient	
	Normal	Caesarean	Complications
Occupancy and feeding			
Patient days	7,000	2,000	1,000
Cost assigned (@ $100)	$700,000	$200,000	$100,000
Nursing care			
Nursing hours	17,500	12,500	20,000
Cost assigned (@$20)	$350,000	$250,000	$400,000
Total cost	$1,050,000	$450,000	$500,000
Patient days	7,000	2,000	1,000
Cost per patient day	$150	$225	$500

4-23 continued

3. The cost of the activity of the laundry department would be assigned to the user departments at a rate of $0.50 per kilogram [$500,000 ÷ 1,000,000]. Maternity would be assigned $100,000 of laundry cost [$0.50 × 200,000 kilograms]. On a functional-basis, the cost per patient day would increase by $10 [$100,000 ÷ 10,000 patient days].

   On an activity-basis, we would need to determine whether the use of laundry varied with the type of patient. If all patients required the same amount of laundry activity, the $10 average cost is appropriate. If some patients (for example patients with complications) required a greater amount of the laundry activity, we would want to gather information on the kilograms of laundry due to each patient type in order to get a more accurate cost assignment.

   Activity-based costing will provide more accurate cost assignments when the operation has a significant amount of nonunit-level costs and different products consume different proportions of the activities.

4-25

1. The average cost per account is $81.40:

Total cost	$4,070,000	
Number of accounts	50,000	[38,000 + 8,000 + 4,000]
Average cost per account	$81.40	

   The average fee to cover the cost of chequing accounts is $6.78 [$81.40 ÷ 12].

2. The average cost per account using activity rates is $87.37 for low-balance accounts, $67.50 for medium-balance accounts, and $52.50 for high-balance accounts:

   The first step is to calculate activity rates for each activity:

Opening and closing accounts cost	$200,000
Activity [15,000 + 3,000 + 2,000]	20,000
Activity rate per transaction	$10.00
Issuing monthly statement cost	$300,000
Activity [450,000 + 100,000 + 50,000]	600,000
Activity rate per statement	$0.50
Processing transactions cost	$2,050,000
Activity [18,000,000 + 2,000,000 + 500,000]	20,500,000
Activity rate per account transaction	$0.10
Customer inquiries cost	$400,000
Activity [1,000,000 + 600,000 + 400,000]	2,000,000
Activity rate per minute	$0.20
Providing ATM services cost	$1,120,000
Activity [1,350,000 + 200,000 + 50,000]	1,600,000
Activity rate per ATM transaction	$0.70

4-25 continued

The next step is to assign activity costs to the customer categories using the activity rates:

all numbers in '000s	Low-balance		Medium-balance		High-balance	
	Activity	Cost	Activity	Cost	Activity	Cost
Opening and closing accounts (@$10.00)	15	$150	3	$30	2	$20
Issuing statements (@$0.50)	450	225	100	50	50	25
Processing transactions (@$0.10)	18,000	1,800	2,000	200	500	50
Customer inquiries (@$0.20)	1,000	200	600	120	400	80
Providing ATM service (@$0.70)	1,350	945	200	140	50	35
Total		$3,320		$540		$210
Number of accounts		38		8		4
Average cost per account		$87.37		$67.50		$52.50

3. Average profit per account:

Average interest revenue	$90.00
Cost	81.40
Profit	$ 8.60

Average profit per account using the account-based cost assignment method:

	Low-balance	Medium-balance	High-balance
Interest revenue	$80.00	$100.00	$165.00
Cost	81.40	81.40	81.40
Profit	–$ 1.40	$ 18.60	$ 83.60

Average profit per account using the activity-based cost assignment method:

	Low-balance	Medium-balance	High-balance
Interest revenue	$80.00	$100.00	$165.00
Cost	87.37	67.50	52.50
Profit	–$ 7.37	$ 32.50	$112.50

4. Activity-based costing will assist in evaluating the president's argument:

*   activity-based costing can be used to calculate the profit from low-balance customers from lost "cross-sales" (loans, credit cards, investment accounts, and other bank products) by tracing the costs of providing these products to different types of account customers.

*   activity-based costing can be used to analyze how the loss of a significant number of customers – if the president is correct, 19,000 customers may switch banks if free-chequing is eliminated – impacts the activity costs of serving chequing account customers. In particular, identifying any fixed and step-fixed costs is important if the amount of the activity is substantially reduced.

4-27

1. The activity-based cost per starter is calculated by (1) determining activity rates for the supplier-related activities and (2) assigning these costs to each supplier.

Activity rates:

Cost of replacing starters	$1,600,000
Activity (starters replaced) [1,980 + 20]	2,000
Activity rate per starter	$ 800
Cost of expediting orders	$2,000,000
Activity (late or failed shipment) [198 + 2]	200
Activity rate per late or failed shipment	$ 10,000
Cost of warranty repairs	$3,600,000
Activity (warranty repairs) [2,440 + 60]	2,500
Activity rate per account transaction	$ 1,440

Supplier Cost:

	Watson	*Johnson*
Purchase cost:		
Units purchased	36,000	8,000
Purchase price paid	$900	$1,000
Purchase cost	$32,400,000	$8,000,000
Replacing starters:		
Starters replaced	1,980	20
Cost assigned (@ $800)	$1,584,000	$20,000
Expediting orders:		
Late or failed shipments	198	2
Cost assigned (@ $10,000)	$1,980,000	$20,000
Warranty repairs:		
Number of warranty repairs	2,440	60
Cost assigned (@ $1,440)	$3,513,600	$86,400
Total supplier cost	$39,477,600	$8,122,400
Units purchased	36,000	8,000
Cost per unit	$1,096.60	$1,015.30

This activity cost analysis shows that Johnson is the low-cost supplier even though its invoice price is higher. Watson is the caused of most of the supplier-related costs and its overall cost is significantly higher when costs related to its poorer quality and reliability and poorer delivery performance are considered.

2. Levy should buy the maximum possible from Johnson (and encourage Johnson to increase its capacity – a long term supply contract could be negotiated). Levy could work with Watson to improve its quality and delivery performance; or request a lower price (approximately $820) to compensate for the higher supplier-related activity costs related to purchases from Watson.

MANAGERIAL DECISION CASES

4-29

1. Chuck Davis has given Leonard Bryner poor advice. His comments indicate that he doesn't understand what activity-based management and costing are about. Activity-based management is most beneficial when used in the type of situation described in this case. Chuck states that it is impossible to increase product-costing accuracy because "so many of our costs are indirect costs." This is exactly the problem activity-based costing is designed to solve.

2. As explained in part 1, Chuck does not seem to be well informed about activity-based management and costing. It may seem strange to ask if Chuck's behaviour is ethical. After all, what is wrong with expressing an opinion, albeit uninformed? However, when others rely on a person's expertise to make decisions or take actions that could be wrong or harmful to themselves or their organizations, a question of professional and ethical conduct arises. Management accountants are expected to act competently and to maintain their knowledge and skills. Chuck has not done this and is not meeting the standard of conduct expected.

MANAGEMENT ACCOUNTING
CANADIAN SIXTH EDITION
SOLUTIONS MANUAL

CHAPTER 5
JOB-ORDER COSTING

ANSWERS TO ODD-NUMBERED QUESTIONS FOR WRITING AND DISCUSSION

1. Job-order costing treats each product as a different cost object and accumulates costs by a job. Process costing treats products as the output of common processes and accumulates costs by process or operation. Job order costing is appropriate for companies that produce products that receive different doses of manufacturing costs. Process costing is appropriate for companies that produce homogeneous products that receive similar doses of manufacturing costs in each process.

3. Job-order costing requires more detailed information to be accumulated and analyzed. A separate job-order cost sheet is used for each job to accumulate the costs of that job. Direct material costs are traced to jobs using material requisition forms and direct labour costs are traced to jobs using time cards for each employee. In process costing, direct material and direct labour costs are traced to a process (operation or department) in a more summarized form and then evenly assigned to the products manufactured. A process costing system does not require specific detail of material and labour use.

5. A lawn mowing service is the type of organization that is well suited for job-order costing. Each customer's lawn is different and requires a different amount of activity. We can define each time a customer's lawn was mowed as a job, or each customer as a job. Labour time tickets could be used as the source document to keep track of the labour hours spent on lawn care (and used to trace costs to each job as well as keep track of each worker's time). Any materials used on a job (fertilizer, weed control, etc.) could be traced using material requisitions or directly on the job cost sheet.

    If the business becomes more complicated – lawn aeration and de-thatching, planting and trimming shrubs and trees, etc. – more use of source documents will be required to keep track of labour time, materials, and use of equipment.

7. A manual job-order costing system will depend on paper source documents and records to track costs. Forms are filled out when the activity takes place, are then collected and used to assign costs to particular jobs. In an automated system, data is recorded directly, and the need for source documents such as time tickets and material requisitions is eliminated. Even if forms are used and entered on a batch basis, the job-order cost sheet is replaced with an electronic record. Instead of job-order cost sheets, collections of job records are stored in electronic files.

SOLUTIONS TO ODD-NUMBERED EXERCISES, PROBLEMS, AND CASES

EXERCISES

5-1

a.	paint manufacturing	process
b.	auto manufacturing	process
c.	toy manufacturing	process
d.	custom cabinet making	job
e.	airplane manufacturing (e.g. 767s)	job
f.	personal computer assembly	process
g.	furniture making	process
h.	custom furniture making	job
i.	dental services	job
j.	hospital services	job
k.	paper manufacturing	process
l.	auto repair	job
m.	architectural services	job
n.	landscape design services	job
o.	light bulb manufacturing	process

5-3

1. Overhead has been applied to Jobs 345 and 346 using an overhead rate based on direct labour cost. The rate can be calculated from the information in the May 1 job cost sheets and is 85% of direct labour cost.

	Job 345	Job 346
Overhead applied	$6,800	$18,700
Direct labour	8,000	22,000
Overhead rate	85%	85%

2. The overhead applied to each job in May is the overhead rate of 85% of direct labour cost multiplied by the direct labour cost added to a job in May:

Job	Direct labour cost	Overhead applied
345	$13,800	$11,730
346	10,000	8,500
347	1,500	1,275
348	4,000	3,400

3. The job cost sheets at the end of May are:

Job 345	Direct materials	Direct labour	Overhead applied	Total
May 1	$5,720	$8,000	$6,800	$20,520
Added in May	13,960	13,800	11,730	39,490
May 31	$19,680	$21,800	$18,530	$60,010

Job 346	Direct materials	Direct labour	Overhead applied	Total
May 1	$15,400	$22,000	$18,700	$56,100
Added in May	7,000	10,000	8,500	25,500
May 31	$22,400	$32,000	$27,200	$81,600

Job 347	Direct materials	Direct labour	Overhead applied	Total
May 1	$ 0	$ 0	$ 0	$ 0
Added in May	350	1,500	1,275	3,125
May 31	$ 350	$1,500	$1,275	$3,125

Job 348	Direct materials	Direct labour	Overhead applied	Total
May 1	$ 0	$ 0	$ 0	$ 0
Added in May	4,800	4,000	3,400	12,200
May 31	$4,800	$4,000	$3,400	$12,200

4. Work in process at May 31 is $75,335 and consists of the cost of the jobs not competed at May 31. Job 346 was completed in May and the remaining jobs remain in process:

Job 345	$60,010
Job 347	3,125
Job 348	12,200
Total	$75,335

5. Job 346 was sold for $122,400. Corbin billed the client the cost of the job plus 50% or $81,600 × 150%.

5-5

1. The total cost of the job is $780. The unit cost is $30 [$780 ÷ 26].

Job Cost

Direct materials	$234	
Direct labour	390	[39 × $10]
Overhead applied	156	[39 × $4]
Total cost	$780	

2. The price charged to each member of the dance class is $45 [$30 × 1.5].

5-7

1. Department 1 uses process costing because each class ring is considered to be essentially the same and use similar amounts of material and conversion costs.

   Department 2 uses job-order costing because each jewellery order is different and requires different materials, labour, and other conversion costs.

2. The pin for John Calvin's wife is a job with a cost of $1,000:

Job Cost

Direct materials	$ 500	
Direct labour	250	
Overhead applied	250	[100% × $250]
Total cost	$1,000	

5-9

1. Job-order cost sheets:

Job 14	
Balance, July1	$12,450
Costs added in July:	
Direct materials	6,000
Direct labour	10,000
Overhead applied:	
Power [$3 × 200]	600
Material handling [$25 × 50]	1,250
Purchasing [$40 × 10]	400
	$18,250
Balance, July 31	$30,700

Job 15	
Balance, July1	$3,770
Costs added in July:	
Direct materials	7,900
Direct labour	8,500
Overhead applied:	
Power [$3 × 150]	450
Material handling [$25 ×10]	250
Purchasing [$40 × 40]	1,600
	$18,700
Balance, July 31	$22,470

Job 16	
Balance, July1	$ 0
Costs added in July:	
Direct materials	15,350
Direct labour	23,000
Overhead applied:	
Power [$3 × 1,000]	3,000
Material handling [$25 × 200]	5,000
Purchasing [$40 × 10]	400
	$46,750
Balance, July 31	$46,750

Job 17	
Balance, July1	$ 0
Costs added in July:	
Direct materials	1,000
Direct labour	900
Overhead applied:	
Power [$3 × 10]	30
Material handling [$25 × 5]	125
Purchasing [$40 × 20]	800
	$ 2,855
Balance, July 31	$ 2,855

5-9 continued

2. Work in process inventory on July 31 has a total cost $49,605 and consists of the cost of the jobs not completed in the month (Jobs 16 and 17):

Job 16	$46,750
Job 17	2,855
Total	$49,605

3. The cost of goods transferred to Finished goods inventory during July is $53,170 and consists of the cost of the jobs completed in the month (Jobs 14 and 15):

Job 14	$30,700
Job 15	22,470
Total	$53,170

Note: the t-account for Work in process inventory shows the relationship between the answers to parts 2 and 3.

	Work in process		
July1 (Jobs 14 and 15)	$16,220		
Costs added in July			
Direct materials	30,250	$53,170	Cost of goods manufactured
Direct labour	42,400		(Jobs 14 and 15)
Overhead applied	13,905		
July 31 (Jobs 16 and 17)	$49,605		

4. During July, Job 15 was the only Job sold. The cost of goods sold is $22,470.

5-11

1. Journal entries (a) through (e):

		Debit	Credit
(a)	Raw materials inventory	$3,000	
	Accounts payable		$3,000

		Debit	Credit
(b)	Work in process inventory	$1,700	
	Raw materials inventory		$1,700

		Debit	Credit
(c)	Work in process inventory	$1,200	
	Wages payable		$1,200

$[(50 + 100) \times \$8.00]$

		Debit	Credit
(d)	Work in process inventory	$1,125	
	Overhead control		$1,125

$[(50 + 100) \times \$7.50]$

		Debit	Credit
(e)	Overhead control	$1,230	
	Cash		$1,230

5-11 continued

2. Job order cost sheets and journal entries (f) and (g):

Job 443	
Direct materials	$ 500
Direct labour [50 × $8]	400
Overhead applied [50 × $7.50]	375
Total cost	$1,275

Job 444	
Direct materials [$1,700 – 500]	$1,200
Direct labour [100 × $8]	800
Overhead applied [100 × $7.50]	750
Total cost	$2,750

		Debit	Credit
(f)	Finished goods inventory	$1,275	
	Work in process inventory		$1,275

[Job 443 is completed]

		Debit	Credit
(g)	Cost of goods sold	$2,000	
	Finished goods inventory		$2,000
	Accounts receivable	$2,500	
	Sales revenue		$2,500

[Job 442 is sold for $2,000 × 125%]

3. Statement of cost of goods manufactured:

Kearney Company
Statement of Cost of Goods Manufactured
for the month ended April 30

Manufacturing costs:		
Direct materials:		
Raw materials inventory, April 1	$1,400	
Purchases	3,000	
Raw materials inventory, April 30 (i)	(2,700)	$1,700
Direct labour		1,200
Overhead applied		1,125
Total manufacturing cost		$4,025
Work in process inventory, April 1		0
Work in process inventory, April 30 (ii)		(2,750)
Cost of goods manufactured		$1,275

(i) $1,400 + 3,000 – 1,700   (ii) Job 443

5-13

See the calculations below for each missing item (shown in bold)

	Job 213	*Job 214*	*Job 217*	*Job 225*
Total sales revenue	**$1,200**	$4,375	$5,600	$1,150
Price per unit	12	**12.50**	14	5
Material used in production	365	**1,453**	488	207
Direct labour cost, Department 1	**150**	700	2,000	230
Machine hours, Department 1	15	35	50	12
Direct labour cost, Department 2	50	100	**100**	0
Machine hours, Department 2	25	50	**20**	**0**
Overhead applied, Department 1	90	**420**	1,200	138
Overhead applied, Department 2	**200**	400	160	0
Total manufacturing cost	855	3,073	**3,948**	575
Number of units	**100**	350	400	**230**
Unit cost	8.55	**8.78**	9.87	**2.50**

Calculations:

Job 213:

Number of units	100	[$855 ÷ $8.55]
Total sales revenue	$1,200	[$12 × 100]
Overhead applied, Department 2	$200	[$8 × 25]
Direct labour cost, Department 1	$150	[$855 – (365 + 50 + 90 + 200)] or [($90 ÷ $6) × $10]

Job 214:

Price per unit	$12.50	[$4,375 ÷ 350]
Unit cost	$8.78	[$3,073 ÷ 350]
Overhead applied, Department 1	$420	[$6 × ($100 ÷ 10)]
Material used in production	$1,453	[$3,073 – (700 + 100 + 420 400)]

Job 217:

Total manufacturing cost	$3,948	[$9.87 × 400]
Machine hours, Department 2	20	[$160 ÷ $8]
Direct labour cost, Department 2	$100	[$3,948 – (488 + 2,000 + 1,200 + 160)]

Job 225:

Number of units	230	[$1,150 ÷ $5]
Unit cost	$2.50	[$575 ÷ 230]
Machine hours, Department 2	0	[0 ÷ $8]

5-15

1. The job cost sheets are:

Job 644	Direct materials	Direct labour	Overhead applied	Total
May 1	na	na	na	$10,000
Added in May (i)	$12,500	$10,920	$7,800	31,220
May 31	na	na	na	$41,220

(i) Direct labour: 780 hours @ $14; Applied overhead 780 hours @ $10

Job 648	Direct materials	Direct labour	Overhead applied	Total
May 1	$ 0	$ 0	$ 0	$ 0
Added in May (ii)	14,500	15,400	11,000	40,900
May 31	$14,500	$15,400	$11,000	$40,900

(ii) Direct materials: $27,000 – 12,500; Direct labour: 1,100 hours @ $14; Applied overhead 1,100 hours @ $10

2. May 31 balances:

Direct materials inventory:

Balance, May 1	$ 6,070
Purchases	42,630
Materials available	$48,700
Materials used	27,000
Balance, May 31	$21,700

Work in process inventory consists of Job 648 (still in process at May 31) with a cost of $40,900.

Finished goods inventory consists of Job 644 (completed in May but not sold) with a cost of $41,220.

5-17

1. Activity rates:

Activity	Cost	Driver	Amount of Driver	Activity Rate
Engineering design	$120,000	Engineering hours	3,000	$40.00
Purchasing	80,000	Number of parts	10,000	8.00
Other	250,000	Direct labour hours	40,000	6.25

5-17 continued

2. Job-order cost sheets:

Job 60	Direct materials	Direct labour	Overhead applied	Total
July 1	na	na	na	$ 32,450
Added in July	$26,000	$40,000	$17,625	83,625
July 31	na	na	na	$116,075

Activity	Amount	Rate	Overhead applied	
Engineering design	20	$40.00	$ 800	
Purchasing	150	8.00	1,200	
Other	2,500	6.25	15,625	
Total			$17,625	

Job 61	Direct materials	Direct labour	Overhead applied	Total
July 1	na	na	na	$ 40,770
Added in July	$37,900	$38,500	$16,840	93,240
July 31	na	na	na	$134,010

Activity	Amount	Rate	Overhead applied	
Engineering design	10	$40.00	$ 400	
Purchasing	180	8.00	1,440	
Other	2,400	6.25	15,000	
Total			$16,840	

Job 62	Direct materials	Direct labour	Overhead applied	Total
July 1	na	na	na	$ 29,090
Added in July	$25,350	$43,000	$18,450	86,800
July 31	na	na	na	$115,890

Activity	Amount	Rate	Overhead applied	
Engineering design	15	$40.00	$ 600	
Purchasing	200	8.00	1,600	
Other	2,600	6.25	16,250	
Total			$18,450	

Job 63	Direct materials	Direct labour	Overhead applied	Total
July 1	$ 0	$ 0	$ 0	$ 0
Added in July	11,000	20,900	15,500	47,400
July 31	$11,000	$20,900	$15,500	$47,400

Activity	Amount	Rate	Overhead applied	
Engineering design	100	$40.00	$ 4,000	
Purchasing	500	8.00	4,000	
Other	1,200	6.25	7,500	
Total			$15,500	

Job 64	Direct materials	Direct labour	Overhead applied	Total
July 1	$ 0	$ 0	$ 0	$ 0
Added in July	13,560	18,000	17,275	48,835
July 31	$13,560	$18,000	$17,275	$48,835

Activity	Amount	Rate	Overhead applied	
Engineering design	200	$40.00	$ 8,000	
Purchasing	300	8.00	2,400	
Other	1,100	6.25	6,875	
Total			$17,275	

5-17 continued

3. Work in process on July 31 consists of the cost of the jobs not completed in July (Jobs 61, 63, and 64) with a cost of $230,245:

Job 61	$134,100
Job 63	47,400
Job 64	48,835
	$230,245

4. Cost of goods sold for July consists of the cost of the jobs sold in July (Jobs 60 and 62) with a cost of $231,965:

Job 60	$116,075
Job 62	115,890
	$231,965

5-19

1. Mrs. Lucky won't understand (or like) being charged more for two jobs when the same number of announcements was produced in the other job. Each job is the same in all essential ways and it is reasonable to expect the production cost to be approximately the same.

2. Each month an actual overhead rate was computed by dividing the total overhead costs ($20,000) by the direct labour hours for the month (500 hours in May, 250 hours in June and July). This rate was multiplied by the actual direct hours worked for each job (5 hours for each job) to calculate the amount of overhead applied to the job.

    May: Actual rate = $20,000 ÷ 500 = $40 per hour
    Overhead assigned (Job 115): $40 × 5 = $200

    June and July: Actual rate = $20,000 ÷ 250 = $80 per hour
    Overhead assigned (Jobs 116, 117): $80 × 5 = $400

3. Using an annual predetermined rate (normal costing) is better since it avoids the effect of the non-uniform level of production activity problem revealed in the first two requirements.

    Predetermined rate = $240,000 ÷ (500 × 12) = $40 per hour

Cost of each job:	
Direct materials	$250
Direct labour	25
Overhead (5 × $40)	200
Total cost	$475

The price of each job would have been $593.75 (125% × $475).

The recommended method of pricing is better because each job bears a more representative application of overhead, without regard to seasonal fluctuations in activity. The jobs in the summer would be priced more fairly.

5-21

1. The per unit cost of Job 34 is $246.20:

Direct materials	$ 1,240
Direct labour	6,150
Applied overhead	4,920 [410 × $12]
Total cost	$12,310
Units produced	50
Unit cost	$246.20

2. The balance in work in process inventory on October 31 is $16,726 – only Job 35 is not competed at the end of October:

Direct materials	$ 985
Direct labour	8,745
Applied overhead	6,996 [583 × $12]
Total cost	$16,726

3. The journal entries are:

Completion of Job 34:

	Debit	Credit
Finished goods inventory	$12,310	
Work in process inventory		$12,310

Sale of Job 34:

	Debit	Credit
Cost of goods sold	$12,310	
Finished goods inventory		$12,310

	Debit	Credit
Accounts receivable	$19,696	
Sales revenue		$19,696

Calculation: $12,310 × 160%

5-23

1. b

2. b

3. a   (see calculation below)

Cost of Job 17		
June 1	$100	
June costs added		
Direct materials	250	
Direct labour	300	
Applied overhead	210	[70% × $300]
Total	$860	

Selling price is 150% of cost or $1,290

5-23 continued

4. d

5. b

PROBLEMS

5-25

1. The plantwide rate (based on machine hours) is $900 per machine hour:

Purchasing	$30,000
Setups	15,000
Engineering	20,000
Other	25,000
Total overhead	$90,000
Machine hours	10,000
Overhead rate	$9.00

Courtney Company's bids are $9,490 for Job 1 and $16,120 for Job 2.

	Job 1		Job 2	
Direct materials	$4,500		$ 8,600	
Direct labour	1,000		2,000	
Applied overhead	1,800	[200 × $9]	1,800	[200 × $9]
Total cost	$7,300		$12,400	
Markup (30%)	2,190		3,720	
Bid price	$9,490		$16,120	

2. The activity rates are:

Activity	Cost	Activity Driver	Amount of Activity	Activity Rate
Purchasing	$30,000	Purchase orders	5,000	$6.00
Setups	15,000	Number of setups	1,000	15.00
Engineering	20,000	Engineering hours	500	40.00
Other	25,000	Machine hours	10,000	2.50

Courtney Company's bids are $9,256 for Job 1 and $15,165 for Job 2.

	Job 1		Job 2	
Direct materials	$4,500		$ 8,600	
Direct labour	1,000		2,000	
Overhead applied				
Purchasing	90	[15 × $6.00]	120	[20 × $6.00]
Setups	30	[2 × $15.00]	45	[3 × $15.00]
Engineering	1,000	[25 × $40.00]	400	[10 × $40.00]
Other	500	[200 × $2.50]	500	[200 × $2.50]
Total cost	$7,120		$11,665	
Markup (30%)	2,136		3,500	
Bid price	$9,256		$15,165	

3. The activity rates better reflect the differences in how Job 1 and Job 2 use overhead activities. Although both jobs use the same amount of machine hours, each uses different amounts of the nonunit-level activities. The use of a plantwide rate overcosts both jobs (and may result in unsuccessful bids).

5-27

1. The plantwide overhead rate is $9.04 per direct labour hour [$4,068,000 ÷ 450,000].

    The estimated unit cost of the job is $2,449.10:

Direct materials	$24,000	
Direct labour	36,900	
Applied overhead	37,064	[4,100 × $9.04]
Total cost	$97,964	
Units produced	40	
Cost per unit	$2,449.10	

    The gross margin per unit is $50.90 [$2,500 – 2,449.10]. The gross margin for the order is $2,036 [40 × $50.90].

    Under normal operating conditions, the order would not be accepted because the price of $2,500 is less than the price of $2,694.10 required by Ferguson's policy [$2,449.10 × 110%].

2. The activity rates are:

Activity	Cost	Activity Driver	Activity Amount	Activity Rate
Machining	$1,000,000	Machine hours	100,000	$10.00
Material handling	800,000	Material moves	10,000	$80.00
Inspection and rework	250,000	Rework hours	5,000	$50.00
Setup	640,000	Number of setups	1,000	$640.00
Purchasing	118,000	Number of purchase orders	20,000	$5.90
General factory	1,260,000	Direct labour hours	450,000	$2.80

    The estimated unit cost of the job is $2,128.70:

Direct materials	$24,000	
Direct labour	36,900	
Applied overhead		
Machining	10,000	[$10 × 1,000]
Material handling	480	[$80 × 6]
Inspection and rework	250	[$50 × 5]
Setup	1,920	[$640 × 3]
Purchasing	118	[$5.90 × 20]
General factory	11,480	[$2.80 × 4,100]
Total cost	$85,148	
Units produced	40	
Cost per unit	$2,128.70	

    The gross margin per unit is $371.30 [$2,500 – 2,128.70]. The gross margin for the order is $14,852 [40 × $371.30].

    At a price of $2,500 per unit, the job would be accepted because the price is higher than the price of $2,341.79 [$2,128.70 × 110%] required by Ferguson's policy.

3. For companies with significant nonunit-level overhead costs and product diversity, activity rates provide better product costing. More accurate product costs, in turn, provide better information for pricing decisions. In this example, the company would reject a profitable job because of inaccurate product cost information (and potentially accept an unprofitable job that is undercosted) and an opportunity to expand into a profitable market would have been lost.

5-29

1. The cost category – general conditions – corresponds to overhead for a manufacturing company. Many of these costs are related to the overall project (for example, field office salaries and cleanup costs) and not to any particular house. Butter allocates this cost on the basis of units produced with an equal amount allocated to each house built. This may distort the costs of different houses. For example, larger houses may place greater demands on site utilities, insurance, etc. Allocating these costs on the size of the house may provide more accurate cost assignments.

    Hard costs are direct costs similar to direct materials and direct labour. Land costs may be traced by the size of a lot. We can consider these to be similar to product costs for a manufacturing company.
    Finance costs are traceable to each house and are part of the cost of building a house – we can treat these as product costs.

    Marketing costs are mostly traceable to a particular house (sales commissions and appraisal fees) but we would treat these as period costs. Some of the marketing costs (for example, advertising) may be for the total project and are not traceable to any particular house.

2. The job cost sheet for Job 3 is:

    Hard costs:
Direct materials	$ 28,000
Direct labour	36,000
Subcontractor	44,000
Total hard costs	$108,000
Land (i)	7,813
General conditions (ii)	6,000
Finance	4,765
Marketing	3,800
Total job cost	$130,378

    (i) The cost of land is assigned to a house based on the size of the lot. 4 hectares of land cost $250,000 or an average of $62,500 per hectare [$250,000 ÷ 4]. The lot for Job 3 is 0.125 hectares with an assigned cost of $7,813 [$62,500 × 0.125].

    (ii) Butter assigns this cost based on the number of lots in the project – a cost of $6,000 per lot [$120,000 ÷ 20].

5-31

1. The plantwide rate is $10 per direct labour hour [$2,500,000 ÷ 250,000]. The bid prices are $18.75 for Job SS and $60.00 for Job TT:

    Job SS

Prime costs	$120,000	
Applied overhead	60,000	[6,000 × $10]
Total costs	$180,000	
Units produced	14,400	
Unit cost	$12.50	
Markup (50%)	6.25	
Bid price	$18.75	

    Job TT

Prime costs	$50,000	
Applied overhead	10,000	[1,000 × $10]
Total costs	$60,000	
Units produced	1,500	
Unit cost	$40.00	
Markup (50%)	20.00	
Bid price	$60.00	

2. The overhead rate for Department A is $2.50 per direct labour hour [$500,000 ÷ 200,000] and the overhead rate for Department B is $16.67 per machine hour [$2,000,000 ÷ 120,000]. The bid prices are $14.67 for Job SS and $101.01 for Job TT:

    Job SS

Prime costs	$120,000	
Applied overhead		
Department A	12,500	[5,000 × $2.50]
Department B	8,335	[500 × $16.67]
Total costs	$140,835	
Units produced	14,400	
Unit cost	$ 9.78	
Markup (50%)	4.89	
Bid price	$14.67	

    Job TT

Prime costs	$50,000	
Applied overhead		
Department A	1,000	[400 × $2.50]
Department B	50,010	[3,000 × $16.67]
Total costs	$101,010	
Units produced	1,500	
Unit cost	$ 67.34	
Markup (50%)	33.67	
Bid price	$101.01	

5-31 continued

3. If Retlief bids based on its plantwide rate, its bid for Job SS would be unsuccessful and its bid for Job TT would be successful.

	Job SS	*Job TT*
Plantwide-based bid	$18.75	$ 60.00
Difference to lowest competing bid	(3.00)	43.00
Lowest competing bid	$15.75	$103.00

Its gross margin would be $30,000 [($60.00 × 1,500) – 60,000].

Note: Based on the departmental rates in part 2, the cost of Job TT is $101,010 and its gross margin is –$11,010 [$90,000 – 101,010].

If Retlief bids based on its departmental rates, it would have been successful for both jobs and earned a gross margin of $120,918.

	Job SS	*Job TT*
Department-based bid	$14.67	$101.01
Lowest competing bid	$15.75	$103.00

Revenue		
Job SS	$211,248	[14,400 × $14.67]
Job TT	151,515	[1,500 × $101.01]
Total	$362,763	
Cost of goods sold	241,845	[$140,835 + 101,010]
Gross margin	$120,918	

4. The departments differ in their overhead activity with Department B being more automated. Jobs (such as Job TT) that spend more time in Department B (as measured by machine hours) should be assigned more overhead cost. The use of departmental rates using better activity drivers will accomplish this.

5-33

1. Overhead is applied at a rate of 60 percent of direct labour cost. We can calculate the rate from the job cost information in work in process and finished goods – for example, Job 204 has applied overhead of $4,326 for $7,210 of direct labour cost with a ratio of 60% [$4,326 ÷ $7,210].

2. The unit cost of Job 204 is $414.72 [$20,736 ÷ 50].

Job 204	*Direct materials*	*Direct labour*	*Overhead applied*	*Total*
October 1	$3,190	$ 7,210	$4,326	$14,726
Added in October	410	3,500	2,100	6,010
October 31	$3,600	$10,710	$6,426	$20,736

5-33 continued

3. (a) The cost of raw materials inventory at October 31 is $4,760:

October 1	$7,800
Purchases in October	8,500
Available	$16,300
Used in October	
Jobs 206, 207 208	8,980
Jobs 202, 204, 205	2,560]
October 31	$4,760

(b) The cost of work in process inventory at October 31 is $22,800 (consisting of jobs 207 and 208):

	Job 207	Job 208
Direct materials	$ 3,600	$1,200
Direct labour	8,340	2,910
Applied overhead	5,004	1,746
Total cost	$16,944	$5,856

Total: $22,800 [$16,944 + 5,856]

(c) The cost of finished goods inventory at October 31 is $21,600 (consisting of job 205):

Job 205	Direct materials	Direct labour	Overhead applied	Total
October 1	$2,800	$ 6,500	$3,900	$13,200
Added in October	1,200	4,500	2,700	8,400
October 31	$4,000	$11,000	$6,600	$21,600

4. The cost of goods manufactured in October is $83,186 (Jobs 202, 204, 205, and 206 are completed in October):

	Direct materials	Direct labour	Overhead applied	Total
Job 202				
October 1	$4,200	$8,500	$5,100	$17,800
Added in October	950	2,000	1,200	4,150
October 31	$5,150	$10,500	$6,300	$21,950
Job 204	(from 2)			$20,736
Job 205	(from 3)			$21,600
Job 206				
October 1	$ 0	$ 0	$ 0	$ 0
Added in October	4,180	9,200	5,520	18,900
October 31	$4,180	$9,200	$5,520	$18,900
Total				$83,186

5-33 continued

5. The total overhead applied to jobs in October is $18,270 [(20,450 + 10,000) × 60%].

Actual overhead in October is $17,660:

Supervisory salaries	$ 4,000	
Factory rent	2,000	
Amortization (machines)	3,000	
Indirect labour	5,000	
Supplies (factory)	1,100	
CPP, EI, and other benefits*	2,560	[$3,200 × 80%]
Total	$17,660	

Overhead is $610 overapplied in October [$18,270 – 17,660].

5-35

1. The overhead rate used last year is $5.00 per bike-rental-day.

The overhead rate for this year is $10.00 per bike-rental-day [$100,000 ÷ 10,000].

The cost of the Carson "job" was $202.00 last year and $252.00 this year. The price charged was $282.80 last year and $352.80 this year (see below for calculations).

The price of the job has increased by $70.00 (or 24.8%). Likely the Carsons will not be pleased with the higher price and may decide to do something else for their annual vacation.

Calculations:

	Last Year	This Year
Bike cost:		
Level 2 (3 × $12 × 2); (3 × $12 × 2)	$72.00	$72.00
Level 3 (2 × $20 × 2); (2 × $20 × 2)	80.00	80.00
Overhead: (5 × $5 × 2); (5 × $10 × 2)	50.00	100.00
Total cost	$202.00	$252.00
Price charged (@140%)	$282.80	$352.80

2. The activity rates are:

Activity	Cost	Activity Driver	Quantity	Rate
Purchasing	$30,000	Purchase orders	10,000	$ 3.00
Power	20,000	Kilowatt-hours	50,000	0.40
Maintenance	6,000	Maintenance hours	600	10.00
Other	44,000	Labour hours	22,000	2.00

$50,000 of overhead is assigned to the bike rental operation and $50,000 is assigned to the catering operation:

Overhead applied	Bike rental	Catering operation
Purchase orders	7,000	3,000
@ $3.00	$21,000	$ 9,000
Kilowatt-hours	5,000	45,000
@ $0.40	$ 2,000	$18,000
Maintenance hours	500	100
@$10.00	$ 5,000	$ 1,000
Labour hours	11,000	11,000
@ $2.00	$22,000	$22,000
Total	$50,000	$50,000

5-35 continued

3. When overhead costs are first assigned to the bike rental and picnic catering operations with activity rates, the overhead rate for bike rentals is $5.00 per bike-rental-day [$50,000 ÷ 10,000].

    Because the overhead rate is the same as last year, the Carson job will have the same cost ($202.00) and the same price ($282.00) as last year:

    Bike cost:

Level 2 (3 × $12 × 2)	$72.00
Level 3 (2 × $20 × 2)	80.00
Overhead: (5 × $5 × 2)	50.00
Total cost	$202.00
Price charged (@140%)	$282.80

4. The overhead rate for the picnic catering operation is $4.55 per labour hour [$50,000 ÷ 11,000].

    The cost of the Estes job is $41.55.

    Bike cost:

Level 1 (2 × $7.50)	$15.00
Overhead: (2 × $5)	10.00
Picnic:	
Materials	12.00
Overhead (1 × $4.55)	4.55
Total cost	$41.55

5. The use of activity-based costing gives the managers of Mountain View Rentals a better idea of the activities (and their costs) used in their business. The addition of Level 4 bikes will increase the average purchasing and maintenance activities related to the bike rentals and increase the average overhead per bike-rental-day.

    Mountain View can use the activity-based approach to assign the overhead costs to the different types of bikes. They can compare the cost of providing a Level 4 bike rental to the price their customers are willing to pay to determine whether the new type of bike will be a profitable addition.

MANAGERIAL DECISION CASES

5-37

1. Doug Adams proposed solution is not ethical. Maintaining the current plantwide rate is not illegal but its continuation has only one purpose – to extract extra profit from government business. Doug knows that the plantwide rate is not accurately assigning overhead costs to the various jobs and is willing to alter the assignments on an "unofficial" basis for purposes of bidding on private-sector jobs. Ethical behaviour is concerned with choosing between right and wrong action. To knowingly overcharge the government certainly seems wrong. To continue overpricing with the knowledge that the new overhead rates would more than make up any lost profits from the government work (through more competitive bidding in the private sector) is a clear indication of greed. While managers have a responsibility to maximize profits, this obligation must be within ethical boundaries.

2. The standards of ethical conduct for management accountants prohibit Tonya Martin from participating in the scheme outlined by Doug Adams. Tonya should refrain from any conduct that would discredit the profession. Management accountants have a responsibility to communicate information fairly and objectively and to disclose all relevant information that could reasonably be expected to influence an intended user's understanding of the reports, comments, and recommendations presented. This requirement would present a significant dilemma for Tonya when government auditors examine the records of the company.

3. If Tonya cannot persuade Doug to refrain from implementing his scheme, she should present her objections to Doug's immediate supervisor. If a resolution cannot be reached at this level, then Tonya should go to the next higher management level. If no resolution is possible after appealing to all higher levels, then Tonya's only remaining option may be to resign.

CHAPTER 6
PROCESS COSTING

ANSWERS TO ODD-NUMBERED QUESTIONS FOR WRITING AND DISCUSSION

1. In sequential processing products pass through a series of processes or operations, one after the other in sequence. A product is worked on in an operation and then, when complete, passes to the next operation.

    In parallel processing, subcomponents of a product are produced simultaneously (in two or more sequential processing operations). The subcomponents are combined in a later operation (or sequence of operations) for final assembly.

3. Equivalent units are the complete units that could have been produced with the amount of direct materials, direct labour, and overhead used during the period.

    Equivalent units are used in a process costing system to measure the amount of output for a process in a period when there are both completed units and partially completed units (i.e. work-in-process inventory at the beginning and/or end of the period). Equivalent units are used as the denominator to calculate the process unit cost for the period.

5. The weighted-average and FIFO methods will give the same results if prior-period unit costs are the same as current-period unit costs.

7. Transferred-in costs are like separate material costs for the receiving department (added at the beginning of the process) with a cost based on the cost of goods completed in the prior (producing) department.

9. The first step is the analysis of the flow of physical units – completed units and partially complete units with different degrees of completion.

    The second step is to calculate equivalent units based on the information in the physical flow schedule (prepared in the first step).

    The third step is the calculation of unit cost by dividing the cost of the process by the equivalent units produced (from the second step).

    The fourth step is to assign costs to completed units (cost of goods transferred out) and partially complete units (cost of ending work-in-process inventory) using the unit costs (from the third step).

    The fifth and final step is a cost reconciliation to check that the costs assigned (in the fourth step) equal the costs to account for (from beginning work-in-process inventory and current period costs).

11. The weighted-average method uses the same unit cost to assign process costs to all the units completed during a period (cost of goods transferred out).

    The FIFO method assigns costs to the units completed from beginning work-in-process inventory based on prior-period and current period unit costs. FIFO assigns costs to the units started and completed based only on current period unit costs.

13. Service companies often have no work-in-process inventories. Process costing for services can be very simple – unit cost is simply the total costs of the service for the period divided by the quantity of service provided during the period.

SOLUTIONS TO ODD-NUMBERED EXERCISES, PROBLEMS, AND CASES

EXERCISES

6-1

1. Cost flow analysis:

	Cutting	*Sewing*	*Packaging*
Direct materials	$5,400	$ 900	$ 225
Direct labour	150	1,800	900
Applied overhead	750	3,600	900
Transferred in from Cutting	---	6,300	---
Transferred in from Sewing	---	---	12,600
Total manufacturing cost	$6,300	$12,600	$14,625

2. The total unit product cost of a pair of jeans is $24.375 [$14,625 ÷ 600].

   This is the total manufacturing cost (from all departments) divided by the total output of 600 pairs of jeans.

6-3

1. 21,900 units were transferred out during May.

Units at May 1	13,500
Units started	16,500
Units in process	30,000
Units at May 31	8,100
Units completed	21,900

2. 8,400 units were started and completed during May.

Units completed	21,900
Units at May 1	13,500
Units started and completed in May	8,400

   or

Units started	16,500
Units at May 31	8,100
Units started and completed in May	8,400

3. Physical flow schedule

   Units to account for:

Work-in-process, May 1	13,500
Started in May	16,500
Total units to account for	30,000

   Units accounted for:

Completed and transferred out in May	21,900
Work-in-process, May 31	8,100
Total units accounted for	30,000

6-3 continued

4. The weighted-average equivalent units for May are 30,000 for materials and 23,925 for conversion costs.

	Materials	*Conversion cost*
Completed and transferred out	21,900	21,900
Work-in-process, May 31*	8,100	2,025
Equivalent units	30,000	23,925

* 8,100 × 100%; 8,100 × 25%

6-5

1. a. 240 units were transferred from Department 1 to Department 2.

Work-in-process, June 1	0
Started in June	540
Units to account for	540
Work-in-process, June 30	300
Completed and transferred out	240

  b. Department 1's equivalent units were 540 for material and 390 for conversion cost.

	Materials	*Conversion cost*
Completed and transferred out	240	240
Work-in-process, June 30*	300	150
Equivalent units	540	390

* 300 × 100%; 300 × 50%

2. a. 290 units were transferred from Department 2 to Finished goods.

Work-in-process, June 1	100
Started in June (from Department 1)	240
Units to account for	340
Work-in-process, June 30	50
Completed and transferred out	290

  b. Department 2's weighted-average equivalent units were 290 for material and 310 for conversion cost.

	Materials	*Conversion cost*
Completed and transferred out	290	290
Work-in-process, June 30*	0	20
Equivalent units	290	310

* 50 × 0%; 50 × 40%

Note: Department 2's work-in-process has no material because all material is added at the end of Department 2's process.

Department 2 would also have 340 equivalent units transferred in from Department 1 [290 + 50]

6-7

Mino Company – Production Report
Mixing Department
for the month of March
(weighted-average method)

Unit Information

Units to account for:

Work-in-process, March 1	20,000
Started in March	40,000
Total units to account for	60,000

Units accounted for:	Physical Flow	Equivalent Units
Completed and transferred out in March	50,000	50,000
Work-in-process, March 31	10,000	2,000
Total units accounted for	60,000	52,000

Cost Information

Cost to account for:

Work-in-process, March 1	$ 93,600
Cost added in March	314,600
Total cost to account for	$408,200

Cost per equivalent unit	$7.85

Cost accounted for:

Completed and transferred out	$392,500
Work-in-process, March 31	15,700
Total cost accounted for	$408,200

6-9

Gilroy, Inc. – Production Report
Department 1

Unit Information

Units to account for:

Work-in-process, beginning	0		
Started in period	43,000		
Total units to account for	43,000		

		Equivalent Units	
Units accounted for:	*Physical Flow*	*Material*	*Conversion cost*
Completed and transferred out	35,500	35,500	35,500
Work-in-process, ending (1)	7,500	7,500	6,000
Total units accounted for	43,000	43,000	41,500

Cost Information

Cost to account for:	*Material*	*Conversion cost*	*Total*
Work-in-process, beginning	$ 0	$ 0	$ 0
Cost added in period (2)	16,340	90,420	106,760
Total cost to account for	$16,340	$90,420	$106,760
Cost per equivalent unit	$0.38	$2.18	$2.56
Cost accounted for:			
Completed and transferred out (3)	$13,490	$77,390	$ 90,880
Work-in-process, ending (4)	2,850	13,080	15,930
Total cost accounted for	$16,340	$90,470	$106,810

Notes:

1. conversion cost equivalent units: 7,000 × 80%

2. conversion cost added: $27,126 + 63,294

3. 35,500 × $0.38; 35,500 × $2.18

4. 7,500 × $0.38; 6,000 × $2.18

6-11

1. Physical flow schedule:

    Units to account for:

Work-in-process, December 1	6,000
Started in December	18,000
Total units to account for	24,000

    Units accounted for:

Completed and transferred out in December	20,000
Work-in-process, December 31	4,000
Total units accounted for	24,000

2. The equivalent units produced are (a) 22,800 for materials and (b) 22,000 for conversion cost.

	Material	Conversion cost
Completed and transferred out	20,000	20,000
Work-in-process, December 31*	2,800	2,000
Total equivalent units	22,800	22,000

    * 4,000 × 70%; 4,000 × 50%

3. (a) The unit cost for materials is $7.67.

Direct materials cost:	
Work-in-process, December 1	$ 18,000
Added in December	156,925
Total cost of materials	$174,925
Equivalent units	22,800
Unit cost	$7.67

    (b) The unit cost for conversion cost is $6.50.

Conversion cost:	
Work-in-process, December 1	$ 18,820
Added in December	124,180
Total conversion cost	$143,000
Equivalent units	22,000
Unit cost	$6.50

    (c) The total manufacturing unit cost is $14.17 [$7.67 + 6.50].

4. The total cost of units transferred out is $283,400. The cost assigned to ending work-in-process inventory is $34,476.

    Calculations:

Units completed and transferred out	20,000
Unit cost	$14.17
Cost of units completed and transferred out	$283,400
Work-in-process, December 31	
Materials (2,800 × $7.67)	$21,476
Conversion cost (2,000 × $6.50)	13,000
Cost of work-in-process inventory	$34,476

6-13

Equivalent units:

	A	B	C	D
Units in beginning inventory	3,200	1,000	0	30,000
Units started	17,000	23,000	40,000	40,000
Units to account for	20,200	24,000	40,000	70,000
Units in ending inventory	4,000	0	9,000	10,000
Units completed	16,200	24,000	31,000	60,000
Units completed from beginning inventory	3,200	1,000	0	30,000
Units started and completed (i)	13,000	23,000	31,000	30,000
Beginning inventory percentage to complete	70%	60%	na	25%
Beginning inventory equivalent units (ii)	2,240	600	0	7,500
Ending inventory percentage complete	25%	0%	10%	25%
Ending inventory equivalent units (iii)	1,000	0	900	2,500
Total equivalent units (i + ii + iii)	16,240	23,600	31,900	40,000

6-15

Terry Linens – Bath Linens Department
Production Report
for the month of June

Unit Information

Units to account for:			
Work-in-process, June 1	10,000		
Started in June	70,000		
Total units to account for	80,000		

		Equivalent Units	
Units accounted for:	*Physical Flow*	*Material*	*Conversion cost*
Completed and transferred out	60,000	60,000	60,000
Work-in-process, June 30	20,000	20,000	12,000
Total units accounted for	80,000	80,000	72,000

Cost Information

Cost to account for:	*Material*	*Conversion cost*	*Total*
Work-in-process, June 1	$ 49,000	$ 2,625	$ 51,625
Cost added in June	351,000	78,735	429,735
Total cost to account for	$400,000	$81,360	$481,360
Cost per equivalent unit	$5.00	$1.13	$6.13
Cost accounted for:			
Completed and transferred out	$300,000	$67,800	$367,800
Work-in-process, June 30	100,000	13,560	113,560
Total cost accounted for	$400,000	$81,360	$481,360

6-17

1. Physical flow schedule:

    Units to account for:

Work-in-process, July 1	180,000
Started in July	360,000
Total units to account for	540,000

    Units accounted for:

Completed and transferred out in July	450,000
Work-in-process, July 31	90,000
Total units accounted for	540,000

2. The equivalent units of production are 337,500.

Started and completed	270,000	[450,000 – 180,000]
Complete work-in-process, July 1	45,000	[180,000 × 25%]
Work-in-process, July 31	22,500	[90,000 × 25%]
Total equivalent units	337,500	

3. The unit cost of production for July is $4.45 [$1,501,875 ÷ 337,500].

4. The cost of units transferred out is $1,982,250 and the cost of work-in-process (July 31) is $100,125

    Cost of units transferred out:

Started and completed	$1,201,500	[270,000 × $4.45]
Work-in-process, July 1		
Prior-period cost	580,500	
Cost to complete	200,250	[45,000 × $4.45]
Total cost of units transferred out	$1,982,250	
Cost of work-in-process, July 31	$100,125	[22,500 × $4.45]

5. Cost reconciliation

    Cost to account for:

Work-in-process, July 1	$ 580,500
Cost added in July	1,501,875
Total cost to account for	$2,082,375

    Cost accounted for:

Completed and transferred out	$1,982,250
Work-in-process, June 30	100,125
Total cost accounted for	$2,082,375

6-19

1. The unit cost is $5.00 for materials, $8.75 for conversion cost, and $13.75 in total [$5.00 + 8.75].

	Materials	Conversion cost
Cost of work-in-process, May 1	$30,000	$ 5,000
Added in May	25,000	65,000
Total cost	$55,000	$70,000
Equivalent units	11,000	8,000
Unit cost	$5.00	$8.75

2. The cost of work-in-process, May 31 is $56,250 and the cost of goods transferred out is $68,750.

Work-in-process, May 31		
Materials	$30,000	(6,000 × $5.00)
Conversion cost	26,250	(3,000 × $8.75)
Cost of work-in-process, May 31	$56,250	
Completed and transferred out	$68,750	(5,000 × $13.75)

6-21

1. Equivalent units schedule

	Transferred in	Materials	Conversion cost
Completed (a)	10,000	10,000	10,000
Work-in-process, July 31 (b)	4,000	2,000	2,000
Total equivalent units	14,000	12,000	12,000

a. Calculation of units completed:

Work-in-process, July 1	2,000
Started	12,000
Units to account for	14,000
Work-in-process, July 31	4,000
Completed	10,000

b. 4,000 × 100%; 4,000 × 50%; 4,000 × 50%

2. Unit cost schedule:

	Transferred In	Material	Conversion cost	Total
Work-in-process, July 1	$ 4,000	$ 3,200	$ 3,120	$10,320
Cost added in July	20,500	16,000	24,960	61,460
Total cost	$24,500	$19,200	$28,080	$71,780
Equivalent units	14,000	12,000	12,000	
Cost per equivalent unit	$1.75	$1.60	$2.34	$5.69

6-23

1. The unit cost of a loaf of bread is $0.50.

Cost of materials	$ 675
Conversion cost	1,575
Total production cost	$2,250
Units produced	4,500
Unit cost	$0.50

2. Wholesome Bread does not need to worry about using the FIFO or weighted-average method. The six operations required to produce a loaf of bread are completed within a short period of time – consequently it does not have work-in-process inventory at the end of each day. Without work-in-process inventory, the FIFO and weighted-average methods (and equivalent unit calculations) are not needed.

    Many food processors also have little work-in-process inventory because of short production cycles – inventories of partially completed product are not typical with perishable products. Process costing is straightforward – the denominator in the unit cost calculation is the quantity produced in the period and the use of equivalent unit concepts is unnecessary.

3. If Wholesome Bread also produces rolls and buns, it might use an operation costing approach. As in job order costing, material costs are traced to each batch (of bread, rolls, or buns) but as in process costing, the conversion cost of each operation (mixing, shaping, rising, baking, cooling, and slicing and wrapping) is assigned to each batch uniformly using an appropriate operation measure. Costs of each operation would be assigned using average costs in a manner very similar to an activity-based costing approach.

6-25

1. Physical flow analysis:

Units to account for:	
Work-in-process, April 1	6,000
Started in April	14,000
Total units to account for	20,000
Units accounted for:	
Completed and transferred out in April	18,000
Work-in-process, April 30	2,000
Total units accounted for	20,000

2. The equivalent units of production are 14,000 for materials and 17,300 for conversion cost.

	Material	Conversion cost
Completed and transferred out	18,000	18,000
From work-in-process, April 1	6,000	6,000
Started and completed (i)	12,000	12,000
To complete work-in-process, April 1		
Units	6,000	6,000
Percentage to complete	0	80%
Equivalent units (ii)	0	4,800
Work-in-process, April 30		
Units	2,000	2,000
Percentage completed	100%	25%
Equivalent units (iii)	2,000	500
Total equivalent units (i + ii + iii)	14,000	17,300

6-25 continued

3. The unit cost is $0.2714 for materials, $0.5028 for conversion cost, and $0.7742 in total.

	Material	Conversion cost	Total
Cost added in April	$ 3,800	$ 8,698	$12,498
Equivalent units of production	14,000	18,500	
Cost per equivalent unit	$0.2714	$0.5028	$0.7742

4. The total cost of units transferred to finishing is $14,055. The cost assigned to ending work-in-process inventory is $794.

Units completed and transferred out		
Started and completed	$ 9,290	[12,000 × $0.7742]
Work-in-process, April 1		
Prior-period costs	2,352	[$1,800 + 552]
Cost to complete	2,413	[4,800 × $0.5028]
Cost of units completed and transferred out	$14,055	
Work-in-process, April 30		
Materials	$543	[2,000 × $0.2714]
Conversion cost	251	[500 × $0.5028]
Cost of work-in-process inventory	$794	

PROBLEMS

6-27

Ellis Company – Production Report
Assembly Department
for the month of November
(weighted-average method)

Unit Information

Units to account for:
Work-in-process, November 1	24,000	
Started in November	56,000	
Total units to account for	80,000	

Units accounted for:	Physical Flow	Equivalent Units
Completed and transferred out in November	69,200	69,200
Work-in-process, November 30	10,800	7,560
Total units accounted for	80,000	76,760

Cost Information

Cost to account for:
Work-in-process, November 1	$ 142,760	[$93,128 + 32,432 + 17,200]
Cost added in November	333,152	[$133,760 + 140,640 + 58,752]
Total cost to account for	$475,912	

Cost per equivalent unit	$6.20	[$475,912 ÷ 76,760]

Cost accounted for:
Completed and transferred out	$429,040	[69,200 × $6.20]
Work-in-process, November 30	46,872	[7,560 × $6.20]
Total cost accounted for	$475,912	

6-29

1. (a) Physical flow schedule:

Units to account for:
Work-in-process, August 1	20,000
Started in August	510,000
Total units to account for	530,000

Units accounted for:
Completed and transferred out in August	500,000
Work-in-process, August 31	30,000
Total units accounted for	530,000

(b) Equivalent units schedule:

	Paraffin	Pigment	Conversion cost
Completed and transferred out	500,000	500,000	500,000
Work-in-process, August 31*	30,000	30,000	21,000
Total equivalent units	530,000	530,000	521,000

* 30,000 × 100%; 30,000 × 100%; 30,000 × 70%

2. The unit cost is $0.60 for paraffin, $0.50 for pigment, $1.017 for conversion cost, and $2.117 in total.

	Paraffin	Pigment	Conversion cost	Total
Work-in-process, August 1	$ 12,000	$ 10,000	$ 13,000	$ 35,000
Cost added in August	306,000	255,000	517,000	1,078,000
Total cost	$318,000	$265,000	$530,000	$1,113,000
Equivalent units	530,000	530,000	521,000	
Cost per equivalent unit	$0.60	$0.50	$1.017	$2.117

3. The cost of ending work-in-process inventory is $54,357. The total cost of units transferred out is $1,058,500 [500,000 × $2.117].

Work-in-process, August 31
Paraffin (30,000 × $0.60)	$18,000
Pigment (30,000 × $0.50)	15,000
Conversion cost (21,000 × $1.017)	21,357
Total cost	$54,357

4. Cost reconciliation:

Cost to account for:
Work-in-process, August 1	$ 35,000
Cost added in August	1,078,000
Total cost to account for	$1,113,000

Cost accounted for:
Completed and transferred out	$1,058,500
Work-in-process, August 31	54,357
Total cost accounted for	$1,112,857

Note: the small difference is due to rounding in calculating the unit cost.

6-31

Chang Manufacturing Company
Production Report
for the month of April
(weighted-average method)

Unit Information

Units to account for:

Work-in-process, April 1	8,000
Started in April	42,000
Total units to account for	50,000

			Equivalent Units	
Units accounted for:	*Physical Flow*	*Chemicals*	*Cans*	*Conversion cost*
Completed and transferred out	40,000	40,000	40,000	40,000
Work-in-process, April 30	10,000	10,000	0	8,000
Total units accounted for	50,000	50,000	40,000	48,000

Cost Information

	Chemicals	*Cans*	*Conversion cost*	*Total*
Cost to account for:				
Work-in-process, April 1	$ 68,400	$ 0	$ 23,750	$ 92,150
Cost added in April	342,600	10,500	133,000	486,100
Total cost to account for	$411,000	$10,500	$156,750	$578,250
Cost per equivalent unit	$8.22	$0.2625	$3.2656	$11.7481
Cost accounted for:				
Completed and transferred out	$328,800	$10,500	$130,624	$469,924
Work-in-process, April 30	82,200	0	26,125	108,325
Total cost accounted for	$411,000	$10,500	$156,749	$578,249

Notes:

Completed and transferred out: 40,000 × $8.22; 40,000 × $0.2625; 40,000 × $3.2556

Work-in-process, April 30: 10,000 × $8.22; 0 × $0.2625; 8,000 × $3.2556

6-33

Keating Company – Department C
Production Report
for the month of January
(weighted-average method)

Unit Information

Units to account for:
Work-in-process, January 1	4,000			
Started in January	20,000			
Total units to account for	24,000			

			Equivalent Units	
Units accounted for:	Physical Flow	Transferred in	Material	Conversion cost
Completed and transferred out	21,000	21,000	21,000	21,000
Work-in-process, January 31	3,000	3,000	0	1,000
Total units accounted for	24,000	24,000	21,000	22,000

Cost Information

Cost to account for:	Transferred in	Materials	Conversion cost	Total
Work-in-process, January 1	$14,970	$ 0	$11,760	$ 26,730
Cost added in January	70,350	40,635	87,900	198,885
Total cost to account for	$85,320	$40,635	$99,660	$225,615
Cost per equivalent unit	$3.555	$1.935	$4.53	$10.02
Cost accounted for:				
Completed and transferred out	$74,655	$40,635	$95,130	$210,420
Work-in-process, January 31	10,665	0	4,530	15,195
Total cost accounted for	$85,320	$40,635	$99,660	$225,615

Notes:

Units completed: 24,000 – 3,000

Conversion cost:

Work-in-process, January 1: $7,560 + 4,200; Added in January: $58,500 + 29,400

Completed and transferred out: 21,000 × $3.555; 21,000 × $1.935; 21,000 × $4.53

Work-in-process, January 31: 3,000 × $3.555; 0 × $1.935; 1,000 × $4.53

6-35

Merrifield, Inc.
Production Report
Mixing Department
(weighted-average method)

Unit Information

Units to account for:

Work-in-process, beginning	9,000
Started in period	45,000
Total units to account for	54,000

			Equivalent Units	
	Physical Flow	*Transferred in*	*Materials*	*Conversion cost*
Units accounted for:				
Completed and transferred out	46,125	46,125	46,125	46,125
Work-in-process, ending	7,875	7,875	7,875	1,575
Total units accounted for	54,000	54,000	54,000	47,700

Cost Information

	Transferred in	*Materials*	*Conversion cost*	*Total*
Cost to account for:				
Work-in-process, beginning	$ 5,700	$ 804	$ 1,800	$ 8,304
Cost added in period	28,800	4,200	9,080	42,080
Total cost to account for	$34,500	$5,004	$10,880	$50,384
Cost per equivalent unit	$0.639	$0.093	$0.228	$0.96
Cost accounted for:				
Completed and transferred out	$29,474	$4,290	$10,517	$44,281
Work-in-process, ending	5,032	732	359	6,123
Total cost accounted for	$34,506	$5,022	$10,876	$50,404

Notes:

46,125 units were completed (54,000 – 7,875)

Completed and transferred out: 46,125 × $0.639; 46,125 × $0.093; 46,125 × $0.228

Work-in-process, ending: 7,875 × $0.639; 7,875 × $0.093; 1,575 × $0.228

6-37

1. (a) Physical flow schedule:

Units to account for:
Work-in-process, November 1	5,000
Started in November	25,000
Total units to account for	30,000

Units accounted for:
Completed and transferred out in November	28,000
Work-in-process, November 30	2,000
Total units accounted for	30,000

Work-in-process, November 30: 30,000 – 28,000

(b) Equivalent units schedule:

	Material	Conversion cost
Started and completed	23,000	23,000
Completed work-in-process, November 1	0	3,000
Work-in-process, November 30	2,000	1,600
Total equivalent units	25,000	27,600

Started and completed: 28,000 – 5,000
Completed work-in-process, November 1: 5,000 × 0%; 5,000 × 60%
Work-in-process, November 30: 2,000 × 100%; 2,000 × 80%

(c) Unit cost schedule:

	Material	Conversion cost	Total
Work-in-process, November 1	$10,000	$ 6,900	$ 16,900
Cost added in November	57,800	95,220	153,020
Total cost to account for	$67,800	$102,120	$169,920
Equivalent units of production	25,000	27,600	
Current cost per equivalent unit	$2.312	$3.45	$5.762

(d) The cost of ending work-in-process inventory is $10,144.

Work-in-process, November 30
Materials (2,000 × $2.312)	$ 4,624
Conversion cost (1,600 × $3.45)	5,520
Cost of work-in-process inventory	$10,144

The total cost of units transferred is $159,776.

Started and completed (23,000 × $5.762)	$132,526
Completed work-in-process, November 1	
Prior-period costs	16,900
Current cost added (3,000 × $3.45)	10,350
Cost of goods completed and transferred out	$159,776

6-37 continued

    (e) Cost reconciliation:

        Cost to account for:

Work-in-process, November 1	$ 16,900
Cost added in November	153,020
Total cost to account for	$169,920

        Cost accounted for:

Completed and transferred out	$159,776
Work-in-process, November 30	10,144
Total cost accounted for	$169,920

2. (a) Physical flow schedule:

      Units to account for:

Work-in-process, November 1	8,000
Started in November	28,000
Total units to account for	36,000

      Units accounted for:

Completed and transferred out in November	33,000
Work-in-process, November 30	3,000
Total units accounted for	36,000

Work-in-process, November 30: 36,000 – 33,000

    (b) Equivalent units schedule:

	Transferred in	Material	Conversion cost
Started and completed	25,000	25,000	25,000
Complete work-in-process, November 1	0	8,000	4,000
Work-in-process, November 30	3,000	0	1,500
Total equivalent units	28,000	33,000	30,500

      Started and completed: 33,000 – 8,000
      Complete work-in-process, November 1: 8,000 × 0%; 8,000 × 100%; 8,000 × 50%
      Work-in-process, November 30: 3,000 × 100%; 3,000 × 0%; 3,000 × 50%

    (c) Unit cost schedule:

	Transferred in	Material	Conversion cost	Total
Work-in-process, November 1	$45,320	$ 0	$ 16,800	$ 62,120
Cost added in November	159,776	37,950	128,100	328,826
Total cost to account for	$205,096	$37,950	$144,900	$387,946
Equivalent units of production	28,000	33,000	30,500	
Cost per equivalent unit	$5.706	$1.15	$4.20	$11.056

6-37 continued

(d) The cost of ending work-in-process inventory is $23,418.

Work-in-process, November 30	
Transferred-in (3,000 × $5.706)	$17,118
Materials (0 × $1.15)	0
Conversion cost (1,500 × $4.20)	6,300
Cost of work-in-process inventory	$23,418

The total cost of units transferred is $364,520.

Started and completed (25,000 × $11.056)	$276,400
Completed work-in-process, November 1	
Prior-period costs	62,120
Current material cost added (8,000 × $1.15)	9,200
Current conversion cost added (4,000 × $4.20)	16,800
Cost of goods completed and transferred	$364,520

(e) Cost reconciliation:

Cost to account for:	
Work-in-process, November 1	$ 62,120
Cost added in November	325,826
Total cost to account for	$387,946

Cost accounted for:	
Completed and transferred out	$364,520
Work-in-process, November 30	23,418
Total cost accounted for	$387,938

6-39

1.   Picking Department production report:

Benson Pharmaceuticals.
Production Report
Picking Department
for the month of March
(FIFO method)

Unit Information

Units to account for:
  Work-in-process, March 1   10
  Started in March   150
  Total units to account for   160

		Equivalent Units	
Units accounted for:	*Physical Flow*	*Materials*	*Conversion cost*
Started and completed	130	130	130
Complete work-in-process, March 1	10	0	6
Work-in-process, March 31	20	20	10
Total units accounted for	160	150	146

Cost Information

Cost to account for:	*Materials*	*Conversion cost*	*Total*
Work-in-process, March 1	$ 252	$ 846	$ 1,098
Cost added in March	3,636	13,854	17,490
Total cost to account for	$3,888	$14,700	$18,588
Current cost per equivalent unit	$24.24	$94.89	$119.13
Cost accounted for:			
Started and completed	$3,151	$12,336	$15,487
Work-in-process, March 1 prior-period	252	846	1,098
Work-in-process, March 1 current	0	569	569
Total cost of goods transferred out	$3,403	$13,751	$17,154
Work-in-process, March 31	485	949	1,434
Total cost accounted for	$3,888	$14,700	$18,588

Notes:

Units started and completed: 140 – 10; Complete work-in-process, March 1: 10 × 0%; 10 × 60%;

Work-in-process, March 31: 20 × 100%; 20 × 50%

Conversion cost: March 1, $282 + $282 × 200%; Added in March, $4,618 + $4,618 × 200%

Started and completed: 130 × $24.24; 130 × $94.89

Complete work-in-process, March 1: 0 × $24.24; 6 × $94.89

Work-in-process, March 31: 20 × $24.24; 10 × $94.89

6-39 continued

2. Encapsulating Department production report:

Benson Pharmaceuticals.
Production Report
Encapsulating Department
for the month of March
(FIFO method)

Unit Information

Units to account for:

Work-in-process, March 1	4,000
Started in March	210,000
Total units to account for	214,000

	Physical Flow	Transferred in	Equivalent Units	
			Materials	Conversion cost
Units accounted for:				
Started and completed	204,000	204,000	204,000	204,000
Complete work-in-process, March 1	4,000	0	0	2,000
Work-in-process, March 31	6,000	6,000	6,000	2,400
Total units accounted for	214,000	210,000	210,000	208,400

Cost Information

	Transferred in	Materials	Conversion cost	Total
Cost to account for:				
Work-in-process, March 1	$ 140	$ 32	$ 50	$ 222
Cost added in March	17,154	1,573	4,860	23,587
Total cost to account for	$17,294	$1,605	$4,910	$23,809
Current cost per equivalent unit	$0.0817	$0.0075	$0.0233	$0.1125
Cost accounted for:				
Started and completed	$16,667	$1,530	$4,753	$22,950
Work-in-process, March 1 prior-period	140	32	50	222
Work-in-process, March 1 current	0	0	47	47
Total cost of goods transferred out	$16,807	$1,562	$4,850	$23,219
Work-in-process, March 31	490	45	56	591
Total cost accounted for	$17,297	$1,607	$4,906	$23,810

Notes:

Started (transferred from picking): 140 × 1,500; Started and completed: 208,000 – 4,000

Complete work-in-process, March 1: 4,000 × 0%; 4,000 × 0%, 4,000 × 50%

Work-in-process, March 31: 6,000 × 100%; 6,000 × 100%; 6,000 × 40%

Conversion cost: March 1, $20 + $20 × 200%; Added in March, $1,944 + $1,944 × 200%

Started and completed: 204,000 × $0.0817; 204,000 × $0.0075; 204,000 × $0.0233

Complete work-in-process, March 1: 0 × $0.0817; 0 × $0.0075; 2,000 × $0.0233

Work-in-process, March 31: 6,000 × $0.0817; 6,000 × $0.0075; 2,400 × $0.0233

6-41

2. (a) Equivalent unit schedule – Moulding Department

	Material	Conversion cost
Started and completed	800	800
Complete work-in-process, February 1	0	350
Work-in-process, February 28	200	40
Total equivalent units	1,000	1,190

Notes:

Started and completed: 1,000 – 200
Complete work-in-process, February 1: 500 × 0%; 500 × 70%
Work-in-process, February 28: 200 × 100%; 200 × 20%

(b) Equivalent unit schedule – Assembly Department

	Transferred in	Material	Conversion cost
Started and completed	900	900	900
Work-in-process, February 28*	400	160	160
Total equivalent units	1,300	1,060	1,060

Notes:

Started and completed: 1,300 – 400
Work-in-process, February 28: 400 × 100%; 400× 40%; 400 × 40%

6-41 continued

(c) Equivalent unit schedule – Packaging Department

	Transferred in	Material	Conversion cost
Started and completed	900	900	900
Complete work-in-process, February 1	0	0	75
Work-in-process, February 28*	0	0	0
Total equivalent units	900	900	975

Notes:

Complete work-in-process, February 1: 150 × 0%; 150 × 50%

3.   Unit cost chart:

	Moulding	Assembly	Packaging
Unit prior-department cost	$ 0	$11.502	$13.062
Unit direct material cost	5.000	0.460	2.675
Unit conversion cost	6.437	1.100	3.054
Total unit cost	$11.437	$13.062	$18.791

Calculations:

Moulding:	Material	Conversion cost
Cost added in February	$5,000	$7,660
Equivalent units of production	1,000	1,190
Cost per equivalent unit	$5.00	$6.437

Assembly:	Transferred in	Material	Conversion cost
Cost added in February	$14,953	$48,760	$1,166
Equivalent units of production	1,300	1,060	1,060
Cost per equivalent unit	$11.502	$0.46	$1.10

Packaging:	Transferred in	Material	Conversion cost
Cost added in February	$11,756.00	$2,782.50	$2,977.50
Equivalent units of production	900	900	975
Cost per equivalent unit	$13.062	$2.675	$3.054

Notes:

The cost of goods transferred from moulding to assembly is $14,953:

Started and completed	$ 9,150	(800 × $11.437)
From work-in-process, February 1	3,550	($2,550 + 1,050)
Current cost to complete work-in-process, February 1	2,253	(350 × $6.437)
Cost of goods transferred	$14,953	

The cost of goods transferred from assembly to packaging is $11,756 [900 × $13.062].

6-41 continued

4. Moulding Department:

Work-in-process, February 28
Materials	$1,000	(200 × $5.00)
Conversion cost	257	(40 × $6.437)
Cost of ending work-in-process inventory	$1,257	

Cost of goods transferred out in February	$14,953	(see part 3)

Assembly Department:

Work-in-process, February 28
Transferred-in	$4,601	(400 × $11.502)
Materials	74	(160 × $0.46)
Conversion cost	176	(160 × $1.10)
Cost of ending work-in-process inventory	$4,851	

Cost of goods transferred out in February	$11,756	(see part 3)

Packaging Department:

Work-in-process, February 28	$0	(no units)

Started and completed	$ 16,912	(900 × $18.791)
From work-in-process, February 1	2,559	($1,959 + 375 + 225)
Current cost to complete work-in-process, February 1	229	(75 × $3.054)
Cost of goods transferred out in February	$19,700	

5. Cost reconciliation:

	Moulding	Assembly	Packaging
Cost to account for:			
Work-in-process, February 1			
Prior-department cost	$ 0	$ 0	$ 1,959
Material	2,500	0	375
Conversion cost	1,050	0	225
Cost added in February			
Prior-department cost	0	14,953	11,756
Material	5,000	488	2,408
Conversion cost	7,660	1,166	2,977
Total cost to account for	$16,210	$16,607	$19,700
Cost accounted for:			
Completed and transferred out	$14,953	$11,756	$19,700
Work-in-process, February 28	1,257	4,851	0
Total cost accounted for	$16,210	$16,607	$19,700

6-43

1. January 1, 2004 balances:

   (a) Raw materials

Units (kilograms)	19,000	[136,000 – 125,000 + 8,000]
Cost	$95,000	[19,000 × $5]

   (b) Work-in-process

Units	26,000	[140,000 + 22,000 – 136,000]
Equivalent units materials	26,000	[26,000 × 100%]
Equivalent units conversion cost	15,600	[26,000 × 60%]
Cost	$364,000	[26,000 × $5 + 15,600 × ($6 + $9)]

   (c) Finished goods

Units	7,000	[102,000 + 45,000 – 140,000]
Cost	$140,000	[7,000 × $20]

   Note: sales are 102,000 units [$4,080,000 ÷ $40].

2. Equivalent units for 2004:

	Materials	Conversion cost	
Completed	140,000	140,000	
Work-in-process, December 31	22,000	7,700	[22,000 × 30%]
Total equivalent units	162,000	147,700	

3. (a) Total cost of material used is $810,000 [162,000 × $5].

   (b) Total cost of conversion applied is $2,215,500 [147,700 × $15].

4. Cost of ending work-in-process is $225,500 [22,000 × $5 + 7,700 × $15].

5. Cost of units completed and transferred is $2,800,000 [140,000 × $20].

MANAGERIAL DECISION CASES

6-45

1. Unit cost calculation:

Units to account for:		Units accounted for:	
Work-in-process, beginning	0	Completed and transferred out	2,500
Started	2,800	Work-in-process, ending	300
Total units to account for	2,800	Total units accounted for	2,800

Equivalent unit schedule:

	Material	Conversion cost
Completed and transferred out	2,500	2,500
Work-in-process, ending	300	240
Total equivalent units	2,800	2,740

* 300 × 100%; 300 × 80%

Unit cost schedule:

	Material	Conversion cost
Costs	$114,000	$82,201
Equivalent units	2,800	2,740
Cost per equivalent unit	$40.71	$30.00

Conversion cost: $45,667 + 0.80 × $45,667

The total unit cost is $70.71 [$40.71 + 30.00].

2. Only the material cost is different between the Econo and Deluxe models – both will have the same conversion cost of $30 per unit.

    For material, separate equivalent unit calculations are required:

	Econo	Deluxe
Completed and transferred out	1,500	1,000
Work-in-process, ending	100	200
Total equivalent units	1,600	1,200
Material cost	$30,000	$84,000
Material unit cost	$18.75	$70.00
Conversion unit cost	30.00	30.00
Total unit cost	$48.75	$100.00

3. The unit costs for Econo and Deluxe models are quite different when material costs are traced to each model. Karen is justified in her belief that a pure process-costing system is not appropriate.

    An operation costing system would be more appropriate – process costing is appropriate for conversion costs in each operation but material costs should be traced to each model separately.

4. The misleading cost information has overstated the cost of the Econo model by almost $22 – the cost of the Deluxe model is understated by more than $29. The Deluxe model appears to be more profitable and the Econo model appears to be less profitable than they actually are. As a result, an incorrect decision has been made about which product to promote. This example illustrates the importance of an accurate costing system.

MANAGEMENT ACCOUNTING
CANADIAN SIXTH EDITION
SOLUTIONS MANUAL

CHAPTER 7
SUPPORT DEPARTMENT COST ALLOCATION

ANSWERS TO ODD-NUMBERED QUESTIONS FOR WRITING AND DISCUSSION

1. In a functional model, departments are usually the initial cost objects. Costs are traced to either producing departments or support departments. The first stage is to assign support department costs to producing departments. Costs are assigned using factors that reflect the consumption of support department output (services) by producing departments. Methods used at this stage include the direct method, the sequential (or step) method, and the reciprocal method. At the end of this stage all manufacturing costs are assigned to the producing departments.

    The second stage is to assign the producing department costs (direct and support department costs assigned in the first stage) to products. Overhead rates are developed to allocate the producing departments' costs to products.

3. Rules of financial reporting (GAAP) require both direct and indirect manufacturing costs to be used for inventory valuation. Support department costs are part of the cost of producing a product and are usually allocated to final products.

5. If a company doesn't allocate support department costs to producing departments, producing department managers may see the support activity as "free" and consume more of the support activity than is optimal. Managers will consume free goods until the marginal benefit of the service is zero. Over consumption of service will cause lower profits for the company because the real marginal cost of a service activity will be greater than its marginal benefit. If the company allocates support department costs and holds the managers of producing departments responsible for profits, managers will use a support service until the marginal benefit of the service equals its allocated cost. Allocating support department costs helps each producing department manager select a better level of support department service consumption.

7. It is important to identify and use causal factors to allocate support department costs because product costs will be more accurate. Managers can make better decisions if they have more accurate cost information. If causal factors are known, managers can better control the consumption of support services.

9. It is better to allocate budgeted support department costs rather than actual support department costs for two fundamental reasons.

    The first reason is that budgeted costs are more useful to develop predetermined overhead rates for product costing purposes.

    The second reason is that budgeted costs are more useful for performance evaluation. Managers of support and producing departments are usually held accountable for the performance of their operations. Their ability to control costs is an important factor in their performance evaluation. Allocating actual costs of support departments tends to allow support departments to pass on their inefficiencies to producing departments. If budgeted costs are used, managers of support departments are held accountable for their results and managers of producing departments are not burdened with higher costs that are beyond their control.

11. The reciprocal method is more accurate than either the direct or sequential method because it considers all of a producing department's use of each support department's service – both direct and indirect. The causal link is complete. The sequential method accounts for only some of the indirect use and the direct method ignores all indirect use by producing departments.

SOLUTIONS TO ODD-NUMBERED EXERCISES, PROBLEMS, AND CASES

EXERCISES

7-1

	Department	*Type*
a.	Power	support
b.	Maintenance	support
c.	Finishing	producing
d.	Landscaping	support
e.	Payroll	support
f.	Quality control of suppliers	support
g.	Cooking	producing
h.	Blending	producing
i.	General factory	support
j.	Timekeeping	support
k.	Packaging	producing
l.	Data processing	support
m.	Engineering	support
n.	Drilling	producing
o.	Cutting	producing

7-3

	Department	*Type*
a.	Janitorial staff	support
b.	Laundry	support
c.	Courier	support
d.	Landscaping	support
e.	Payroll	support
f.	Operating rooms	producing
g.	Laboratory	support
h.	Medical records	support
i.	Admitting	support
j.	Radiology	producing
k.	Pediatrics	producing
l.	Data processing	support
m.	Supplies	support
n.	Purchasing	support
o.	Billing	support

7-5

1. The single charging rate is $25 per hour of labour.

Direct labour cost	$360,000
Overhead cost	240,000
Total cost	$600,000
Direct labour hours	24,000
Rate per hour of labour	$25

2. The charge to the used car sales department by the service department is $678.

Materials cost	$478	
Labour and overhead charge	200	[8 × $25]
Total charge	$678	

3. The total cost charged to the producing departments is $34,600 to the new car sales and $125,390 to the used car sales. The service department charged $563,800 to outside service customers.

	New Car Sales	Used Car Sales	Outside Service
Materials	$ 2,100	$ 7,890	$ 86,300
Labour hours	1,300	4,700	19,100
Cost @ $25	$32,500	$117,500	$477,500
Total cost	$34,600	$125,390	$563,800

7-7

1. Maintenance worked just a little over a day in the assembly department. With a billing rate of $52 (see answer to 7-6), the $520 charge is for 10 hours of maintenance time [$520 ÷ $52]. The charge to the assembly department is correct based on the company's existing system.

2. The charging rate for routine maintenance is $24 per hour and the charging rate for technical maintenance is $108 per hour.

	Routine	Technical	Total
Budgeted maintenance cost	$48,000	$108,000	$156,000
Budgeted maintenance hours	2,000	1,000	3,000
Billing rate	$ 24	$ 108	

    The assembly department would have been charged $240 for routine maintenance under the dual rate system [10 × $24].

3. This experience illustrates the need to carefully select a causal factor when developing charging rates. The cost of an hour of routine maintenance is much lower than the cost of technical maintenance – maintenance hours is not a sufficient measure to properly allocate the cost of the different types of maintenance activity.

7-9

1. The sequential method allocation ratios are:

User	Human Resources Employees	Ratio	Maintenance Hours	Ratio
Maintenance	10	0.1250		
Cutting	35	0.4375	8,000	0.80
Polishing	35	0.4375	2,000	0.20
Total	80		10,000	

2. Sequential method allocation:

	Support Departments Human Resources	Maintenance	Producing Departments Cutting	Polishing
Direct costs	$200,000	$130,000		
Allocation from:				
Human Resources	(200,000)	25,000	$ 87,500	$ 87,500
Maintenance	---	(155,000)	124,000	31,000
Total	$ 0	$ 0	$211,500	$118,500

Notes:

Allocation of Human Resources: 0.1250 × $200,000; 0.4375 × $200,000; 0.4375 × $200,000

Allocation of Maintenance: 0.80 × $155,000; 0.20 × $155,000

7-11

1. The direct method allocation rates are $0.90 per kilowatt hour for power; $5.2188 per square metre for general factory; $8.40 per direct labour hour for human resources.

Calculations:

	Power	General Factory	Human Resources
Direct cost (a)	$90,000	$167,000	$84,000
Usage by			
Shaping	30,000	24,000	4,000
Firing	70,000	8,000	6,000
Total (b)	100,000	32,000	10,000
Rate (a ÷ b)	$0.90	$5.2188	$8.40

Allocation of support department costs:

	Support Departments Power	General Factory	Human Resources	Producing Departments Shaping	Firing
Direct costs	$90,000	$167,000	$ 84,000		
Allocation from:					
Power	(90,000)			$ 27,000	$ 63,000
General Factory		(167,000)		125,251	41,750
Human Resources	--	--	(84,000)	33,600	50,400
Total	$ 0	$ 0	$ 0	$185,851	$155,150

7-11 continued

Notes:

Allocation of Power: 30,000 × $0.90; 70,000 × $0.90

Allocation of General Factory: 24,000 × $5.2188; 8,000 × $5.2188

Allocation of Human Resources: 4,000 × $8.40; 6,000 × $8.40

2.   The overhead rates for the producing departments are $65.2128 per direct labour hour for shaping and $64.8583 per direct labour hour for firing.

Calculations:

	Shaping	Firing
Direct overhead	$ 75,000	$234,000
Support department cost	185,851	155,150
Total overhead cost	$260,851	$389,150
Direct labour hours	4,000	6,000
Overhead rate	$65.2128	$64.8583

7-13

1.   The reciprocal method allocation ratios are:

	Human Resources		Power	
User	Payroll	Ratio	Hours	Ratio
Human Resources			50,000	0.125
Power	$ 80,000	0.2		
Generating	160,000	0.4	200,000	0.500
Colouring	160,000	0.4	150,000	0.375
Total	$400,000		400,000	

The cost equation for the human resources department is $HR = \$144,000 + 0.125P$.

The cost equation for the power department is $P = \$130,000 + 0.2HR$.

The total support-department costs are $164,359 for the human resources department and $162,872 for the power department.

Calculations:

$$P = \$130,000 + 0.2 \times (\$144,000 + 0.125P)$$
$$P = \$130,000 + 28,800 + 0.025P$$
$$0.975P = \$158,800$$
$$P = \$162,872$$

$$HR = \$144,000 + 0.125P$$
$$HR = \$144,000 + 0.125 \times \$162,872$$
$$HR = \$164,359$$

7-13 continued

Reciprocal method allocation:

| | Support Departments | | Producing Departments | |
	Human Resources	Power	Generating	Colouring
Direct costs	$144,000	$130,000		
Allocation from:				
Human Resources	(164,360)	32,872	$ 65,744	$ 65,744
Power	20,359	(162,872)	81,436	61,077
Total	$(1)	$ 0	$147,180	$126,821

Notes:

Allocation of Human Resources: 0.2 × $164,359; 0.4 × $164,359; 0.4 × $164,359

Allocation of Power: 0.125 × $162,872; 0.5 × $162,872; 0.375 × $162,872

2. The producing department overhead rates are $9.86 per direct labour hour for generating and $6.89 per direct labour hour for colouring.

	Generating	Colouring
Direct overhead	$ 50,000	$ 80,000
Support department cost	147,180	126,821
Total overhead cost	$197,180	$206,821
Direct labour hours	20,000	30,000
Overhead rate	$9.86	$6.89

7-15

1. We need to choose a sequence to allocate the support departments for the sequential method. We will allocate human resources first and then power. The sequential method allocation is summarized below:

| | Support Departments | | Producing Departments | |
	Human Resources	Power	Generating	Colouring
Direct costs	$144,000	$130,000		
Allocation from:				
Human Resources	(144,000)	28,800	$ 57,600	$ 57,600
Power	--	(158,795)	90,740	68,055
Total	$ 0	$(5)	$148,340	$125,655

Notes:

Human resources costs are allocated first to power, generating, and colouring. The overhead rate for human resources is $0.36 per payroll dollar [$144,000 ÷ ($80,000 + 160,000 + 160,000)] with human resources cost allocated as $80,000 × $0.36; $160,000 × $0.36; $160,000 × $0.36.

Power costs are allocated next to generating and colouring. The overhead rate for power is $0.4537 per kilowatt-hour [($130,000 + 28,800) ÷ (200,000 + 150,000)] with power cost allocated as 200,000 × $0.4537; 150,000 × $0.4537.

7-15 continued

2. The producing department overhead rates are $9.92 per direct labour hour for generating and $6.86 per direct labour hour for colouring.

	Generating	Colouring
Direct overhead	$ 50,000	$ 80,000
Support department cost	148,340	125,655
Total overhead cost	$198,340	$205,655
Direct labour hours	20,000	30,000
Overhead rate	$9.92	$6.86

The sequential method rates are more accurate because some indirect use of support department services is recognized. The direct method recognizes only direct use of support department service. How important the increased accuracy is for this example is debatable. Some may argue that the departmental rates are not that different and the use of a more complicated method is not justified.

7-17

1. The direct method allocation rates are $2.857 per kilowatt for power and $2.857 per maintenance hour for maintenance.

Calculations:

	Power	Maintenance
Direct cost (a)	$20,000	$12,000
Usage by		
Assembly	4,000	2,500
Finishing	3,000	1,700
Total (b)	7,000	4,200
Rate (a ÷ b)	$2.857	$2.857

Direct method support department allocations are:

	Support Departments		Producing Departments	
	Power	Maintenance	Assembly	Finishing
Direct costs	$20,000	$12,000		
Allocation from:				
Power	(19,999)		$11,428	$ 8,571
Maintenance	--	(12,000)	7,143	4,857
Total	$ 1	$ 0	$18,571	$13,428

Notes:

Allocation of Power: 4,000 × $2.857; 3,000 × $2.857

Allocation of Maintenance: 2,500 × $2.857; 1,700 × $2.857

7-17 continued

2. The reciprocal method allocation ratios are:

	Power		Maintenance	
User	Hours	Ratio	Hours	Ratio
Power			800	0.16
Maintenance	2,000	0.222		
Assembly	4,000	0.444	2,500	0.50
Finishing	3,000	0.333	1,700	0.34
Total	9,000		5,000	

The cost equation for the power department is P = $20,000 + 0.16M.

The cost equation for the maintenance department is M = $12,000 + 0.222P.

The total support-department costs are $22,727 for the human resources department and $17,045 for the maintenance department.

Calculations:

$$P = \$20,000 + 0.16\ (\$12,000 + 0.222P)$$
$$P = \$20,000 + 1,920 + 0.03552P$$
$$0.96448P = \$21,920$$
$$P = \$22,727$$

$$M = \$12,000 + 0.222P$$
$$M = \$12,000 + 0.222 \times \$22,727$$
$$M = \$17,045$$

Reciprocal method allocation:

	Support Departments		Producing Departments	
	Power	Maintenance	Assembly	Finishing
Direct costs	$20,000	$12,000		
Allocation from:				
Power	(22,704)	5,045	$10,091	$ 7,568
Maintenance	2,727	(17,045)	8,523	5,795
Total	$ 23	$ 0	$18,614	$13,363

Notes:

Allocation of Power: 0.222 × $22,727; 0.444 × $22,727; 0.333 × $22,727

Allocation of Maintenance: 0.16 × $17,045; 0.5 × $17,045; 0.34 × $17,045

7-17 continued

3. Memo:

The direct method of allocating support department costs is based on the amount of support service used by each producing department directly. It is simple and easy to use. The reciprocal method of allocating support department costs is based on both the direct support service used by a producing department and its indirect use. Indirect use occurs when a producing department uses the service of a support department that uses another support department's service. The use of service of one support department flows through to the producing department.

Although the reciprocal method better traces the support department costs to the producing department causing the cost, it is more complicated and difficult for managers to understand. In this case the small difference in allocated cost likely does not justify its use.

17-19

1. We need to choose a sequence to allocate the support departments for the sequential method. We will allocate general factory first and then power. The sequential method allocation is summarized below:

	Support Departments		Producing Departments	
	Power	General Factory	Grinding	Assembly
Direct costs	$60,000	$100,000		
Allocation from:				
Power	(93,330)		$74,664	$18,666
General factory	33,332	(99,997)	16,666	49,999
Total	$____2	$(____3)	$91,330	$68,665

Notes:

General factory costs are allocated first to power, grinding, and assembly. The rate for general factory is $8.333 per square metre [$100,000 ÷ (4,000 + 2,000 + 6,000)] with general factory cost allocated as 4,000 × $8.333; 2,000 × $8.333; 6,000 × $8.333.

Power costs are allocated next to grinding and assembly. The rate for power is $9.333 per machine-hour [($60,000 + 33,332) ÷ (8,000 + 2,000)] with power cost allocated as 8,000 × $9.333; 2,000 × $9.333.

2. The producing department overhead rates are $24.29 per machine hour for grinding and $3.84 per direct labour hour for assembly.

	Grinding	Assembly
Direct overhead	$103,000	$ 85,000
Support department cost	91,330	68,665
Total overhead cost	$194,330	$153,665
Activity	8,000	40,000
Overhead rate	$24.29	$3.84

7-19 continued

3. The unit cost is $49.47.

Prime cost	$17.50	
Grinding overhead	24.29	[1 × $24.29]
Assembly overhead	7.68	[2 × $3.84]
Total cost	$49.47	

7-21

1. The direct method allocation rates are $8.40 per hour for SDX and $8.00 per hour for SDY.

    Calculations:

	SDX	SDY
Direct cost (a)	$6,300	$5,600
Usage by		
Fabricating	300	500
Assembly	450	200
Total (b)	750	700
Rate (a ÷ b)	$8.40	$8.00

    Direct method support department allocations are:

	Support Departments		Producing Departments	
	SDX	SDY	Fabricating	Assembly
Direct costs	$6,300	$5,600		
Allocation from:				
SDX	(6,300)		$2,520	$3,780
SDY	--	(5,600)	4,000	1,600
Total	$ 0	$ 0	$6,520	$5,380

    Notes:

    Allocation of SDX: 300 × $8.40; 450 × $8.40

    Allocation of SDY: 500 × $8.00; 200 × $8.00

2. We need to choose a sequence to allocate the support departments for the sequential method. We will allocate SDX first and then SDY. The sequential method allocation is summarized below:

	Support Departments		Producing Departments	
	SDX	SDY	Fabricating	Assembly
Direct costs	$6,300	$5,600		
Allocation from:				
SDX	(6,300)	1,050	$2,100	$3,150
SDY	--	(6,650)	4,750	1,900
Total	$ 0	$ 0	$6,850	$5,050

7-21 continued

Notes:

SDX are allocated first to SDY, fabricating, and assembly. The rate for SDX is \$7.00 per hour [\$6,300 ÷ (150 + 300 + 450)] with SDX cost allocated as 150 × \$7.00; 300 × \$7.00; 450 × \$7.00.

SDY are allocated next to fabricating and assembly. The rate for SDY is \$9.50 per hour [(\$5,600 + 1,050) ÷ (500 + 200)] with SDY cost allocated as 500 × \$9.50; 200 × \$9.50.

3. The reciprocal method allocation ratios are:

	SDX		SDY	
User	Hours	Ratio	Hours	Ratio
SDX			100	0.125
SDY	150	0.167		
Fabricating	300	0.333	500	0.625
Assembly	450	0.500	200	0.250
Total	900		800	

The cost equation for SDX is SDX = \$6,300 + 0.125SDY.

The cost equation for SDY is SDY = \$5,600 + 0.167SDX.

The total support-department costs are \$7,149 for SDX and \$6,794 for SDY.

Calculations:

$$
\begin{aligned}
SDX &= \$6,300 + 0.125\,(\$5,600 + 0.167SDX) \\
SDX &= \$6,300 + 700 + 0.0209SDX \\
0.9791SDX &= \$7,000 \\
SDX &= \$7,149 \\[6pt]
SDY &= \$5,600 + 0.167SDX \\
SDY &= \$5,600 + 0.167 \times \$7,149 \\
SDY &= \$6,794
\end{aligned}
$$

Reciprocal method allocation:

	Support Departments		Producing Departments	
	SDX	SDY	Fabricating	Assembly
Direct costs	\$ 6,300	\$ 5,600		
Allocation from:				
SDX	(7,150)	1,194	\$2,381	\$3,575
SDY	849	(6,794)	4,246	1,699
Total	\$(1)	\$ 0	\$6,627	\$5,274

Notes:

Allocation of SDX: 0.167 × \$7,149; 0.333 × \$7,149; 0.500 × \$7,149

Allocation of SDY: 0.125 × \$6,794; 0.625 × \$6,794; 0.250 × \$6,794

7-21 continued

4. The reciprocal method gives the most complete allocation because it considers both the direct use of a support department's service by each producing department and all indirect use (through use by other support departments). Whether this benefit is enough to justify the additional complexity of the reciprocal method depends on the significance of support department interrelationships. This is a matter of a cost-benefit tradeoff the more complex an allocation process, the greater its cost in terms of calculation, chance of error, and difficulty of understanding.

    The following table shows the costs allocated to the producing departments using the three methods:

	Fabricating	*Assembly*
Direct method	$6,520	$5,380
Sequential method	6,850	5,050
Reciprocal	6,627	5,274

7-23

We need to choose a sequence to allocate the support departments for the sequential method. We will allocate S1 first and then S2. The sequential method allocation is summarized below

	Support Departments		Producing Departments	
	S1	*S2*	*P1*	*P2*
Direct costs	$50,000	$25,000		
Allocation from:				
S1	(50,000)	5,000	$15,000	$30,000
S2	--	(30,000)	24,000	6,000
Total	$ 0	$ 0	$39,000	$36,000

First S1's cost is allocated to S2, P1, and P2. The overhead rate for S1 is $250 per employee [$50,000 ÷ (20 + 60 +120)] with S1's cost allocated as 20 × $250; 60 × $250; 120 × $250.

Next S2's cost is allocated to P1 and P2. The overhead rate for S2 is $0.60 per machine hour [($25,000 + 5,000) ÷ (40,000 + 10,000)] with S2's cost allocated as 40,000 × $0.60 + 10,000 × $0.60.

The producing department overhead rates are $5.975 per machine-hour for P1 and $5.60 per direct labour hour for P2.

Calculations:

	P1	*P2*
Direct cost	$200,000	$300,000
Allocated from support departments	39,000	36,000
Total	$239,000	$336,000
Hours	40,000	60,000
Rate	$5.975	$5.60

The overhead cost of Job 49 is $29.13 [3 × $5.975 + 2 × $5.60].

CHAPTER SEVEN

Support Department Cost Allocation

PROBLEMS

7-25

1. The direct method allocation rates are $2.051 per sample for delivery and $7.105 per transaction for accounting.

Calculations:

	Delivery	Accounting
Direct cost (a)	$240,000	$270,000
Usage by		
Laboratory	70,200	24,700
Tissue Pathology	46,800	13,300
Total (b)	117,000	38,000
Rate (a ÷ b)	$2.051	$7.105

Direct method support department allocations are:

	Support Departments		Operating Departments	
	Delivery	Accounting	Laboratory	Tissue Pathology
Direct costs	$240,000	$270,000		
Allocation from:				
Delivery	(239,967)		$143,980	$ 95,987
Accounting	--	(269,991)	175,494	94,497
Total	$ 33	$ 9	$319,474	$190,484

Notes:

Allocation of delivery: 70,200 × $2.051; 46,800 × $2.051

Allocation of accounting: 24,700 × $7.105; 13,300 × $7.105

2. We need to choose an order to allocate the support departments for the sequential method. We will allocate accounting first and then delivery. The sequential method allocation is summarized below:

	Support Departments		Operating Departments	
	Delivery	Accounting	Laboratory	Tissue Pathology
Direct costs	$ 240,000	$270,000		
Allocation from:				
Delivery	(253,539)		$152,123	$ 101,416
Accounting	13,500	(270,000)	166,725	89,775
Total	$(39)	$ 0	$318,848	$191,191

First accounting cost is allocated to delivery, laboratory, and tissue pathology. The overhead rate for accounting is $6.75 per transaction [$270,000 ÷ (2,000 + 24,700 + 13,300)] and its cost is allocated as 2,000 × $6.75; 24,700 × $6.75; 13,300 × $6.75.

Next delivery cost is allocated to laboratory and tissue pathology. The overhead rate for delivery is $2.167 per sample [($240,000 + 13,500) ÷ (70,200 + 46,800)] and its cost is allocated as 70,200 × $2.167; 46,800 × $2.167.

7-25 continued

3. The reciprocal method allocation ratios are:

User	Delivery Samples	Ratio	Accounting Transactions	Ratio
Delivery			2,000	0.0500
Accounting				
Laboratory	70,200	0.60	24,700	0.6175
Tissue pathology	46,800	0.40	13,300	0.3325
Total	117,000		40,000	

The cost equation for delivery is D = $240,000 + 0.0500A.

The cost equation for accounting is A = $270,000.

The total support-department costs are $253,500 for delivery and $270,000 for accounting.

Calculations:

D = $240,000 + 0.0500 ($270,000)
D = $253,500

The reciprocal method allocation is:

	Support Departments		Operating Departments	
	Delivery	Accounting	Laboratory	Tissue Pathology
Direct costs	$240,000	$270,000		
Allocation from:				
Delivery	(253,500)		$152,100	$ 101,400
Accounting	13,500	(270,000)	166,725	89,775
Total	$ 0	$ 0	$318,825	$191,175

Notes:

Allocation of delivery: $253,500 × 60%; $253,500 × 40%

Allocation of accounting: $270,000 × 5%; $270,000 × 61.75%; $270,000 × 33.25%

7-27

1. The sequential method allocation (maintenance first, then power) is summarized below:

	Support Departments		Operating Departments	
	Maintenance	*Power*	*Cutting*	*Sewing*
Direct costs	$ 240,000	$380,000		
Allocation from:				
Maintenance	(240,000)	90,000	$120,000	$ 30,000
Power	--	(469,980)	46,998	422,982
Total	$ 0	$ 20	$166,998	$452,982

Maintenance costs are allocated first to power, cutting, and sewing. The overhead rate for maintenance is $3.00 per machine-hour [$240,000 ÷ (30,000 + 40,000 + 10,000)] with maintenance cost allocated as 30,000 × $3.00; 40,000 × $3.00; 10,000 × $3.00.

Power costs are allocated next to cutting and sewing. The overhead rate for power is $2.611 per kilowatt-hour [($380,000 + 90,000) ÷ (18,000 + 162,000)] with power cost allocated as 18,000 × $2.611; 162,000 × $2.611.

The overhead rates for the producing departments are $5.80 per machine-hour for cutting and $18.00 per direct labour hour for sewing.

Calculations:

	Cutting	*Sewing*
Direct cost	$ 65,000	$ 87,000
Allocated from support departments	166,998	452,982
Total	$231,998	$539,982
Hours	40,000	30,000
Rate	$5.80	$18.00

The bid price for a batch of the uniforms is $3,411.38.

Calculations:

Prime cost	$1,817.50	
Overhead – cutting	11.60	[2 × $5.80]
Overhead – sewing	900.00	[50 × $18.00]
Total cost	$2,729.10	
Bid price	$3,411.38	[$2,694.57 × 125%]

7-27 continued

2. The sequential method allocation (power first, then maintenance) is summarized below:

	Support Departments		Operating Departments	
	Maintenance	Power	Cutting	Sewing
Direct costs	$ 240,000	$380,000		
Allocation from:				
Maintenance	(278,000)		$222,400	$ 55,600
Power	38,000	(380,000)	34,200	307,800
Total	$ 0	$ 0	$256,600	$363,400

Power costs are allocated first to maintenance, cutting, and sewing. The overhead rate for power is $1.90 per machine-hour [$380,000 ÷ (20,000 + 18,000 + 162,000)] with power cost allocated as 20,000 × $1.90; 18,000 × $1.90; 162,000 × $1.90.

Maintenance costs are allocated next to cutting and sewing. The overhead rate for maintenance is $5.56 per kilowatt-hour [($240,000 + 38,000) ÷ (40,000 + 10,000)] with maintenance cost allocated as 40,000 × $5.56; 10,000 × $5.56.

The overhead rates for the producing departments are $8.04 per machine-hour for cutting and $15.013 per direct labour hour for sewing.

Calculations:

	Cutting	Sewing
Direct cost	$ 65,000	$ 87,000
Allocated from support departments	256,600	363,400
Total	$321,600	$450,400
Hours	40,000	30,000
Rate	$8.04	$15.013

The bid price for a batch of the uniforms is $3,230.29.

Calculations:

Prime cost	$1,817.50	
Overhead – cutting	16.08	[2 × $8.04]
Overhead – sewing	750.65	[50 × $15.013]
Total cost	$2,584.23	
Bid price	$3,230.29	[$2,584.23× 125%]

7-27 continued

3. Yes, there is a difference in the bids. The bid based on allocating maintenance first is $181.09 higher than the bid based on allocating power first [$3,411.38 – 3,230.29]. The difference between the bids is caused by the amount of indirect support department service included in the cost allocation. Power uses a larger share of maintenance's service than maintenance uses of power's service. This higher use then flows to a greater degree to the sewing department (which uses a greater proportion of power) and this higher cost allocation is reflected in the cost of the job (which uses a greater proportion of the sewing operation. We can look at the reciprocal method-based bid (see answer to 7-26) to see the effect of including the complete interaction – this bid is $3,368.20 and fits between the two sequential method-based bids.

7-29

1. The unit cost of power is $0.10 per kilowatt-hour [$50,000 ÷ (100,000 + 300,000 + 100,000)]. The price of buying is greater ($0.11) and Watterman would reject the offer.

2. The cost of operating the power department, using the reciprocal method is $63,158 and the cost per kilowatt-hour is $0.1263 [$63,158 ÷ 500,000].

Calculations;

The reciprocal method allocation ratios are:

	Maintenance		Power	
User	Hours	Ratio	Hours	Ratio
Maintenance			100,000	0.20
Power	5,000	0.25		
Machining	10,000	0.50	300,000	0.60
Assembly	5,000	0.25	100,000	0.20
Total	20,000		500,000	

The cost equation for power is P = $50,000 + 0.25M.

The cost equation for maintenance is M = $40,000 + 0.20P.

The total support-department costs are $63,158 for power and $52,632 for maintenance.

Calculations:

$$
\begin{aligned}
P &= \$50,000 + 0.25\,(\$40,000 + 0.20P) \\
P &= \$40,000 + 10,000 + 0.05P \\
0.95P &= \$50,000 \\
P &= \$63,158
\end{aligned}
$$

$$
\begin{aligned}
M &= \$40,000 + 0.20 \times \$63,158 \\
P &= \$52,632
\end{aligned}
$$

When we consider the interactions between the support departments, we see that the average cost of producing power internally is greater than the external price offer. Some of the costs of operating the power department are incurred in the maintenance department and were not considered when only direct costs were included in our analysis.

The company will have lower costs if it buys its power externally.

7-29 continued

3. Analysis of savings:

Savings realized if power department is eliminated:

Direct cost of power	$50,000	
Savings from direct cost of maintenance	10,000	[$40,000 ÷ 20,000 × 5,000]
Total savings	$60,000	

New demand for power:

Current demand	500,000	
Reduced demand from maintenance	25,000	[100,000 ÷ 20,000 × 5,000]
New demand	475,000	

Savings per kilowatt-hour: $0.1263 [$60,000 ÷ 475,000]. This is the same as the cost per hour calculated from the reciprocal method in Requirement 2.

The new cost of power, purchased externally, is $52,250 [475,000 × $0.11], providing a decrease in power cost of $7,750 [$60,000 – 52,250].

7-31

1. Purchasing costs allocated on the basis of 2003 sales revenue:

	2003 Revenues	2004 Hours	Cost Allocated
Kenora	$ 337,500	1,475	$ 16,504
Brandon	360,000	938	17,604
Portage la Prairie	450,000	400	22,005
Winnipeg (West)	562,500	375	27,506
Winnipeg (South)	540,000	562	26,406
Total	$2,250,000	3,750	$110,025

Notes:

The cost of purchasing in 2004 is $110,000 [$50,000 + $16 × 3,750] or $0.0489 per sales dollar [$110,000 ÷ $2,250,000].

2. Fixed purchasing costs allocated on the basis of 2003 sales revenue and variable costs on the basis of 2004 hours of use:

	2003 Revenues	Fixed Cost	2004 Hours	Variable Cost	Total Cost
Kenora	$ 337,500	$7,493	1,475	$23,600	$ 31,093
Brandon	360,000	7,992	938	15,008	23,000
Portage la Prairie	450,000	9,990	400	6,400	16,390
Winnipeg (West)	562,500	12,488	375	6,000	18,488
Winnipeg (South)	540,000	11,988	562	8,992	20,980
Total	$2,250,000	$49,951	3,750	$60,000	$109,951

Notes:

Fixed cost is allocated as $0.0222 per sales dollar and variable cost is allocated as $16 per hour.

7-31 continued

3. The first method based on sales revenue is simple and easy to use but it may not accurately reflect the amount of the purchasing activity used by a restaurant. It is an "ability to pay" approach rather than one that is based on usage. The second method uses hours as a causal factor to allocate the variable cost and is more of a "cause and effect" approach. This method is more likely to encourage managers to use purchasing department time efficiently. With the first method, a manager has less control over purchasing costs because the amount allocated depends on the sales of other restaurants. With the second method, a restaurant manager has more control over purchasing cost.

7-33

1. Using the direct method, the support department overhead rates are

	Maintenance	Power	Setups	General Factory
Direct cost (a)	$500,000	$225,000	$150,000	$625,000
Used by				
Dept. A	1,000	10,000	40	35,360
Dept. B	7,000	50,000	160	94,640
Total (b)	8,000	60,000	200	130,000
Rate (a ÷ b)	$62.50	$3.75	$750	$4.808

Direct method support department cost allocations are:

		Support Departments			Producing Departments	
	Main	Power	Setups	General	Dept. A	Dept. B
Direct costs	$500,000	$225,000	$150,000	$625,000		
Allocation from:						
Maintenance	(500,000)				$62,500	$437,500
Power		(225,000)			37,500	187,500
Setups			(150,000)		30,000	120,000
General Factory				(625,040)	170,011	455,029
Total	$ 0	$ 0	$ 0	$(40)	$300,011	$1,200,029

Notes:

Allocation of maintenance: 1,000 × $62.50; 7,000 × $62.50

Allocation of power: 10,000 × $3.75; 50,000 × $3.75

Allocation of setups: 40 × $750; 160 × $750

Allocation of general factory: 35,360 × $4.808; 94,640 × $4.808

The producing department overhead rates are:

	Dept. A	Dept. B
Direct cost	$200,000	$ 800,000
Support department cost	300,011	1,200,029
Total	$500,011	$2,000,029
Activity	200,000	120,000
Overhead rate	$2.50	$16.67

These are the same as Alden calculated.

7-33 continued

2. We will use an allocation order of general factory, maintenance, power, and setups for the sequential method. This is based on the amount of each support department's direct cost. The allocation ratios are:

		General	Support Departments Maintenance	Power	Setups	Producing Departments Dept. A	Dept. B
General	Activity	--	25,000	40,000	5,000	35,360	94,640
	Ratio	--	0.125	0.20	0.025	0.1768	0.4732
Main	Activity	--	--	1,500	500	1,000	7,000
	Ratio	--	--	0.15	0.05	0.10	0.70
Power	Activity	--	--	--	500	10,000	50,000
	Ratio	--	--	--	0.008	0.165	0.826
Setups	Activity	--	--	--	--	40	160
	Ratio	--	--	--	--	0.2	0.8

Sequential method support department allocation:

	General	Support Departments Main	Power	Setups	Producing Departments Dept. A	Dept. B
Direct costs	$625,000	$500,000	$225,000	$150,000		
Allocation from:						
General factory	(625,000)	78,125	125,000	15,625	$110,500	$295,750
Maintenance		(578,126)	86,719	28,906	57,813	404,688
Power			(436,283)	3,494	72,059	360,730
Setups				(198,025)	39,605	158,420
Total	$ 0	$(1)	$ 436	$ 0	$279,977	$1,219,588

Notes:

Allocation of general factory: $625,000 × 0.125; × 0.20; × 0.025; × 0.1768; × 0.4732

Allocation of maintenance: $578,125 × 0.15; × 0.05; × 0.10; × 0.70

Allocation of power: $436,719 × 0.008; × 0.165; × 0.826

Allocation of setups: $198,025 × 0.2; × 0.8

The producing department overhead rates are:

	Dept. A	Dept. B
Direct cost	$200,000	$ 800,000
Support department cost	279,977	1,219,588
Total	$479,977	$2,019,588
Activity	200,000	120,000
Overhead rate	$2.40	$16.83

7-33 continued

The bids, using the sequential method cost allocations, are $14.63 for Job SS and $ for Job TT.

Calculations:

	Job SS	Job TT
Prime cost	$120,000	$50,000
Overhead		
Dept. A (5,000 × $2.40; 400 × $2.40)	12,000	960
Dept. B (500 × $16.83; 3,000 × $16.83)	8,415	50,490
Total cost	$140,415	$101,450
Bid @ 150%	$210,623	$152,175
Units	14,400	1,500
Bid per unit	$14.63	$101.45

3. The sequential method will give Alden a more accurate cost of the different jobs and will make his bids more useful (Retlief will find that the jobs they "win" are profitable).

4. The best competing bid is $14.65 [$18.75 – 4.10]. The bid based on the sequential method is $14.63 and is competitive and the cost allocation appears to be giving Alden good information on which to base his bids.

MANAGERIAL DECISION CASES

7-35

1. Although all allocations are to some extent arbitrary, Emma's proposal has little merit. Even if an allocation is arbitrary, changing it to exploit a customer is wrong. They are using an allocation system based on an analysis of causal factors and they decided that maintenance hours is more closely related to maintenance cost than machine hours. If we accept cause and effect as a reasonable criterion for designing an allocation system, then switching to a factor that is less related to overhead consumption will decrease the accuracy of the product cost. Emma should price the new order using the most accurate cost information available and the current allocation approach should be kept.

2. Larry should refuse to make the change in allocation base requested by Emma. He should try to persuade Emma that her idea is wrong and would be unethical. As a management accountant, Larry has a responsibility to act ethically – including an obligation to provide accurate and fair information.

3. Larry should pursue all levels of internal review until a satisfactory resolution is achieved. If he fails in this attempt he should look for another job.

4. Larry's decision to contact the customer after he resigned was inappropriate. As a management accountant he has an obligation to keep any information acquired in the course of his work confidential and not reveal it unless authorized.

7-37

The report should cover the following points:

Plant-wide or departmental rates:

- a plant-wide rate uses a single rate (and base) to allocate all overhead to jobs. Departmental rates would use a separate for each producing department using the activity driver most appropriate for the department's activity. In this case the machining department is machine-intensive and the fabrication department is more labour-intensive. It is unlikely a single activity measure will be adequate to capture the essence of both of these operations.
- departmental rates provide better cost information if different jobs use the producing department operations to varying degrees. Plant-wide rates are adequate if products are more homogeneous. In this case a wide variety of products are produced.

Recommendation: use departmental rates

Direct, sequential, or reciprocal method to allocate support department costs:

- the difference between these methods is the extent to which support departments use the service of other support departments (or indirect use). The direct method ignores all indirect use; the sequential method recognizes some indirect use; the reciprocal method recognizes all indirect use. The other difference is in the complexity of use – the direct method is simple and easy to use; the sequential method is more complicated; the reciprocal method is the most involved and difficult for managers to understand.
- the computer department is the only support department that is used by other support departments

Recommendation: use the sequential method with computer department costs allocated first

Variable and fixed or a single charging rate for support department costs:

- the support departments have significant amounts of both variable and fixed cost
- separate variable and fixed rates will allow for more detailed allocations (variable costs linked to current use and fixed costs linked to long-term or capacity needs)

Recommendation: use separate rates for variable and fixed support department costs if there is an identifiable long-term capacity need

Allocation bases:

Computer Department: fixed costs based on long-term capacity required by other departments; variable costs based on current use (hours used for example).

Product Design Department: design time required by jobs (unlikely to be a long-term relationship if jobs are unique)

Purchasing Department: purchase requisitions or direct material cost

Machining Department: machine hours worked on a job

Fabrication Department: direct labour hours worked on each job

CHAPTER 8

VARIABLE COSTING: SEGMENTED REPORTING AND PERFORMANCE EVALUATION

ANSWERS TO ODD-NUMBERED QUESTIONS FOR WRITING AND DISCUSSION

1. The only difference between the way costs are assigned under variable and absorption costing is the treatment of fixed overhead. Under variable costing, fixed overhead is treated as a period cost and expensed in the period incurred. Under absorption costing, fixed overhead is treated as a product cost and included as part of the inventoriable cost of production. Fixed overhead cost is expensed in the period the product is sold.

3. Variable costing is a more descriptive term than direct costing because all variable manufacturing costs (direct materials, direct labour, and variable overhead) are assigned to products, not just direct manufacturing costs.

5. If sales are greater than production (and inventory decreases), variable-costing income is greater than absorption-costing income because variable-costing income includes only the current period fixed overhead cost but absorption-costing income will include prior period fixed overhead cost from inventory.

7. If the fixed overhead expense on an income statement was $100,000 and the fixed overhead for the period was $80,000, the statement must have been prepared using absorption costing. Under variable costing, the fixed overhead incurred in the period is the amount expensed on the income statement. Under absorption costing, there can be a difference. In this case, the additional fixed overhead cost expensed would have come from beginning inventory.

9. Variable costing is better than absorption costing for evaluating segment performance because variable costing better reflects the cost behaviour of a segment's activities. Variable costing does not assign fixed overhead cost to products and shows fixed overhead costs separately. Absorption costing assigns fixed overhead costs to each product and the segment's fixed overhead costs are buried in cost of goods sold (and in inventory). Managers are better able to evaluate the segment contributions from variable costing information.

11. The difference between a direct fixed cost and a common fixed cost is traceability. A direct fixed cost is a fixed cost that is traceable to one (and only one) segment (or cost object). A common fixed cost cannot be traced to a single segment (or cost object) but is common to two or more segments.

    The difference is important because a direct fixed cost will be avoided if its segment is dropped but a common fixed cost will continue although one of the segments is dropped.

13. Absorption-costing income can increase from one period to the next (although unit sales, selling prices, and costs have remained the same) if more units are produced in the second period than in the first period. More production will cause a greater increase in inventory, more fixed overhead deferred in inventory, and greater income.

15. Activity-based costing can be applied to segmented reporting by identifying different activities and activity levels associated with each segment.

SOLUTIONS TO ODD-NUMBERED EXERCISES, PROBLEMS, AND CASES

EXERCISES

8-1

1. Under absorption costing, the unit cost is $15.46.

	Total	Per unit
Direct materials	$162,500	$ 6.50
Direct labour	132,500	5.30
Variable overhead	26,500	1.06
Fixed overhead	65,000	2.60
Total cost	$386,500	$15.46

   Note: unit costs are total cost divided by units produced (25,000)

   The cost of finished goods inventory is $54,110 [(25,000 – 21,500) × $15.46].

2. Under variable costing, the unit cost is $12.86.

	Total	Per unit
Direct materials	$162,500	$ 6.50
Direct labour	132,500	5.30
Variable overhead	26,500	1.06
Total cost	$321,500	$12.86

   Note: unit costs are total cost divided by units produced (25,000)

   The cost of finished goods inventory is $45,010 [(25,000 – 21,500) × $12.86].

3. Most companies will use absorption costing to value inventories for external reporting – and will report a finished goods inventory cost of $54,110.

8-3

1. Absorption-costing income statements:

	Year 1		Year 2	
Sales		$384,000		$480,000
Cost of goods sold				
Beginning inventory	$ 0		$ 52,000	
Cost of goods manufactured	260,000		232,000	
Cost of goods available for sale	$260,000		$284,000	
Ending inventory	52,000		0	
Cost of goods sold		208,000		284,000
Gross margin		$176,000		$196,000
Selling and administration expenses		24,300		24,300
Operating income		$151,700		$171,700

8-3 continued

Notes:

Sales: 16,000 × $24; 20,000 × $24

Cost of goods manufactured: 20,000 × ($4 + 2 + 1) + $120,000; 16,000 × ($4 + 2 + 1) + $120,000

Ending inventory: ($260,000 ÷ 20,000) × (20,000 – 16,000)

Irvine has done slightly better in Year 2 in terms of operating income.

2. Variable-costing income statements:

	Year 1		Year 2	
Sales		$384,000		$480,000
Variable expenses				
Product costs				
Beginning inventory	$ 0		$ 28,000	
Cost of goods manufactured	140,000		112,000	
Cost of goods available for sale	$140,000		$140,000	
Ending inventory	28,000		0	
Variable product costs	$112,000		$140,000	
Variable selling costs	0		0	
Total variable expenses		112,000		140,000
Contribution margin		$272,000		$340,000
Fixed expenses				
Fixed overhead	$120,000		$120,000	
Fixed selling and administrative	24,300		24,300	
Total fixed expenses		144,300		144,300
Operating income		$127,700		$195,700

Notes:

Sales: 16,000 × $24; 20,000 × $24

Cost of goods manufactured: 20,000 × ($4 + 2 + 1); 16,000 × ($4 + 2 + 1)

Ending inventory: ($4 + 2 + 1) × (20,000 – 16,000)

Irvine has done much better in Year 2 in terms of operating income.

8-5

1. Denham Company absorption-costing income statement:

Sales	$1,512,000
Cost of goods sold	1,048,000
Gross margin	$ 464,000
Selling and administration expenses	444,000
Net income	$ 20,000

8-5 continued

Notes:

Calculation of cost of goods sold:

Fixed overhead rate: $4.00 per unit [$300,000 ÷ 75,000]

Applied fixed overhead: $296,000 [$4.00 × 74,000]

Under applied fixed overhead: $4,000 [$300,000 – 296,000]

Cost of goods sold

Variable cost of goods sold	$ 756,000	
Fixed overhead	288,000	[72,000 × $4.00]
Underapplied fixed overhead	4,000	
Absorption cost of goods sold	$1,048,000	

Selling and administrative expenses: $444,000 [$360,000 + 84,000]

2. The difference between the $12,000 variable-costing net income and the $20,000 absorption-costing net income is the $8,000 of fixed overhead deferred in ending inventory under absorption costing [$4 × (0 + 74,000 – 72,000)].

8-7

1. Louise would see this as a positive step. The 30% increase in sales of the scented line will produce $900 additional contribution margin [$3,000 × 30%] for an additional cost of $250. The scented line's segment margin would increase by $650 [$900 – 250]. The 30% increase in sales of the musical line will also produce $900 additional contribution margin [$3,000 × 30%] for an additional cost of $750. The musical line's segment margin would increase by $150 [$900 – 750]. The new segmented income statement is shown below. FunTime will still have an overall loss and both the scented and musical lines will continue to have negative segment margins. Louise would have to consider dropping these two lines.

	Scented	Musical	Regular	Total
Sales	$13,000	$19,500	$25,000	$57,500
Less: Variable expenses	9,100	15,600	12,500	37,200
Contribution margin	$ 3,900	$ 3,900	$12,500	$20,300
Less: Direct fixed expenses	4,250	5,750	3,000	13,000
Segment margin	$(350)	$(1,850)	$ 9,500	$ 7,300
Common fixed expenses				7,500
Net profit (loss)				$ (200)

Notes:

Sales: Scented line 130% × $10,000; Musical line 130% × $15,000

Variable expenses: Scented line 130% × $7,000; Musical line 130% × $12,000

8-7 continued

2. If FunTime drops both the scented and musical lines it will avoid the negative segment margins of $3,000 [$1,000 + 2,000]. If the scented and musical lines are dropped, the sales of the regular line are expected to be 20% lower. The contribution margin of the regular line will be $2,500 less (as will its segment margin and the company's profit) [20% × $12,500]. The income statement for this option is shown below.

	Regular
Sales	$20,000
Less: Variable expenses	10,000
Contribution margin	$10,000
Less: Fixed expenses	10,500
Net profit (loss)	$ (500)

Notes:

Sales: $25,000 × 80%

Variable expenses: $12,500 × 80%

Fixed expenses: $3,000 + 7,500

FunTime will have a smaller loss (by $500) then its current result but it will be worse off (by $300) than if it increased advertising for the scented and musical lines as proposed in Requirement 1.

3. If the sales of the regular line are expected to be 10% lower if either line is dropped, its contribution margin would drop by $1,250 [10% × $12,500]. The musical line's segment margin (with the increased advertising) is a loss of $1,850. FunTime's profit will increase by $600 [$1,850 – 1,250] if it drops the musical line. The scented line's segment margin (with the increased advertising) is a loss of $350 – a smaller saving than the loss in profit from the decrease in regular sales. Thus FunTime should drop the musical line, keep the scented line and increase its advertising. It will have a profit of $400 from this option. The income statement for this option is shown below.

	Scented	*Regular*	*Total*
Sales	$13,000	$22,500	$35,500
Less: Variable expenses	9,100	11,250	20,350
Contribution margin	$ 3,900	$11,250	$15,150
Less: Direct fixed expenses	4,250	3,000	7,250
Segment margin	$(350)	$ 8,250	$ 7,900
Common fixed expenses			7,500
Net profit (loss)			$ 400

Notes:

Sales: Scented line 130% × $10,000; Regular line 90% × $25,000

Variable expenses: Scented line 130% × $7,000; Regular line 90% × $12,500

8-9

1. Emby's absorption-costing income is $534,100 and its variable-costing income is $531,130 . See the income statements for calculations.

    Absorption costing:

Sales	$1,770,300
Cost of goods sold	1,121,190
Gross margin	$ 649,110
Selling and administrative expenses	115,010
Net income	$ 534,100

    Notes:

    Sales: 196,700 × $9.00

    Cost of goods sold: 196,700 × $5.70 (last year's costs were the same)

    Selling and administrative expenses: 196,700 × $0.30 + $56,000

    Variable costing:

Sales		$1,770,300
Variable expenses		
Cost of goods sold	$944,160	
Selling	59,010	1,003,170
Contribution margin		$ 767,130
Fixed expenses		
Overhead	$180,000	
Selling and administrative	56,000	236,000
Net income		$ 531,130

    Notes:

    Sales: 196,700 × $9.00

    Variable expenses: Cost of goods sold 196,700 × $4.80; Selling 196,700 × $0.30

2. Emby's variable-costing income is $2,970 lower than its absorption-costing income [$534,100 − 531,130]. The difference is the result of Emby selling 3,300 fewer units than it produced. Its inventory increased by 3,300 units and $2,970 of fixed overhead was deferred in inventory [3,300 × $0.90] and not expensed during the year.

Overhead	$ 37,500	
Selling and administrative	120,000	157,500
Net income		$163,500

    Notes:

    Cost of goods sold: 53,500 × $2.50

    Fixed overhead: 55,000 × $0.50 + $10,000

    Sugarsmooth's variable-costing income is $750 less than its absorption-costing income [$164,250 − 163,500]. This is because it produced 1,500 more units than it sold. These units are left in inventory and are assigned $750 of fixed overhead cost [1,500 × $0.50] which is deferred and not expensed in the current period.

8-11

1. Segmented variable-costing income statement:

	Drugstores and Supermarkets	Discount Stores	Beauty Shops	Total
Sales	$454,750	$135,000	$90,000	$679,750
Variable expenses				
Cost of goods sold	$133,750	$ 50,000	$25,000	$208,750
Return penalties	--	1,350	--	1,350
Commissions	--	--	9,000	9,000
Packing	--	--	5,000	5,000
Total variable expenses	$133,750	$ 51,350	$39,000	$224,100
Contribution margin	$321,000	$ 83,650	$51,000	$455,650
Direct fixed expenses	--	75,000	--	75,000
Segment margin	$321,000	$ 8,650	$51,000	$380,650
Common fixed expenses				157,500
Net income				$223,150

Notes:

Sales: 53,500 × $8.50; 20,000 × $6.75; 10,000 × $9.00

Cost of goods sold: 53,500 × $2.50; 20,000 × $2.50; 10,000 × $2.50

Return penalties: 1% × $135,000

Commissions: 10% × $90,000

Packing: 10,000 × $0.50

Direct fixed expenses: $45,000 + 30,000

Common fixed expenses: $37,500 + 120,000

2. The segmented income statement shows that all the customer groups have positive segment margins and are making a contribution to the company's common fixed expenses. The discount stores group has the lowest segment margin and requires a commitment to new fixed costs. Sugarsmooth should carefully look at its estimates for this group before deciding to go ahead with this expansion.

8-13

1. Summerside's November absorption-costing income statement:

Sales		$6,300,000
Cost of goods sold		
Beginning inventory	$ 340,000	
Cost of goods manufactured	4,080,000	
Cost of goods available for sale	$4,420,000	
Ending inventory	136,000	
Cost of goods sold		4,284,000
Gross margin		$2,016,000
Selling and administration expenses		530,000
Operating income		$1,486,000

Notes:

Sales: 315,000 × $20.00

Fixed overhead rate: $1.60 [$480,000 ÷ 300,000]

Beginning inventory: 25,000 × ($3.00 + 5.00 + 4.00 + 1.60)

Cost of goods manufactured: 300,000 × ($3.00 + 5.00 + 4.00 + 1.60)

Ending inventory: (25,000 + 300,000 – 315,000) × ($3.00 + 5.00 + 4.00 + 1.60)

Selling and administrative expenses: $280,000 + 250,000

2. Summerside's November variable-costing income statement:

Sales		$6,300,000
Variable cost of goods sold		
Beginning inventory	$ 300,000	
Cost of goods manufactured	3,600,000	
Cost of goods available for sale	$3,900,000	
Ending inventory	120,000	
Variable cost of goods sold		3,780,000
Contribution margin		$2,520,000
Fixed expenses		
Overhead	$480,000	
Selling and administration expenses	530,000	1,010,000
Operating income		$1,510,000

Notes:

Sales: 315,000 × $20.00

Beginning inventory: 25,000 × ($3.00 + 5.00 + 4.00)

Cost of goods manufactured: 300,000 × ($3.00 + 5.00 + 4.00)

Ending inventory: (25,000 + 300,000 – 315,000) × ($3.00 + 5.00 + 4.00)

Selling and administrative expenses: $280,000 + 250,000

8-13 continued

3. Summerside's variable-costing income is $24,000 higher than its absorption-costing income [$1,510,000 1,486,000] because it sold 15,000 more units than it produced. The reduction in inventory caused fixed overhead costs from prior periods to be released and expensed in November. The difference in income is reconciled below.

Variable-costing income	$1,510,000	
Less fixed overhead released from beginning inventory	(40,000)	[25,000 × $1.60]
Plus fixed overhead deferred in ending inventory	16,000	[10,000 × $1.60]
Absorption-costing income	$1,486,000	

8-15

1. Grenada's variable-costing income statement is:

Sales		$450,000
Variable expenses		
Variable cost of goods sold		
Beginning inventory	$ 24,000	
Cost of goods manufactured	168,000	
Cost of goods available for sale	$192,000	
Ending inventory	12,000	
Variable cost of goods sold	$180,000	
Selling expenses	45,000	
Variable expenses		225,000
Contribution margin		$225,000
Fixed expenses		
Overhead	$60,000	
Selling and administration expenses	20,000	80,000
Operating income		$145,000

Notes:

Sales: 45,000 × $10.00

Beginning inventory: 6,000 × $4.00

Cost of goods manufactured: 42,000 × $4.00

Ending inventory: (6,000 + 42,000 – 45,000) × $4.00

Variable selling expenses: 45,000 × $1.00

8-15 continued

2. Grenada's absorption-costing income statement is:

Sales		$450,000
Cost of goods sold		
Beginning inventory	$ 33,000	
Cost of goods manufactured	231,000	
Cost of goods available for sale	$264,000	
Ending inventory	16,500	
Cost of goods sold	247,500	
Less overapplied overhead	3,000	
Adjusted cost of goods sold		244,500
Gross margin		$205,500
Selling and administration expenses		65,000
Operating income		$140,500

Notes:

Sales: 45,000 × $10.00

Fixed overhead rate: $1.50 [$60,000 ÷ 40,000]

Cost of goods manufactured: 42,000 × ($4.00 + 1.50)

Ending inventory: (6,000 + 42,000 – 45,000) × ($4.00 + 1.50)

Selling and administrative expenses: 45,000 × $1.00 + $20,000

Overapplied fixed overhead: $60,000 – (42,000 × $1.50)

3. The following is a reconciliation of Grenada's variable-costing and absorption-costing income:

Variable-costing income	$145,000	
Less fixed overhead released from beginning inventory	(9,000)	[6,000 × $1.50]
Plus fixed overhead deferred in ending inventory	4,500	[3,000 × $1.50]
Absorption-costing income	$140,500	

Grenada sold 3,000 more units than it produced and expensed $4,500 of its prior-period fixed overhead costs from inventory [(6,000 – 3,000) × $1.50].

8-17

1. Copper Company's variable-costing segmented income statement:

Copper Company
Variable Costing Income Statement
(dollars in thousands)

	Western	Eastern	Total
Sales	$15,000	$12,000	$27,000
Less variable expenses: cost of goods sold	6,020	8,380	14,400
Contribution margin	$ 8,980	$ 3,620	$12,600
Less direct fixed expenses:			
Direct fixed overhead	1,080	720	1,800
Direct selling and administrative	1,000	1,500	2,500
Segment margin	$ 6,900	$ 1,400	$ 8,300
Less common fixed expenses:			
Common fixed overhead			1,800
Common selling and administrative			2,000
Net income			$ 4,500

Supporting calculations:

Fixed overhead costs: $3,600 [20% of cost of goods sold: 20% × $18,000]
  Direct fixed overhead costs: $1,800 [50% of $3,600]
    Western Region direct fixed overhead costs: $1,080 [30% × $3,600]
    Eastern Region direct fixed overhead costs: $720 [20% × $3,600]
  Common fixed overhead costs: $1,800 [50% of $3,600]

Total applied fixed overhead costs under absorption costing:
  Western Region: $1,980 [$1,080 + (50% × $1,800)]
  Eastern Region: $1,620 [$720 + (50% × $1,800)]

Variable cost of goods sold:
  Western Region: $6,020 [$8,000 – 1,980]
  Eastern Region: $8,380 [$10,000 – 1,620]

Selling & administrative costs:
  Common costs: $2,000
  Direct costs: $2,500 [$4,500 – $2,000]
    Western Region: $1,000 [40% × $2,500]
    Eastern Region: $1,500 [60% × $2,500]

The company should not eliminate its Eastern Region. The Eastern Region's segment margin is large and positive.

8-17 continued

2. Ratios based on original information:

	Western	Eastern
Contribution margin	59.9%	30.2%
Segment margin	46.0%	11.7%

Revised income statement with 10% increase in sales:

Copper Company
Variable Costing Income Statement
(dollars in thousands)

	Western	*Eastern*	*Total*
Sales	$16,500	$13,200	$29,700
Less variable expenses: cost of goods sold	6,622	9,218	15,840
Contribution margin	$ 9,878	$ 3,982	$13,860
Less direct fixed expenses:			
Direct fixed overhead	1,080	720	1,800
Direct selling and administrative	1,000	1,500	2,500
Segment margin	$ 7,798	$ 1,762	$ 9,560
Less common fixed expenses:			
Common fixed overhead			1,800
Common selling and administrative			2,000
Net income			$ 5,760

Note: Sales, variable costs, and contribution margin increase by 10% in each region. Fixed costs, direct and common, are unchanged.

Ratios based on increased activity:

	Western	Eastern
Contribution margin	59.9%	30.2%
Segment margin	47.3%	13.3%

The contribution margin ratio remained constant as a percentage of sales, but the segment margin increased. By definition, we would expect variable costs to increase in proportion to increases in sales, thus leaving the contribution margin ratio unchanged. However, we would expect the segment margin to increase as a percentage as sales increase, simply because direct fixed costs do not change as volume changes.

8-19

1. Wetzel's absorption-costing income statement for January 2004 is:

Sales (8,800 × $6.20)	$54,560	
Variable expenses (8,800 × $4.90)	43,120	
Gross margin	$11,440	
Selling and administration expenses	18,926	[10% × $54,560 + $13,470]
Net income	$(7,486)	

8-19 continued

2. Wetzel's variable-costing income statement for January 2004 is:

Sales (8,800 × $6.20)	$54,560	
Cost of goods sold (8,800 × $2.52)	22,176	
Contribution margin	$32,384	
Fixed expenses	40,470	[$27,000 + 13,470]
Net income	$(8,086)	

3. The following is a reconciliation of Wetzel's absorption-costing and variable-costing income for January 2004

Absorption-costing income	$(7,486)
Plus fixed overhead released from beginning inventory	0
Less fixed overhead deferred in ending inventory	(600)
Variable-costing income	$(8,086)

Ending inventory includes $600 of fixed overhead cost [$980 – 380]. (See the answer to 8-18.)

8-21

Answers in **bold**.

	A	B	C
Unit information:			
Price	$22	**$15**	$17
Direct materials	4	2	6
Direct labour	3	4	1
Variable overhead	1	1	1
Fixed overhead	**$5**	3	1
Contribution margin	14	**$6.75**	**$6**
Gross profit	9	**$5**	**$8**
Units sold	2,000	7,600	**8,000**
Units produced	2,000	8,000	**6,000**
Beginning inventory, units	500	0	3,000
Total information:			
Sales	**$44,000**	$114,000	$136,000
Cost of goods sold	**$26,000**	**$76,000**	$72,000
Gross profit	**$18,000**	$38,000	**$64,000**
Variable marketing	**$0**	$ 9,500	$24,000
Fixed marketing	$5,000	$8,000	**$15,000**
Fixed administrative	$3,000	**$20,000**	$8,300
Net income	**$10,000**	$500	$16,700
Value of ending inventory	$6,500	**$4,000**	$9,000

8-21 continued

Calculations:

Fixed overhead, A: **$5** [$22 – ($4 + 3 + 1 +9)]; Sales, A: **$44,000** [2,000 × $22];

Cost of goods sold, A: **$26,000** [2,000 × ($22 – 9); Variable marketing, A: **$0** [2,000 × ($22 – (4 + 3 +1) – 14)]

Price, B: **$15** [$144,000 ÷ 7,600]; Contribution margin, B: **$6.75** [$15 – ($2 + 4 + 1 + ($9,500 ÷ 7,600))]

Gross profit, B: **$5** [$15 – ($2 + 4 + 1 +3)]; Cost of goods sold, B: **$76,000** [$114,000 – 38,000]

Fixed administrative, B: **$20,000** [$38,000 – (9,500 + 8,000) – 500]

Value of ending inventory, B: **$4,000** [($2 + 4 + 1 +3) × (0 + 8,000 – 7,600)]

Units sold, C: **8,000** [$72,000 ÷ ($6 + 1 + 1 +1)]; Price, C: **$17** [$136,000 ÷ 8,000]

Gross profit, C: **$8** [$17 – ($6 + 1 + 1 +1)]; Contribution margin, C: **$6** [$17 – ($6 + 1 + 1 + ($24,000 ÷ 8,000))]

Units produced, C: **6,000** [8,000 + ($9,000 ÷ ($6 + 1 + 1 +1)) – 3,000]

Fixed marketing, C: **$15,000** [$64,000 – ($24,000 + 8,300) – $16,700]

8-23

1. Telster's direct labour cost per unit is $10.85, its variable overhead cost per unit is $21.70, and its fixed overhead cost per unit is $3.45. Its variable manufacturing cost per unit is $56.55. Total manufacturing cost per unit is $60.00 (given). See below for calculations.

    Calculations:

    Fixed overhead rate: $41,400 ÷ 12,000

    Direct labour per unit:

Cost of goods sold	=	Direct materials + Direct labour + Variable overhead + Fixed overhead
$60	=	$24 + DL$ + VOH$ + $3.45
$32.55	=	DL$ + VOH$

    but VOH$ = 2 × DL$

$32.55	=	DL$ + 2DL$
3DL$	=	$32.55
DL$	=	$10.85

    Variable overhead per unit: 2 × $10.85

    Variable cost per unit: $24 + 10.85 + 21.70

8-23 continued

2. Telster's absorption-costing income is $113,000.

Sales	$850,000
Cost of goods sold	600,000
Gross margin	$250,000
Selling and administrative expenses	137,000
Net income	$113,000

Notes:

Unit sales: 10,000 [12,000 – 2,000]

Sales: $850,000 [10,000 × $85]

Cost of goods sold: $600,000 [10,000 × $60]

Telster's variable-costing income is $106,100.

Sales	$850,000
Variable expenses	565,500
Contribution margin	$284,500
Fixed expenses	178,400
Net income	$106,100

Notes:

Variable expenses: $565,500 [10,000 × $56.55]

Fixed expenses: $178,400 [$41,400 + 137,000]

We can also find the variable-costing income if we adjust the absorption-costing income for the $6,900 of fixed overhead deferred in ending inventory [2,000 × $3.45]. This fixed overhead is the difference between absorption-costing income and variable-costing income – $113,000 – 6,900 = $106,100.

3. The value of ending inventory under absorption costing is $120,000 [$60 × 2,000]. The value of ending inventory under variable-costing is $113,100 [$56.55 × 2,000].

8-25

The profit earned by Woolywear is a loss of $27,500 for the specialty shops and is a profit of $4,500 for Giga-Mart.

Calculations:

Specialty Shops:

Sales		$450,000	[50,000 × $9.00]
Variable expenses:			
Variable cost of goods sold	$312,500		[50,000 × ($1.75 + 1.50 + 3.00)]
Special design	100,000		[50,000 × $2.00]
Commissions	45,000		[50,000 × $0.90]
Total variable expenses		457,500	
Contribution margin		$ (7,500)	
Fixed expenses:			
Shipping		20,000	
Net loss		$(27,500)	

Giga-Mart:

Sales		$450,000	[50,000 × $9.00]
Discount		50,000	[50,000 × $1.00]
Net sales		$400,000	
Variable expenses:			
Variable cost of goods sold	$312,500		[50,000 × ($1.75 + 1.50 + 3.00)]
Return penalties	3,000		[$400,000 × 15% × 5%]
Total variable expenses		315,500	
Contribution margin		$ 84,500	
Fixed expenses:			
Delivery		80,000	
Profit		$ 4,500	

PROBLEMS

8-27

1. Eckel's absorption-costing income statement is:

Sales		$643,200	
Cost of goods sold		289,440	[$643,200 × 45%]
Gross margin		$353,760	
Selling and administrative expenses			
Selling	$123,360		[183,360 – 60,000]
Administrative	60,000		
Total		183,360	[$353,760 – 170,400]
Net income		$170,400	

8-27 continued

2. Eckel's variable-costing income statement is:

Sales		$643,200	
Variable expenses:			
Cost of goods sold	$231,552		[$289,440 × 80%]
Selling	61,680		[$123,360 × 50%]
Total		293,232	
Contribution margin		$349,968	
Fixed expenses			
Overhead	$57,888		[$289,440 × 20%]
Selling	61,680		[$123,360 × 50%]
Administrative	60,000		
Total		179,568	
Net income		$170,400	

3. The total variable cost per motor is $5.47 [$293,232 ÷ 53,600]. The variable production cost per motor is $4.32 [$231,552 ÷ 53,600].

8-29

1. Pro forma variable-costing income statement:

Sales	$19,350,000	[21,500 × $900]
Variable cost of goods sold	11,287,500	[21,500 × $525]
Variable marketing	1,612,500	[21,500 × $75]
Contribution margin	$ 6,450,000	
Fixed expenses	6,600,000	
Net income (loss)	$ (150,000)	

2. Pro forma variable-costing income statement based on change in technology:

Sales		$19,350,000	[21,500 × $900]
Variable cost of goods sold			
Direct materials	$3,870,000		[21,500 × $240 × 75%]
Direct labour	4,644,000		[21,500 × $180 × 120%]
Variable overhead	1,693,125		[21,500 × $105 × 75%]]
Total		10,207,125	
Variable marketing		1,612,500	[21,500 × $75]
Contribution margin		$ 7,530,375	
Fixed expenses		7,260,000	[$6,600,000 × 110%]
Net income (loss)		$ 270,375	

8-31

1. Variable-costing income statement for six months ended May 31, 2004:

Sales		$330,000	[22,000 × $15]
Variable expenses:			
Direct materials	$ 67,500		
Direct labour	101,250		
Variable overhead	54,000		
Variable manufacturing costs	$222,750		
Less ending inventory	41,250		[$222,750 ÷ 27,000 × (27,000 – 22,000)]
Variable cost of goods sold	$181,500		
Variable selling and administrative	16,500		[$330,000 × 5%]
Total variable expenses		198,000	
Contribution margin		$132,000	
Fixed expenses:			
Overhead	$189,000		
Selling and administrative	30,000		
Total fixed expenses		219,000	
Operating income (loss)		$ (87,000)	

Absorption-costing income statement for six months ended May 31, 2004

Sales		$330,000	[22,000 × $15]
Cost of goods sold:			
Direct materials	$ 67,500		
Direct labour	101,250		
Variable overhead	54,000		
Fixed overhead	189,000		
Total manufacturing costs	$411,750		
Less ending inventory	76,250		[$411,750 ÷ 27,000 × (27,000 – 22,000)]
Cost of goods sold		335,500	
Gross margin		$ (5,500)	
Selling and administrative expenses		46,500	[$30,000 + $330,000 × 5%]
Operating income (loss)		$ (52,000)	

2. The $35,000 difference between variable-costing income and absorption-costing income is the fixed overhead cost applied to ending inventory under absorption costing.

   The fixed overhead rate is $7.00 per unit [$189,000 ÷ 27,000]. Ending inventory is 5,000 units [27,000 – 22,000] with fixed overhead of $35,000 [5,000 × $7.00].

3. The costing method Jarrett should use depends on how it will use the information.

   Absorption costing is usually preferred for external reporting and may be better for long-term pricing decisions because it includes a share of all production costs.

   Variable costing provides better information for short-term pricing decisions and is usually preferred for planning and control purposes because it highlights cost behaviour patterns. Income is more closely related to sales activity and is not affected by changes in production activity.

   Jarrett can use variable costing for management purposes and easily convert its information to absorption costing for external reporting purposes.

8-33

1. B.T. Company's 2004 income statement:

Sales		$400,000	
Cost of goods sold			
Direct materials	$100,000		[$80,000 ÷ 20,000 × 25,000]
Direct labour	75,000		[$60,000 ÷ 20,000 × 25,000]
Variable overhead	50,000		[$40,000 ÷ 20,000 × 25,000]
Fixed overhead	100,000		
Cost of goods manufactured	$325,000		
Ending inventory	65,000		[$325,000 ÷ 25,000 × (25,000 – 20,000)]
Total cost of goods sold		260,000	
Gross profit		$140,000	
Selling and administrative expenses			
Variable	$30,000		
Fixed	40,000		
Total selling and administration		70,000	
Net income		$ 70,000	

2. B. T. Company's 2004 net income is different from expected because it produced 25,000 units rather than 20,000 units as planned. Inventory increased by 5,000 units [25,000 – 20,000] and these units carried fixed overhead in future periods. Under its original plan all fixed overhead would have been expensed in 2004. The fixed overhead rate is $4.00 per unit [$100,000 ÷ 25,000] and $20,000 of fixed overhead is applied to units in inventory [$4.00 × 5,000]. This is the $20,000 difference between its expected income and its actual income.

3. If B. T. Company used variable costing it would have avoided this difference in income – its income would depend on sales and management of costs (which were as expected) and not on amount of production (which was different). All fixed overhead would be expensed when incurred – as expected – and its net income would be as expected. Only the additional cost of production would be deferred as a cost of inventory. B. T. Company's variable-costing 2004 income statement is shown below.

Sales		$400,000	
Variable expenses			
Direct materials	$100,000		[$80,000 ÷ 20,000 × 25,000]
Direct labour	75,000		[$60,000 ÷ 20,000 × 25,000]
Variable overhead	50,000		[$40,000 ÷ 20,000 × 25,000]
Variable cost of goods manufactured	$225,000		
Ending inventory	45,000		[$225,000 ÷ 25,000 × (25,000 – 20,000)]
Total variable cost of goods sold	$180,000		
Variable selling and administrative	30,000		
Total variable expenses		210,000	
Contribution margin		$190,000	
Fixed expenses			
Fixed overhead	$100,000		
Fixed selling and administration	40,000		
Total fixed expenses		140,000	
Net income		$ 50,000	

8-35

1. Unit costs under absorption costing and variable costing:

Month 1:	Absorption	Variable	
Unit (product) costs:			
Direct materials	$4.00	$4.00	
Direct labour	2.00	2.00	
Variable overhead	2.00	2.00	
Fixed overhead	1.60	---	($960,000 ÷ 12) ÷ 50,000
Total	$9.60	$8.00	
Period costs:			
Fixed overhead	---	$80,000	($960,000 ÷ 12)
Variable selling	$1.00	$1.00	
Fixed selling and administrative	$25,000	$25,000	($300,000 ÷ 12)

Month 2:	Absorption	Variable	
Unit (product) costs:			
Direct materials	$4.00	$4.00	
Direct labour	2.00	2.00	
Variable overhead	2.00	2.00	
Fixed overhead	2.00	---	($960,000 ÷ 12) ÷ 40,000
Total	$10.00	$8.00	
Period costs:			
Fixed overhead	---	$80,000	($960,000 ÷ 12)
Variable selling	$1.00	$1.00	
Fixed selling and administrative	$25,000	$25,000	($300,000 ÷ 12)

Month 3:	Absorption	Variable	
Unit (product) costs:			
Direct materials	$4.00	$4.00	
Direct labour	2.00	2.00	
Variable overhead	2.00	2.00	
Fixed overhead	2.00	---	($960,000 ÷ 12) ÷ 40,000
Total	$10.00	$8.00	
Period costs:			
Fixed overhead	---	$80,000	($960,000 ÷ 12)
Variable selling	$1.00	$1.00	
Fixed selling and administrative	$25,000	$25,000	($300,000 ÷ 12)

2. The difference between absorption-costing income and variable-costing income is the fixed overhead deferred in beginning and ending inventory.

    In month 1 inventory increased by 10,000 units [50,000 – 40,000] with $16,000 of fixed overhead deferred under absorption costing [10,000 × $1.60] – absorption-costing income will be $16,000 higher than variable-costing income. In month 2, ending inventory remains at 10,000 units [10,000 + 40,000 – 40,000], $16,000 of fixed overhead is released from beginning inventory, and $20,000 of fixed overhead cost is deferred in ending inventory [10,000 × $2.00] – the net effect is to defer $4,000 of fixed overhead [$20,000 – 16,000] and absorption-costing income is $4,000 higher than variable-costing income. In month 3, ending inventory increased to 20,000 units [10,000 + 40,000 – 30,000], $20,000 of fixed overhead is released from beginning inventory, and $40,000 of fixed overhead cost is deferred in ending inventory [20,000 × $2.00] – the net effect is to defer $20,000 of fixed overhead [$40,000 – 20,000] and absorption-costing income is $20,000 higher than variable-costing income.

8-35 continued

3. Absorption-costing and variable-costing income statements:

Absorption-Costing Income Statement: Month 1

Sales (40,000 × $14)		$560,000
Cost of goods sold:		
Beginning inventory	$ 0	
Cost of goods manufactured (50,000 × $9.60)	480,000	
Less ending inventory ((50,000 – 40,000) × $9.60)	96,000	384,000
Gross margin		$176,000
Selling and administrative expenses:		
Variable (40,000 × $1.00)	$40,000	
Fixed	25,000	
Total selling and administrative expenses		65,000
Net income		$111,000

Absorption-Costing Income Statement: Month 2

Sales (40,000 × $14)		$560,000
Cost of goods sold:		
Beginning inventory	$ 96,000	
Cost of goods manufactured (40,000 × $10.00)	400,000	
Less ending inventory (10,000 × $10.00)	100,000	396,000
Gross margin		$164,000
Selling and administrative expenses:		
Variable (40,000 × $1.00)	$40,000	
Fixed	25,000	
Total selling and administrative expenses		65,000
Net income		$ 99,000

Absorption-Costing Income Statement: Month 3

Sales (30,000 × $14)		$420,000
Cost of goods sold:		
Beginning inventory	$100,000	
Cost of goods manufactured (40,000 × $10.00)	400,000	
Less ending inventory (20,000 × $10.00)	200,000	300,000
Gross margin		$120,000
Selling and administration expenses:		
Variable (30,000 × $1.00)	$30,000	
Fixed	25,000	
Total selling and administrative expenses		55,000
Net income		$ 65,000

8-35 continued

Variable-Costing Income Statement: Month 1

Sales (40,000 × $14)			$560,000
Variable expenses:			
Cost of goods sold:			
Beginning inventory	$ 0		
Cost of goods manufactured (50,000 × $8.00)	400,000		
Less ending inventory ((50,000 – 40,000) × $8.00)	80,000	$320,000	
Selling (40,000 × $1.00)		40,000	
Total variable expenses			360,000
Contribution margin			$200,000
Fixed expenses:			
Fixed overhead		$80,000	
Fixed selling and administrative		25,000	
Total fixed expenses			105,000
Net income			$ 95,000

Variable-Costing Income Statement: Month 2

Sales (40,000 × $14)			$560,000
Variable expenses:			
Cost of goods sold:			
Beginning inventory	$ 80,000		
Cost of goods manufactured (40,000 × $8.00)	320,000		
Less ending inventory (10,000 × $8.00)	80,000	$320,000	
Selling (40,000 × $1.00)		40,000	
Total variable expenses			360,000
Contribution margin			$200,000
Fixed expenses:			
Fixed overhead		$80,000	
Fixed selling and administrative		25,000	
Total fixed expenses			105,000
Net income			$ 95,000

Variable-Costing Income Statement: Month 3

Sales (30,000 × $14)			$420,000
Variable expenses:			
Cost of goods sold:			
Beginning inventory	$ 80,000		
Cost of goods manufactured (40,000 × $8.00)	320,000		
Less ending inventory (20,000 × $8.00)	160,000	$240,000	
Selling (30,000 × $1.00)		30,000	
Total variable expenses			270,000
Contribution margin			$150,000
Fixed expenses:			
Fixed overhead		$80,000	
Fixed selling and administrative		25,000	
Total fixed expenses			105,000
Net income			$ 45,000

8-35 continued

Reconciliation:

	Month 1	Month 2	Month 3
Variable-costing net income	$ 95,000	$95,000	$45,000
Plus: fixed overhead deferred in ending inventory	16,000	20,000	40,000
Less: fixed overhead released from beginning inventory	---	16,000	20,000
Absorption costing net income	$111,000	$99,000	$65,000

8-37

1. Absorption-costing income statement:

Sales		$725,000
Cost of goods sold		
Cost of goods manufactured	$448,000	
Ending inventory	42,000	
Cost of goods sold	$406,000	
Overapplied overhead	6,000	
Adjusted cost of goods sold		400,000
Gross margin		$325,000
Selling and administrative expenses		209,000
Net income		$116,000

Notes:

Sales: 29,000 × $25

Cost of goods manufactured: ($4.00 + 5.00 + 2.00 + 3.00) × 32,000

Ending inventory: ($4.00 + 5.00 + 2.00 + 3.00) × (32,000 – 29,000)

Overapplied overhead: ($3.00 × 30,000) – ($3.00 × 32,000)

Selling and administrative expenses: ($1.00 × 29,000) + ($6.00 × 30,000)

8-37 continued

2. Variable-costing income statement:

Sales		$725,000
Variable expenses:		
Cost of goods sold		
Cost of goods manufactured	$352,000	
Ending inventory	33,000	
Cost of goods sold	$319,000	
Selling	29,000	
Total variable expenses		348,000
Contribution margin		$377,000
Fixed expenses:		
Overhead	$ 90,000	
Administrative	180,000	
Total fixed expenses		270,000
Net income		$107,000

Notes:

Sales: 29,000 × $25

Cost of goods manufactured: ($4.00 + 5.00 + 2.00) × 32,000

Ending inventory: ($4.00 + 5.00 + 2.00) × (32,000 – 29,000)

Variable selling expenses: $1.00 × 29,000

Fixed overhead: $3.00 × 30,000

Fixed administrative expenses: $6.00 × 30,000

3. There is a difference between the absorption-costing net income and the variable-costing net income because of the $9,000 [$3.00 × 3,000] of fixed overhead applied to ending inventory by absorption costing – an amount that is expensed under variable-costing. A reconciliation is shown below:

Absorption-costing income	$116,000
Fixed overhead from beginning inventory	0
Fixed overhead deferred in ending inventory	(9,000)
Variable-costing income	$107,000

8-39

1. Kathy lost her bonus because the increase in sales activity was offset by the decrease in inventory and the expensing of fixed overhead cost carried forward from years 1 and 2. This is the result of her company using absorption costing. Profit will be affected by changes in inventory – as occurred in this case. In year 2, Kathy showed a large increase in income because she increased sales and increased the fixed overhead deferred in inventory. In year 3, she also increased sales but liquidated the previously deferred fixed overhead cost. As a result her income was not as high as it would have been if she had not reduced inventory.

   The fixed overhead expensed in year 3 from previous years is $8,800.

from year 1	$5,800	[$2.90 × (10,000 – 8,000)]
from year 2	3,000	[$3.00 × (11,000 – 10,000)]
Total	$8,800	

   In addition, Kathy didn't defer any of her fixed overhead incurred in year 3. So although she incurred the same amount of fixed overhead cost in years 2 and 3, more was expensed in year 3, her income was lower and she lost her bonus. Variable-costing income statements would do a better job of showing how much Kathy's good management has contributed to her company's welfare.

2. Variable-costing income statements:

	Year 1	Year 2	Year 3
Sales revenue	$80,000	$100,000	$120,000
Variable expenses			
Cost of goods sold	31,200	40,000	47,800
Variable selling	3,200	5,000	6,000
Total variable expenses	34,400	45,000	53,800
Contribution margin	$45,600	$ 55,000	$ 66,200
Fixed expenses			
Overhead	29,000	30,000	30,000
Other	9,000	10,000	10,000
Total fixed expenses	38,000	40,000	40,000
Net income	$ 7,600	$ 15,000	$ 26,200

   Notes:

   Variable cost of goods sold, Year 1: ($1.00 + 1.90 +1.00) × 8,000

   Variable cost of goods sold, Year 2: ($1.00 + 2.00 +1.00) × 10,000

   Variable cost of goods sold, Year 3:

Produced in year 3	$36,000	[($1.00 + 2.00 +1.00) × 9,000]
Produced in year 2	4,000	[($1.00 + 2.00 +1.00) × 1,000]
Produced in year 1	7,800	[($1.00 + 1.90 +1.00) × 2,000]
Total	$47,800	

   Variable selling expenses: 8,000 × $0.40; 10,000 × $0.50; 12,000 × $0.50

8-39 continued

To reconcile the absorption-costing and variable-costing net income, we track the fixed overhead cost applied to inventory. The fixed overhead in ending inventory is summarized below:

	Year 1	*Year 2*	*Year 3*
From year 1 (2,000 × $2.90)	$5,800	$5,800	--
From year 2 (1,000 × $3.00)	--	3,000	--
Total fixed overhead in ending inventory	$5,800	$ 8,800	--

The reconciliation of the absorption-costing and variable-costing net income is shown below:

	Year 1	*Year 2*	*Year 3*
Absorption-costing income	$13,400	$18,000	$17,400
Fixed overhead from beginning inventory	0	5,800	8,800
Fixed overhead deferred in ending inventory	(5,800)	(8,800)	0
Variable-costing income	$ 7,600	$15,000	$26,200

3. The vice-president of Kathy's company would prefer to use the variable-costing income statements to evaluate Kathy's performance. Variable costing provides a more consistent signal of a manager's performance. Kathy will receive her bonus based on her success in increasing sales, controlling costs, and reducing inventories. With absorption costing, Kathy's success in increasing sales while controlling costs is overshadowed by the effect of reducing inventories (usually a favourable result) because of the liquidation of previously deferred fixed overhead cost. Variable costing will also prevent a manager from inflating his income by increasing production to increase inventory and defer more fixed overhead to future periods. Overall variable-costing income is a better gauge of a manager's contribution to the company's profitability.

8-41

1. Lion Company produced 20,000 units in 2004.

    The difference in absorption costing income from what was expected for the sale of 15,000 units is caused by an increase in inventory and deferral of fixed overhead costs. Thus there is $3,000 of fixed overhead cost applied to ending inventory. This represents 25% of the fixed overhead cost [$3,000 ÷ 12,000] – and the 15,000 units sold would have 75% of the fixed overhead cost, or $9,000 [75% × $12,000]. The fixed overhead rate is $0.60 per unit [$9,000 ÷ 15,000] and 20,000 units were produced [$12,000 ÷ $0.60].

2. If the company used variable costing there would be no discrepancy between expected and actual income if all revenues and costs behaved as expected. The difference under absorption costing is caused because some of the fixed overhead is applied to inventory, deferred to future periods, and not expensed in the current period. Thus income can be affected by differences between sales and production. Under variable costing all fixed overhead is expensed as incurred and differences between sales and production will not affect income.

8-43

1. The total amount of fixed overhead incurred in 2004 is $100,100.

Fixed overhead in cost of goods sold	$ 85,800	
Fixed overhead added to ending inventory	5,720	[($85,800 ÷ 12,000) × (12,800 – 12,000)]
Underapplied fixed overhead	8,580	[underapplied overhead is all from fixed overhead]
Total fixed	$100,100	

8-43 continued

2. The total contribution margin is $216,000.

Sales	$540,000	
Variable expenses		
Cost of goods sold	(261,000)	[$102,000 + 84,000 + 75,000]
Selling and administrative	(63,000)	
Contribution margin	$216,000	

3. If Lampton Green Industries has used variable costing, its 2004 net income would be $35,900.

Contribution margin	$216,000
Fixed overhead	(100,100)
Fixed selling and administrative	(80,000)
Net income	$ 35,900

4. The difference between absorption-costing net income and variable-costing net income is the fixed overhead applied to units in inventory. The fixed overhead rate is $7.15 per unit [$85,800 ÷ 12,000]. Under absorption costing fixed overhead is expensed when the units are sold. Under variable costing fixed overhead is expensed when incurred. The difference is reconciled below.

Variable-costing income	$35,900	
Fixed overhead from beginning inventory	(6,793)	[950 × $7.15]
Fixed overhead deferred in ending inventory	12,513	[(950 + 12,800 – 12,000) × $7.15]
Absorption-costing income	$41,620	

5. The value of ending inventory under absorption costing is $50,575. The value of ending inventory under variable costing is $38,062.50.

Units in ending inventory	1,750	[950 + 12,800 – 12,000]
Variable cost per unit	$21.75	[$261,000 ÷ 12,000]
Variable-costing inventory	$38,062.50	[1,750 × $21.75]
Fixed overhead applied	12,512.50	[1,750 × $7.15]
Absorption-costing inventory	$50,575.00	

8-45

1. The unit cost using absorption costing is $32.50. The unit cost using variable costing is $26.00 [$32.50 – 6.50]

2. Absorption-costing income statement:

Sales		$1,370,000	[27,400 × $50]
Cost of goods sold	$890,500		[27,400 × $32.50]
Underapplied overhead	15,000		[$10,000 + 5,000]
Adjusted cost of goods sold		905,500	
Gross margin		$ 464,500	
Selling and administrative expenses		435,500	[$230,000 + 15% × $1,370,000]
Net income		$ 29,000	

8-45 continued

3. Variable-costing income statement:

Sales		$1,370,000	[27,400 × $50]
Variable expenses:			
Cost of goods sold	$712,400		[27,400 × $26.00]
Underapplied overhead	5,000		[$10,000 + 5,000]
Adjusted cost of goods sold	$717,400		[15% × $1,370,000]
Selling and administrative	205,500		
Total variable expenses		922,900	
Contribution margin		$ 447,100	
Fixed expenses:			
Overhead	$205,000		[30,000 × $6.50 + $10,000]
Selling and administrative	230,000		
Total fixed expenses		435,000	
Net income		$ 12,100	

4. The difference between the absorption-costing income and the variable-costing income is the fixed overhead cost applied to inventory and deferred to future periods rather than expensed in the current period.

Reconciliation:

Absorption-costing income	$29,000	
Fixed overhead from beginning inventory	0	
Fixed overhead deferred in ending inventory	(16,900)	[(30,000 – 27,400) × $6.50]
Variable-costing income	$12,100	

MANAGERIAL DECISION CASES

8-47

The report should cover the following items

- evaluation of current system
- design of new system
- variable costing versus absorption costing

Evaluation of current system

- designed for annual reporting and inventory valuation
- little information provided for management decision use; cost control, planning and control, product pricing, customer profitability analysis, etc. – no cost traced to specific products or jobs with average cost used for inventory valuation
- expanding business has created new need for accounting information – in a small operation information may be gathered on an informal basis (for example, cost control may be by direct observation) but as the operation grows this is no longer adequate and formal costing and reporting systems are needed
- new markets require more information to evaluate and compare existing and new opportunities

8-47 continued

Design of new system

- characteristics of operations, products, and markets should be considered
- some operations are similar across products and markets (frames, springs, etc.) but other items are specific to the product or market (upholstery)
- a mixture of process costing and job order costing is appropriate – possibly with an activity-based system to handle overhead cost
- cost (additional effort and staff) and benefit (cost information specific to operation and product available to managers) evaluation

Variable costing versus absorption costing

- variable-costing information (for management purposes) and absorption-costing information (for financial reporting) can be provided by a well-designed accounting system
- variable costing provides information about cost behaviour – useful to managers for planning and control, pricing, and other decisions

8-49

1. Absorption-costing income statement:

Sales		$90,000
Cost of goods sold	$55,000	
Underapplied overhead	4,000	
Adjusted cost of goods sold		59,000
Gross margin		$31,000
Selling and administrative expenses		34,500
Net income (loss)		$ (3,500)

Notes:

Sales: 100,000 × $0.90

Cost of goods sold: 100,000 × $0.55

Underapplied overhead: $14,000 – (100,000 × 0.10)

Selling and administrative expenses: $10,000 + 5% × $90,000 + $20,000

8-49 continued

Variable-costing income statement:

Sales		$90,000
Variable expenses		
Cost of goods sold	$45,000	
Selling	4,500	
Total variable expenses		49,500
Contribution margin		$40,500
Fixed expenses		
Overhead	$14,000	
Selling and administrative	30,000	44,000
Net income (loss)		$ (3,500)

Notes:

Sales: 100,000 × $0.90

Variable cost of goods sold: 100,000 × ($0.22 + 0.14 + 0.09)

Variable selling expenses: 5% × $90,000

Selling and administrative expenses: $10,000 + $20,000

Although the income statements show the same amount of net income (because units sold and produced are the same and there is no deferred fixed overhead cost), Norma can point to the clear separation of variable and fixed cost as an advantage of variable costing – information that is useful in evaluating the profitability of different products.

2. The gross margin of the order of 30,000 concrete blocks is $(300) [30,000 × ($0.54 – 0.55)]. The contribution margin of the order of 30,000 concrete blocks is $1,890 [30,000 × ($0.54 – 0.45) – 30,000 × $0.54 ×5%].

The order's gross margin and contribution margin differ because of two factors. Contribution margin considers only the costs that change with the order. Gross margin includes fixed overhead cost – a cost that remains the same in total regardless of whether the order is accepted or not. The fixed overhead cost causes a difference of $3,000 [30,000 × $0.10]. Contribution margin considers both product and period costs while gross margin considers only product costs. There is a variable selling cost of $810 [30,000 × $0.54 ×5%] associated with the order.

Together these differences explain the $2,190 difference between gross margin and contribution margin [$3,000 – 810 = $1,890 – (300)].

8-49 continued

3. Absorption-costing income statement with special order:

Sales		$106,200
Cost of goods sold	$71,500	
Underapplied overhead	1,000	
Adjusted cost of goods sold		72,500
Gross margin		$33,700
Selling and administrative expenses		35,310
Net income (loss)		$ (1,610)

Notes:

Sales: $100,000 \times \$0.90 + 30,000 \times \$0.54$

Cost of goods sold: $130,000 \times \$0.55$

Underapplied overhead: $\$14,000 - (130,000 \times 0.10)$

Selling and administrative expenses: $\$10,000 + 5\% \times \$106,200 + \$20,000$

Variable-costing income statement with special order:

Sales		$106,200
Variable expenses		
Cost of goods sold	$58,500	
Selling	5,310	
Total variable expenses		63,810
Contribution margin		$42,390
Fixed expenses		
Overhead	$14,000	
Selling and administrative	30,000	44,000
Net income (loss)		$ (1,610)

Notes:

Sales: $100,000 \times \$0.90 + 30,000 \times \$0.54$

Variable cost of goods sold: $130,000 \times (\$0.22 + 0.14 + 0.09)$

Variable selling expenses: $5\% \times \$106,200$

Selling and administrative expenses: $\$10,000 + \$20,000$

The contribution margin shows exactly the effect on profit of accepting the order at $0.54 per block. With the order the company's net income increases by $1,890 – the contribution margin. Gross margin signals that the order would cause a loss – because of the fixed overhead cost that is applied to the order (a cost that doesn't change with the decision). The gross margin also ignores the increase in selling expense. Contribution margin correctly signals that the order will increase the company's net income and properly excludes the fixed overhead and includes the change in selling expenses.

8-49 continued

4. The example in Requirements 2 and 3 should convince Eric of the merits of variable costing. Absorption costing provides incomplete information and the wrong signal for pricing decisions. Variable costing provides complete and consistent information and the correct signal for pricing decisions. An income statement that reveals cost behaviour provides information that is more useful in many cases than the information provided by absorption costing.

    Eric is correct that all costs must be covered or the company will eventually go out of business but often a price based on variable costs (rather than average total costs) is appropriate to allow a company to meet this objective. Variable costing does a better job of meeting a manager's information needs because it does consider all costs (which absorption costing doesn't) and shows each cost's cost behaviour so that managers can correctly see the expected consequences of their decisions.

CHAPTER 9
COST-VOLUME-PROFIT ANALYSIS:
A MANAGERIAL PLANNING TOOL

ANSWERS TO ODD-NUMBERED QUESTIONS FOR WRITING AND DISCUSSION

1. CVP analysis emphasizes the interrelationships between costs, cost behaviour, quantity sold, and price. Managers can use CVP analysis to ask different "what if" questions to assess the effect on profits of changes in these key variables. This sensitivity analysis is an integral part of a manager's planning activity.

3. The breakeven point is the sales level (in units or revenue) where total revenue equals total cost or where zero profits are earned. At the breakeven point total contribution margin is equal to total fixed cost.

5. At the breakeven point of 10,000 units, the total contribution margin is equal to total fixed cost. If 15,000 units are sold, the contribution margin from the 5,000 additional units [15,000 – 10,000] will provide an operating income of $35,000 [5,000 × $7].

7. To breakeven sales revenue is $50,000 [$20,000 ÷ 0.4].

9. Sales mix is the relative combination of products sold by a company. For example a sales mix of 4 to 3 (or 4:3) means that 4 units of one product are sold for every three units of another product.

11. 2,400 units of A and 1,200 units of B must be sold to break even.

    Calculation:

Product	A	B	Package
Unit contribution margin	$10	$5	
Sales mix	2	1	
Package contribution margin	$20	$5	$25

Breakeven point:			
Fixed cost	$30,000		
Package contribution margin	25		
Breakeven in packages	1,200		
Units of A	2,400	[1,200 × 2]	
Units of B	1,200	[1,200 × 1]	

13. A change in sales mix will change the amount of contribution margin from each product in the "package" and thus the package's contribution margin. This can change the number of packages, and the units of each product, at the breakeven point.

15. Operating leverage is the use of fixed cost to extract higher percentage changes in operating income as sales activity changes. Operating leverage is measured by the degree of operating leverage (calculated as Contribution margin ÷ Operating income). The greater a company's degree of operating leverage, the greater will be the effect of changes in its sales activity on its operating income. A company that faces greater increases or decreases in its operating income caused by increases or decrease in its sales activity has more operating risk. A company that faces smaller increases or decreases in its operating income caused by increases or decrease in its sales activity has less operating risk.

17. Conventional CVP analysis assumes that all cost of a company can be divided into two categories: those that vary with sales volume (costs that vary at a unit level) and those that do not (fixed costs). In an activity-based costing system, costs are divided into unit-based and two or more nonunit-based categories. Activity-based costing recognizes that some costs vary with units and other costs do not. Many nonunit-based costs vary with respect to other activity drivers. We see the fixed costs of conventional CVP analysis with a better understanding of nonunit cost behaviour when we use CVP in conjunction with activity-based costing.

SOLUTIONS TO ODD-NUMBERED EXERCISES, PROBLEMS, AND CASES

EXERCISES

9-1

Column A	*Column B*
1. Contribution margin	e. Price minus variable cost per unit
2. Contribution margin ratio	c. Contribution margin per unit divided by price
3. Variable cost ratio	d. Total variable cost divided by total revenue
4. Break-even units	b. Total fixed costs divided by the contribution margin per unit
5. Operating income	a. Sales minus total variable costs minus total fixed costs

9-3

1. Dorian Company's breakeven point is 1,800 units.

Fixed expenses	$18,000	
Contribution margin per unit	$10	[$20,000 ÷ 2,000]
Breakeven point	1,800	[$18,000 ÷ $10]

2. Dorian Company's income statement at breakeven is:

Sales revenue	$45,000	[1,800 × $25]
Variable expenses	27,000	[1,800 × ($30,000 ÷ 2,000)]
Contribution margin	$18,000	
Fixed expenses	18,000	
Operating income	$ 0	

3. To earn an operating income of $15,000, Dorian must sell 3,300 units.

Calculation:

Fixed expenses	$18,000
Target operating income	15,000
Total contribution margin required	$33,000
Contribution margin per unit	$10
Units required	3,300

9-5

1. To earn an operating income equal to 20 percent of revenue, Dorian Company must sell 3,600 units.

    Calculation:

$$
\begin{aligned}
X &= (\$18,000 + 0.2 \times \$25X) \div \$10 \\
\$10X &= \$18,000 + \$5X \\
\$5X &= \$18,000 \\
X &= 3,600 \text{ units}
\end{aligned}
$$

2. Dorian Company's income statement at 3,600 units is:

Sales revenue	$90,000	[3,600 × $25]
Variable expenses	54,000	[3,600 × $15]
Contribution margin	$36,000	
Fixed expenses	18,000	
Operating income	$18,000	

   Operating income of $18,000 is 20 percent of Dorian Company's revenue [$18,000 ÷ $90,000].

9-7

1. Lacy Company's sales mix is 1A:3B.

2. Lacy must sell 600 units of Product A and 1,800 units of Product B to break even.

    Calculation:

Product	A	B	Package
Unit contribution margin	$4	$3	
Sales mix	1	3	
Package contribution margin	$4	$9	$13

Breakeven point:		
Fixed cost	$7,800	[$4,700 + 3,100]
Package contribution margin	13	
Breakeven in packages	600	
Units of A	600	[600 × 1]
Units of B	1,800	[600 × 3]

   Notes:

   Product A's contribution margin per unit is $4 [$4,000 ÷ 1,000].

   Product B's contribution margin per unit is $3 [$9,000 ÷ 3,000].

3. Lacy Company's breakeven revenue is $27,601.

Fixed expenses	$ 7,800	
Contribution margin ratio	0.2826	[$13,000 ÷ $46,000]
Breakeven revenue	$27,601	

9-9

1. Fremont Company's breakeven point is 10,000 units.

   Calculation:

Fixed expenses	$100,000	
Contribution margin per unit	$10	[$20 – 10]
Breakeven point	10,000	[$100,000 ÷ $10]

2. Fremont Company's breakeven point using the ABC approach is 10,000 units.

   Calculation:

Fixed expenses	$ 40,000	
Setup cost	30,000	[$600 × 50]
Engineering cost	30,000	[$60 × 500]
Total contribution margin required	$100,000	
Contribution margin per unit	$10	[$20 – 10]
Breakeven point	10,000	[$100,000 ÷ $10]

3. Fremont's new breakeven point using the ABC approach is 9,500 units.

Fixed expenses	$40,000	
Setup cost	25,000	[($600 – 100) × 50]
Engineering cost	30,000	[$60 × 500]
Total contribution margin required	$95,000	
Contribution margin per unit	$10	[$20 – 10]
Breakeven point	9,500	[$95,000 ÷ $10]

   Under the traditional approach, the reduction in the setup costs may not be noticed and the fixed cost of $100,000 would not be adjusted. The breakeven point would remain at 10,000 units.

9-11

1. With a tax rate of 40 percent, Loewen must earn a before-tax income of $42,000 to have after-tax income of $25,200 [$25,200 ÷ (1 – 0.4)].

   Loewen must sell 240,000 bottles to earn an after-tax income of $25,200 [($136,000 + 14,000 + 42,000) ÷ $0.80].

2. With a tax rate of 30 percent, Loewen must earn a before-tax income of $36,000 to have after-tax income of $25,200 [$25,200 ÷ (1 – 0.3)].

   Loewen must sell 232,500 bottles to earn an after-tax income of $25,200 [($136,000 + 14,000 + 36,000) ÷ $0.80].

3. With a tax rate of 50 percent, Loewen must earn a before-tax income of $50,400 to have after-tax income of $25,200 [$25,200 ÷ (1 – 0.5)].

   Loewen must sell 250,500 bottles to earn an after-tax income of $25,200 [($136,000 + 14,000 + 50,400) ÷ $0.80].

9-11 continued

4. Loewen's margin of safety is 27,500 bottles [215,000 – 187,500] and $74,800 in sales dollars [27,500 × $2.72].

   Notes:

   Loewen's breakeven point is 187,500 bottles [($136,000 + 14,000) ÷ $0.80] and $510,000 [187,500 × $2.72].

9-13

	A	B	C	D
Sales	$5,000	$15,600	$16,250	$9,000
Total variable expenses	4,000	11,700	9,750	5,400
Contribution margin	$1,000	$ 3,900	$ 6,500	$3,600
Total fixed costs	500	4,000	6,100	750
Operating income (loss)	$ 500	$ (100)	$ 400	$2,850
Units sold	1,000	1,300	125	90
Price per unit	$5	$12	$130	$100
Variable cost per unit	$4	$9	$78	$60
Contribution margin per unit	$1	$3	$52	$40
Contribution margin ratio	20%	25%	40%	40%
Breakeven in units	500	1,334	118	19

Notes and calculations:

For A: total fixed cost [$1,000 – 500]; units sold [$5,000 ÷ $5]; variable cost per unit [$4,000 ÷ 1,000]; contribution margin per unit [$5 – 4]; contribution margin ratio [$1 ÷ $5]; breakeven in units [$500 ÷ $1]

For B: sales [$11,700 + 3,900]; operating income [$3,900 – 4,000]; price per unit [$15,600 ÷ 1,300]; contribution margin ratio [$3 ÷ $12]; breakeven in units [$4,000 ÷ $3]

For C: sales [$130 × 125]; contribution margin [$16,250 – 9,750]; total fixed cost [$6,500 – 400]; variable cost per unit [$9,750 ÷ 125]; contribution margin per unit [$130 – 78]; breakeven in units [$6,100 ÷ $52]

For D: contribution margin [$2,850 + 750]; total variable expenses [$9,000 – 3,600]; selling price per unit [$9,000 ÷ 90]; variable cost per unit [$5,400 ÷ 90]; contribution margin per unit [$100 – 60]; contribution margin ratio [$40 ÷ $100]; breakeven in units [$750 ÷ $40]

9-15

1. Thiessen Company charged a price of $380.

   Calculation:

Unit contribution margin	$ 80	[$120,000 ÷ 1,500]
Variable cost per unit	300	
Selling price per unit	$380	

2. Jesper Company's variable cost per unit is $2.25.

Selling price per unit	$3.50	
Unit contribution margin	1.25	[$160,000 ÷ 128,000]
Variable cost per unit	$2.25	

9-17

1. The contribution margin per unit for a box of praline fudge is $1.40. The contribution margin ratio is 25% [$1.40 ÷ $5.60].

    Calculation:

Selling price		$5.60
Variable expenses:		
Pecans	$0.70	
Sugar	0.35	
Butter	1.85	
Other ingredients	0.34	
Box, packing material	0.76	
Selling commission	0.20	
Total variable expenses		4.20
Contribution margin per unit		$1.40

2. 32,000 boxes must be sold to break even. The breakeven sales revenue is $179,200.

    Calculations:

    $$X = (\$32,300 + 12,500) \div \$1.40$$
    $$X = \$44,800 \div \$1.40$$
    $$X = 32,000 \text{ boxes}$$

    $$R = \$44,800 \div 0.25$$
    $$R = \$179,200$$

3. Candyland's operating income last year was $4,200 [35,000 × $1.40 – $44,800].

4. Candyland's margin of safety is 3,000 boxes [35,000 – 32,000] and $16,800 [3,000 × $5.60].

5. Candyland's new breakeven point is 22,400 boxes.

    Calculations:

    New contribution margin per unit is $2.00 [$6.20 – 4.20].

    $$X = \$44,800 \div \$2.00$$
    $$X = 22,400 \text{ boxes}$$

Candyland should raise the price. It will earn an operating income of $18,200 [31,500 × $2.00 – $44,800], an increase of $14,000 [$18,200 – 4,200] and have less risk with a larger margin of safety of 9,100 boxes [31,500 22,400].

9-19

1. The selling price required to earn an after-tax profit of $144,000 is $25.50.

    Calculations:

Before-tax profit	=	After-tax profit ÷ (1 – tax rate)
	=	$144,000 ÷ (1 – 0.4)
	=	$240,000

2004 unit sales	=	$1,800,000 ÷ $22.50
	=	80,000 units

Variable cost per unit	=	$2.00 + 4.00 + 1.00 + 3.00
	=	$10.00

Fixed cost	=	$400,000 + 600,000
	=	$1,000,000

Before tax profit	=	(Selling price – Variable cost) × X – Fixed cost
$240,000	=	(Selling price – $10.00) × 80,000 – $1,000,000
Selling price × 80,000	=	$2,040,000
Selling price	=	$25.50

2. At a sales price of $25.00, Brisbane's breakeven point is 66,667 units [$1,000,000 ÷ ($25.00 – 10.00)].

3. The selling price (for 70,000 units) required to earn an operating income of 10% of revenue is $26.99.

    Calculation:

70,000 × (Selling price – $10.00) – $1,000,000	=	0.10 × (70,000 × Selling price)
(70,000 × Selling price) – $1,700,000	=	7,000 × Selling price
63,000 × Selling price	=	$1,700,000
Selling price	=	$26.99

9-21

1. Sales revenue of $60,000 must be earned to produce operating income equal to 20 percent of sales revenue.

    Calculation:

0.2 R	=	(1 – 0.4)R – $24,000
0.4 R	=	$24,000
R	=	$60,000

    The variable-costing income statement is shown below.

Sales revenue	$60,000	
Variable expenses	24,000	[$60,000 × 0.4]
Contribution margin	$36,000	
Fixed expenses	24,000	
Operating income	$12,000	

    The operating revenue of $12,000 is 20 percent of sales revenue [$12,000 ÷ $60,000].

9-21 continued

2. If the selling price is $10 per bucket, 6,000 buckets must be sold to earn an operating income equal to 20 percent of revenue [$60,000 ÷ $10].

    Alternative calculation:

    $$
    \begin{aligned}
    X &= (\$24{,}000 + 0.2 \times \$10 \times X) \div (\$10 - \$4) \\
    \$6\,X &= \$24{,}000 + \$2\,X \\
    \$4\,X &= \$24{,}000 \\
    X &= 6{,}000
    \end{aligned}
    $$

    If the selling price is $10 per bucket, 6,857 buckets must be sold to earn an operating income equal to 25 percent of revenue.

    Calculation:

    $$
    \begin{aligned}
    X &= (\$24{,}000 + 0.25 \times \$10 \times X) \div (\$10 - \$4) \\
    \$6\,X &= \$24{,}000 + \$2.5\,X \\
    \$3.5\,X &= \$24{,}000 \\
    X &= 6{,}857
    \end{aligned}
    $$

    The variable-costing income statement for sales of 6,857 buckets is shown below.

Sales revenue	$68,570	[6,857 × $10]
Variable expenses	27,428	[6,857 × $4]
Contribution margin	$41,142	
Fixed expenses	24,000	
Operating income	$17,142	

    Operating revenue of $17,142 is 25 percent of sales revenue [$17,142 ÷ $68,570].

3. Tom must have sales revenue of $89,989 to earn after-tax net income of 20 percent of sales revenue.

    Calculation:

    $$
    \begin{aligned}
    0.2\,R \div (1 - 0.4) &= (1 - 0.4)R - \$24{,}000 \\
    0.2667\,R &= \$24{,}000 \\
    R &= \$89{,}989
    \end{aligned}
    $$

9-23

1. Company A's degree of operating leverage is 2. Company B's degree of operating leverage is 6.

    Calculations:

	Company A	Company B
Contribution margin	$100,000	$300,000
Operating income	50,000	50,000
Degree of operating leverage	2	6

9-23 continued

2.   Company A's breakeven point is $250,000. Company B's breakeven point is $416,667.

Calculations:

	Company A	Company B
Contribution margin	$100,000	$300,000
Sales revenue	$500,000	$500,000
Contribution margin ratio	20%	60%
Fixed expenses	$50,000	$250,000
Contribution margin ratio	20%	60%
Breakeven point	$250,000	$416,667

Company B's breakeven point is higher because it is more highly leveraged – its fixed costs are higher.

3.   With a 50 percent increase in sales, Company A's profits will increase by 100 percent [50% × 2] and Company B's profits will increase by 300 percent [50% × 6]. The increase in Company B's profit is much larger because it is more highly leveraged with more fixed costs and a larger contribution margin ratio. 60 percent of Company B's revenue above its breakeven point is additional operating income. Only 20 percent of Company A's revenue above its breakeven point is additional operating income.

9-25

1.   Serenity Products sales mix is 2 videos sold for each equipment set sold (or 2:1).

2.   The breakeven point is 5,600 videos and 2,800 equipment sets.

Calculation:

	Videos	Equipment Sets	Package
Selling price	$12.00	$15.00	
Variable cost	4.00	6.00	
Contribution margin	$ 8.00	$ 9.00	
Sales mix	2	1	
Package contribution margin	$16.00	$9.00	$25.00

Breakeven point:

$$X = \$70,000 \div \$25.00$$
$$= 2,800 \text{ packages}$$

Videos	5,600	[2 × 2,800]
Equipment sets	2,800	[1 × 2,800]

9-25 continued

3. Serenity's income statement for last year:

	Videos	*Equipment sets*	*Total*
Sales revenue	$120,000	$75,000	$195,000
Variable expenses	40,000	30,000	70,000
Contribution margin	$ 80,000	$45,000	$125,000
Fixed expenses			70,000
Operating income			$ 55,000

Notes:

Sales revenue: $12.00 × 10,000; $15.00 × 5,000

Variable expenses: $4.00 × 10,000; $6.00 × 5,000

Serenity's contribution margin ratio is 64.1 percent [$125,000 ÷ $195,000]. Serenity's breakeven point is $109,204 [$70,000 ÷ 0.641].

4. Serenity's margin of safety is $85,796 [$195,000 – 109,204].

9-27

1. Roy's breakeven point is 79,301 units and $475,807.

Calculations:

Contribution margin per unit	$3.72	[$372,000 ÷ 100,000]
Contribution margin ratio	62%	[$372,000 ÷ 600,000]

Breakeven point:

$$X = \$295,000 \div \$3.72$$
$$= 79,301 \text{ units}$$

$$R = \$295,000 \div 0.62$$
$$= \$475,807$$

2. If the selling price increases by 10 percent, the breakeven point will decrease because the contribution margin increases. The new breakeven point is 68,287 units and $450,382.

Calculations:

Contribution margin per unit	$4.32	[($600,000 × 110% – 228,000) ÷ 100,000]
Contribution margin ratio	65.5%	[$4.32 ÷ $6.60]

Breakeven point:

$$X = \$295,000 \div \$4.32$$
$$= 68,287 \text{ units}$$

$$R = \$295,000 \div 0.655$$
$$= \$450,382$$

9-27 continued

3. If the variable cost per unit increases by $0.35, the breakeven point will increase because the contribution margin decreases. The new breakeven point is 87,537 units and $524,911.

    Calculations:

Contribution margin per unit	$3.37	[($372,000 ÷ 100,000) – $0.35]
Contribution margin ratio	56.2%	[$3.37 ÷ $6.00]

    Breakeven point:

    $$X = \$295,000 \div \$3.37$$
    $$= 87,537 \text{ units}$$

    $$R = \$295,000 \div 0.562$$
    $$= \$524,911$$

4. If both the selling price and the variable cost increase, we can predict the effect on breakeven point only if we know the size of the increase. The important change is the effect on contribution margin. In this case the increase in selling price ($0.60) is larger than the increase in variable cost ($0.35) and contribution margin increases by $0.25 [$0.60 – 0.35]. An increase in contribution margin will cause the breakeven point in units to decrease. The new breakeven point is 74,307 units. Interestingly, the contribution margin ratio decreases (because the percentage increase in selling price is less than the percentage increase in variable cost). The new breakeven point in sales dollars is higher at $490,033.

    Calculations:

Contribution margin per unit	$3.97	[($372,000 ÷ 100,000) + $0.25]
Contribution margin ratio	60.2%	[$3.97 ÷ $6.60]

    Breakeven point:

    $$X = \$295,000 \div \$3.97$$
    $$= 74,307 \text{ units}$$

    $$R = \$295,000 \div 0.602$$
    $$= \$490,033$$

5. If total fixed costs increase by $50,000 the breakeven point will increase because more total contribution margin is required to break even. The new breakeven point is 92,742 units and $556,452.

    Calculations:

Contribution margin per unit	$3.72	[$372,000 ÷ 100,000]
Contribution margin ratio	62%	[$372,000 ÷ 600,000]
Fixed cost	$345,000	[$295,000 + 50,000]

    Breakeven point:

    $$X = \$345,000 \div \$3.72$$
    $$= 92,742 \text{ units}$$

    $$R = \$345,000 \div 0.62$$
    $$= \$556,452$$

9-29

1. Suriname's unit contribution margin is $18.90 [$945,000 ÷ 50,000]. Its breakeven point is 43,000 units. [$812,700 ÷ $18.90]. If it sells 30,000 units above the breakeven point, its operating income is $567,000 [30,000 × $18.90].

2. Suriname's contribution margin ratio is 42 percent [$945,000 ÷ $2,250,000]. Its breakeven point is $1,935,000 [$812,700 ÷ 0.42]. If its revenues are $200,000 more than expected its operating income is $216,300 [$132,300 + $200,000 × 0.42].

3. Suriname's margin of safety is 7,000 units [50,000 – 43,000] and $315,000 [$2,250,000 – 1,935,000].

4. Suriname's degree of operating leverage is 7.143 [$945,000 ÷ 132,300]. If its sales are 20 percent higher than expected, its operating income is $321,304 [$132,300 + $132,300 × 0.20 × 7.143]. In other words, operating income will increase by 142.9 percent [20% × 7.143] or $189,057 [142.9% × $132,300].

5. Suriname must sell 56,438 units to earn an operating income equal to 10 percent of sales.

Calculation:

$$
\begin{aligned}
0.1 \times \$45 \times X &= \$18.90 \times X - \$812,700 \\
\$4.50 \times X &= \$18.90 \times X - \$812,700 \\
\$14.40 \times X &= \$812,700 \\
X &= 56,438 \text{ units}
\end{aligned}
$$

6. Suriname must sell 58,873 units to earn an after-tax profit of $180,000.

Calculation:

Target operating income: $300,000   [$180,000 ÷ (1 – 0.4)]

$$
\begin{aligned}
\$300,000 &= \$18.90 \times X - \$812,700 \\
\$18.90 \times X &= \$1,112,700 \\
X &= 58,873 \text{ units}
\end{aligned}
$$

9-31

1. d

2. c

3. a

4. d

5. e

6. b

7. c

PROBLEMS

9-33

1. Unicorn Enterprises must sell 7,400 Mystical Wars games and 37,000 Magical Dragons games to break even [7,400 × 1; 7,400 × 5].

    Calculations:

    Unicorn Enterprises expects to sell 10,000 Mystical Wars games [$300,000 ÷ $30] and 50,000 Magical Dragons games [$2,500,000 ÷ $50]. The contribution margin per unit is $20 for the Mystical Wars game [$200,000 ÷ 10,000] and $40 for the Magical Dragons game [$2,000,000 ÷ 50,000]. Its total fixed cost is $1,628,000 [$1,528,000 + 100,000].

    Package contribution margin based on expected sales mix:

	Wars	Dragons	Package
Contribution margin per unit	$20	$40	
Sales mix*	1	5	
Total contribution margin	$20	$200	$220

    * based on sales of 10,000 and 50,000

    Packages to breakeven: 7,400   [$1,628,000 ÷ $220]

2. Unicorn must have revenue of $2,373,178 to produce an operating income of 10 percent of sales revenue.

    Calculations:

    Unicorn's overall contribution margin ratio is 78.6 percent [$2,200,000 ÷ $2,800,000].

    Its required sales revenues are:

    $$0.1R = 0.786R - \$1,628,000$$
    $$0.686R = \$1,628,000$$
    $$R = \$2,373,178$$

3. If the sales mix changes to 3 Wars: 5 Dragons, Unicorn Enterprises must sell 18,785 Mystical Wars games and 31,308 Magical Dragons games to break even [6,261.5 × 3; 6,261.5 × 5].

    Calculations:

    Package contribution margin based on new sales mix:

	Wars	Dragons	Package
Contribution margin per unit	$20	$40	
Sales mix*	3	5	
Total contribution margin	$60	$200	$260

    Packages to breakeven: 6,261.5   [$1,628,000 ÷ $260]

    Unicorn must have revenue of $2,448,120 to produce an operating income of 10 percent of sales revenue

    Calculations:

    Unicorn's package selling price is $340 [3 × $30 + 5 × $50] and its overall contribution margin ratio is 76.5 percent [$260 ÷ $340].

9-33 continued

Its required sales revenues are:

$$0.1R = 0.765R - \$1,628,000$$
$$0.665R = \$1,628,000$$
$$R = \$2,448,120$$

4. Unicorn will be better off with this strategy because its operating income will increase by $455,000.

    Calculations:

Increased contribution margin from additional sales of Dragons	$600,000	[15,000 × $40]
Decreased contribution margin from lost sales of Wars	(100,000)	[5,000 × $20]
Additional advertising expense	(45,000)	
Net increase in operating income	$455,000	

9-35

1. Laraby's breakeven point was 15,000 units.

    Calculation:

Selling price	$25	[$625,000 ÷ 25,000]
Variable cost per unit	15	[$375,000 ÷ 25,000]
Contribution margin per unit	$10	

$$X = \$150,000 \div \$10$$
$$X = 15,000 \text{ units}$$

2. Laraby must sell 29,000 units to earn $77,000 in net income after taxes.

    Calculation:

Tax rate	45%	[$45,000 ÷ 100,000]
Target operating income	$140,000	[$77,000 ÷ (1 – 0.45)]

$$X = (\$150,000 + 140,000) \div \$10$$
$$X = 29,000 \text{ units}$$

3. Laraby's breakeven point after the proposed changes is 19,125 units.

    Calculation:

New contribution margin per unit	$8.00	[$10.00 + 2.50 – 4.50]
New fixed costs	$153,000	[$150,000 + ($18,000 ÷ 6)]

$$X = \$153,000 \div \$8$$
$$X = 19,125 \text{ units}$$

4. Laraby must sell 31,625 units after the proposed changes to earn the same net income after taxes as last year.

    Calculation:

$$X = (\$153,000 + 100,000) \div \$8$$
$$X = 31,625 \text{ units}$$

9-35 continued

5. Laraby must charge a selling price of $28.33 to maintain last year's contribution margin ratio after the increase in materials cost.

   Calculation:

   Last year's variable cost ratio is 60 percent [$375,000 ÷ 625,000]. To maintain the variable cost ratio with the $2.00 increase in variable cost (and thus the contribution margin ratio), the selling price would have to be increased by $3.33 [$2 ÷ 0.6]. Last year's selling price was $25 [$625,000 ÷ 25,000] and the new price is $28.33 [$25.00 + 3.33].

9-37

1. KC's 2003 breakeven point is 47,059 flowerpots.

   Calculations:

Selling price per flowerpot	$10.00	
Variable cost per flowerpot	5.75	[$8.00 – 2.25]
Contribution margin per flowerpot	$ 4.25	
Fixed cost	$200,000	[$180,000 + $20,000]

   $$X = \$200,000 \div \$4.25$$
   $$X = 47,059 \text{ flowerpots}$$

   Note: applied overhead includes fixed overhead of $2.25 [$180,000 ÷ 80,000].

2. Jack and Katie would be better off remaining self-employed because KC's 2004 operating income of $140,000 exceeds their joint salaries of $70,000.

   Calculation:

   $$I = 80,000 \times \$4.25 - \$200,000$$
   $$I = \$140,000$$

3. KC's breakeven revenue from the sales of flowerpots and lawn ornaments is $581,258.

   Calculations:

	Flowerpot	Lawn Ornament	Package
Selling price	$10.00	$12.00	
Variable cost per unit	5.75	7.00	
Contribution margin per unit	$ 4.25	$ 5.00	
Sales mix	5	3	
Total contribution margin	$21.25	$15.00	$36.25

   KC's revenue from the sale of a package is $86.00 [$10.00 × 5 + $12.00 × 3]. Its contribution margin ratio is 42.15 percent [$36.25 ÷ $86.00]. Its breakeven point is $581,258 [$245,000 ÷ 0.4215].

9-37 continued

4. Adopting the marketing plan will increase KC's breakeven point by $37,054 [$618,312 – 581,258].

   Calculations:

   New contribution margin:

	Flowerpot	*Lawn Ornament*	*Package*
Contribution margin per unit	$ 4.25	$ 5.00	
Sales mix	4	4	
Total contribution margin	$17.00	$20.00	$37.00

   KC's revenue from the sale of the new package is $88.00 [$10.00 × 4 + $12.00 × 4]. Its new contribution margin ratio is 42.05 percent [$37 ÷ $88]. Its new breakeven point is $618,312 [($245,000 + 15,000) ÷ 0.4205]

9-39

1. Dalhart Company's contribution margin ratio is 54 percent [$302,616 ÷ $560,400].

2. Dalhart must have sales revenue of $277,778 in order to break even [$150,000 ÷ 0.54].

3. Dalhart must have sales revenue of $358,166 in order to earn an after-tax income equal to 8 percent of sales.

   Calculation:

   Target operating income: $0.1212R$ $[0.08R ÷ (1 – 0.34)]$

   $$0.1212R = 0.54R – \$150,000$$
   $$0.4188R = \$150,000$$
   $$R = \$358,166$$

4. The contribution margin ratio will not change if the unit selling price and unit variable cost each increase by 10 percent – contribution margin per unit will also increase by 10 percent and the ratio will not change. The contribution margin ratio after the change is $(1.1P – 1.1V) ÷ (1.1P)$; after eliminating the common term, 1.1, in the numerator and denominator, the contribution margin ratio is $(P – V) ÷ P$, as before.

5. The new contribution margin ratio is 51 percent [0.54 – 0.03] – variable cost increases by 3 percent of revenue and the contribution margin ratio falls by that amount. The new breakeven point will be higher with a lower contribution margin ratio. The new breakeven point is $294,118 [$150,000 ÷ 0.51] (higher than the old breakeven point of $277,778.

6. It is a good decision to introduce the 3 percent commission if sales revenue increases by $80,000. Dalhart's operating income increases by $23,988.

   Calculation:

Increase in contribution margin from increased sales	$40,800	[$80,000 × 0.51]
Decrease in contribution margin from sales commission	16,812	[$560,400 × 0.03]
Net increase in operating income	$23,988	

9-41

1. Artistic Woodcrafting expects to sell 224 Grade I and 524 Grade II cabinets during 2004.

    Calculations:

    Let C be a "package" of 3 Grade I and 7 Grade II cabinets with total revenue of $1,600,000.

    $1,600,000 = 3C × $3,400 + 7C × $1,600
    $1,600,000 = $21,400C
       C = 74.8 packages

    74.8 packages are 224 Grade I and 524 Grade II cabinets [74.8 × 3; 74.8 × 7]

2. Artistic Woodcrafting must sell 167 Grade I and 389 Grade II cabinets during 2004 to break even.

    Calculations:

	Grade I	Grade II	Package
Selling price per unit	$3,400	$1,600	
Variable cost per unit	2,686	1,328	
Contribution margin per unit	$ 714	$ 272	
Sales mix	3	7	
Total contribution margin	$2,142	$1,904	$4,046

    Total fixed cost $225,000 [$95,000 + 95,000 +35,000]

    X = $225,000 ÷ $4,046
    X = 55.6 packages

    55.6 packages are 167 Grade I and 389 Grade II cabinets [55.6 × 3; 55.6 × 7]

3. Artistic Woodcrafting will have $73,137 more operating income in 2004 with the new equipment. Its new breakeven point is 144 Grade I and 335 Grade II cabinets.

    Calculations:

	Grade I	Grade II	Package
Selling price per unit	$3,400	$1,600	
Variable cost per unit	2,444	1,208	
Contribution margin per unit	$ 956	$ 392	
Sales mix	3	7	
New total contribution margin	$2,868	$2,744	$5,612

    Note: new variable cost $2,686 × 0.91; $1,328 × 0.91

    New fixed cost $269,000 [$225,000 + 44,000]

    Increase in operating income

Increase in contribution margin	$117,137	[74.8 × ($5,612 – 4,046)] (from Requirements 1 and 2)
Less increase in fixed cost	44,000	
Net increase in operating income	$ 73,137	

    New breakeven point

    X = $269,000 ÷ $5,612
    X = 47.9 packages

    47.9 packages are 144 Grade I and 335 Grade II cabinets [47.9 × 3; 47.9 × 7]

9-41 continued

4. Artistic Woodcrafting will have $106,752 more operating income in 2004 with the addition of a retail outlet. Its new breakeven point is 299 Grade I and 299 Grade II cabinets

Calculations:

	Grade I	Grade II	Package
Selling price per unit	$3,400	$1,600	
Variable cost per unit	2,686	1,328	
Contribution margin per unit	$ 714	$ 272	
Sales mix	5	5	
New total contribution margin	$3,570	$1,360	$4,930

New total fixed cost $295,000   [$225,000 +70,000]

Increase in operating income

Increase in contribution margin from change in sales mix	$ 66,123	[74.8 × ($4,930 – 4,046)]
Increase in contribution margin from increased sales	110,629	[74.8 × 30% × $4,930]
Less increase in fixed cost	70,000	
Net increase in operating income	$106,752	

New breakeven point

X = $295,000 ÷ $4,930
X =   59.8 packages

59.8 packages are 299 Grade I and 299 Grade II cabinets [59.8 × 5; 59.8 × 5]

9-43

1. Carlyle's breakeven sales revenue is $450,045.

Calculation:

Contribution margin ratio   33.33 percent   [$200,000 ÷ $600,000]

R = $150,000 ÷ 0.3333
R = $450,045

2. Carlyle must sell 9,000 floor lamps and 9,000 table lamps to break even.

Calculation:

	Floor lamps	Table lamps
Percentage of sales	60%	40%
Total breakeven sales	$450,045	$450,045
Product sales	$270,027	$180,018
Selling price	$ 30	$ 20
Unit sales	9,000	9,000

3. Carlyle's degree of operating leverage is 4 [$200,000 ÷ 50,000]. If its actual revenue is 40% higher than projected, its operating income will increase by 160 percent [40% × 4].

9-45

1. Victoria Company's breakeven point is 21,429 units and sales revenue of $900,090.

    Calculations:

    Contribution margin per unit $14.00   [$406,000 ÷ 29,000]

    Contribution margin ratio   33.33 percent   [$406,000 ÷ $1,218,000]

    X = $300,000 ÷ $14
    X = 21,429 units

    R = $300,000 ÷ 0.3333
    R = $900,090

2. Victoria's margin of safety was 7,571 units [29,000 – 21,429] and $317,910 [$1,218,000 – 900,090]

3. Victoria's budgeted income statement is:

Sales	$1,218,000	
Variable expenses	548,100	[$1,218,000 × 45%]
Contribution margin	$ 669,900	
Fixed expenses	550,000	[$300,000 + 250,000]
Operating income	$ 119,900	

    Victoria Company's new breakeven point is 23,810 units and sales revenue of $1,000,000.

    Calculations:

    Contribution margin per unit $23.10   [$669,900 ÷ 29,000]

    Contribution margin ratio   55 percent   [1 – 0.45]

    X = $550,000 ÷ $23.10
    X = 23,810 units

    R = $550,000 ÷ 0.55
    R = $1,000,000

9-47

1. Marston's breakeven sales revenue (with its own sales force and new advertising) is $18,025,000.

    Calculations:

    Contribution margin ratio:

Sales	$26,000,000	
Variable expenses:		
Cost of goods sold	$11,700,000	
Sales commissions (at 10%)	2,600,000	[$26,000,000 × 10%]
Total variable expenses	$14,300,000	
Contribution margin	$11,700,000	
Contribution margin ratio	45 percent	[$11,700,000 ÷ $26,000,000]

    Fixed expenses:

Cost of goods sold	$2,870,000	
Advertising	1,250,000	[$750,000 + 500,000]
Administrative	1,850,000	
Interest	650,000	
Sales staff salaries	640,000	[$80,000 × 8]
Sales manager and secretary salaries	150,000	
Travel and entertainment	600,000	
Total fixed expenses	$8,010,000	

    Note: for sales above $2,000,000 per salesperson (and $16,000,000 in total), the commission rate is 15%.

    Breakeven point:

    $$0.45R = \$8,010,000 + 0.05 (R - \$16,000,000)$$
    $$0.45R = \$8,010,000 - 800,000 + 0.05R$$
    $$0.40R = \$7,210,000$$
    $$R = \$18,025,000$$

2. Marston would require sales of $30,062,500 to earn the same net income in 2004 with the higher sales commission rate.

    Calculations:

Contribution margin ratio	32 percent	[(($26,000,000 – 11,700,0000) ÷ $26,000,000) – 0.23]

    Fixed costs:

Cost of goods sold	$2,870,000
Advertising	750,000
Administrative	1,850,000
Interest	650,000
Total fixed expenses	$6,120,000

    $$R = (\$6,120,000 + \$3,500,000) \div 0.32$$
    $$R = \$30,062,500$$

3. In this case the assumption that all costs can be divided into variable and fixed elements affects the usefulness of Marston's breakeven analysis. The sales commission rate Marston would pay to its own sales force changes for sales above $2,000,000 for each salesperson. We were able to modify our basic analysis in Requirement 1 to fit in this different cost behaviour pattern.

MANAGERIAL DECISION CASES

9-49

1. The expected revenues from the scheduled performances are:

	Dream	Petrushka	Nutcracker	Sleeping Beauty	Bugaku	Total
A Seats	114	114	114	114	114	
Price	$35	$35	$35	$35	$35	
Revenue A	$3,990	$3,990	$3,990	$3,990	$3,990	
B Seats	605	605	756	605	605	
Price	$25	$25	$25	$25	$25	
Revenue B	$15,125	$15,125	$18,900	$15,125	$15,125	
C Seats	738	738	984	738	738	
Price	$15	$15	$15	$15	$15	
Revenue C	$11,070	$11,070	$14,760	$11,070	$11,070	
Total A + B + C	$30,185	$30,185	$37,650	$30,185	$30,185	
Performances	5	5	20	10	5	
Total revenues	$150,925	$150,925	$753,000	$301,850	$150,925	$1,507,625

The Ballet's variable-costing segment income statement is:

	Dream	Petrushka	Nutcracker	Sleeping Beauty	Bugaku	Total
Total revenues	$ 150,925	$150,925	$753,000	$ 301,850	$150,925	$1,507,625
Variable expenses	42,500	42,500	170,000	85,000	42,500	382,500
Contribution margin	$ 108,425	$108,425	$583,000	$ 216,850	$108,425	$1,125,125
Direct fixed expenses	275,500	145,500	70,500	345,000	155,500	992,000
Segment margin	$(167,075)	$(37,075)	$512,500	$(128,150)	$(47,075)	$ 133,125
Common fixed expenses						401,000
Operating income						$(267,875)

Notes:

Variable expenses are $8,500 for each performance of a ballet.

2. The breakeven number of performances for each ballet are:

	Dream	Petrushka	Nutcracker	Sleeping Beauty	Bugaku
Revenue	$30,185	$30,185	$37,650	$30,185	$30,185
Variable expense	8,500	8,500	8,500	8,500	8,500
Contribution margin	$21,685	$21,685	$29,150	$21,685	$21,685
Direct fixed expenses	$275,500	$145,500	$70,500	$345,000	$155,500
Breakeven point	13	7	3	16	8

Note: each ballet's breakeven point is calculated to the next whole number.

9-49 continued

3. The breakeven number of performance for the company are:

Package contribution:	Dream	Petrushka	Nutcracker	Sleeping Beauty	Bugaku	Total
Revenue	$30,185	$30,185	$ 37,650	$30,185	$30,185	
Variable expense	8,500	8,500	8,500	8,500	8,500	
Contribution margin	$21,685	$21,685	$ 29,150	$21,685	$21,685	
Sales mix	1	1	4	2	1	
Total contribution	$21,685	$21,685	$116,600	$43,370	$21,685	$225,025

Total fixed expenses	$1,393,000	[$992,000 + 401,000]
Contribution margin	225,025	
Breakeven point	6.19 "packages"	

Breakeven point	Dream	Petrushka	Nutcracker	Sleeping Beauty	Bugaku
Sales mix	1	1	4	2	1
Performances	7	7	25	13	7

Note: each ballet's breakeven point is calculated to the next whole number.

I would alter the performance schedule to reflect the breakeven mix – assuming that the community will support the additional performances without decreasing the expected attendance for the performances already scheduled.

4. The company's operating income will increase by $72,000 from the matinee performances. Its overall breakeven point will decrease as shown below.

Calculations:

Revenue from the 5 added matinee performances:

A Seats	91
Price	$30
Revenue A	$2,730
B Seats	605
Price	$20
Revenue B	$12,100
C Seats	787
Price	$10
Revenue C	$7,870
Total A + B + C	$22,700

The additional contribution margin is $14,400 per performance [$22,700 – (8,500 – 200)] and $72,000 for 5 performances [5 × $14,400].

With the matinee performances the new package contribution margin is $239,425 [$225,025 + 14,400] and 5.8 "packages" are required to breakeven [$1,393,000 ÷ $239,425]. The breakeven points for each ballet are:

	Dream	Petrushka	Nutcracker	Sleeping Beauty	Bugaku	Matinee
Sales mix	1	1	4	2	1	1
Performances	6	6	24	12	6	6

Note: each ballet's breakeven point is calculated to the next whole number.

9-49 continued

5. The company will not break even with the additional matinees and the grants and contributions – there will be a shortfall of $135,875.

Calculation:

Original operating income	$(267,875)	[from Requirement 1]
Added contribution margin from matinees	72,000	[from Requirement 4]
Grants and contributions	60,000	
Revised operating income	$(135,875)	

It is difficult to decide what the company should do to bring revenues in line with costs and eliminate the projected loss. The company can act to increase revenues, reduce costs, or a combination of increased revenues and reduced costs. The segmented income statement and CVP analysis are valuable tools to managers as they consider these options. Increasing the number of performances should provide more contribution margin but if attendance for the original performances drops, there may be little gain. The company may consider increasing the price of some seats (for example, the A seats) to generate more revenue from the current performances, but the gains may be lost if the price increase shifts the mix of demand for seats A, B, and C. The segmented income statement shows that the *Nutcracker's* segment margin covers the company's common costs by itself. Would the ballet be viable if it only presented this ballet? A less radical option is to look at the other ballets and their segment margins. The direct fixed costs of *Sleeping Beauty* are high – dropping this ballet and increasing the number of performances of the others may enable the company to break even. The company should also look at its common costs for opportunities to save costs.

MANAGEMENT ACCOUNTING
CANADIAN SIXTH EDITION
SOLUTIONS MANUAL

CHAPTER 10
TACTICAL DECISION MAKING

ANSWERS TO ODD-NUMBERED QUESTIONS FOR WRITING AND DISCUSSION

1. Tactical decision-making consists of choosing among alternatives with an immediate or limited consequence. Strategic decision-making is the choice among alternative strategies so that a long-term competitive advantage is established. Tactical decisions should support the company's strategic objectives. Tactical decisions tend to be short run in nature but may have longrun consequences. Tactical decisions are often small-scale actions that serve a larger purpose.

3. In order for a future cost to be relevant, it must be different under some alternative. Any future cost that is not different, regardless of the decision made, would not be relevant.

    For example, in a make-or-buy decision for a component used in manufacturing a company's final product, overhead costs such as heat, light, and power that are not expected to be different, regardless of whether the decision is to make or buy the component, are not relevant for the decision.

5. Relevant cost analysis is often not enough to identify the alternative that should be chosen. Decisions are based on a manager's evaluation of quantitative and qualitative factors. Relevant cost analysis is focused on quantitative factors. A manager may decide to reject an alternative that is favoured by quantitative factors because of less favourable qualitative factors.

7. A relevant cost is a future cost that differs across alternatives. A differential cost is the difference in cost between two alternatives.

9. Past costs, by definition, are not relevant costs because a past cost cannot be different in the future. Past costs are useful in relevant-cost analysis as information to estimate future costs. An activity's cost in the past is often the best indicator of its cost in the future.

11. Complementary effects in a keep-or-drop decision are important because managers should consider all the consequences of their decisions. If a product is dropped, customers may move to other products as a replacement purchase or may change their purchase behaviour for the company's other products. The decision whether to drop a product may affect not only that product's revenues and costs but the revenues and costs of related products.

13. Joint costs should not be considered in a sell-or-process-further decision. Joint costs occur before the split-off point and the same cost will be incurred regardless of whether the product is sold or processed further. Thus joint costs are irrelevant to the sell-or-process-further decision.

15. Fixed costs are never relevant in a product-mix decision because fixed costs (within the relevant range) are the same regardless of how many units are produced. Fixed cost doesn't change with different product mixes and isn't relevant to a product-mix decision.

17. A company would be willing to sell a product for less than its full cost when it has idle capacity and the special price does not displace the sale of other units. Any price greater than the product's variable cost will increase the company's contribution margin and operating income. The product's full cost includes an allocation of fixed costs – costs that are not relevant if they don't change with the decision whether to sell the product or not.

19. Managers who are influenced by sunk costs are not necessarily irrational. There are many rational reasons to use sunk costs in decision-making. Performance evaluation systems are often retrospective and managers are concerned with how past costs will affect their performance. Generally accepted accounting principles are primarily based on historical (sunk) costs and managers are held accountable to financial results. When sunk costs are used by decision makers as inputs in cost prediction models, it may appear that sunk costs are being used in decision making.

21. An objective function is the equation for the objective to be maximized given the set of constraints. It is usually expressed in terms of the contribution margins of the products included in the product mix. A constraint is a limit placed on the solution. Some constraints involve resources that are in scarce or limited supply. These resource constraints are usually equations expressed in terms of the amount of the available resource and the amount required by the products included in the product mix. Other constraints involve the maximum demand for the products in the product mix. In addition there are usually constraints that recognize the impossibility of negative production – referred to as nonnegativity constraints. A constraint set is the collection of all constraints – resource, demand, and nonnegativity – that apply to the product mix problem.

23. Four steps are followed to solve a linear programming problem graphically. The first step is to graph each constraint – lines that represent the maximum use of each scarce resource by the products, the maximum demand for each product, and nonnegativity. The second step is to identify the feasible set of solutions – the combinations of the products that satisfy all of the constraint relationships. The third step is to identify all of the corner-point values in the feasible set. A corner point is a feasible solution formed by the intersection of two (or more) constraint lines. The optimal solution will be a corner point for problems with linear constraints. The fourth and final step is to calculate the value of the objective function for each corner point. The optimal solution is the corner point with the largest value for the objective function.

When the problem includes more than two or three products, the optimal solution is usually found by using an algorithm called the simplex method. The simplex method algorithm is available as a computer program to solve larger linear programming problems.

SOLUTIONS TO ODD-NUMBERED EXERCISES, PROBLEMS, AND CASES

EXERCISES

10-1

The correct order for the steps in the tactical decision model is:

D. Recognize and define the problem.

E. Identify alternatives as possible solutions to the problem.

B. Identify the costs and benefits associated with each feasible alternative.

F. Total the relevant costs and benefits for each alternative.

C. Assess qualitative factors.

A. Select the alternative with the greatest overall benefit.

10-3

1. If product C is dropped, the relevant items are product C's contribution margin, $60,000, and its avoidable direct fixed expenses, $40,000 [$70,000 – 30,000]. The net effect is a decrease in Uintah's operating income of $20,000 [$60,000 – 40,000]. The amortization on product C's dedicated equipment is not relevant because it is the same whether the product is kept or dropped. The revenues and expenses of the other products, and the common fixed expenses, are not relevant because none of these items change with the decision.

2. If product C is dropped and 10 percent of Uintah's customers for product B stop buying from it, Uintah's operating income will decrease by $100,000 to $300,000 [$400,000 – 100,000].

    Calculation:

Dropping product C	$ (20,000)	[see Requirement 1]
Lost sales of product B	(80,000)	[10% × $800,000]
Net change	$(100,000)	

10-5

1. The $11,300 Heather has spent on the Grand Am is a sunk cost and not relevant to her decision whether to repair the Grand Am or buy the Neon. Her past decisions do not change regardless of what she decides to do now.

2. Heather should buy the Neon because it will cost her $500 less.

    Relevant cost analysis:

Repair Grand Am	$3,500	
Purchase Neon	3,000	[$9,400 – 6,400]
Advantage to purchase Neon	$ 500	

    Note: there may be other factors that Heather should consider. We are told that she would be equally happy with either car but there may be differences in operating expenses – fuel, maintenance, insurance, etc. – she should consider.

10-7

1. If all fixed overhead is common fixed overhead (unchanged and irrelevant for the decision), Fontaro should continue to make Part K96 because it will cost $52,500 more to buy its needs than its cost to make [$385,000 · 332,500].

	Make		Buy	
Direct materials	$210,000	[$6 × 35,000]	$ 0	
Direct labour	70,000	[$2 × 35,000]	0	
Variable overhead	52,500	[$1.50 × 35,000]	0	
Purchase cost	0		385,000	[$11 × 35,000]
Total relevant costs	$332,500		$385,000	

Note: Fontaro's common fixed overhead is not relevant.

2. The most that Fontaro would be willing to pay an outside supplier is a price of $9.50, equal to its average cost of making 35,000 units based on the above relevant costs [$332,500 ÷ 35,000].

3. Fontaro's operating income would decrease by $52,500 (the difference between the cost of making and the cost of buying).

10-9

1. If Pomona buys the portable power washer from Schering, its operating income will decrease by $40,000 [$2,600,000 – 2,560,000].

    Calculations:

    Cost of making 40,000 units:

Variable costs	$2,560,000	[40,000 × ($25.00 + 33.50 + 5.50)]

    Cost of buying 40,000 units:

Purchase cost	$2,600,000	[40,000 × $65]

    Note: Pomona's fixed costs are assumed not to change – and are not relevant for its make-or-buy decision.

2. If Pomona buys the portable power washer from Schering, its operating income will increase by $320,000 [$2,920,000 – 2, 600,000].

    Calculations:

    Cost of making 40,000 units:

Variable costs	$2,560,000	[40,000 × ($25.00 + 33.50 + 5.50)]
Nonunit level activity costs		
Materials handling	55,000	[2,200 × $25]
Purchasing	60,000	[4,000 × $15]
Setups	160,000	[800 × $200]
Engineering	50,000	[1,000 × $50]
Maintenance	35,000	[7,000 × $5]
Total cost to make	$2,920,000	

    Cost of buying 40,000 units:

Purchase cost	$2,600,000	[40,000 × $65]

    Note: Pomona's nonunit level activity costs are assumed to be avoidable if it buys the power washers – and are relevant to its make-or-buy decision.

10-11

1. Specialty Paper Products should reject the offer as the additional revenue is less than the additional costs (fixed overhead is allocated and will not increase with the special order). It will have a loss of $250 on the order.

Incremental revenue per calendar	$4.20	
Incremental cost per calendar	4.25	[$1.15 + 2.00 + 1.10]
Incremental loss per calendar	$(0.05)	

    Total loss on order: $250 [$0.05 × 5,000]

2. Specialty Paper Products should accept the order. The cost savings of $18,100 from avoiding layoffs more than compensates the company for the loss of $250 on this order.

    Costs associated with layoffs:

Loss of productivity	$14,600	[1% × $1,460,000]
Layoff notification	500	[$25 × 20]
Rehiring and training	3,000	[$150 × 20]
Total	$18,100	

    If the idle capacity is viewed as a temporary state, then accepting an order that shows a loss in order to maintain labour stability and community image may be justifiable. Qualitative factors often outweigh quantitative (at least in the short run).

    Are labour costs relevant if layoffs are ruled out? In this case Specialty Paper Products treat the consequences of layoffs as a quantitative, rather than a qualitative, factor. There are very real out-of-pocket costs associated with laying-off workers. These include the costs of notification, rehiring, retraining, etc.. The personnel manager is aware of these costs and has some idea of their magnitude. Of course, these "layoff costs" are in favour of accepting the special order.

10-13

1. If Kohata can manufacture 2,000 units of Juno and 4,000 units of Hera, its total contribution margin is $300,000. [($30 × 2,000) + ($60 × 4,000)]

2. Kohata should produce 2,000 units of Juno and 2,400 units of Hera. Its contribution margin from this plan would be $204,000 [($30 × 2,000) + ($60 × 2,400) OR (4,000 × $15) + (12,000 × $12)].

    Analysis:

    If Kohata looks only at the unit contribution margins of each product, it might decide that Hera (with a unit contribution margin of $60) is a better choice than Juno (with a contribution margin of $30) and produce 3,200 units of Hera [16,000 ÷ 5] and earn a contribution margin of $192,000 [3,200 × $60]. This decision doesn't consider that Hera requires more of the scarce resource per unit.

    To take this factor into account, Kohata should calculate each product's contribution per kilogram (of the scarce resource). Juno's contribution per kilogram is $15 [$30 ÷ 2] and Hera's contribution per kilogram is $12 [$60 ÷ 5].

    Juno has a higher contribution per kilogram of the scarce material and should be produced first. A total of 8,000 units of Juno could be produced [16,000 ÷ 2] but Kohata must also consider the demand for its products.

10-13 continued

In its original plan only 2,000 units of Juno were scheduled to be produced, and this might indicate the maximum demand for Juno. In that case, Kohata will use 4,000 kilograms to produce 2,000 units of Juno [2,000 × 2] and use the remaining 12,000 kilograms [16,000 – 4,000] to produce 2,400 units of Hera [12,000 ÷ 5].

10-15

1. a.   If Bruning sells 8,000 units to the customer at $35, its operating income will increase by $94,400.

Calculation:

Incremental revenue		$280,000	[8,000 × $35]
Incremental costs			
Direct materials	$60,000		[8,000 × $300,000 ÷ 40,000]
Direct labour	80,000		[8,000 × $400,000 ÷ 40,000]
Variable overhead	40,000		[8,000 × $200,000 ÷ 40,000]
Sales commissions	5,600		[$280,000 × 2%]
Total incremental costs		185,600	
Increase in operating income		$ 94,400	

Notes:

Fixed overhead, delivery costs, sales salaries, administrative salaries, and office rental are not affected by the decision whether to accept or reject the order and are not relevant for Bruning's decision.

b.   If Bruning sells 14,000 units to the customer at $35, its operating income will increase by $61,200.

Note: selling 14,000 units will exceed Bruning's current capacity of 50,000 units. It can fill the order by either increasing its capacity by 4,000 units [40,000 + 14,000 – 50,000] at a cost of $120,000 [$60,000 × 4,000 ÷ 2,000] or by reducing regular sales by 4,000 units. Bruning's operating income will decrease by $104,000 if it reduces regular sales by 4,000 units (see calculation below). Reducing regular sales has a lower cost to Bruning and is the option it should use.

Calculation of effect on operating income of reduced regular sales:

Reduction in revenue		$200,000	[4,000 × $2,000,000 ÷ 40,000]
Reduction in costs			
Direct materials	$30,000		[4,000 × $300,000 ÷ 40,000]
Direct labour	40,000		[4,000 × $400,000 ÷ 40,000]
Variable overhead	20,000		[4,000 × $200,000 ÷ 40,000]
Delivery costs	2,000		[4,000 × $20,000 ÷ 40,000]
Sales commissions	4,000		[$200,000 × 2%]
Total reduction in costs		96,000	
Decrease in operating income		$104,000	

Calculation of effect on operating income of accepting order:

Incremental revenue		$490,000	[14,000 × $35]
Incremental costs			
Direct materials	$105,000		[14,000 × $300,000 ÷ 40,000]
Direct labour	140,000		[14,000 × $400,000 ÷ 40,000]
Variable overhead	70,000		[14,000 × $200,000 ÷ 40,000]
Sales commissions	9,800		[$490,000 × 2%]
Total incremental costs		324,800	
Decrease in regular sales		104,000	[see above]
Increase in operating income		$ 61,200	

10-15 continued

2. The qualitative factors that Bruning should consider include the effect on regular sales if it offers discounts to some customers, whether customers will be lost if sales to regular customers are reduced to fill the special order, and whether the new customer will continue to purchase in the future at the regular price.

10-17

1. Based on gross profit only, cavasol should be processed further into cavasette. Lastivika's revenues will increase by $6,000 [($32 – 26) × 1,000] with an added cost of $2,300 – a net benefit of $3,700.

2. Based on a value-chain analysis, cavasol should not be processed further into cavasette but should be sold at the split-off point. When distribution costs of $900 [$0.90 × 1,000] and sales commissions of $3,200 [$32,000 × 10%] are included in the analysis the net benefit is $400 in favour of selling cavasol at the split-off point [$3,200 + 900 – 3,700]. As well the qualitative factor of increased legal liability with the production of cavasette favours the sale of cavasol.

10-19

1. If an unlimited number of each model can be sold, O'Connor should produce 6,000 units of Model 33-P [12,000 ÷ 2]. Model 33-P has a contribution of $5.00 per machine hour [$10 ÷ 2] and Model 14-D has a contribution of $3.00 per machine hour [$12 ÷ 4]. O'Connor will have $24,000 more operating income from producing Model 33-P rather than Model 14-D [12,000 × ($5.00 – 3.00)].

2. If no more than 5,000 units of each model can be sold, O'Connor should produce the maximum of 5,000 units of Model 33-P and use the remaining machine hours to produce 500 units of Model 14-D [(12,000 – 5,000 × 2) ÷ 4].

10-21

1. Jamil is using a markup of 170 percent [$81,900 ÷ $48,100].

2. Jamil's initial bid price is $11,340.

    Calculation:

Direct materials	$ 1,800	
Direct labour	1,600	
Overhead	800	
Cost of goods sold	$ 4,200	
Markup	7,140	[$4,200 × 170%]
Bid price	$11,340	

10-23

1. Variable costs (production, selling, and administrative) would be the only relevant costs for pricing the special order – fixed costs are not affected because the company has idle capacity.

2. Variable costs (production, selling, and administrative) and the opportunity cost of the displaced regular sales would be the relevant costs for pricing the special order. The opportunity cost of the lost regular sales can be measured by the total contribution margin that would have been earned on the regular sales. Fixed costs are not affected because capacity is not increased.

3. Variable and fixed costs (production and selling and administrative) would be relevant costs for pricing regular production orders. An effective pricing strategy for the company would be to base its prices on a production order's variable cost of plus a markup to cover fixed cost and allow the company to earn a reasonable profit. The markup would be based on the expected volume of production during the period.

4. The avoidable costs of production would be relevant costs for a company's decision whether to produce or buy a component. These may include variable costs (direct material, direct labour, and variable overhead) and direct fixed costs of the component. If the production capacity has an alternative use there may also be relevant opportunity costs – the company may be able to use its capacity to expand production of its main product line or produce more of other components.

PROBLEMS

10-25

1. The following are the relevant costs associated with each site – for two years and for three years. The centre's best choice will depend on whether it will operate for two or three years. Site 1 is the least expensive alternative over two years but the most expensive over three years. Site 3 is the most expensive over two years but the least expensive over three years.

For two years:	Site 1	Site 2	Site 3
Rent	$11,400	$12,000	$ 0
Partitions	2,040	1,500	0
Repairs	0	0	15,000
Total costs	$13,440	$13,500	$15,000

Notes:

Rent: Site 1: 24 × $475; Site 2: 24 × $500

Partitions: Site 1: 24 × $85

For three years:	Site 1	Site 2	Site 3
Rent	$17,100	$18,000	$ 0
Partitions	3,060	1,500	0
Repairs	0	0	15,000
Total costs	$20,160	$19,500	$15,000

Notes:

Rent: Site 1: 36 × $475; Site 2: 36 × $500

Partitions: Site 1: 36 × $85

10-25 continued

2.   The memo to Alice should cover the following points:

 • the best choice quantitatively for a new site will depend on whether the centre will continue for two years or three years. The sites are ranked quantitatively as follows:

	Two Years		Three Years	
Rank	Site	Cost	Site	Cost
1	1	$13,400	3	$15,000
2	2	13,500	2	19,500
3	3	15,000	1	20,160

 • location is a key qualitative factor – site 2 is close to the caseworkers' homes but farther from its clients; site 1 is downtown and closer to the centre's clients.

 • acceptability in the neighbourhood is another qualitative factor – the centre may be more welcome at site 1 because the other businesses (law office, bail bond agency) are compatible with the centre's activities; stores in the strip mall in site 2 may oppose having the drug centre as a neighbour and try to prevent the centre from moving in or delay its opening.

 • space is another qualitative factor – site 3 is the largest and site 1 is the smallest. A related factor is the privacy available to caseworkers and their clients – site 3 offers the best privacy and site 1 the least.

 • site 3 requires time to make the required repairs and modifications for use – the centre only has two months to move without disruption of service.

10-27

1.   Zanda should process the depryl into tablets – it will have $12,615 more contribution from each batch [$19,716 – 7,101].

Analysis:

Contribution from sale of depryl at split-off:

Revenue	$7,200	[600 × $12]
Cost of bags	(39)	[600 ÷ 20 × $1.30]
Shipping	(60)	[600 × $0.10]
Contribution	$7,101	

Contribution from processing of depryl into tablets:

Revenue	$24,000	[600 × 10 × $4]
Processing cost	(1,500)	[600 × $2.50]
Cost of bottles	(2,400)	[600 × 10 × $0.40]
Shipping	(384)	[600 × 10 ÷ 25 × $1.60]
Contribution	$19,716	

2.   If Zanda normally sells 265,000 kilograms of depryl per year, its profits will be higher by $5,571,625 if it processes depryl into tablets [$12,615 ÷ 600 × 265,000].

10-29

1. Hoboe should drop A – its net income will increase by $450 to $4,800.

    Analysis:

    Assume that product A has no direct fixed costs and total fixed costs are unchanged if Hoboe drops product A. Assume that its operations related to B and C are unaffected.

    The only relevant items are the sales revenue and variable costs of A – these can be summarized as A's contribution margin.

Selling price	$ 3.50	
Variable costs	3.60	[$3.25 + 0.35]
Contribution margin	$(0.10)	

    Hoboe has sold 4,500 units of A [$15,750 ÷ $3.50] and will avoid a loss (negative contribution margin) of $450 if A is dropped [4,500 × $0.10]. Its total net income will increase to $4,800 [$4,350 + 450].

2. Hoboe should keep product A if product C's sales drop by more than 78 units.

    Analysis:

    C's contribution margin per unit is $5.70 [$7.50 – 1.50 – 0.30]. Hoboe's lost contribution margin from C is greater than its cost savings from dropping A when the sales of C drop more than 78 units [$450 ÷ $5.70].

    Note: this analysis is similar to a breakeven calculation.

10-31

Small Bear should accept the order because its operating income will increase by $12,200.

Incremental analysis:

Revenue from special order	$144,000	[$18 × 8,000]
Variable costs of special order:		
Direct material	(52,800)	[$270,000 ÷ 45,000 × 110% × 8,000]
Direct labour	(42,000)	[$225,000 ÷ 45,000 × 105% × 8,000]
Variable overhead	(24,000)	[$3 ×8,000]
Added fixed costs of special order	(1,000)	
Increase in profit from special order	$ 24,200	
Lost contribution margin due to reduced regular sales	12,000	[see calculation below]
Increase in profits if special order is accepted	$ 12,200	

Calculation of lost contribution margin:

Regular sales without special order	45,000 units	
Regular sales with special order	42,000 units	[50,000 – 8,000]
Reduction in regular sales	3,000 units	
Contribution margin on regular sales	$4	[$20 – 6 – 5 – 3 – 2]
Reduction in contribution margin	$12,000	

10-33

Home Security should not accept the First Alarm special order because the contribution from displaced regular orders is grater than the contribution from the special order. Home Security should not accept the Bar-the-Door special order because its direct costs are greater than its revenues.

Analysis:

The special order from First Alarm will require 6,250 machine hours [25,000 × 0.25] and the special order from Bar the-Door will require 4,000 machine hours [8,000 × 0.5]. Home Security has a capacity of 21,750 machine hours in the quarter [7,250 × 3] and regular orders for 17,400 machine hours [21,750 × 0.80]. It will not be able to produce the First Alarm order without affecting regular sales but will be able to produce the Bar-the-Door order with available capacity.

The overhead rate is $8.00 per machine hour (based on plant capacity of 87,000 machine hours). Fixed overhead is $4.80 per machine hour [$417,600 ÷ 87,000] and variable overhead is $3.20 per machine hour [$8.00 – 4.80].

The contribution margin per unit of regular orders is $6.20 [$18.00 – ($5.00 + 6.00 + 0.25 × 3.20)] or $24.80 per machine hour [$6.20 ÷ 0.25].

The contribution from the First Alarm special order is:

Revenue	$300,000	[25,000 × $12.00]
Raw materials	(112,500)	[25,000 × $4.50]
Direct labour	(150,000)	[25,000 × $6.00]
Variable overhead	(20,000)	[25,000 × 0.25 × $3.20]
Contribution	$ 17,500	

If the First Alarm special order is accepted, 15,500 machine hours will be left for regular orders [21,750 – 6,250], 1,900 machine hours less than originally expected [17,400 – 15,500]. If the special order is produced rather than regular orders, Home Security would have $47,120 less contribution from its regular orders [1,900 × $24.80]. This opportunity cost is greater than the contribution from the First Alarm special order – the order should not be accepted.

The contribution from the Bar-the-Door special order is:

Revenue	$120,000	[8,000 × $15.00]
Raw materials	(52,000)	[8,000 × $6.50]
Direct labour	(48,000)	[8,000 × 0.5 × $12.00]
Variable overhead	(12,800)	[8,000 × 0.5 × $3.20]
Contribution	$ 7,200	
Additional setup costs	(3,600)	
Special device	(5,200)	
Net benefit	$ (1,600)	

The direct costs of the Bar-the-Door special order are more than its revenues – the order should not be accepted.

10-35

1. The division is making a contribution of $228,350 to the company's operating income.

Sales		$3,751,500
Variable expenses		
Cost of goods sold	$1,902,400	
Selling	102,500	[20,500 × $5]
Total variable expenses		2,004,900
Contribution margin		$1,746,600
Direct fixed expenses		
Fixed overhead	$820,000	
Fixed selling and administrative	698,250	
Total direct fixed expenses		1,518,250
Segment margin		$ 228,350

    Notes:

    The division sells 20,500 units to outside customers and 20,500 units to another division – a total of 41,000 units [20,500 + 20,500].

    Calculation:

    $$\begin{aligned} \$100X + \$83X &= \$3,751,500 \\ \$183X &= \$3,751,500 \\ X &= 20,500 \text{ units} \end{aligned}$$

    The division's variable production cost per unit is $46.40 [$1,902,400 ÷ 41,000].

    Calculation:

Cost of goods sold	$2,722,400	
Fixed overhead applied	820,000	[41,000 × $20]
Variable production cost	$1,902,400	

    The division's direct fixed selling and administrative expenses are $698,250.

    Calculation:

Total selling and administrative expenses	$1,100,000	
Variable selling expenses	102,500	[20,500 × $5]
Fixed selling and administrative expenses	$ 997,500	
Direct fixed selling and administrative expenses	$ 698,250	[$997,500 × (1 – 0.3)]

2. Ira should not shut down the division. Not only is the division making a contribution of $228,350 from its operations, the other division will incur additional costs of $348,500 if it is required to purchase externally the part supplied to it by the division [20,500 × ($100 – 83)]. The lost contribution and extra costs are greater than the benefit of $100,000 from the sale of the division's facilities and equipment. The total effect will be a decrease in the company's profits of $476,850 [$228,350 + 348,500 – 100,000].

10-37

1. The effect of Alternative A on Triangle's net income before income taxes is:

Decrease in Isosceles variable cost	$74,000	[$925,000 × 52% – (285,000 + 270,000)]
Increase in fixed cost	(50,000)	[$480,000 – (304,200 + 125,800)]
Increase in net income	$24,000	

Note: The purchase of the new machinery is included in the analysis as part of the increased fixed expenses of the Isosceles product.

The effect of Alternative B on Triangle's net income before income taxes is:

Increased Scalene contribution margin	$172,500	[($575,000 – 150,000 – 80,000) × 50%]
Decreased Isosceles contribution margin	(370,000)	[$925,000 – (285,000 + 270,000)]
Decreased fixed cost	30,000	
Rent revenue	157,500	
Decrease in net income	$(10,000)	

Note: The rent allocated to Isosceles production is unchanged and not relevant.

2. If the cash outlay for the new equipment was $700,000, the increase in fixed cost would be higher due to higher future amortization expenses.

3. A relevant cost is a future cost that is different depending on the decision made. Historical (sunk) costs are irrelevant for decision-making purposes but are often the basis for predicting the amount of future costs.

10-39

1. Olat's variable-costing segmented income statement is:

	D-gauge	P-gauge	T-gauge	Total
Sales	$900,000	$1,600,000	$900,000	$3,400,000
Variable expenses	710,000	1,008,000	900,000	2,618,000
Contribution margin	$190,000	$ 592,000	$ 0	782,000
Direct fixed expenses	100,000	210,000	40,000	350,000
Segment margin	$ 90,000	$ 382,000	$(40,000)	$ 432,000
Common fixed expenses				490,000
Operating income				$ (58,000)

Notes:

Olat sold 10,000 D-gauges [$900,000 ÷ $90], 8,000 P-gauges [$1,600,000 ÷ $200] and 5,000 T-gauges [$900,000 ÷ $180].

The variable expenses are: D-gauge, 10,000 × [$17 + 20 + 30 + 4]; P-gauge, 8,000 × [$31 + 40 + 45 + 10]; T-gauge, 5,000 × [$50 + 60 + 60 + 10].

Olat's common fixed expenses are $490,000. This is made up of fixed overhead of $320,000 [10,000 × $10 + 8,000 × $15 + 5,000 × $20] and selling and administrative expenses of $170,000 [$690,000 – (10,000 × $4 + 8,000 × $10 + 5,000 × $10) – 350,000].

10-39 continued

2. As the segmented income statement shows, the T-gauge has a negative segment margin – its contribution margin is zero. Olat will be better off if it drops this product, as long as its other sales are not affected. It will still have a loss of $18,000 [$(58,000) + 40,000].

3. Olat will be worse off if it drops its T-gauges, increases its sales of P-gauges by 25 percent, and decreases its sales of D-gauges by 50 percent. Its loss will be $45,000 [$(58,000) + 13,000] compared to a loss of $18,000 if it only drops its T-gauges.

    Analysis:

Increase in contribution margin of P-gauges	$148,000	[$592,000 × 25%]
Increase in promotion expenses of P-gauges	(100,000)	
Decrease in contribution margin of D-gauges	(95,000)	[$190,000 × 50%]
Decrease in advertising expenses of D-gauges	20,000	
Gain from elimination of negative segment margin of T-gauges	40,000	
Change in operating income	$ 13,000	

10-41

Phylex's linear programming problem is:

Maximize	$Z = \$16.66A + \$17.84B + \$13.11C$	[Objective function]
Subject to:	$3A + 6B + 8C \leq 18,000$	[metal quantity constraint]
	$4A + 2B + 2C \leq 15,000$	[plastic quantity constraint]
	$4A + 6B + 6.5C \leq 85,200$	[direct labour constraint (minutes)]
	$4A + 6B + 10C \leq 10,080$	[machine time constraint (minutes)]
	$A \leq 2,800$	[A's demand constraint]
	$B \leq 2,100$	[B's demand constraint]
	$C \leq 700$	[C's demand constraint – including contract]
	$C \geq 400$	[current contract for C]
	$A \geq 0, B \geq 0$	[Nonnegativity constraints for A and B]
Where:	A = number of units of A; B = number of units of B; C = number of units of C	

Analysis:

Unit contribution margin:

	A	B	C
Selling price	$62.00	$84.00	$120.00
Direct materials			
Metal	$ 1.20	$ 2.40	$ 3.20
Plastic	2.00	1.00	1.00
Direct labour	1.04	1.56	1.69
Machining	38.00	57.00	95.00
Selling	3.10	4.20	6.00
Total variable expenses	$45.34	$66.16	$106.89
Contribution margin	$16.66	$17.84	$ 13.11

Notes:

Metal: 3 × $0.40; 6 × $0.40; 8 × $0.40   Plastic: 4 × $0.50; 2 × $0.50; 2 × $0.50

Direct labour: 4 × $15.60 ÷ 60; 6 × $15.60 ÷ 60; 6.5 × $15.60 ÷ 60

Machining: 4 × $570 ÷ 60; 6 × $570 ÷ 60; 10 × $570 ÷ 60

Selling: 5% × $62.00; 5% × $84.00; 5% × $120.00;

10-43

1. Sportway should use its production capacity to first produce, its expected sales of 17,500 skateboards because skateboards earn a higher contribution per direct labour hour than tackle boxes. Skateboards will require 8,750 direct labour hours [17,500 × 0.50]; 1,250 hours will be left to produce tackle boxes. Sportway should produce 1,000 tackle boxes [1,250 ÷ 1.25] with the remaining direct labour capacity. Sportway should buy 9,000 tackle boxes – this is the maximum it can buy although it expects to be able to sell 2,000 more [12,000 – (1,000 + 9,000)].

Sportway's contribution margin from this product mix is $500,250 [17,500 × $19.50 + 1,000 × $33.00 + 9,000 × $14.00], $236,250 higher than its current contribution margin of $264,000 [8,000 × $33.00].

Analysis and notes:

Unit contribution margin calculation:	Purchased tackle boxes	Manufactured tackle boxes	Skateboards
Selling price	$86.00	$86.00	$45.00
Variable expenses			
Purchase cost	68.00		
Materials			
Moulded plastic		8.00	5.50
Hinges, latches, handle		9.00	
Wheels, hardware			7.00
Direct labour		18.75	7.50
Variable overhead		6.25	2.50
Variable selling and administrative	4.00	11.00	3.00
Total variable expenses	72.00	53.00	25.50
Contribution margin per unit	$14.00	$33.00	$19.50
Direct labour hours per unit	na	1.25	0.50
Contribution per direct labour hour	na	$26.40	$39.00

Direct labour hours per unit:	Manufactured tackle boxes	Skateboards
Direct labour expense	$18.75	$7.50
Direct labour rate per hour	15.00	15.00
Direct labour hours	1.25	0.50

Variable overhead rate:

Fixed overhead	$50,000	
Direct labour denominator	10,000	[8,000 × 1.25]
Fixed overhead rate	$5 per direct labour hour	
Total overhead rate	$10 per direct labour hour	[$12.50 ÷ 1.25]
Variable overhead rate	$5 per direct labour hour	[$10 – 5]

Variable overhead (tackle boxes): $5 × 1.25; Variable overhead (skateboards): $5 × 0.50

Variable selling and administrative:	Purchased tackle boxes	Manufactured tackle boxes	Skateboards
Total selling and administrative	$10.00	$17.00	$9.00
Fixed selling and administrative	6.00	6.00	6.00
Variable selling and administrative	$ 4.00	$11.00	$3.00

10-43 continued

2. Sportway should also consider qualitative factors such as the quality of the purchased tackle boxes, the reliability of the supplier, technical problems of switching from production of tackle boxes to skateboards, and the confidence it has in the skateboard market study.

MANAGERIAL DECISION CASES

10-45

1. Valerie has violated the standards of ethical behaviour by revealing the impending decision concerning the power department. She received the information in confidence – it was stressed that the deal be kept quiet until a decision was made. By talking with Quentin about the decision, she breached the standard of confidentiality.

2. Valerie should have declared the conflict of interest due to her romantic relationship with Quentin and withdrawn from any active role in the decision concerning the power department.

   Valerie has a duty to provide the correct data concerning the power department. It is not her role to make a decision for the company concerning its responsibility for the decision's effect on its work force.

   Valerie could provide qualitative arguments of the effect of the elimination of the power department on its employees and community relations. She may also point out the issues of reliability of supply and the short-term nature of the agreement versus the long-term effects of closing the power department.

RESEARCH ASSIGNMENTS

10-47

Students' answers will vary depending on their research.

MANAGEMENT ACCOUNTING
CANADIAN SIXTH EDITION
SOLUTIONS MANUAL

CHAPTER 11

CAPITAL INVESTMENT DECISIONS

ANSWERS TO ODD-NUMBERED QUESTIONS FOR WRITING AND DISCUSSION

1. Independent projects are projects that, if accepted or rejected, do not affect the cash flows of other projects. Mutually exclusive projects are projects that, if accepted, preclude accepting other competing projects.

3. Ignoring the time value of money is a major deficiency of both the payback period and the accounting rate of return models because a manager may choose investments that do not maximize a company's profits. Good projects may be rejected and bad projects accepted. Present value allows a manager to assess each project in terms of today's dollars, and to make valid comparisons between projects.

5. Three possible reasons why the payback period is used to help make capital investments decisions are:

    1. Payback period is a rough measure of risk – the longer a project's payback period, the riskier it is. A company with risky cash flows will prefer shorter a payback period to minimize its risk.

    2. Payback period is associated with a company's liquidity. Companies with liquidity problems will prefer earlier cash flows and shorter payback periods.

    3. Payback period is associated with obsolescence. In industries where the risk of obsolescence is high, companies would be interested in recovering funds quickly – and prefer shorter payback periods.

7. Future value is the amount that accumulates by the end of the investment's life, assuming a specified compound return.

9. Present value is the current value of a future cash flow. It is the amount that must be invested now to produce a specific future cash flow, assuming compounding at a given interest rate.

11. Yes, net present value is the profit of a project expressed in present dollars. Net present value is the difference in the present value of a project's cash inflows and cash outflows. It is the return in excess of the investment and its cost of capital.

13. The required rate of return is used as the discount rate in the NPV model.

    The required rate of return is the minimum return (or benchmark) for the IRR model – if a project's IRR is greater than the required rate of return it is accepted but if a project's IRR is less than the required rate of return it is rejected.

15. If NPV is greater than zero, the investment is profitable and acceptable. If NPV equals zero, the decision maker is indifferent between accepting or rejecting the investment. If NPV is negative, the investment should be rejected because it is earning less than the required rate of return.

17. A project that requires an investment of $299,100 and provides a return of $100,000 a year for four years has an IRR of 12.75%.

    Calculation:

Discount factor	=	$299,100 ÷ $100,000
df	=	2.991

    $$2.991 = 1/(1 + i) + 1/(1 + i)^2 + 1/(1 + i)^3 + 1/(1 + i)^4$$
    $$i = 12.75\% \text{ (found by trial and error)}$$

try $i = 0.10$	df	=	3.1698
try $i = 0.13$	df	=	2.9745
try $i = 0.125$	df	=	3.0056
try $i = 0.1275$	df	=	2.9900

    IRR can also be calculated using a financial calculator or the IRR function in Excel (IRR = 12.734%).

19. A postaudit is a follow-up analysis of an investment decision once it is implemented, comparing actual benefits and costs with expected benefits and costs.

    A postaudit is useful by providing feedback that may help improve future decisions. Managers are held accountable for their decisions and the estimates they used in making their decisions. Corrective action may be needed to improve performance or a project may be abandoned.

21. A company may be choosing between two mutually exclusive projects with negative NPVs because it is looking for the least cost alternative to provide an activity or output (revenues are identical and not relevant for the analysis). Thus the NPV of both projects will be negative. The company will maximize its profits by selecting the project with the largest (or least negative) NPV.

23. It is important for a manager to conduct a careful review of the assumptions and methods used to in forecasting cash flows because the quality and reliability of the projections of cash flows are directly affected. If the assumptions and forecasting methods are poor, then cash forecasts will be of poor quality and unreliable. Inaccurate estimates of cash flows may lead to incorrect investment decisions.

25. Sensitivity analysis (often referred to as what-if analysis) changes the assumptions on which the capital investment analysis relies and assesses the effect of the assumptions on the cash-flow pattern. Sensitivity analysis is useful in capital investment decisions because it helps a manager consider the element of uncertainty. Even with good estimates, there will be some level of uncertainty, and a manager can see whether her decision is affected by this uncertainty.

27. The project's annual after-tax operating cash inflow is $50,000 [$40,000 + 10,000].

29. The significant differences between accounting amortization and capital cost allowances for tax purposes are:

    - Accounting amortization may be calculated on a straight-line, declining-balance, units of production, or other acceptable basis. Maximum capital cost allowance (CCA) is calculated on a declining-balance for most asset classes.

    - The income tax act specifies the maximum CCA rate; there is more freedom in selecting accounting amortization rates.

    - In the year of acquisition, assets are subject to the one-half rule – CCA is limited to one-half of the usual rate.

31. The one-half rule restricts the amount of CCA that can be claimed in the year of acquisition to one-half of the CCA rate for the class.

    The effect of the one-half rule is to decrease the NPV of the CCA tax shield because some of the tax shield is deferred during the first year.

33. In the new manufacturing environment attention must be paid to the inputs used in capital investment decisions. Definitions of investment, estimates of operating cash flows, salvage values, and discount rates are all affected. Benefits and costs are often more intangible and indirect than in traditional investment decisions and linked to a company's strategic objectives – flexibility, diversification, product quality, etc.. Investment is more complex to assess – often composed of soft costs like software and process development rather than machines and buildings. Operating cash flow effects are often indirect rather than direct cost differences.

SOLUTIONS TO ODD-NUMBERED EXERCISES, PROBLEMS, AND CASES

EXERCISES

11-1

1. The payback period is 2.6 years.

    Analysis:

Year	Unrecovered investment	Annual cash flow
1	$200,000	$ 60,000
2	140,000	80,000
3	60,000	100,000
4	0	120,000
5		140,000

    In year 3, only $60,000 is needed to recover the remaining original investment; it will take 0.6 years to earn this amount [$60,000 ÷ $100,000].

2. The accounting rate of return using the original investment is 30 percent [$60,000 ÷ $200,000].

    Analysis:

Year	Annual cash flow
1	$ 60,000
2	80,000
3	100,000
4	120,000
5	140,000
Total	$500,000
Average	$100,000

    Average amortization: $40,000 [$200,000 ÷ 5]

    Average net income $60,000 [$100,000 – 40,000]

11-3

The project has an IRR of 12%.

Analysis:

The project has a discount factor of 2.4024 [$300,000 ÷ 124,875].

Its discount factor is $(1 \div (1 + i)) + (1 \div (1 + i)^2) + (1 \div (1 + i)^3) = 2.4024$.

This can be solved by trial and error, using a financial calculator, or spreadsheet function.

Trial and error:

try $i = 0.10$	df	=	2.4869
try $i = 0.13$	df	=	2.3612
try $i = 0.12$	df	=	2.4018

By spreadsheet function: IRR = 11.986%

11-5

1. The annual cash flow is $280,000 [$180,000 + 100,000].

    Analysis:

Revenues	$900,000
Cash expenses	500,000
Amortization	100,000
Operating income	$300,000
Income taxes	120,000 [$300,000 × 40%]
Net income	$180,000

2. The after-tax cash flows for each item on the income statement are:

	Before tax	After tax	
Revenues	$900,000	$540,000	[$900,000 × (1 – 40%)]
Cash expenses	500,000	(300,000)	[$500,000 × (1 – 40%)]
Amortization	100,000	40,000	[$100,000 × 40%]
Total		$280,000	

11-7

1. Project I's NPV is $13,991. Project II's NPV is $46,690.

    Analysis:

	Cash Flow			PV	
Year	Project I	Project II	df	Project I	Project II
1	$5,000	$30,000	0.86207	$ 4,310	$25,862
2	5,000	20,000	0.74316	3,716	14,863
3	5,000	5,000	0.64066	3,203	3,203
4	5,000	5,000	0.55229	2,761	2,761
Total			2.79818	$13,991	$46,690

    Note: $df = 1/(1.16)^n$.

2. To have $50,000 after six years, the couple would have to invest $31,508 at 8 percent, $25,332 at 12 percent and $20,522 at 16 percent.

    Analysis:

Interest rate	0.08	0.12	0.16
Discount factor	0.63017	0.50663	0.41044
Future value	$50,000	$50,000	$50,000
Present value	$31,508	$25,332	$20,522

    Note: the discount factor is $1/(1 + i)^6$ where i is the interest rate.

11-7 continued

3. The most the company should pay for the new equipment is $226,009; the amount where the equipment's NPV is equal to zero.

    Analysis:

Year	df
1	0.8928571
2	0.7971939
3	0.7117802
4	0.6355181
5	0.5674269
6	0.5066311
7	0.4523492
8	0.4038832
9	0.3606100
10	0.3219732
Total	5.6502230

    Note: $df = 1/(1.12)^n$.

    PV of savings is $226,009 [$40,000 × 5.6502230].

4. The minimum savings in operating expense that must be earned each year to justify the acquisition is $99,998; the amount where the equipment's NPV is equal to zero.

    Analysis:

Year	df
1	0.8771930
2	0.7694675
3	0.6749715
4	0.5920803
5	0.5193687
Total	3.4330810

    Note: $df = 1/(1.14)^n$.

    Minimum annual savings in operating expense is $99,998 [$343,300 ÷ 3.4330810].

11-9

1. Project A's payback period is 2.6 years; Project B's payback period is 2.5 years. If rapid payback is important, Project B should be chosen because it has a shorter payback period. Project A is more profitable for Wei – it has higher cash flows in years 4 and 5.

    Analysis:

Project A	Year 0	Year 1	Year 2	Year 3	Year 4	Year 5
Cash flow		$3,000	$4,000	$5,000	$10,000	$10,000
Investment remaining	$10,000	$7,000	$3,000	$ 0	$ 0	$ 0

    In year 3, only $3,000 is needed to recover the remaining original investment; it will take 0.6 years to earn this amount [$3,000 ÷ $5,000)].

Project B	Year 0	Year 1	Year 2	Year 3	Year 4	Year 5
Cash flow		$3,000	$4,000	$6,000	$3,000	$3,000
Investment remaining	$10,000	$7,000	$3,000	$ 0	$ 0	$ 0

    In year 3, only $3,000 is needed to recover the remaining original investment; it will take 0.5 years to earn this amount [$3,000 ÷ $6,000)].

2. Project A's accounting rate of return is 44%; Project B's accounting rate of return is 38%. Project A should be chosen because it has a higher accounting rate of return.

    Analysis:

Project A	Year 1	Year 2	Year 3	Year 4	Year 5	Total
Cash flow	$3,000	$4,000	$5,000	$10,000	$10,000	$32,000
Amortization	2,000	2,000	2,000	2,000	2,000	10,000
Net income	$1,000	$2,000	$3,000	$ 8,000	$ 8,000	$22,000

    Amortization (straight-line) is $2,000 per year [$10,000 ÷ 5].

    Average net income is $4,400 [$22,000 ÷ 5].

    Accounting rate of return (original investment) is 44% [$4,400 ÷ 10,000].

Project B	Year 1	Year 2	Year 3	Year 4	Year 5	Total
Cash flow	$3,000	$4,000	$6,000	$3,000	$3,000	$19,000
Amortization	2,000	2,000	2,000	2,000	2,000	10,000
Net income	$1,000	$2,000	$4,000	$1,000	$1,000	$ 9,000

    Amortization (straight-line) is $2,000 per year [$10,000 ÷ 5].

    Average net income is $3,800 [$19,000 ÷ 5].

    Accounting rate of return (original investment) is 38% [$3,800 ÷ 10,000].

11-9 continued

3. Wilma should take the 20-year, $24,000 annuity because it has a higher present value ($235,636) than the lump sum payment ($225,000). [Alternate calculation: 9.8181474 × $24,000]

Analysis:

Year	df	Cash Flow	PV
1	0.9259259	$24,000	$ 22,222
2	0.8573388	24,000	20,576
3	0.7938322	24,000	19,052
4	0.7350299	24,000	17,641
5	0.6805832	24,000	16,334
6	0.6301696	24,000	15,124
7	0.5834904	24,000	14,004
8	0.5402689	24,000	12,966
9	0.5002490	24,000	12,006
10	0.4631935	24,000	11,117
11	0.4288829	24,000	10,293
12	0.3971138	24,000	9,531
13	0.3676979	24,000	8,825
14	0.3404610	24,000	8,171
15	0.3152417	24,000	7,566
16	0.2918905	24,000	7,005
17	0.2702690	24,000	6,486
18	0.2502490	24,000	6,006
19	0.2317121	24,000	5,561
20	0.2145482	24,000	5,149
Total	9.8181474		$235,636

Note: $df = 1/(1.08)^n$.

4. Darryl should invest in the tools and equipment because the investment's NPV is $7,737.

Year	df	Cash Flow	PV
0	1.0000000	$(20,000)	$(20,000)
1	0.9259259	6,000	5,556
2	0.8573388	6,000	5,144
3	0.7938322	6,000	4,763
4	0.7350299	6,000	4,410
5	0.6805832	6,000	4,083
6	0.6301696	6,000	3,781
NPV			$ 7,737

Note: $df = 1/(1.08)^n$.

5. The project's internal rate of return is 14%. Zara should acquire the equipment because its IRR is greater than her cost of capital (of 10%).

Analysis:

The investment's discount factor is 5.216 [$130,400 ÷ 25,000].

Its discount factor is $(1 \div (1 + i)) + (1 \div (1 + i)^2) + (1 \div (1 + i)^3) + \ldots + (1 \div (1 + i)^9) + (1 \div (1 + i)^{10}) = 5.216$.

11-9 continued

This can be solved by trial and error, using a financial calculator, or spreadsheet function.

Trial and error:

i	0.1	0.15	0.125	0.14
1	0.9090909	0.8695652	0.8888889	0.8771930
2	0.8264463	0.7561437	0.7901235	0.7694675
3	0.7513148	0.6575162	0.7023320	0.6749715
4	0.6830135	0.5717532	0.6242951	0.5920803
5	0.6209213	0.4971767	0.5549290	0.5193687
6	0.5644739	0.4323276	0.4932702	0.4555865
7	0.5131581	0.3759370	0.4384624	0.3996373
8	0.4665074	0.3269018	0.3897443	0.3505591
9	0.4240976	0.2842624	0.3464394	0.3075079
10	0.3855433	0.2471847	0.3079461	0.2697438
df	6.1445671	5.0187686	5.5364308	5.2161156

By spreadsheet function: IRR = 14.0%

11-11

1. Project A's NPV is $48,686; Project B's NPV is $123,034.

	Cash Flow			PV	
Year	Project A	Project B	df	Project A	Project B
0	$(200,000)	$(200,000)	1.0000	$(200,000)	$(200,000)
1	120,000	20,000	0.8929	107,143	17,857
2	60,000	20,000	0.7972	47,832	15,944
3	80,000	120,000	0.7118	56,942	85,414
4	40,000	160,000	0.6355	25,421	101,683
5	20,000	180,000	0.5674	11,349	102,137
Total				$ 48,686	$123,034

Note: $df = 1/(1.12)^n$.

11-11 continued

2. Project A's payback period is 2.25 years; Project B's payback period is 3.25 years. Timtell would accept project A because its payback period is less than 3 years. Timtell would reject project B because its payback period is more than 3 years.

   Timtell may use payback period as a rough measure of risk to evaluate projects. A project with a shorter payback period may be less risky than a project with a longer payback period. Timtell may also have liquidity problems and need to invest only in projects that provide immediate cash flows. Although project B is more profitable than project A, Timtell would not accept it because its payback period is too long.

   Analysis:

Project A	Year 0	Year 1	Year 2	Year 3	Year 4	Year 5
Cash flow		$120,000	$60,000	$80,000	$40,000	$20,000
Investment remaining	$200,000	$ 80,000	$20,000	$ 0	$ 0	$ 0

   In year 3, only $20,000 is needed to recover the remaining original investment; it will take 0.25 years to earn this amount [$2,000 ÷ $80,000)].

Project B	Year 0	Year 1	Year 2	Year 3	Year 4	Year 5
Cash flow		$ 20,000	$ 20,000	$120,000	$160,000	$180,000
Investment remaining	$200,000	$180,000	$160,000	$ 40,000	$ 0	$ 0

   In year 4, only $40,000 is needed to recover the remaining original investment; it will take 0.25 years to earn this amount [$40,000 ÷ $160,000)].

3. Project A's accounting rate of return is 12% using the original investment [$24,000 ÷ 200,000] and 24% using the average investment [$24,000 ÷ 100,000]; Project B's accounting rate of return is 30% using the original investment [$60,000 ÷ 200,000] and 60% using the average investment [$60,000 ÷ 100,000].

   Analysis:

Project A	Year 1	Year 2	Year 3	Year 4	Year 5	Total
Cash flow	$120,000	$60,000	$80,000	$40,000	$20,000	$320,000
Amortization	40,000	40,000	40,000	40,000	40,000	200,000
Net income	$ 80,000	$20,000	$40,000	$ 0	$(20,000)	$120,000

   Amortization (straight-line) is $40,000 per year [$200,000 ÷ 5].

   Average net income is $24,000 [$120,000 ÷ 5].

   Average investment is $100,000 [$200,000 ÷ 2].

Project B	Year 1	Year 2	Year 3	Year 4	Year 5	Total
Cash flow	$ 20,000	$ 20,000	$120,000	$160,000	$180,000	$500,000
Amortization	40,000	40,000	40,000	40,000	40,000	200,000
Net income	$(20,000)	$(20,000)	$ 80,000	$120,000	$140,000	$300,000

   Amortization (straight-line) is $40,000 per year [$200,000 ÷ 5].

   Average net income is $60,000 [$300,000 ÷ 5].

   Average investment is $100,000 [$200,000 ÷ 2].

11-13

1. The cost of capital for the project is 10% [60% × 5% + 40% × 17.5%].

   Analysis:

Source	Amount	Percent	Rate
Borrowing	$150,000	60%	5.0%
Stock	100,000	40%	17.5%
Total	$250,000	100%	

   Note: The cost of borrowing is 5% [$7,500 ÷ 150,000].

2. The project's NPV is $60,856. It is not necessary to subtract interest and dividend payments from the annual cash flows because these payments are included in the company's cost of capital (used as the discount rate in the NPV calculation).

   Analysis:

Year	df	Cash Flow	PV
0	1.0000000	$(250,000)	$(250,000)
1	0.9090909	125,000	113,636
2	0.8264463	125,000	103,306
3	0.7513148	125,000	93,914
NPV			$ 60,856

   Note: $df = 1/(1.1)^n$.

   Note: there is an error in the information in the question – the project will produce cash inflows of $125,000 per year for the next three years (not two years).

11-15

1. The system's payback period is 6.145 years. Torront would not accept the project because its payback period is more than the five-year period specified by Torront's policy.

   Analysis:

   The benefits associated with the system are $200,000 a year, for 10 years [$80,000 + 90,000 + 30,000].

Year	Cash flow	Remaining investment
0		$1,229,000
1	$200,000	1,029,000
2	200,000	829,000
3	200,000	629,000
4	200,000	429,000
5	200,000	229,000
6	200,000	29,000
7	200,000	0
8	200,000	0
9	200,000	0
10	200,000	0

   In year 7, only $29,000 is needed to recover the remaining original investment; it will take 0.145 years to earn this amount [$29,000 ÷ $200,000)].

   Alternate calculation: $1,229,000 ÷ 200,000 = 6.145 years.

11-15 continued

2. The project's NPV is $(98,955). Torront should reject the project because its NPV is negative and it doesn't cover the company's 12% cost of capital.

    Analysis:

Year	Cash flow	df	PV
0	$(1,229,000)	1.00000	$(1,229,000)
1	200,000	0.89286	178,571
2	200,000	0.79719	159,439
3	200,000	0.71178	142,356
4	200,000	0.63552	127,104
5	200,000	0.56743	113,485
6	200,000	0.50663	101,326
7	200,000	0.45235	90,470
8	200,000	0.40388	80,777
9	200,000	0.36061	72,122
10	200,000	0.32197	64,395
NPV		6.65022	$ (98,955)

    Note: $df = 1/(1.12)^n$.

    Alternate calculation: NPV = ($200,000 × (6.65022 – 1)) – $1,229,000 = $(98,955).

3. With the revised information, the project's payback period is 4.916 years and its NPV is $215,753. Torront would now accept the project because its payback period is shorter than the five-year period specified by Torront's policy and its NPV is positive.

    Analysis:

    The benefits associated with the system are $250,000 a year, for 10 years [$200,000 + 50,000] with an additional salvage value of $100,000 in year 10.

    Payback period:

Year	Cash flow	Remaining investment
0		$1,229,000
1	$250,000	979,000
2	250,000	729,000
3	250,000	479,000
4	250,000	229,000
5	250,000	0
6	250,000	0
7	250,000	0
8	250,000	0
9	250,000	0
10	350,000	0

    In year 5, only $229,000 is needed to recover the remaining original investment; it will take 0.916 years to earn this amount [$229,000 ÷ $250,000)].

    Alternate calculation: $1,229,000 ÷ 250,000 = 4.916 years.

11-15 continued

NPV:

Year	Cash flow	df	PV
0	$(1,229,000)	1.00000	$(1,229,000)
1	250,000	0.89286	223,214
2	250,000	0.79719	199,298
3	250,000	0.71178	177,945
4	250,000	0.63552	158,880
5	250,000	0.56743	141,857
6	250,000	0.50663	126,658
7	250,000	0.45235	113,087
8	250,000	0.40388	100,971
9	250,000	0.36061	90,153
10	350,000	0.32197	112,691
NPV			$ 215,753

Note: $df = 1/(1.12)^n$.

11-17

1. Project I's NPV is $11,281 and its IRR is 16%. Project II's NPV is $10,826 and its IRR is18%.

    Analysis:

	Cash Flow			PV	
Year	Project I	Project II	df	Project I	Project II
0	$(100,000)	$(100,000)	1.0000	$(100,000)	$(100,000)
1	0	63,857	0.9091	0	58,052
2	134,650	63,857	0.8264	111,281	52,774
Total				$ 11,281	$ 10,826

For Project I $100,000 = $134,650 \div (1 + i)^2$.

$(1 + i)^2 = 1.3465[\$134,650 \div 100,000]$.

This can be solved by trial and error, using a financial calculator, or spreadsheet function.

Trial and error:

i	0.1	0.2	0.15	0.16
$(1 + i)^2$	1.21	1.44	1.3225	1.3456

By spreadsheet function: 16.039%

Project II's discount factor is 1.566 [$100,000 ÷ 63,857].

Its discount factor is $(1 \div (1 + i)) + (1 \div (1 + i)^2) = 1.566$.

This can be solved by trial and error, using a financial calculator, or spreadsheet function.

11-17 continued

Trial and error:

i	0.1	0.2	0.15	0.16	0.18
$(1 \div (1 + i))$	0.9090909	0.8333333	0.8695652	0.862069	0.8474576
$(1 \div (1 + i)^2)$	0.8264463	0.6944444	0.7561437	0.7431629	0.7181844
df	1.7355372	1.5277778	1.6257089	1.6052319	1.5656421

By spreadsheet function: 17.982%

2. We can show that project I is better than project II by modifying the cash flows for project II to reflect reinvestment of year 1 cash flows at the company's cost of capital. Project II's cash flow in year 2 is now $134,100 [$63,857 + $63,857 × 1.1], which is less than project I's year 2 cash flows of $134,650.

   Note that NPV correctly signals the best investment but IRR gives an incorrect signal.

11-19

1. The present value of the CCA tax shield (including the one-half rule) is $2,696.

   Analysis:

   $$[(R \times C \times T) \div (R + i)] \times [(1 + 0.5i) \div (1 + i)] = [(0.2 \times \$12,000 \times 0.38) \div (0.2 + 0.12)]$$
   $$\times [(1 + 0.5 \times 0.12) \div 1.12]$$
   $$= \$2,850 \times 0.946$$
   $$= \$2,696$$

2. With a salvage value of $2,500, the present value of the CCA tax shield (including the one-half rule) is $2,359

   Analysis:

   The CCA adjustment for salvage value is:

   $$[(R \times S \times T) \div (R + i)] \times [1 \div (1 + i)^n] = [(0.2 \times \$2,500 \times 0.38) \div (0.2 + 0.12)] \times [1 \div 1.12^5]$$
   $$= \$594 \times 0.567$$
   $$= \$337$$

   The tax shield, with salvage adjustment, is $2,359 [$2,696 – 337].

11-21

1. The project's NPV (unadjusted cash flows) is $(1,224).

   Analysis:

	Year 0	Year 1	Year 2	NPV
Investment	$(40,000)			
Cash inflow		$22,000	$24,000	
df	1.00000	0.89286	0.79719	
PV	$(40,000)	$19,643	$19,133	$(1,224)

   df is $(1 \div (1.12)^n)$

2. The project's NPV (inflation-adjusted cash flows) is $1,719.

   Analysis:

	Year 0	Year 1	Year 2	NPV
Investment	$(40,000)			
Cash inflow		$22,000	$24,000	
Adjusted cash flow		23,100	26,460	
df	1.00000	0.89286	0.79719	
PV	$(40,000)	$20,625	$21,094	$1,719

   Adjusted cash flow: year 1 $22,000 × 1.05; year 2 $24,000 × 1.05 × 1.05

   df is $(1 \div (1.12)^n)$

11-23

Craddock should purchase the machine because it has a NPV of $248,862. The investment's positive NPV indicates that it is expected to earn a return in excess of the company's cost of capital.

Analysis:

The machine will increase Craddock's annual after-tax cash flow by $214,520 a year for five years. The NPV of the investment (before the CCA tax shield) is $51,827. With the tax shield, the NPV of the machine is $248,862 [$51,827 + 202,091 − 5,056].

Increase in revenues	$760,000	[(50,000 – 30,000) × ($950,000 ÷ 25,000)]
Increase in variable production costs	(294,400)	[(50,000 – 30,000) × ($575,000 × 80% ÷ 25,000) × 80%]
Savings in variable production costs	110,400	[30,000 × ($575,000 × 80% ÷ 25,000) × 20%]
Increase in variable selling costs	(200,000)	[(50,000 – 30,000) × ($250,000 ÷ 25,000)]
New machine operator	(30,000)	
Increase in operating cash flows	$346,000	
Increase in income taxes	(131,480)	[$346,000 × 38%]
Increase in after-tax cash flow	$214,520	

	Year 0	Year 1	Year 2	Year 3	Year 4	Year 5	NPV
Purchase machine	$(780,000)						
After-tax cash flows		$214,520	$214,520	$214,520	$214,520	$214,520	
Salvage value						30,000	
Total	$(780,000)	$214,520	$214,520	$214,520	$214,520	$244,520	
df	1.00000	0.90909	0.82645	0.75131	0.68301	0.62092	
PV	$(780,000)	$195,018	$177,289	$161,172	$146,520	$151,828	$51,827

The present value of the CCA tax shield (including the one-half rule) is $202,091.

$$[(R \times C \times T) \div (R + i)] \times [(1 + 0.5i) \div (1 + i)] = [(0.25 \times \$780,000 \times 0.38) \div (0.25 + 0.10)]$$
$$\times [(1 + 0.5 \times 0.10) \div 1.10]$$
$$= \$202,091$$

The CCA adjustment for salvage value is $5,056.

$$[(R \times S \times T) \div (R + i)] \times [1 \div (1 + i)^n] = [(0.25 \times \$30,000 \times 0.38) \div (0.25 + 0.10)] \times [1 \div 1.10^5]$$
$$= \$5,056$$

11-25

1. The NPV of the standard equipment is $273,997; the NPV of the CAM equipment is $198,548.

   Analysis:

Year	df	Standard Cash Flow	PV	CAM Cash Flow	PV
0	1.00000	$(500,000)	$(500,000)	$(2,000,000)	$(2,000,000)
1	0.87719	300,000	263,158	100,000	87,719
2	0.76947	200,000	153,894	200,000	153,894
3	0.67497	100,000	67,497	300,000	202,491
4	0.59208	100,000	59,208	400,000	236,832
5	0.51937	100,000	51,937	400,000	207,747
6	0.45559	100,000	45,559	400,000	182,235
7	0.39964	100,000	39,964	500,000	199,819
8	0.35056	100,000	35,056	1,000,000	350,559
9	0.30751	100,000	30,751	1,000,000	307,508
10	0.26974	100,000	26,974	1,000,000	269,744
NPV			$273,997		$ 198,548

   df is $(1 \div (1.14)^n)$

2. The NPV of the standard equipment with the new information is $95,524. The company would change its decision – now the CAM project has a higher NPV and the company would choose it rather than the standard equipment. The reversal in the decision is due to the benefit of maintaining market share because of improved quality. Managers must consider all aspects of an investment decision – in this case, the intangible benefit affects the decision.

   Analysis:

Year	df	Standard Cash Flow	PV
0	1.00000	$(500,000)	$(500,000)
1	0.87719	300,000	263,158
2	0.76947	200,000	153,894
3	0.67497	50,000	33,749
4	0.59208	50,000	29,604
5	0.51937	50,000	25,968
6	0.45559	50,000	22,779
7	0.39964	50,000	19,982
8	0.35056	50,000	17,528
9	0.30751	50,000	15,375
10	0.26974	50,000	13,487
NPV			$ 95,524

PROBLEMS

11-27

1. The cash flows for the proposed project are:

	Year 0	Year 1	Year 2	Year 3	Year 4	Year 5	Year 6	Year 7
Purchase equipment	$(300,000)							
Increase in working capital	(30,000)							
Revenues		$255,000	$255,000	$255,000	$255,000	$255,000	$255,000	$255,000
Production costs		(120,000)	(120,000)	(120,000)	(120,000)	(120,000)	(120,000)	(120,000)
Cash operating expenses		(60,000)	(60,000)	(60,000)	(60,000)	(60,000)	(60,000)	(60,000)
Machine overhaul						(20,000)		
Salvage value of equipment								24,000
Recovery of working capital								30,000
Total cash flow	$(330,000)	$ 75,000	$ 75,000	$ 75,000	$ 75,000	$ 55,000	$ 75,000	$129,000

Revenues: 1,500 × $170; Production costs: 1,500 × $80

2. The project's NPV is $50,424. The product should be produced because the project has a positive NPV and earns a return greater than the company's cost of capital.

	Year 0	Year 1	Year 2	Year 3	Year 4	Year 5	Year 6	Year 7	NPV
Total	$(330,000)	$75,000	$75,000	$75,000	$75,000	$55,000	$75,000	$129,000	
df	1.00000	0.90909	0.82645	0.75131	0.68301	0.62092	0.56447	0.51316	
PV	$(330,000)	$68,182	$61,983	$56,349	$51,226	$34,151	$42,336	$ 66,197	$50,424

df is $(1 \div (1.10)^n)$

11-29

1. Proposal A's NPV is $40,171; Proposal B's NPV is $46,904.

   Analysis:

Year	df	Proposal A Cash Flow	PV	Proposal B Cash Flow	PV
0	1.00000	$(90,000)	$(90,000)	$(130,000)	$(130,000)
1	0.90909	60,000	54,545	(15,000)	(13,636)
2	0.82645	50,000	41,322	(10,000)	(8,264)
3	0.75131	20,000	15,026	(5,000)	(3,757)
4	0.68301	15,000	10,245	85,000	58,056
5	0.62092	10,000	6,209	110,000	68,301
6	0.56447	5,000	2,822	135,000	76,204
NPV			$40,171		$46,904

2. Proposal A's payback period is 1.6 years; Proposal B's payback period is 4.68 years.

   Analysis:

Year	Proposal A Cash Flow	Investment	Proposal B Cash Flow	Investment
0		$(90,000)		$(130,000)
1	$60,000	(30,000)	$(15,000)	(145,000)
2	50,000	0	(10,000)	(155,000)
3	20,000	0	(5,000)	(160,000)
4	15,000	0	85,000	(75,000)
5	10,000	0	110,000	0
6	5,000	0	135,000	0

   In year 2, Proposal A requires $30,000 to recover the remaining investment. It will take 0.6 years to earn this amount [$30,000 ÷ 50,000]. In year 5, Proposal B requires $75,000 to recover the remaining investment. It will take 0.68 years to earn this amount [$75,000 ÷ 110,000].

3. Both proposals are acceptable because they have positive net present values and earn returns greater than the branch's cost of capital.

4. Dominic accepted Proposal A because it has a positive NPV and a short payback period. The proposal will cause an immediate increase in his branch's net income in the next three years. Dominic will improve his chances of getting his bonus and promotion with this project.

   Dominic rejected Proposal B, although it has a positive NPV that is bigger than Proposal A's, because it has a long payback period and has negative cash flows in its early years. Dominic's branch's net income will be lower over the next three years if he accepts Proposal B and his chances of a bonus and promotion will be lower.

   Dominic may have considered Proposal B to be too risky to accept – it has a long payback period and negative cash flows in the first three years. Most of its returns will not arrive until the later years. Dominic may feel that these cash flows are more uncertain than the cash flows promised by Proposal A – cash flows that occur early in the life of the project.

   Dominic's decision to accept Proposal A and reject Proposal B is not unethical. He may have legitimate concerns about Proposal B's risk even though it seems to offer a good return to the credit union. He is likely influenced by the vice-president's promise of a bonus and promotion if he improves the short-term profits of his branch but acting on these incentives is not unethical.

The credit union's performance evaluation approach may be promoting short planning decisions by its managers. Proposal B is not attractive in the short term and is only profitable far down the road. Perhaps, if the credit union wants to encourage these types of development projects, it should exclude them from the routine evaluation of managers. Projects with a longer payback period could follow a different approval process and only enter into the performance evaluation when up and running.

11-31

1. The aircraft's NPV is $22,525,500. PrairieJet should buy it because its NPV is positive and the investment earns a return greater than the company's required rate of return.

    Analysis:

    The aircraft's annual operating cash flows are $18,500,000 per year for 20 years.

Flights per year	700	[(365 – 15) × 2]
Revenue per flight	$ 30,000	[$200 × 150]
Revenue per year	$21,000,000	
Operating costs	2,500,000	
Operating cash flows	$18,500,000	

    The discount factor for an annuity with a 14% required rate of return and 20 years is 6.623. [This is calculated as $\sum(1/(1 + i)^n)$ and can be calculated using a financial calculator, in a spreadsheet, or found in present value tables.] The present value of the operating cash flows is $122,525,500 [6.623 × $18,500,000] and the aircraft's NPV is $22,525,500 [$122,525,500 – 100,000,000].

2. With the revised information, the aircraft's NPV is $(5,291,100). PrairieJet should not buy it because its NPV is negative and the investment earns a return less than the company's required rate of return.

    Analysis:

    The aircraft's annual operating cash flows are $18,500,000 per year for 20 years.

Flights per year	700	[(365 – 15) × 2]
Revenue per flight	$ 24,000	[$200 × 150 × 80%]
Revenue per year	$16,800,000	
Operating costs	2,500,000	
Operating cash flows	$14,300,000	

    The discount factor for an annuity with a 14% required rate of return and 20 years is 6.623. [This is calculated as $\sum(1/(1 + i)^n)$ and can be calculated using a financial calculator, in a spreadsheet, or found in present value tables.] The present value of the operating cash flows is $94,708,900 [6.623 × $14,300,000] and the aircraft's NPV is $(5,291,100) [$94,708,900 – 100,000,000].

3. The average seating rate that would be needed so that the aircraft's NPV = 0 is 83.8%.

    Analysis:

    When the aircraft's NPV = 0, the present value of its operating cash flows will be $100,000,000 or 6.623 × CF. Thus its CF is $15,098,897 [$100,000,000 ÷ 6.623]. The revenue required for this cash flow is $17,598,897 [$15,098,897 + 2,500,000]. The revenue per flight is $25,141 [$17,598,897 ÷ 700] or 83.8% of full capacity [$25,141 ÷ 30,000].

4. With an increase in price of 10%, the average seating rate that would be needed so that the aircraft's NPV = 0 is 76.2%. This is slightly below the most likely capacity of 80% and it is likely that the investment will have a positive NPV. There is some risk that the actual rate will be as low as 70% and the aircraft will have a negative NPV. The company should take the risk and purchase the aircraft.

11-31 continued

Analysis:

The revenue per flight is $25,141 [same as Requirement 3]. Revenue at full capacity with the higher price is $33,000 [$30,000 × 110%]. The required capacity is 76.2% of full capacity [$25,141 ÷ 33,000].

11-33

The old computer system's NPV is $(155,090); the new computer system's NPV is $(339,552). Dinocare should keep the old computer because it has a lower cost over the next five years.

Analysis:

The NPV of keeping the old computer system (before the CCA tax shield) is $(210,612). The NPV of buying the new computer system (before the CCA tax shield) is $(501,401).

Keep Old

Year	0	1	2	3	4	5	NPV
df	1.00000	0.89286	0.79719	0.71178	0.63552	0.56743	
After-tax cash costs		$(60,000)	$(60,000)	$(60,000)	$(60,000)	$(60,000)	
Salvage value						10,000	
Total cash flow	$0	$(60,000)	$(60,000)	$(60,000)	$(60,000)	$(50,000)	
PV	$0	$(53,571)	$(47,832)	$(42,707)	$(38,131)	$(28,371)	$(210,612)

Buy New

Year	0	1	2	3	4	5	NPV
df	1.00000	0.89286	0.79719	0.71178	0.63552	0.56743	
Purchase new	$(500,000)						
Salvage value old	50,000						
After-tax cash costs		$(30,000)	$(30,000)	$(30,000)	$(30,000)	$(30,000)	
Salvage value new						100,000	
Total cash flow	$(450,000)	$(30,000)	$(30,000)	$(30,000)	$(30,000)	$70,000	
PV	$(450,000)	$(26,786)	$(23,916)	$(21,353)	$(19,066)	$39,720	$(501,401)

Notes:

df is $(1/(1.12)^n)$

after-tax cash costs (old): $100,000 × (1 – 0.4); after-tax cash costs (new): $50,000 × (1 – 0.4)

The present value of the remaining CCA tax shield of the old computer (adjusted for its salvage value) is $55,522 [$57,143 – 1,621] for a total NPV of $(155,090) [$(210,612) + $55,522].

$$[(R \times C \times T) \div (R + i)] = [(0.3 \times \$200,000 \times 0.40) \div (0.3 + 0.12)]$$
$$= \$57,143$$

$$[(R \times S \times T) \div (R + i)] \times [1 \div (1 + i)^n] = [(0.3 \times \$10,000 \times 0.40) \div (0.3 + 0.12)] \times [1 \div 1.12^5]$$
$$= \$1,621$$

11-33 continued

The present value of the CCA tax shield of the new computer (with one-half rule and adjusted for its salvage value) is \$118,992 [\$135,204 – 16,212] for a total NPV of \$(382,409) [\$(501,401) + \$118,992].

$$[(R \times C \times T) \div (R + i)] \times [(1 + 0.5i) \div (1 + i)] = [(0.3 \times \$500,000 \times 0.40) \div (0.3 + 0.12)]$$
$$\times [(1 + 0.5 \times 0.12) \div 1.12]$$
$$= \$135,204$$

$$[(R \times S \times T) \div (R + i)] \times [1 \div (1 + i)^n] = [(0.3 \times \$100,000 \times 0.40) \div (0.3 + 0.12)] \times [1 \div 1.12^5]$$
$$= \$16,212$$

If the company buys the new computer system, it will have a remaining tax shield for the old computer based on its unamortized capital cost of \$200,000 less the immediate salvage value of \$50,000. The present value of this tax shield is \$42,857.

$$[(R \times C \times T) \div (R + i)] = [(0.3 \times \$150,000 \times 0.40) \div (0.3 + 0.12)]$$
$$= \$42,857$$

The total NPV of buying the new computer system is \$(339,552) [\$(382,409) + 42,857].

11-35

1. The after-tax cash flows for each alternative are as follows:

   Purchase machine:

Year	Revenues	After-tax Operating costs	CCA tax shield	After-tax Cash flow
1	\$33,000	\$(12,000)	\$4,000	\$25,000
2	33,000	(12,000)	7,200	28,200
3	33,000	(12,000)	5,760	26,760
4	33,000	(12,000)	4,608	25,608
5	33,000	(12,000)	3,686	24,686
6	33,000	(12,000)	2,949	23,949
7	33,000	(12,000)	2,359	23,359
8	33,000	(12,000)	1,887	22,887
9	33,000	(12,000)	1,510	22,510
10	33,000	(12,000)	1,208	22,208

Year	Remaining capital cost	CCA rate	CCA	CCA tax shield
1	\$100,000	0.1	\$10,000	\$4,000
2	90,000	0.2	18,000	7,200
3	72,000	0.2	14,400	5,760
4	57,600	0.2	11,520	4,608
5	46,080	0.2	9,216	3,686
6	36,864	0.2	7,373	2,949
7	29,491	0.2	5,898	2,359
8	23,593	0.2	4,719	1,887
9	18,874	0.2	3,775	1,510
10	15,099	0.2	3,020	1,208

11-35 continued

Note: After-tax revenues are $55,000 × (1 – 0.4); after-tax operating costs are $20,000 × (1 – 0.4).

There is also a cash outflow of $100,000 in year 0 to purchase the machine and a cash inflow of $20,000 at the end of year 10 for the machine's salvage value.

Lease machine (no service contract):

Year	Revenues	After-tax Operating costs	Lease	Cash flow
0			$(12,420)	$(12,420)
1	$33,000	$(12,000)	(12,420)	8,580
2	33,000	(12,000)	(12,420)	8,580
3	33,000	(12,000)	(12,420)	8,580
4	33,000	(12,000)	(12,420)	8,580
5	33,000	(12,000)	(12,420)	8,580
6	33,000	(12,000)	(12,420)	8,580
7	33,000	(12,000)	(12,420)	8,580
8	33,000	(12,000)	(12,420)	8,580
9	33,000	(12,000)	(12,420)	8,580
10	33,000	(12,000)		21,000

Note: After-tax revenues are $55,000 × (1 – 0.4); after-tax operating costs are $20,000 × (1 – 0.4); after-tax lease payments are $20,700 × (1 – 0.4). The first lease payment is due in year 0 and the last at the beginning of year 10.

There is also a cash outflow of $5,000 in year 0 as a deposit on the leased machine and a cash inflow of $5,000 at the end of year 10 for the return of the deposit.

Lease machine (with service contract):

Year	Revenues	After-tax Operating costs	Lease	Tax shield	After-tax Cash flow
0			$(12,420)		$(12,420)
1	$33,000	$(6,000)	(12,420)	$1,200	15,780
2	33,000	$(6,000)	(12,420)	1,200	15,780
3	33,000	$(6,000)	(12,420)	1,200	15,780
4	33,000	$(6,000)	(12,420)	1,200	15,780
5	33,000	$(6,000)	(12,420)	1,200	15,780
6	33,000	$(6,000)	(12,420)	1,200	15,780
7	33,000	$(6,000)	(12,420)	1,200	15,780
8	33,000	$(6,000)	(12,420)	1,200	15,780
9	33,000	$(6,000)	(12,420)	1,200	15,780
10	33,000	$(6,000)		1,200	28,200

Note: After-tax revenues are $55,000 × (1 – 0.4); after-tax operating costs are $10,000 × (1 – 0.4); after-tax lease payments are $20,700 × (1 – 0.4). The first lease payment is due in year 0 and the last at the beginning of year 10.

There is also a cash outflow of $5,000 in year 0 as a deposit on the leased machine and a cash inflow of $5,000 at the end of year 10 for the return of the deposit.

There is a cash outflow in year 0 of $30,000 for the service contract. The contract is amortized at $3,000 per year [$30,000 ÷ 10]; with a tax shield of $1,200 per year [$3,000 × 40%].

11-35 continued

2. The NPV of the purchase alternative is $37,824. The NPV of the lease alternative (without service contract) is $32,033. Moore should purchase the machine because it is has a higher net present value. Revenues and operating costs are not included in the analysis because these items are the same regardless of the decision and therefore not relevant.

Analysis:

Purchase machine:

Year	Cash flow	df	PV
0	$(100,000)	1.00000	$(100,000)
1	25,000	0.87719	21,930
2	28,200	0.76947	21,699
3	26,760	0.67497	18,062
4	25,608	0.59208	15,162
5	24,686	0.51937	12,821
6	23,949	0.45559	10,911
7	23,359	0.39964	9,335
8	22,887	0.35056	8,023
9	22,510	0.30751	6,922
10	42,208	0.26974	11,385
NPV			$ 36,251

Note: df is $(1/(1.14)^n)$.

There is also a remaining CCA tax shield effect to consider and the reduction in tax shield from the salvage at the end of year 10.

The remaining capital cost at the end of year 10 is $12,079 [$15,099 – 3,020] with a present value of the CCA tax shield of $2,842.

$$[(R \times C \times T) \div (R + i)] = [(0.2 \times \$12,079 \times 0.40) \div (0.2 + 0.14]$$
$$= \$2,842$$

The reduction in the CCA tax shield from the $20,000 has a present value of $1,269.

$$[(R \times S \times T) \div (R + i)] \times [1 \div (1 + i)^n] = [(0.2 \times \$20,000 \times 0.40) \div (0.2 + 0.14)] \times [1 \div 1.14^{10}]$$
$$= \$1,269$$

Summary:

NPV of cash flows	$36,251
Remaining CCA tax shield	2,842
Reduction from salvage	(1,269)
Total NPV	$37,824

11-35 continued

Lease machine (no service contract):

Year	Cash flow	df	PV
0	$(17,420)	1.00000	$(17,420)
1	8,580	0.87719	7,526
2	8,580	0.76947	6,602
3	8,580	0.67497	5,791
4	8,580	0.59208	5,080
5	8,580	0.51937	4,456
6	8,580	0.45559	3,909
7	8,580	0.39964	3,429
8	8,580	0.35056	3,008
9	8,580	0.30751	2,638
10	26,000	0.26974	7,013
NPV			$32,033

Note: df is $(1/(1.14)^n)$.

3. The NPV of the lease alternative with the service contract is $39,589. This is now the alternative with the highest NPV and should be chosen by Moore. Revenues are not included in the analysis because this item is the same regardless of the decision made.

Analysis:

Year	Cash flow	df	PV
0	$(47,420)	1.00000	$(47,420)
1	15,780	0.87719	13,842
2	15,780	0.76947	12,142
3	15,780	0.67497	10,651
4	15,780	0.59208	9,343
5	15,780	0.51937	8,196
6	15,780	0.45559	7,189
7	15,780	0.39964	6,306
8	15,780	0.35056	5,532
9	15,780	0.30751	4,852
10	33,200	0.26974	8,955
NPV			$39,589

Note: df is $(1/(1.14)^n)$.

11-37

1. The old system's NPV is $(1,113,094); the flexible system's NPV is $(1,364,135).

    Analysis:

    Old system

Year	Cash flows	Tax shield	Total	df	PV
1	$(231,000)	34,000	$(197,000)	0.89286	$ (175,893)
2	(231,000)	34,000	(197,000)	0.79719	(157,047)
3	(231,000)	34,000	(197,000)	0.71178	(140,221)
4	(231,000)	34,000	(197,000)	0.63552	(125,197)
5	(231,000)	34,000	(197,000)	0.56743	(111,783)
6	(231,000)	34,000	(197,000)	0.50663	(99,806)
7	(231,000)	34,000	(197,000)	0.45235	(89,113)
8	(231,000)	34,000	(197,000)	0.40388	(79,565)
9	(231,000)	34,000	(197,000)	0.36061	(71,040)
10	(231,000)	34,000	(197,000)	0.32197	(63,429)
NPV					$(1,113,094)

    Notes:

    Cash flows (after-tax): $350,000 \times (1 - 0.34)$

    Tax shield: $100,000 \times 0.34$

    df: $(1/(1.12)^n)$

    Flexible system

Year	Cash flows	Tax shield	Total	df	PV
0	$(1,250,000)		$(1,250,000)	1.00000	$(1,250,000)
1	(62,700)	42,500	(20,200)	0.89286	(18,036)
2	(62,700)	42,500	(20,200)	0.79719	(16,103)
3	(62,700)	42,500	(20,200)	0.71178	(14,378)
4	(62,700)	42,500	(20,200)	0.63552	(12,837)
5	(62,700)	42,500	(20,200)	0.56743	(11,462)
6	(62,700)	42,500	(20,200)	0.50663	(10,234)
7	(62,700)	42,500	(20,200)	0.45235	(9,137)
8	(62,700)	42,500	(20,200)	0.40388	(8,158)
9	(62,700)	42,500	(20,200)	0.36061	(7,284)
10	(62,700)	42,500	(20,200)	0.32197	(6,504)
NPV					$(1,364,135)

    Notes:

    Cash flows (after-tax): $95,000 \times (1 - 0.34)$

    Tax shield: straight-line amortization $125,000 [$1,250,000 ÷ 10]; tax shield $125,000 \times 0.34$

    df: $(1/(1.12)^n)$

11-37 continued

2. When adjusted for inflation, the old system's NPV is $(1,379,665); the flexible system's NPV is $(1,436,490).
    Analysis:
    Old system

Year	Cash flows	Tax shield	Total	df	PV
1	$(240,240)	34,000	$(206,240)	0.89286	$ (184,143)
2	(249,850)	34,000	(215,850)	0.79719	(172,074)
3	(259,844)	34,000	(225,844)	0.71178	(160,751)
4	(270,237)	34,000	(236,237)	0.63552	(150,133)
5	(281,047)	34,000	(247,047)	0.56743	(140,181)
6	(292,289)	34,000	(258,289)	0.50663	(130,857)
7	(303,980)	34,000	(269,980)	0.45235	(122,125)
8	(316,139)	34,000	(282,139)	0.40388	(113,951)
9	(328,785)	34,000	(294,785)	0.36061	(106,302)
10	(341,936)	34,000	(307,936)	0.32197	(99,147)
NPV					$(1,379,665)

Notes:

Cash flows (after-tax): $350,000 \times (1 - 0.34) \times (1.04)^n$

Tax shield: $100,000 \times 0.34$

df: $(1/(1.12)^n)$

Flexible system

Year	Cash flows	Tax shield	Total	df	PV
0	$(1,250,000)		$(1,250,000)	1.00000	$(1,250,000)
1	(65,208)	42,500	(22,708)	0.89286	(20,275)
2	(67,816)	42,500	(25,316)	0.79719	(20,182)
3	(70,529)	42,500	(28,029)	0.71178	(19,950)
4	(73,350)	42,500	(30,850)	0.63552	(19,606)
5	(76,284)	42,500	(33,784)	0.56743	(19,170)
6	(79,336)	42,500	(36,836)	0.50663	(18,662)
7	(82,509)	42,500	(40,009)	0.45235	(18,098)
8	(85,809)	42,500	(43,309)	0.40388	(17,492)
9	(89,242)	42,500	(46,742)	0.36061	(16,856)
10	(92,811)	42,500	(50,311)	0.32197	(16,199)
NPV					$(1,436,490)

Cash flows (after-tax): $95,000 \times (1 - 0.34) \times (1.04)^n$

Tax shield: straight-line amortization $125,000 [$1,250,000 ÷ 10]; tax shield $125,000 \times 0.34$

df: $(1/(1.12)^n)$

3. It is important to adjust cash flows for inflationary effects. The company's required rate of return includes an inflationary component; the future cash flows should also be adjusted for expected increases.

11-39

1. The new system's NPV is $91,572 [NPV of cash flows, $(85,972) + CCA tax shield, $177,544].

   Analysis:

Year	Initial cost	Cost savings	df	PV
0	$(860,000)		1.00000	$(860,000)
1		178,200	0.86207	153,621
2		178,200	0.74316	132,432
3		178,200	0.64066	114,165
4		178,200	0.55229	98,418
5		178,200	0.47611	84,843
6		178,200	0.41044	73,141
7		178,200	0.35383	63,052
8		178,200	0.30503	54,356
NPV				$ (85,972)

   df is $(1/(1.16)^n)$.

   Cost savings (after-tax): $270,000 \times (1 - 0.34)$

   CCA tax shield:

   $$[(R \times C \times T) \div (R + i)] \times [(1 + 0.5i) \div (1 + i)] = [(0.3 \times \$860,000 \times 0.34) \div (0.3 + 0.16)] \times [(1 + 0.5 \times 0.16) \div 1.16]$$
   $$= \$177,544$$

2. The new system's NPV with the new information is $(13,377) [NPV of cash flows, $(203,308) + CCA tax shield, $189,931]. Based on this new information, the company did not make the right decision. The project has a negative NPV and is not earning the company's minimum return.

   Analysis:

Year	Initial cost	Cost savings	df	PV
0	$(920,000)		1.00000	$(920,000)
1		165,000	0.86207	142,241
2		165,000	0.74316	122,622
3		165,000	0.64066	105,709
4		165,000	0.55229	91,128
5		165,000	0.47611	78,559
6		165,000	0.41044	67,723
7		165,000	0.35383	58,382
8		165,000	0.30503	50,329
NPV				$(203,308)

   df is $(1/(1.16)^n)$.

   Revised initial cost: $860,000 + 60,000$

   Revised cost savings (after-tax): $(\$270,000 - 20,000) \times (1 - 0.34)$

   CCA tax shield:

   $$[(R \times C \times T) \div (R + i)] \times [(1 + 0.5i) \div (1 + i)] = [(0.3 \times \$920,000 \times 0.34) \div (0.3 + 0.16)] \times [(1 + 0.5 \times 0.16) \div 1.16]$$
   $$= \$189,931$$

11-39 continued

3.   The increase in revenue of $100,000 will produce additional after tax cash flows of $66,000 per year [$100,000 × (1 – 0.34)]. The present value of these cash flows is $286,677. This additional present value makes the project's NPV positive and acceptable. [The company should also consider the additional variable costs to earn this additional revenue.]

Analysis:

Year	After-tax revenue	df	PV
1	$66,000	0.86207	$ 56,897
2	66,000	0.74316	49,049
3	66,000	0.64066	42,283
4	66,000	0.55229	36,451
5	66,000	0.47611	31,423
6	66,000	0.41044	27,089
7	66,000	0.35383	23,353
8	66,000	0.30503	20,132
Total			$286,677

df is $(1/(1.16)^n)$.

4.   A postaudit is beneficial to Rutherford because Rutherford can use the postaudit to assess whether its resources are being used effectively.

Rutherford may find that additional resources ought to be invested or that it should take corrective action to improve the performance of the investment. The postaudit may signal the need to abandon the project or replace it with a more viable alternative.

Managers may obtain information from a postaudit that they can use to improve their future capital investment decisions – improved understanding of the costs and benefits of a project.

Postaudits can be used to hold managers accountable for the results of their capital investment decisions.

11-41

1.   The after-tax cash flows for each alternative are:

	Overhaul Service		Diesel Service	
	Before-tax	After-tax	Before-tax	After-tax
Year 0 – investment	$(280,000)	$(280,000)	$(420,000)	$(420,000)
Years 1 – 10:				
Revenues	$120,000	$72,000	$250,000	$150,000
Labour costs	(24,000)	(14,400)	(30,000)	(18,000)
Material costs	(20,190)	(12,114)	(100,000)	(60,000)
Amortization tax shield	28,000	11,200	42,000	16,800
Total	$103,810	$56,686	$162,000	$ 88,800

After-tax = Before-tax × (1 – 0.4).

Amortization: overhaul service, $280,000 ÷ 10; diesel service, $420,000 ÷ 10

Amortization tax shield: overhaul service, $28,000 × 0.4; diesel service, $42,000 × 0.4

11-41 continued

2. The overhaul service's NPV is $(6,024) and its IRR is 15.4%; the diesel service's NPV is $9,191 and its IRR is 16.6%. The diesel service has a larger NPV and IRR and should be chosen.

   In this case, NPV and IRR signal the same decision. This will not always be the case – IRR does not always signal the more profitable project.

   Analysis:

   NPV

		Overhaul Service		Diesel Service	
Year	df	Cash flow	PV	Cash flow	PV
0	1.00000	$(280,000)	$(280,000)	$(420,000)	$(420,000)
1	0.86207	56,686	48,867	88,800	76,552
2	0.74316	56,686	42,127	88,800	65,993
3	0.64066	56,686	36,316	88,800	56,890
4	0.55229	56,686	31,307	88,800	49,043
5	0.47611	56,686	26,989	88,800	42,279
6	0.41044	56,686	23,266	88,800	36,447
7	0.35383	56,686	20,057	88,800	31,420
8	0.30503	56,686	17,291	88,800	27,086
9	0.26295	56,686	14,906	88,800	23,350
10	0.22668	56,686	12,850	88,800	20,130
NPV			$ (6,024)		$ 9,191

   $df = (1/(1.16)^n)$

11-41 continued

IRR

The overhaul service's discount factor is 4.9395 [$280,000 ÷ 56,686]; the diesel service's discount factor is 4.7298 [$420,000 ÷ 88,800].

The discount factor is $(1 \div (1 + i)) + (1 \div (1 + i)^2) + (1 \div (1 + i)^3) + \ldots + (1 \div (1 + i)^9) + (1 \div (1 + i)^{10})$.

This can be solved by trial and error, using a financial calculator, or spreadsheet function. By trial and error:

i	15%	16%	15.5%	16.5%	15.4%	16.6%
Year						
1	0.86957	0.86207	0.86580	0.85837	0.86655	0.85763
2	0.75614	0.74316	0.74961	0.73680	0.75091	0.73553
3	0.65752	0.64066	0.64901	0.63244	0.65070	0.63082
4	0.57175	0.55229	0.56192	0.54287	0.56387	0.54101
5	0.49718	0.47611	0.48651	0.46598	0.48862	0.46399
6	0.43233	0.41044	0.42122	0.39999	0.42341	0.39793
7	0.37594	0.35383	0.36469	0.34334	0.36691	0.34128
8	0.32690	0.30503	0.31575	0.29471	0.31795	0.29269
9	0.28426	0.26295	0.27338	0.25297	0.27552	0.25102
10	0.24718	0.22668	0.23669	0.21714	0.23875	0.21529
df	5.01877	4.83323	4.92458	4.74460	4.94319	4.72720

The overhaul service's IRR is 15.4%; the diesel service's IRR is 16.6%.

3. The diesel service's NPV with CCA instead of straight-line amortization is $14,889. Its NPV changed by $5,698 [$14,889 – $9,191].

Analysis:

Diesel service
annual after-tax cash
flows

	Before-tax	After-tax
Revenues	$250,000	$150,000
Labour costs	(30,000)	(18,000)
Material costs	(100,000)	(60,000)
Total	$120,000	$ 72,000

NPV

Year	df	Cash flow	PV
0	1.00000	$(420,000)	$(420,000)
1	0.86207	72,000	62,069
2	0.74316	72,000	53,508
3	0.64066	72,000	46,127
4	0.55229	72,000	39,765
5	0.47611	72,000	34,280
6	0.41044	72,000	29,552
7	0.35383	72,000	25,476
8	0.30503	72,000	21,962
9	0.26295	72,000	18,933
10	0.22668	72,000	16,321
NPV			$ (72,008)

11-41 continued

CCA tax shield:

$$[(R \times C \times T) \div (R + i)] \times [(1 + 0.5i) \div (1 + i)] \; = \; [(0.2 \times \$420{,}000 \times 0.40) \div (0.2 + 0.16)]$$
$$\times\, [(1 + 0.5 \times 0.16) \div 1.16]$$
$$= \; \$86{,}897$$

The diesel service's total NPV is $14,889 [$(72,008) + $86,897].

11-43

1. The old system's NPV is $21,525,759; the CAM system's NPV is $7,664,068. Meikle should keep its old system because it has a higher NPV.

    Analysis:

    The old system has after-tax cash flows of $4,800,000 per year except for year 10 – year 10's cash flow is $4,560,000 because it will not have an amortization tax shield.

Revenues	$30,000,000	[100,000 × $300]
Costs	22,400,000	[100,000 × ($80 + 90 + 20 + 40 – 6)]
Operating cash flow	$ 7,600,000	
After-tax	4,560,000	[$7,600,000 × (1 – 0.40)]
Amortization tax shield	240,000	[100,000 × $6 × 40%]
Total after-tax cash flow	$ 4,800,000	

The old system's NPV is $21,525,759.

Year	Cash flow	df	PV
0	$ 0	1.00000	$ 0
1	4,800,000	0.84746	4,067,797
2	4,800,000	0.71818	3,447,285
3	4,800,000	0.60863	2,921,428
4	4,800,000	0.51579	2,475,787
5	4,800,000	0.43711	2,098,124
6	4,800,000	0.37043	1,778,071
7	4,800,000	0.31393	1,506,840
8	4,800,000	0.26604	1,276,983
9	4,800,000	0.22546	1,082,189
10	4,560,000	0.19106	871,254
NPV			$21,525,759

df is $(1/(1.18)^n)$.

11-43 continued

The CAM system will have after-tax cash flows of $12,840,000 per year.

Revenues	$30,000,000	[100,000 × $300]
Direct materials cost	6,000,000	[100,000 × $80 × 75%]
Direct labour costs	3,000,000	[100,000 × $90 × 1/3]
Volume-related overhead	1,500,000	[100,000 × ($20 – 5)]
Direct fixed overhead	1,700,000	[100,000 × ($40 – 6 – 17)]
Operating cash flow	$17,800,000	
After-tax	10,680,000	[$17,800,000 × (1 – 0.40)]
Amortization tax shield	2,160,000	
Total after-tax cash flow	$12,840,000	

The CAM system's amortization (straight-line) is $5,400,000 per year [($34,000,000 + 20,000,000) ÷ 10]. Its amortization tax shield is $2,160,000 per year [$5,400,000 × 40%].

Meikle will also have a loss of $2,400,000 on the sale of the old system [$6,000,000 – (100,000 × $6) – 3,000,000]. This will create a tax shield of $960,000 in year 0 [$2,400,000 × 40%].

The CAM system's NPV is $7,664,068.

Year	Cash flow	df	PV
0	$(50,040,000)	1.00000	$(50,040,000)
1	12,840,000	0.84746	10,881,356
2	12,840,000	0.71818	9,221,488
3	12,840,000	0.60863	7,814,820
4	12,840,000	0.51579	6,622,729
5	12,840,000	0.43711	5,612,482
6	12,840,000	0.37043	4,756,341
7	12,840,000	0.31393	4,030,797
8	12,840,000	0.26604	3,415,930
9	12,840,000	0.22546	2,894,856
10	12,840,000	0.19106	2,453,268
NPV			$ 7,664,068

Year 0's cash flow is an outflow of $50,040,000 [$54,000,000 – 3,000,000 – 960,000].

df is $(1/(1.18)^n)$.

11-43 continued

2. With a discount rate of 12%, the old system's NPV is $27,043,797; the CAM system's NPV is $22,508,864. Meikle should still keep its old system but the difference is much smaller.

Analysis:

Old system

Year	Cash flow	df	PV
0	$ 0	1.00000	$ 0
1	4,800,000	0.89286	4,285,714
2	4,800,000	0.79719	3,826,531
3	4,800,000	0.71178	3,416,545
4	4,800,000	0.63552	3,050,487
5	4,800,000	0.56743	2,723,649
6	4,800,000	0.50663	2,431,829
7	4,800,000	0.45235	2,171,276
8	4,800,000	0.40388	1,938,639
9	4,800,000	0.36061	1,730,928
10	4,560,000	0.32197	1,468,198
NPV			$27,043,797

df is $(1/(1.12)^n)$.

CAM system

Year	Cash flow	df	PV
0	$(50,040,000)	1.00000	$(50,040,000)
1	12,840,000	0.89286	11,464,286
2	12,840,000	0.79719	10,235,969
3	12,840,000	0.71178	9,139,258
4	12,840,000	0.63552	8,160,052
5	12,840,000	0.56743	7,285,761
6	12,840,000	0.50663	6,505,144
7	12,840,000	0.45235	5,808,164
8	12,840,000	0.40388	5,185,861
9	12,840,000	0.36061	4,630,233
10	12,840,000	0.32197	4,134,136
NPV			$22,508,864

df is $(1/(1.12)^n)$.

11-43 continued

3. The old system's NPV, with declining sales, is $13,676,098. With this new analysis, the CAM system is more attractive because it has a larger NPV.

Analysis:

The product's contribution margin is $110 per unit [$300 – (80 – 90 – 20)] or $66 after-tax [$110 × (1 – 0.40)]. Meikle has $3,400,000 fixed cash costs (not including amortization) [100,000 × ($40 – 6)] or $2,040,000 after-tax [$3,400,000 × (1 – 0.40)]. Meikle has an amortization tax shield of $240,000 for years 1 through 9. The new after-tax cash flows have a net present value of $13,676,098.

Year	Units	Cont	Fixed	Tax shield	Total	df	PV
1	100,000	$6,600,000	$(2,040,000)	$240,000	4,800,000	0.89286	$ 4,285,714
2	90,000	5,940,000	(2,040,000)	240,000	4,140,000	0.79719	3,300,383
3	80,000	5,280,000	(2,040,000)	240,000	3,480,000	0.71178	2,476,995
4	70,000	4,620,000	(2,040,000)	240,000	2,820,000	0.63552	1,792,161
5	60,000	3,960,000	(2,040,000)	240,000	2,160,000	0.56743	1,225,642
6	50,000	3,300,000	(2,040,000)	240,000	1,500,000	0.50663	759,947
7	40,000	2,640,000	(2,040,000)	240,000	840,000	0.45235	379,973
8	30,000	1,980,000	(2,040,000)	240,000	180,000	0.40388	72,699
9	20,000	1,320,000	(2,040,000)	240,000	(480,000)	0.36061	(173,093)
10	10,000	660,000	(2,040,000)	0	(1,380,000)	0.32197	(444,323)
NPV							$13,676,098

df is $(1/(1.12)^n)$.

4. With the salvage value for the CAM system, its NPV is $22,892,721. The old system's NPV is the same as in Requirement 3, $13,676,098. Meikle should invest in the CAM system because it has a higher NPV.

Analysis:

The salvage value of $4,000,000 will change the amortization each year and increase the cash flows in year 10 by $4,000,000.

The CAM system's amortization (straight-line) is now $5,000,000 per year [($34,000,000 + 20,000,000 – 4,000,000) ÷ 10]. Its amortization tax shield is $2,000,000 per year [$5,400,000 × 40%] – a difference of $160,000 [$2,160,000 – 2,000,000].

The change in cash flows will have a NPV of $383,857 – making the CAM system's NPV $22,892,721 [$22,508,864 + 383,857].

Year	Cash flow	df	PV
1	$(160,000)	0.89286	$ (142,857)
2	(160,000)	0.79719	(127,551)
3	(160,000)	0.71178	(113,885)
4	(160,000)	0.63552	(101,683)
5	(160,000)	0.56743	(90,788)
6	(160,000)	0.50663	(81,061)
7	(160,000)	0.45235	(72,376)
8	(160,000)	0.40388	(64,621)
9	(160,000)	0.36061	(57,698)
10	3,840,000	0.32197	1,236,377
NPV			$ 383,857

df is $(1/(1.12)^n)$.

11-43 continued

5. It is important to use accurate inputs for assessing capital investments in CAM systems. Requirement 2 illustrates the importance of using appropriate discount rates. The high rate of 18% negatively affects the CAM system (which requires a large initial investment) – the CAM system is more attractive when the company's cost of capital is used. In Requirement 3, we see the importance of including indirect and intangible effects – the decline in competitiveness if the new system is not adopted has a significant effect on the relative merits of the alternatives – and in favour of the CAM system. Including the salvage value of the CAM system further increases its edge over the old system.

MANAGERIAL DECISION CASES

11-45

A student should discuss the following points in answer to this question:

- The lower bid meets all the requirements of the company – implied by the statement that Manny would normally have taken the first bid.

- Manny seems to be acting on friendship – offering to let Todd revise his bid – and personal interest. He is not maintaining objectivity and integrity in performing his duties.

- The main standard of ethical conduct that Manny is violating is allowing his friendship with Todd and Todd's offer of a job for Manny's son and a vacation trip to influence his decision – a decision that may not be in his employer's best interests. If Manny awards the contract to Todd and accepts his favours, then Manny's behaviour is clearly unethical.

- Manny may have legitimate concerns about the lower bid – such as ability to deliver or quality of the system – but he should not have contacted Todd to allow him to match the offer.

CHAPTER 12

INVENTORY MANAGEMENT

ANSWERS TO ODD-NUMBERED QUESTIONS FOR WRITING AND DISCUSSION

1. Ordering costs are the costs of placing and receiving an order. Examples include the costs of processing an order (clerical costs and documents), the cost of insurance for shipment, and unloading costs.

3. Carrying costs are the costs of carrying inventory. Examples include insurance, obsolescence, the opportunity cost of funds tied up in inventory, handling costs, and storage space.

5. Minimizing ordering costs favours large, infrequent orders and causes larger inventories. Larger inventories result in larger carrying costs (for insurance, funds invested in inventory, storage costs, etc.).

7. The economic order quantity is the amount that should be ordered (or produced) to minimize the total ordering (or setup) and carrying costs.

9. Safety stock is used to deal with demand uncertainty by carrying extra inventory as insurance against fluctuations in demand. It is the difference between maximum demand and average demand multiplied by the lead time. With safety stock, if maximum demand is experienced, the company will have sufficient inventory on hand to fill all orders.

11. Long-term contractual relationships with suppliers can reduce the acquisition cost of raw materials by reducing the number of orders and ordering costs. With continuous replenishment (and EDI), the supplier assumes the inventory management function for the purchaser. Suppliers may offer lower prices in exchange for long-term purchase commitments.

13. The JIT approach to inventory management deals with the problem of shutdowns by emphasizing total preventative maintenance, total quality control, and close relationships with suppliers to ensure on-time delivery of shipments. These strategies address the primary causes of shutdowns – machine failure, defective production, and unavailability of raw materials or parts.

15. Constraints are a company's limiting factors. An internal constraint is a limiting factor found within a company – such as machine capacity. An external constraint is a limiting factor imposed on the company from external sources – such as market demand.

17. The three measures of organizational performance used by the theory of constraints are throughput, inventory, and operating expenses. Throughput is the rate at which an organization generates money through sales. Inventory is the money the organization spends in turning raw materials into throughput. Operating expenses are all the money an organization spends in turning inventory into throughput. Management's objectives are to increase

19. The five steps used by the theory of constraints to improve organizational performance are (1) identify the organization's constraints, (2) exploit the binding constraints, (3) subordinate everything else to the decisions made in step 2, (4) elevate the binding constraints, and (5) repeat the process.

SOLUTIONS TO ODD-NUMBERED EXERCISES, PROBLEMS, AND CASES

EXERCISES

12-1

1. Snowgo's annual ordering cost is $3,000 [12 × $250].

2. Snowgo's annual carrying cost is $12,000 [(4,000 ÷ 2) × $6].

3. The cost of Snowgo's current inventory policy is $15,000 [$3,000 + 12,000].

12-3

1. Quito's EOQ is 12,000 litres.

   Analysis:

   EOQ = $\sqrt{2PD/C}$ where P is cost per order, D is demand, C carrying cost per litre
       = $\sqrt{2 \times \$5 \times 720,000/\$0.05}$
       = 12,000 litres

2. Quito's annual ordering cost is $300 [(720,000 ÷ 12,000) × $5]; Quito's annual carrying cost is $300 [(12,000 ÷ 2 × $0.50].

12-5

1. Power's EOQ is 18,000 lawn mower engines.

   Analysis:

   EOQ = $\sqrt{2PD/C}$ where P is cost per setup, D is demand, C carrying cost per engine
       = $\sqrt{2 \times \$2,000 \times 162,000/\$2}$
       = 18,000 lawn mower engines

2. Power's setup cost for lawn mower engines is $18,000 [(162,000 ÷ 18,000) × $2,000]; Power's carrying cost for lawn mower engines is $18,000 [(18,000 ÷ 2) × $2]. Power's total setup cost and carrying cost is $36,000 [$18,000 + 18,000].

3. Power's reorder point for lawn mower engines is 7,128 engines [648 × 11].

4. Power's EOQ is 20,000 jet-ski engines.

   Analysis:

   EOQ = $\sqrt{2PD/C}$ where P is cost per setup, D is demand, C carrying cost per engine
       = $\sqrt{2 \times \$2,400 \times 250,000/\$3}$
       = 20,000 jet-ski engines

Power's setup cost for jet-ski engines is $30,000 [(250,000 ÷ 20,000) × $2,400]; Power's carrying cost for jet-ski engines is $30,000 [(20,000 ÷ 2) × $3]. Power's total setup cost and carrying cost is $60,000 [$30,000 + 30,000].

12-5 continued

Notes: *Power's average sales of jet-ski engines is 1,000 [250,000 ÷ 250], not 500 as stated in the question.*

The solution to Power's EOQ problem requires 12.5 setups [250,000 ÷ 20,000]. It is not possible to have a fraction of a setup – Power will either have 12 or 13 setups in the year. If it uses 12 setups, its total cost is $60,050 [12 × $2,400 + (250,000 ÷ 12) ÷ 2 × $3]. If it uses 13 setups, its total cost is $60,046 [13 × $2,400 + (250,000 ÷ 13) ÷ 2 × $3].

Power's reorder point for jet-ski engines is 12,000 engines [1,000 × 12].

5. Lawnmowers require 9 batches per year [162,000 ÷ 18,000] and each batch requires 11 days – 9 workdays [18,000 ÷ 2,000] plus 2 days setup time – for a total time of 99 days [9 × 11].

   Jet-skis require 12 (or 13) batches per year [250,000 ÷ 20,000; see note in Requirement 4] and each batch requires an average of 12.5 days – 10.5 workdays [250,000 ÷ 12 ÷ 2,000] plus 2 days setup time – for a total time of 150 days.

   The total time required to produce the scheduled production is 249 days [99 +150]. Power has 250 days available and can produce the amount that can be sold of each engine.

   Power must develop a production schedule that coordinates production, inventory usage, and sales.

   This is a push system because the production of engines is determined by anticipated demand rather than current demand.

12-7

Pinegar's reorder point is 5,250 units with a safety stock of 750 units.

Analysis:

Reorder point without safety stock	4,500	[6 × 750]
Safety stock	750	[6 × (875 – 750)]
Reorder point with safety stock	5,250	

12-9

1. A withdrawal Kanban controls movement of work through the manufacturing process – it specifies the quantity that a subsequent process should withdraw from the preceding process.

2. A production Kanban specifies the quantity that the preceding process should produce.

3. A vendor Kanban controls movement of parts between outside suppliers and the processes. It is used to notify suppliers to the quantity of parts to deliver and the time of delivery.

12-11

1. Marvel should sell only Type II because it has the highest contribution margin for the limited machine capacity. It can produce 100,000 units of Type II [20,000 ÷ 0.2]. Marvel's contribution margin for this product mix is $1,600,000 [20,000 × $80.00 or 100,000 × $16.00].

   Analysis:

	Type I	Type II	Type III
Selling price	$40.00	$60.00	$75.00
Variable cost per unit	20.00	44.00	34.00
Contribution margin per unit	$20.00	$16.00	$41.00
Machine hours per unit	0.50	0.20	1.50
Contribution margin per machine hour	$40.00	$80.00	$27.33

2. Marvel should produce 75,000 units of Type II, using 15,000 hours [75,000 × 0.2]. Marvel has 5,000 hours remaining [20,000 – 15,000] and can produce 10,000 units of Type I, the product with the next highest contribution margin for the limited machine capacity [5,000 ÷ 0.50]. Marvel's contribution margin for this product mix is $1,400,000 [15,000 × $80.00 + 5,000 × $40.00 or 75,000 × $16.00 + 10,000 × $20.00].

12-13

1. e

2. a

3. d

4. c

PROBLEMS

12-15

1. Parry's EOQ is 600 packages and its reorder point is 80 packages. Its total ordering and carrying cost is $2,190.

   Analysis:

   $$EOQ = \sqrt{2PD/C} \text{ where P is cost per order, D is demand, C carrying cost per package}$$
   $$= \sqrt{2 \times \$90 \times 7,300/\$3.65}$$
   $$= 600 \text{ packages}$$

   Parry's reorder point is 80 [20 × 4].

   Using its EOQ, Parry's cost of ordering is $1,095 [7,300 ÷ 600 × $90]; Parry's cost of carrying inventory is $1,095 [600 ÷ 2 × $3.65]; Parry's total ordering and carrying cost is $2,190 [$1,095 + 1,095].

2. Parry should carry a safety stock of 40 packages [(30 – 20) × 4] with a new reorder point of 120 [80 + 40]. Its cost of ordering is still $1,095 but its cost of carrying inventory is now $1,241 [40 + (600 ÷ 2) × $3.65] for a total ordering and carrying cost of $2,336 [$1,095 + 1,241].

12-17

1. Old Orchard Battery Distributor's expected demand during the lead-time is 400 units.

   Analysis:

Demand	Probability	Demand × Probability
100	0.03	3
200	0.05	10
300	0.20	60
400	0.40	160
500	0.25	125
600	0.07	42
Average		400

2. A reorder point equal to the maximum demand of 600 units during the lead-time will minimize stockouts. If the reorder point is 600 units, the new batteries will always arrive before the inventory is gone.

3. The probability of a stockout with a reorder point of 400 is 32% - this is the probability of demand greater than 400 units during the lead-time.

   Analysis:

Demand	Probability
500	0.25
600	0.07
	0.32

12-19

1. Morning Beverages should produce zero units of Rich Instant and 800,000 units of Diet Instant [800,000 ÷ 1] because Diet Instant has a higher contribution margin per hour of the limited machine time. Morning Beverages will earn a total contribution of $1,200,000 [800,000 × $1.50].

	Rich Instant	Diet Instant
Unit selling price	$5.00	$6.00
Unit variable cost	3.00	4.50
Unit contribution margin	$2.00	$1.50
Machine hours per unit	2.00	1.00
Contribution margin per machine hour	$1.00	$1.50

2. With a maximum demand of 600,000 units of Diet Instant, Morning Beverages should produce 600,000 units of it (using 600,000 machines hours) and produce 100,000 units of Rich Instant with the remaining time [(800,000 − 600,000) ÷ 2]. Morning Beverages will earn a total contribution of $1,100,000 [600,000 × $1.50 + $100,000 × $2.00].

12-21

1. Covey requires 18,000 minutes per day to produce the daily demand for Part A and 45,000 minutes per day to produce the daily demand for Part B. the total time required is 63,000 minutes.

    The major internal constraint Covey faces is the available time in the moulding department. Covey requires 13,000 minutes but only 8,640 minutes are available – a shortfall of 4,360 minutes [13,000 – 8,640]. Covey has excess capacity in the grinding and finishing departments.

    Analysis:

	Part A	Part B	Total
Daily demand (units)	300	500	
Minutes in moulding per unit	10	20	
Total minutes in moulding	3,000	10,000	13,000
Minutes in grinding per unit	20	30	
Total minutes in grinding	6,000	15,000	21,000
Minutes in finishing per unit	30	40	
Total minutes in finishing	9,000	20,000	29,000
Total	18,000	45,000	63,000

	Moulding	Grinding	Finishing
Number of workers	24	--	70
Minutes available (workers × 8 hours × 60 minutes)	11,520	24,000	33,600
Setup time (workers × 2 hours × 60 minutes)	(2,880)	--	--
Available	8,640	24,000	36,600
Required	13,000	21,000	29,000

12-21 continued

2. Covey should exploit its major binding constraint by using the moulding capacity to first produce the product that produces the greatest contribution margin per minute of moulding time. Product A's contribution margin per moulding minute is $10 (greater than Product B's $6 per minute). Covey should produce the daily demand of Product A – 300 units – using 3,000 minutes of moulding time [300 × 10]. Covey can use the remaining 5,640 minutes [8,640 – 3,000] to produce 282 units of Product B [5,640 ÷ 20].

    A product mix of 300 units of Product A and 282 units of Product B will maximize daily throughput with a total daily contribution margin of $63,840 [300 × $100 + 282 × $120].

    Analysis:

	Product A	Product B
Selling price	$180	$220
Variable cost	80	100
Contribution margin	$100	$120
Moulding minutes required	10	20
Contribution margin per moulding minute	$ 10	$ 6

3. Reducing the moulding setup time from 1 hour to 10 minutes will increase the moulding department's capacity by 2,400 minutes [(60 – 10) × 2 × 24]. Covey can use this additional time to produce 120 more units of Product B [2,400 ÷ 20] for a total of 402 units [282 +120].

    The new product mix is 300 units of Product A and 402 units of Product B. Covey's daily throughput increases to a contribution margin of $78,240 [300 × $100 + 402 × $120].

12-23

1. If Bountiful can meet daily market demand, it will have a potential daily contribution margin of $14,000. Bountiful requires 8,000 minutes of cutting, 12,000 minutes of welding, 9,000 minutes of polishing, and 7,000 minutes of painting to meet the daily market demand. It cannot do this because welding does not have enough time to complete the required production. Thus welding is the bottleneck or binding constraint.

    Analysis:

	Frame X	Frame Y	Total
Selling price	$ 80	$ 110	
Variable cost	40	50	
Contribution margin per unit	$ 40	$ 60	
Market demand	200	100	
Total contribution margin	$8,000	$6,000	$14,000

	Cutting	Welding	Polishing	Painting
Minutes per unit of Frame X	30	30	30	20
Minutes for 200 units of Frame X	6,000	6,000	6,000	4,000
Minutes per unit of Frame Y	20	60	30	30
Minutes for 100 units of Frame Y	2,000	6,000	3,000	3,000
Total required	8,000	12,000	9,000	7,000
Total available	9,600	9,600	12,480	9,600

12-23 continued

2. Bountiful's optimal product mix is 200 units of Frame X and 60 units of Frame Y. Bountiful should produce all it can sell of Frame X because it has a higher contribution margin per minute of the welding process than Frame Y. Producing 200 units of Frame X will use 6,000 welding minutes [200 × 30], leaving 3,600 minutes to produce Frame Y [9,600 – 6,000]. Bountiful can produce 60 units of Frame Y [3,600 ÷ 60]. Bountiful's daily contribution margin (throughput) is $11,600 [200 × $40 + 60 × $60].

   Analysis:

	Frame X	Frame Y
Contribution margin per unit	$ 40	$ 60
Minutes of welding per unit	30	60
Contribution margin per minute	$1.333	$1.000

3. In a DBR system, welding is the binding constraint or *drummer*. It will set the production rate for the plant – 200 units of Frame X and 60 units of Frame Y.

   To protect the plant's throughput, a time *buffer* of 2-days production is set up in front of the welding process. Two days is the length of time Bountiful's management has determined it will take to correct any production interruptions. The buffer will be 400 cut units for Frame X and 120 cut units for Frame Y [200 × 2; 60 × 2].

   To control the release of materials to the cutting process, a *rope* will tie the cutting process's production to the drummer's rate of 200 units of Frame X and 60 units of Frame Y.

4. Bountiful's redesign of the polishing and welding processes for Frame X will increase Frame X's polishing time by 3,200 minutes [(46 – 30) × 200] and decrease its welding time by 2,000 minutes [(30 – 20) × 200]. Bountiful can produce 33 more units of Frame Y with the released welding time [2,000 ÷ 60].

   Polishing has enough excess capacity to handle the additional demand (200 × 46 + (60 + 33) × 30 = 11,990 < 12,480).

   Bountiful's contribution margin will increase by $1,980 per day [33 × $60]. It will take 10.1 days for Bountiful to recover its investment of $20,000 [$20,000 ÷ 1,980]. This is an attractive investment for the company.

   This proposal represents the fourth step of the TOC process – elevate the binding constraint. The company has found a way to decrease its current use of the binding constraint, freeing time up for other production. Note that a company doesn't need to add new resources to increase its throughput.

MANAGERIAL DECISION CASE

RESEARCH ASSIGNMENT

12-25

Each student's answers will vary depending on his research.

MANAGEMENT ACCOUNTING
CANADIAN SIXTH EDITION
SOLUTIONS MANUAL

CHAPTER 13
BUDGETING FOR PLANNING AND CONTROL

ANSWERS TO ODD-NUMBERED QUESTIONS FOR WRITING AND DISCUSSION

1. Budgets are financial plans for the future. They identify objectives and the actions needed to achieve them. The development of a budget is part of the planning process and the budget is an output of the planning process.

3. All organizations, regardless of size, benefit from effective planning and control. Large and small organizations need to set goals and determine how they will achieve those goals – this is the essence of planning. Large and small organizations need to monitor their actual results and decide whether changes are required – this is the essence of control. For most organizations, budgets are important tools for carrying out their planning and control activities.

5. A master budget is a comprehensive financial plan for the whole organization, and consists of various individual budgets and schedules. The master budget can be divided into operating and financial budgets.

   An operating budget covers the organization's income generating activities – sales, production, and administrative operations. An operating budget often takes the form of a budgeted income statement and supporting schedules.

   Financial budgets detail the inflows and outflows of cash (the cash budget) and the organization's overall financial position (a budgeted balance sheet).

7. All budgets depend on the sales budget in the sense that production and other activities must be consistent with the planned sales activity. A company must produce enough (considering its inventories) to meet its sales targets. In turn, a company must have the necessary materials, labour, and other production inputs to achieve its planned production. In a similar way, a company's selling and administrative activities must articulate with its planned sales. A company's financial budgets are also determined by its operating activities, and thus the sales budget.

9. Static budgets are budgets prepared for particular activity levels – usually the master budget sales and production activities. Flexible budgets are prepared for different activity levels – taking into account cost behaviour and the amount of sales and production activity. Flexible budgets are superior to static budgets for performance reporting because they allow a company to separate the effects of sales and production volume changes from the effects of price and cost changes. This is important information for evaluating company and manager performance and identifying appropriate control actions.

11. Goal congruence is the alignment of a manager's personal goals with those of the organization. Positive behaviour is more likely to occur when the goals of individual managers are aligned with the goals of an organization, and managers are motivated to achieve the organization's goals. Without goal congruence, a manager's goals (and actions) may be in conflict with the organization's goals (and desired actions).

13. Managers respond to both monetary and nonmonetary incentives and both are used by organizations to motivate desirable behaviour. Monetary incentives appeal to managers' economic needs and nonmonetary incentives appeal to their psychological and social needs. A good budgetary system will include both types of incentives.

15. Easy budget targets can lead to diminished performance because managers will not have to exert much effort to achieve the target and will have little incentive to achieve more.

17. A manager may have an incentive to build slack into budgets to make it easier to achieve budget targets (and compensation) and to reduce risk.

19. Multiple measures of performance, financial and nonfinancial, can be used to discourage myopic behaviour. Some measures will take into account long-term perspectives to alleviate the focus on short-term results

21. Across-the-board cuts fail to recognize the activities that are vital to an organization's success and survival. Cuts that are made without formal analysis may impair the ability of units to perform their functions. With scarce resources, an organization must decide what its goals are, and the activities necessary to achieve those goals. Across-the-board cuts are unlikely to achieve this.

23. The primary difference between an activity flexible budget and a functional-based flexible budget is the number of activity drivers used. A functional-based flexible budget usually uses a single (unit-level) activity driver such as the number of units sold or produced. An activity flexible budget uses many (unit-level and nonunit-level) activity drivers with different activity drivers used for different activities.

SOLUTIONS TO ODD-NUMBERED EXERCISES, PROBLEMS, AND CASES

EXERCISES

13-1

1. Fresh-n-Clean's sales budget is:

Detergent	1st Quarter	2nd Quarter	3rd Quarter	4th Quarter	Total
Sales (boxes)	40,000	55,000	62,000	70,000	227,000
Selling price	$ 3.00	$ 3.00	$ 3.00	$ 3.00	$ 3.00
Sales (revenue)	$120,000	$165,000	$186,000	$210,000	$ 681,000
Presoak					
Sales (boxes)	50,000	50,000	60,000	70,000	230,000
Selling price	$ 3.50	$ 3.50	$ 3.50	$ 3.50	$ 3.50
Sales (revenue)	$175,000	$175,000	$210,000	$245,000	$ 805,000
Total sales revenue	$295,000	$340,000	$396,000	$455,000	$1,486,000

2. Fresh-n-Clean can use this sales budget to plan its production budget and the other budget schedules that depend on its sales and production activity (such as direct materials purchases and selling expenses).

   Fresh-n-Clean can use this sales budget for control purposes – each quarter it can compare actual sales (in boxes) and actual sales revenue to its sales budget to see whether its sales activity is meeting its expectations.

13-3

Pretty-Kitty's production budget is:

	January	February	March	Total
Units sold	100,000	120,000	110,000	330,000
Required ending inventory	42,000	38,500	35,000	35,000
Total required	142,000	158,500	145,000	365,000
Beginning inventory	18,000	42,000	38,500	18,000
Units produced	124,000	116,500	106,500	347,000

Notes:

Required ending inventory is 35% of next month's sales [example, January: 35% × 120,000]. March's required ending inventory is 35% of April's sales or 35% × 100,000.

13-5

Carson's production budget is:

	January	February	March	Total
Units sold	200,000	240,000	220,000	660,000
+ Required ending inventory	36,000	33,000	30,000	30,000
Total required	236,000	273,000	250,000	690,000
– Beginning inventory	18,000	36,000	33,000	18,000
Units produced	218,000	237,000	217,000	672,000

Notes:

Required ending inventory is 15% of the next month's sales [example: January = 15% × 240,000].

Required ending inventory for March is 15% of April's budgeted sales; 15% × 200,000.

13-7

Lester's direct labour budget is:

	March	April	May	Total
Budgeted production (rolls)	5,000	25,000	35,000	65,000
Direct labour per roll (hours)	0.03	0.03	0.03	0.03
Total direct labour required for production (hours)	150	750	1,050	1,950
Cost per hour	$8.00	$8.00	$8.00	$8.00
Cost of direct labour	$1,200	$6,000	$8,400	$15,600

13-9

1.

JENNA'S JAMS AND JELLIES
PRODUCTION BUDGET (in units)

	September	October	November	December
Sales	100	150	170	225
Desired ending inventory	30	34	45	20
Total needed	130	184	215	245
Less: beginning inventory	20	30	34	45
Production	110	154	181	200

Notes:

Ending inventory is 20% of next month's sales [example, September's is 20% × 150 = 30]. September's beginning inventory is 20% of its sales [20% × 100].

13-9 continued

2.

JENNA'S JAMS AND JELLIES
PURCHASES BUDGET (in units)

Fruit:	*September*	*October*	*November*
Production	110	154	181
× Kilograms per jar	0.5	0.5	0.5
Needed for production	55	77	91
Desired ending inventory	4	5	5
Needed	59	82	96
Less: beginning inventory	3	4	5
Purchases	56	78	91

Notes:

Ending inventory is 5% of next month's fruit requirements [example, September's is 5% × 77 = 4 (rounded)]
September's beginning inventory is 5% of its production needs [5% × 55 = 3 (rounded)].

Sugar:	*September*	*October*	*November*
Production	110	154	181
× Kilograms per jar	0.5	0.5	0.5
Needed for production	55	77	91
Desired ending inventory	39	46	50
Needed	94	123	141
Less: beginning inventory	28	39	46
Purchases	66	84	95

Notes:

Ending inventory is 50% of next month's requirements [example, September's is 50% × 77 = 39 (rounded)].
September's beginning inventory is 50% of its production needs [50% × 55 = 28 (rounded)].

Pectin:	*September*	*October*	*November*
Production	110	154	181
× Kilograms per jar	0.1	0.1	0.1
Needed for production	11	15	18
Desired ending inventory	8	9	10
Needed	19	24	28
Less: beginning inventory	6	8	9
Purchases	13	16	19

Notes:

Ending inventory is 50% of next month's requirements [example, September's is 50% × 15 = 8 (rounded)].
September's beginning inventory is 50% of its production needs [50% × 11 = 6 (rounded)].

13-9 continued

Jar Sets:	September	October	November
Production	110	154	181
× 1 jar	1	1	1
Needed for production	110	154	181
Desired ending inventory	77	91	100
Needed	187	245	281
Less: beginning inventory	55	77	91
Purchases	132	168	190

Notes:

Ending inventory is 50% of next month's requirements [example, September's is 50% × 154 = 77]. September's beginning inventory is 50% of its production needs [50% × 110 = 55].

3. A purchases budget for December requires an estimate of January's production (to calculate December's desired ending inventory). We cannot compute January's production because we do not have February's sales forecast.

13-11

ANDREA'S SHOP
SCHEDULE OF CASH RECEIPTS FOR MAY

From May sales:

Cash sales [$60,000 × 25%]		$15,000
Cheques [5% × $60,000]	$3,000	
less bad cheques [1% × $3,000]	(30)	
less service charge [($3,000 ÷ $37.50) × $0.25]	(20)	2,950

From April sales:

VISA/MasterCard [50% × $30,000]	$15,000	
less fee [1.5% × $15,000]	(225)	14,775
American Express [20% × $30,000]	$6,000	
less fee [3.5% × $6,000]	(210)	5,790
Total		$38,515

13-13

Lyman's total activity level for October is 18,000 hours with a budgeted overhead cost of $34,800.

Analysis:

Activity level:

	Part 301	Part 414	Total
Production (units)	48,000	18,000	
Minutes per unit	15	20	
Total minutes required	720,000	360,000	
Total hours required	12,000	6,000	18,000

Flexible overhead budget:	per unit	Total
Hours required		18,000
Variable costs		
Maintenance	$1.00	$18,000
Supplies	0.50	9,000
Power	0.10	1,800
Total variable overhead costs	$1.60	$28,800
Fixed costs		
Amortization		$ 600
Salaries		5,400
Total fixed overhead costs		$ 6,000
Total overhead costs		$34,800

Lyman's October fixed overhead cost is one-twelfth of its annual costs [1/12 × $7,200; 1/12 × $64,800].

13-15

1. Per-Care's expected activity is 55,000 direct labour hours with a budgeted overhead cost of $199,000

   Analysis:

   Budgeted direct labour hours:

	BasicDiet	SpecDiet	Total
Production (bags)	100,000	100,000	
Direct labour hours per bag	0.25	0.30	
Direct labour hours required	25,000	30,000	55,000

   Flexible overhead budget for 55,000 direct labour hours:

		Variable cost		
Overhead item	Fixed cost	Per hour	Total	Total overhead
Maintenance	$17,000	$0.40	$ 22,000	$ 39,000
Power	--	0.50	27,500	27,500
Indirect labour	26,500	1.60	88,000	114,500
Rent	18,000	--	--	18,000
Total	$61,500	$2.50	$137,500	$199,000

13-15 continued

2. If Pet-Care's production is 10% higher than expected, it will require 60,500 direct labour hours and budgeted overhead of $212,750. If Pet-Care's production is 20% lower than expected, it will require 44,000 direct labour hours and budgeted overhead of $171,500.

Analysis:

Budgeted direct labour hours (10% higher):

	BasicDiet	SpecDiet	Total
Production (bags)	110,000	110,000	
Direct labour hours per bag	0.25	0.30	
Direct labour hours required	27,500	33,000	60,500

Flexible overhead budget for 60,500 direct labour hours:

		Variable cost		
Overhead item	Fixed cost	Per hour	Total	Total overhead
Maintenance	$17,000	$0.40	$ 24,200	$ 41,200
Power	--	0.50	30,250	30,250
Indirect labour	26,500	1.60	96,800	123,300
Rent	18,000	--	--	18,000
Total	$61,500	$2.50	$151,250	$212,750

Budgeted direct labour hours (20% lower):

	BasicDiet	SpecDiet	Total
Production (bags)	80,000	80,000	
Direct labour hours per bag	0.25	0.30	
Direct labour hours required	20,000	24,000	44,000

Flexible overhead budget for 44,000 direct labour hours:

		Variable cost		
Overhead item	Fixed cost	Per hour	Total	Total overhead
Maintenance	$17,000	$0.40	$ 17,600	$ 34,600
Power	--	0.50	22,000	22,000
Indirect labour	26,500	1.60	70,400	96,900
Rent	18,000	--	--	18,000
Total	$61,500	$2.50	$110,000	$171,500

13-17

1. The budgeted cash collections in December 2005 from November 2005 credit sales are $91,200 [$240,000 × 0.95 × (1 – 0.6)].

2. The total budgeted cash receipts in January 2006 are $299,400.

   Analysis:

January cash sales	$ 60,000	
Collections on January credit sales	102,600	[$180,000 × 95% × 60%]
Collections on December credit sales	136,800	[$360,000 × 95% × 40%]
Total cash receipts	$299,400	

3. The budgeted cash payments for inventory purchases in December 2005 are $283,500.

   Analysis:

	November	December	January	
Sales	$320,000	$460,000	$240,000	
Purchases	322,000	168,000		[70% of next month's sales]

Payments in December:		
For November purchases	$241,500	[$322,000 × 75%]
For December purchases	42,000	[$168,000 × 25%]
Total	$283,500	

13-19

The flexible budget for 1,650 direct labour hours is:

Maintenance	$13,900	[$4,000 + $6.00 × 1,650]
Amortization	5,000	
Supervision	15,000	
Supplies	2,310	[$1.40 × 1,650]
Power	1,238	[$0.75 × 1,650]
Other	8,165	[$8,000 + $0.10 × 1,650]
Total overhead	$45,613	

Analysis:

We must first determine the cost behaviour for each overhead item from the two flexible overhead budgets. Amortization and supervision are fixed costs because their costs do not change from 1,000 to 2,000 direct labour hours. The other items are variable or mixed costs – we can use the high-low method to find their fixed and variable components.

Maintenance:

Variable cost per direct labour hour	$6.00	[($16,000 – 10,000) ÷ (2,000 – 1,000)]
Fixed cost	$4,000	[$16,000 – (2,000 × $6)]

Supplies:

Variable cost per direct labour hour	$1.40	[($2,800 – 1,400) ÷ (2,000 – 1,000)]
Fixed cost	$0	[$16,000 – (2,000 × $6)]

Power:

Variable cost per direct labour hour	$0.75	[($1,500 – 750) ÷ (2,000 – 1,000)]
Fixed cost	$0	[$16,000 – (2,000 × $6)]

13-19 continued

Other:

Variable cost per direct labour hour	$0.10	[($8,200 – 8,100) ÷ (2,000 – 1,000)]
Fixed cost	$8,000	[$16,000 – (2,000 × $6)]

13-21

Finnco Company's cash payments for August are $150,150.

Analysis:

July purchases	$ 18,750	[$25,000 × 75%]
August purchases	7,500	[$30,000 × 25%]
July direct labour	4,000	[$40,000 × 10%]
August direct labour	45,000	[$50,000 × 90%]
August overhead	64,500	[$70,000 – 5,500]
Loan repayment	10,000	
Interest payment	400	[$10,000 × 12% × 4 ÷ 12]
Total cash payments	$150,150	

PROBLEMS

13-23

1. Schedule 1: Sales Budget

	January	February	March	Total
Units	40,000	50,000	60,000	150,000
Unit selling price	$180	$180	$180	$180
Sales revenue	$7,200,000	$9,000,000	$10,800,000	$27,000,000

2. Schedule 2: Production Budget

	January	February	March	Total
Sales	40,000	50,000	60,000	150,000
Desired ending inventory	40,000	48,000	48,000	48,000
Total needs	80,000	98,000	108,000	198,000
Less beginning inventory	32,000	40,000	48,000	32,000
Units to be produced	48,000	58,000	60,000	166,000

Note: ending inventory is 80% of next month's sales [example: January's is 80% × 50,000 = 40,000]

13-23 continued

3.   Schedule 3: Direct Materials Purchases Budget

Metal:

	January	February	March	Total
Production	48,000	58,000	60,000	166,000
Direct material per unit	10	10	10	10
Production needs	480,000	580,000	600,000	1,660,000
Desired ending inventory	250,000	300,000	300,000	300,000
Total direct material needs	730,000	880,000	900,000	1,960,000
Less: beginning inventory	200,000	250,000	300,000	200,000
Direct material purchases	530,000	630,000	600,000	1,760,000
Cost per unit	$8	$8	$8	$8
Total cost	$4,240,000	$5,040,000	$4,800,000	$14,080,000

Components:

	January	February	March	Total
Production	48,000	58,000	60,000	166,000
Direct material per unit	6	6	6	6
Production needs	288,000	348,000	360,000	996,000
Desired ending inventory	150,000	180,000	180,000	180,000
Total direct material needs	438,000	528,000	540,000	1,176,000
Less: beginning inventory	120,000	150,000	180,000	120,000
Direct material purchases	318,000	378,000	360,000	1,056,000
Cost per unit	$2	$2	$2	$2
Total cost	$636,000	$756,000	$720,000	$2,112,000

Beginning inventory is 50% of material needed for that month's sales [example: January's beginning inventory of metal is 50% × (40,000 × 10) = 200,000].

4.   Schedule 4: Direct Labour Budget

	January	February	March	Total
Production	48,000	58,000	60,000	166,000
Direct labour hours per unit	4	4	4	4
Total hours needed	192,000	232,000	240,000	664,000
Cost per hour	$9.25	$9.25	$9.25	$9.25
Total direct labour cost	$1,776,000	$2,146,000	$2,220,000	$6,142,000

13-23 continued

5. Schedule 5: Overhead Budget

	January	February	March	Total
Budgeted direct labour hours	192,000	232,000	240,000	664,000
Variable overhead:				
Supplies ($1.00/DLH)	$192,000	$232,000	$240,000	$ 664,000
Power ($0.50/DLH)	96,000	116,000	120,000	332,000
Maintenance ($0.40/DLH)	76,800	92,800	96,000	265,600
Other ($1.50/DLH)	288,000	348,000	360,000	996,000
Budgeted variable overhead	$652,800	$788,800	$816,000	$2,257,600
Fixed overhead:				
Maintenance	$ 30,000	$ 30,000	$30,000	$ 90,000
Supervision	16,000	16,000	16,000	48,000
Amortization	200,000	200,000	200,000	600,000
Taxes	12,000	12,000	12,000	36,000
Other	80,000	80,000	80,000	240,000
Budgeted fixed overhead	$338,000	$338,000	$338,000	$1,014,000
Total budgeted overhead	$990,800	$1,126,800	$1,154,000	$3,271,600

6. Schedule 6: Selling and Administrative Expense Budget

	January	February	March	Total
Planned sales	40,000	50,000	60,000	150,000
Variable selling and admin				
Commissions ($2.00/unit)	$ 80,000	$100,000	$120,000	$300,000
Shipping ($1.00/unit)	40,000	50,000	60,000	150,000
Other ($0.60/unit)	24,000	30,000	36,000	90,000
Budgeted variable S&A	$144,000	$180,000	$216,000	$540,000
Fixed selling and admin				
Salaries	$ 50,000	$ 50,000	$ 50,000	$150,000
Amortization	40,000	40,000	40,000	120,000
Other	20,000	20,000	20,000	60,000
Budgeted fixed S&A	$110,000	$110,000	$110,000	$330,000
Total budgeted S&A	$254,000	$290,000	$326,000	$870,000

7. Schedule 7: Ending Finished Goods Inventory Budget

Unit cost computation:

Direct materials	Metal	$ 80.00	[10 × $8]
	Components	12.00	[6 × $2]
Direct labour		37.00	[4 × $9.25]
Overhead:			
Variable		13.60	[4 × $3.40]
Fixed		6.11	[4 × $1,014,000 ÷ 664,000]
Total unit cost		$148.71	

	Units	Cost per unit	Total Amount
Finished goods, March 31	48,000	$148.71	$7,138,080

13-23 continued

8. Schedule 8: Cost of Goods Sold Budget

Direct materials used:

Metal [1,660,000 × $8]	$13,280,000	
Components [996,000 × $2]	1,992,000	$15,272,000
Direct labour used		6,142,000
Overhead		3,271,600
Budgeted cost of goods manufactured		$24,685,600
Add: Beginning finished goods		4,758,720
Goods available for sale		$29,444,320
Less: Ending finished goods		7,138,080
Budgeted cost of goods sold		$22,306,240

Beginning inventory: 32,000 × $148.71.

9. Schedule 9: Budgeted Income Statement

Sales	$27,000,000
Less cost of goods sold	22,306,240
Gross margin	$ 4,693,760
Less S&A expense	870,000
Income before taxes	$ 3,823,760

10. Schedule 10: Cash Budget

	January	*February*	*March*	*Total*
Beginning balance	$ 400,000	$ 0	$ 0	$ 400,000
Cash receipts	7,200,000	9,000,000	10,800,000	27,000,000
Cash available	$7,600,000	$9,000,000	$10,800,000	$27,400,000
Less disbursements:				
Direct materials purchases	$4,876,000	$5,796,000	$ 5,520,000	$16,192,000
Direct labour payroll	1,776,000	2,146,000	2,220,000	6,142,000
Overhead	790,800	926,800	954,000	2,671,600
Selling and administrative	214,000	250,000	286,000	750,000
Total	$7,656,800	$9,118,800	$ 8,980,000	$25,755,600
Ending balance	$ (56,800)	$ (118,800)	$ 1,820,000	$ 1,644,400
Plus borrowing	56,800	118,800	--	175,600
Less repayments	--	--	175,600	175,600
Less interest	--	--	2,324	2,324
Ending balance	$ 0	$ 0	$ 1,642,076	$ 1,642,076

Note: no cash is paid for amortization in overhead and selling and administrative.

Interest: ($56,800 × 12% × 2 ÷ 12) + ($118,800 × 12% × 1 ÷ 12)

13-25

Nepean's cash budget is:

Cash balance, April 1		$ 6,000	
Cash collections:			
from February sales	$ 900		[$15,000 × 6%]
from March sales	13,500		[$45,000 × 30%]
from April sales	21,384		[$36,000 × 60% × 99%]
Total cash collections		35,784	
Total cash available		$41,784	
Cash payments			
for March purchases	$ 9,000		
for April purchases	14,000		[see below]
for selling and administrative expenses	4,960		[see below]
Total cash payments		27,960	
Cash balance, April 30		$13,824	

Analysis:

Nepean's April purchases will be $21,000 and payments will be $14,000.

Cost of April's sales	$24,000	[$36,000 ÷ 15 × 10]
Required ending inventory	9,000	[$27,000 ÷ 15 × 10 × 50%]
Total required	$33,000	
Beginning inventory	12,000	
April's purchases	$21,000	
April's payments	$14,000	[$21,000 × 2/3]

Nepean's April cash payments for selling and administrative expenses will be $4,960.

Fixed expenses (excluding amortization)	$1,000	[(21,000 − 9,000) ÷ 12]
Variable expenses	3,960	[($70,500 − 21,000) ÷ $450,000 × $36,000]
Total cash payments	$4,960	

13-27

1. Laurier's budgeted cash disbursements for August 2006 are $280,445.

Payments for July's purchases	$103,500	[46% × $225,000]
Payments for August's purchases	131,544	[54% × $243,600]
Payments for July's selling and administrative expenses	21,220	[46% × $46,130]
Payments for August's selling and administrative expenses	24,181	[54% × $44,780]
Total budgeted cash disbursements	$280,445	

    Analysis:

    Purchases budget:

	July	August	
Units sold	11,900	11,400	
Required ending inventory	14,820	15,600	[130% × 11,400; 130% × 12,000]
Total required	26,720	27,000	
Beginning inventory	15,470	14,820	[July 1: $309,400 ÷ $20
Units purchased	11,250	12,180	
Purchase cost (@ $20)	$225,000	$243,600	

    Selling and administrative expense budget:

	July	August	
Fixed selling and administrative	$14,000	$14,000	[$16,000 – 2,000]
Variable selling and administrative	32,130	30,780	[9% × $357,000; 9% × $342,000]
Total selling and administrative	$46,130	$44,780	

2. Laurier's budgeted cash collections for July 2006 are $330,384.

Collections on June's sales (within discount period)	$211,266	[$363,000 × 60% × 97%]
Collections on June's sales (after discount period)	90,750	[$363,000 × 25%]
Collections on May's sales	31,860	[$354,000 × 9%]
Total collections	$333,876	

3. Laurier will purchase 12,260 units in September 2006.

Units sold	12,000	
Required ending inventory	15,860	[130% × 12,200]
Total required	27,860	
Beginning inventory	15,600	[130% × 12,000]
Units purchased	12,260	

13-29

1. By involving managers and others in the development of budgets, participative budgeting increases their sense of worth and commitment to the budget. It is believed that managers in a participative environment will perform better because they are more motivated and will work harder to achieve targets they helped set. Goal congruence is often greater and managers take pride in "ownership" of their budget. Managers are able to contribute their local knowledge and creativity to the budget process. As a result the budget planning process is enhanced.

    Participative budgeting may have some disadvantages. Managers may set budgets that are too tight or too loose – decreasing the budget's control value. Managers may attempt to build slack into their budgets to make it easier to show superior performance or to use the company's resources for their own purposes.

13-29 continued

2. Scott Weidner's outline has the following deficiencies that can be corrected as shown:

Deficiency	*Remedy*
Department managers are not involved in setting the targets for their departments.	Managers should be given an opportunity for input into setting the original targets.
Department managers will tend to request spending up to the target – whether needed or not. Spending at the current level for salaries and contracts will also encourage managers to start at that point rather than look for potential savings or efficiencies.	Spending, current and new proposals should be justified as part of the budget process.
Allocation of the approved budget to programs by the controller, under the direction of the deputy minister, defeats the purpose of participatory budgeting.	Managers should participate in the allocation of the approved budget based on the need for different programs.
Management-by-exception reporting identifies excessive expenditures but does not reward or encourage meeting targets or finding cost savings. Managers will tend to spend all funds – whether needed for their programs or not.	Retain the management-by-exception to control overspending but provide recognition (and compensation) for managers who come within their budget allocations or deliver their programs at lower cost.

13-31

Macam Company's revised budgeted income statement (in thousands) is:

Net sales	$32,736	[$186 × 176]
Less: Cost of goods sold	22,104	
Gross margin	$10,632	
Less: Operating expenses	5,400	
Income before taxes	$ 5,232	

Macam Company's revised budgeted cost of goods sold (in thousands) is:

Direct materials:			
Materials inventory, September 1, 2005	$ 1,360		
Materials purchased	15,576		[$3,300 + 3,960 + 8,316]
Available for use	$16,936		
Less: Materials inventory, August 31, 2006	1,628		
Direct materials used		$15,308	
Direct labour		1,190	[($1,134 ÷ 162) × 170
Overhead:			
Indirect materials	$1,531		[$15,308 × 10%]
General	3,320	4,851	
Cost of goods manufactured		$21,349	
Finished goods, September 1, 2005		1,169	
Total goods available		$22,518	
Less: Finished goods, August 31, 2006		414	[($21,349 ÷ 170) × 3.3]
Cost of goods sold		$22,104	

13-31 continued

Analysis:

Revised budgeted net sales:

Macam sold 35,300 units from September to November 2005 [9,300 + 35,000 – 9,000].

Macam expects to sell 140,700 units from December 2005 to August 2006 [9,000 + (170,000 – 35,000) – 3,300].

Macam's revised budgeted sales for the year ended August 31, 2006 are 176,000 units [35,300 + 140,700].

Macam's original budgeted sales for the year ended August 31, 2006 was 168,000 units [9,300 + 162,000 – 3,300].

Macam's budgeted selling price is $186 [$31,248,000 ÷ 168,000].

Revised budgeted materials purchases:

Macam will purchase materials for 172,500 units during the year [170,000 + 18,500 – 16,000]. 37,500 units were purchased to December 1, 2005 at a price of $88 per unit [$3,300,000 ÷ 37,500] and 135,000 will be purchased in the remainder of the year [172,500 – 37,500]. Macam will purchase 45,000 units from December 2005 to February 2006 [135,000 × 1/3] for $3,960,000 [45,000 × $88] and 90,000 units from March to August 2006 [135,000 × 2/3] for $8,316,000 [90,000 × $88 × 105%].

Revised budgeted general overhead:

Macam expects fixed general overhead of $1,620,000 [$3,420,000 × 1/2] and variable general overhead of $1,700,000 [(($3,420,000 × 1/2) ÷ 162,000) × 170,000] for a total revised budgeted general overhead of $3,320,000 [$1,620,000 + 1,700,000].

13-33

1. Amy's performance report using direct-labour-based formulas:

	Actual cost	Budgeted cost	Variance	
Direct labour	$210,000	$200,000	$ 10,000 U	[$10× 20,000]
Power	135,000	85,000	50,000 U	[$5,000 + $4 × 20,000]
Setups	140,000	100,000	40,000 U	
Total	$485,000	$385,000	$100,000 U	

2. Amy's performance report using multiple-cost-driver formulas:

	Actual cost	Budgeted cost	Variance	
Direct labour	$210,000	$200,000	$10,000 U	[$10× 20,000]
Power	135,000	149,000	14,000 F	[$68,000 + $0.90 × 90,000]
Setups	140,000	142,000	2,000 F	[$98,000 + $400 × 110]
Total	$485,000	$491,000	$ 6,000 F	

3. Amy's performance is more accurately shown by the multiple-cost-driver approach because her budget is based on the cause-and-effect relationship between the cost items and the activity measures. Using direct labour hours as the single activity measure does not provide an accurate budget and fails to show her good performance in controlling her costs.

13-35

a. Corella's sales budget:

	First Quarter	Second Quarter	Third Quarter	Fourth Quarter	Year
Unit sales	65,000	70,000	75,000	90,000	300,000
Unit price	$400	$400	$400	$400	$400
Total sales revenue	$26,000,000	$28,000,000	$30,000,000	$36,000,000	$120,000,000

b. Corella's production budget:

	First Quarter	Second Quarter	Third Quarter	Fourth Quarter	Year
Unit sales	65,000	70,000	75,000	90,000	300,000
Desired ending inventory	13,000	15,000	20,000	10,000	10,000
Total needs	78,000	85,000	95,000	100,000	310,000
Less: beginning inventory	0	13,000	15,000	20,000	0
Unit production	78,000	72,000	80,000	80,000	310,000

c. Corella's direct materials purchases budget:

	First Quarter	Second Quarter	Third Quarter	Fourth Quarter	Year
Unit production	78,000	72,000	80,000	80,000	310,000
Materials per unit	3	3	3	3	3
Production needs	234,000	216,000	240,000	240,000	930,000
Desired ending inventory	63,000	67,500	81,000	65,700	65,700
Total needs	297,000	283,500	321,000	305,700	995,700
Less beginning inventory	65,700	63,000	67,500	81,000	65,700
Purchases required	231,300	220,500	253,500	224,700	930,000
Cost per unit	$80	$80	$80	$80	$80
Purchase cost	$18,504,000	$17,640,000	$20,280,000	$17,976,000	$74,400,000

Desired ending inventory = 30% of materials needs of next month's sales:
First quarter: 30% × 70,000 × 3; Second quarter: 30% × 75,000 × 3; Third quarter: 30% × 90,000 × 3

d. Corella's direct labour budget:

	First Quarter	Second Quarter	Third Quarter	Fourth Quarter	Year
Unit production	78,000	72,000	80,000	80,000	310,000
Hours per unit	5	5	5	5	5
Hours needed	390,000	360,000	400,000	400,000	1,550,000
Cost per hour	$10	$10	$10	$10	$10
Total cost	$3,900,000	$3,600,000	$4,000,000	$4,000,000	$15,500,000

e. Corella's overhead budget:

	First Quarter	Second Quarter	Third Quarter	Fourth Quarter	Year
Budgeted hours	390,000	360,000	400,000	400,000	1,550,000
Variable rate	$6	$6	$6	$6	$6
Variable overhead	$2,340,000	$2,160,000	$2,400,000	$2,400,000	$9,300,000
Fixed overhead	1,000,000	1,000,000	1,000,000	1,000,000	4,000,000
Total overhead	$3,340,000	$3,160,000	$3,400,000	$3,400,000	$13,300,000

13-35 continued

f.   Corella's selling and administrative expense budget:

	First Quarter	Second Quarter	Third Quarter	Fourth Quarter	Year
Unit sales	65,000	70,000	75,000	90,000	300,000
Variable rate	$10	$10	$10	$10	$10
Variable expense	$650,000	$700,000	$ 750,000	$ 900,000	$3,000,000
Fixed expense	250,000	250,000	250,000	250,000	1,000,000
Total expense	$900,000	$950,000	$1,000,000	$1,150,000	$4,000,000

g.   Corella's ending finished goods inventory budget:

Unit cost computation:

Direct materials	$240.00	[3 units × $80]
Direct labour	50.00	[5 hours × $10]
Variable overhead:	30.00	[5 hours × $6]
Fixed overhead	12.90	[$4,000,000 ÷ 310,000]
Total unit cost	$332.90	

	Units	Cost per unit	Total Amount
Finished Goods:	10,000	$332.90	$3,329,000

h.   Corella's cost of goods sold budget:

Direct materials used	$ 74,400,000
Direct labour used	15,500,000
Overhead	13,300,000
Budgeted manufacturing costs	$103,200,000
Add: Beginning finished goods	0
Goods available for sale	$103,200,000
Less: Ending finished goods	3,329,000
Budgeted cost of goods sold	$ 99,871,000

i.   Corella's cash budget:

	First Quarter	Second Quarter	Third Quarter	Fourth Quarter	Year
Beginning cash balance	$ 250,000	$ 1,110,000	$ 3,128,000	$ 5,568,000	$ 250,000
Collections on sales:					
Current quarter	22,100,000	23,800,000	25,500,000	30,600,000	102,000,000
Prior quarter	3,300,000	3,900,000	4,200,000	4,500,000	15,900,000
Cash available	$25,650,000	$28,810,000	$32,828,000	$40,668,000	$118,150,000
Less disbursements:					
Direct materials:					
Current quarter	$ 9,252,000	$ 8,820,000	$10,140,000	$ 8,988,000	$ 37,200,000
Prior quarter	7,248,000	9,252,000	8,820,000	10,140,000	35,460,000
Direct labour	3,900,000	3,600,000	4,000,000	4,000,000	15,500,000
Overhead	2,990,000	2,810,000	3,050,000	3,050,000	11,900,000
Selling and administrative	850,000	900,000	950,000	1,100,000	3,800,000
Dividends	300,000	300,000	300,000	300,000	1,200,000
Equipment	0	0	0	2,000,000	2,000,000
Total cash needs	$24,540,000	$25,682,000	$27,260,000	$29,578,000	$107,060,000
Ending cash balance	$ 1,110,000	$ 3,128,000	$ 5,568,000	$11,090,000	$ 11,090,000

13-35 continued

Analysis and calculations:

Collections on sales:

	Prior	*Current*
First quarter	Accounts receivable, December 31, 2004	85% × $26,000,000
Second quarter	15% × $26,000,000	85% × $28,000,000
Third quarter	15% × $28,000,000	85% × $30,000,000
Fourth quarter	15% × $30,000,000	85% × $36,000,000

Payments for direct material purchases:

	Prior	*Current*
First quarter	Accounts payable, December 31, 2004	50% × $18,504,000
Second quarter	50% × $18,504,000	50% × $17,640,000
Third quarter	50% × $17,640,000	50% × $20,280,000
Fourth quarter	50% × $20,280,000	50% × $17,976,000

Payments for overhead:

First quarter	$3,340,000 – 350,000
Second quarter	$3,160,000 – 350,000
Third quarter	$3,400,000 – 350,000
Fourth quarter	$3,400,000 – 350,000

Payments for selling and administrative:

First quarter	$900,000 – 50,000
Second quarter	$950,000 – 50,000
Third quarter	$1,000,000 – 50,000
Fourth quarter	$1,150,000 – 50,000

j. Corella's budgeted income statement for the year ended December 31, 2005 (using absorption costing):

Sales	$120,000,000	[from sales budget]
Less: Cost of goods sold	99,871,000	[from cost of goods sold budget]
Gross margin	$ 20,129,000	
Less: Selling and administrative expenses	4,000,000	[from selling and administrative expenses budget]
Operating income	$ 16,129,000	

k. Corella's budgeted balance sheet, December 31, 2005:

Assets

Cash	$11,090,000	[from cash budget]
Accounts receivable	5,400,000	[15% × $36,000,000]
Direct materials inventory	5,256,000	[65,700 × $80]
Finished goods inventory	3,329,000	[from finished goods inventory budget]
Plant and equipment	33,900,000	[see below for calculation]
Total assets	$58,975,000	

Liabilities and Equity

Accounts payable	$ 8,988,000	[50% × $17,976,000]
Capital stock	27,000,000	
Retained earnings (note 5)	22,987,000	[see below for calculation]
Total liabilities and equity	$58,975,000	

13-35 continued

Calculation of plant and equipment:

Beginning plant and equipment	$33,500,000	
Add: new equipment	2,000,000	
Less: amortization expense	(1,600,000)	[4 × ($350,000 + 50,000)]
Ending plant and equipment	$33,900,000	

Calculation of retained earnings:

Beginning retained earnings	$ 8,058,000	
Plus: net income	16,129,000	[budgeted income statement]
Less: dividends paid	(1,200,000)	[cash budget]
Ending retained earnings	$22,987,000	

13-37

1. ArtDecor's budgeted cash receipts for the second quarter are:

		April	May	June	Second quarter
February sales	[40% × $2,000,000]	$ 800,000	--	--	$ 800,000
March sales	[60% × $1,800,000]	1,080,000	--	--	1,080,000
	[40% × $1,800,000]	--	$ 720,000	--	720,000
April sales	[60% × $2,200,000]	--	1,320,000	--	1,320,000
	[40% × $2,200,000]	--	--	$ 880,000	880,000
May sales	[60% × $2,500,000]	--	--	1,500,000	1,500,000
Total		$1,880,000	$2,040,000	$2,380,000	$6,300,000

ArtDecor's budgeted cash disbursements for the second quarter are:

		April	May	June	Second quarter
Purchases	[see below]	$1,004,000	$1,156,000	$1,310,000	$3,470,000
Wages	[see below]	440,000	500,000	560,000	1,500,000
Salaries	[$480,000 ÷ 12]	40,000	40,000	40,000	120,000
Promotion	[$660,000 ÷ 12]	55,000	55,000	55,000	165,000
Property taxes	[$240,000 ÷ 4]	--	--	60,000	60,000
Insurance	[$360,000 ÷ 12]	30,000	30,000	30,000	90,000
Utilities	[$300,000 ÷ 12]	25,000	25,000	25,000	75,000
Income taxes	[see below]	408,000	--	--	408,000
Total		$2,002,000	$1,806,000	$2,080,000	$5,888,000

Summary of ArtDecor's cash flows:

	April	May	June	Second quarter
Beginning cash balance	$ 100,000	$ 100,000	$ 100,000	$ 100,000
Cash receipts	1,880,000	2,040,000	2,380,000	6,300,000
Cash payments	(2,002,000)	(1,806,000)	(2,080,000)	(5,888,000)
Net cash	$ (22,000)	$ 334,000	$ 400,000	$ 512,000
Borrowing	122,000	--	--	122,000
Investing	--	(234,000)	(300,000)	(534,000)
Ending cash balance	$ 100,000	$ 100,000	$ 100,000	$ 100,000

13-37 continued

Analysis and calculations:

Purchases:		*February*	*March*	*April*	*May*
For February	[40% × 50% × $2,000,000]	$400,000	--	--	--
For March	[60% × 50% × $1,800,000]	540,000	--	--	--
	[40% × 50% × $1,800,000]	--	$ 360,000	--	--
For April	[60% × 50% × $2,200,000]	--	660,000	--	--
	[40% × 50% × $2,200,000]	--	--	$ 440,000	--
For May	[60% × 50% × $2,500,000]	--	--	750,000	--
	[40% × 50% × $2,200,000]	--	--	--	$ 500,000
For June	[60% × 50% × $2,800,000]	--	--	--	840,000
Total		$940,000	$1,020,000	$1,190,000	$1,340,000

Payments:		*April*	*May*	*June*
For February	[20% × $940,000]	$ 188,000	--	--
For March	[80% × $1,020,000]	816,000	--	--
	[20% × $1,020,000]	--	$ 204,000	--
For April	[80% × $1,190,000]	--	952,000	--
	[20% × $1,190,000]	--	--	$ 238,000
For May	[80% × $1,340,000]	--	--	1,072,000
Total		$1,004,000	$1,156,000	$1,310,000

Payments for hourly wages:

April	$440,000	[20% × $2,200,000]
May	500,000	[20% × $2,500,000]
June	560,000	[20% × $2,800,000]

Payments for income taxes:

First quarter's operating income: $1,020,000 [$612,000 ÷ (1 – 40%)].
Income tax payment: $408,000 [$1,020,000 × 40%].

2. Cash budgeting is particularly important for a rapidly growing company because often cash disbursements precede cash receipts. In this case ArtDecor purchases and pays for its product (during the month before and the month of sales) before it makes a sale and collects on its sales (during the two months following a sale). This could create a cash shortage that it should be prepared to manage. Some of ArtDecor's cash payments are lumpy at particular times (property taxes and income taxes). ArtDecor must plan its cash flows to meet these obligations.

13-39

Hosking Company's budgeted cash disbursements for January 2006 are:

Payments for direct material purchases	$171,000	[see calculation below]
Payments for wages and salaries	399,600	[see calculation below]
Payments for indirect supplies	6,900	[$6,000 + 900]
Payment for insurance	12,000	[$1,000 × 12]
Total cash disbursements	$589,500	

Analysis and calculations:

Hosking's production budget:

	January	February	
Unit sales	30,000	25,000	
Units required for ending inventory	5,200	4,200	[200 + 20% × 25,000; 200 + 20% × 20,000]
Units required	35,200	29,200	
Units from beginning inventory	6,200	5,200	[200 + 20% × 30,000]
Unit production	29,000	24,000	

Hosking's direct materials purchase budget:

Unit production	29,000	
Direct material per unit (kilograms)	2	
Direct material required for production (kilograms)	58,000	
Kilograms required for ending inventory	5,800	[1,000 + (10% × 24,000 × 2)]
Direct material required	63,800	
Kilograms in beginning inventory	6,800	[1,000 + (10% × 29,000 × 2)]
Kilograms purchased	57,000	
Direct material cost per kilogram	$3	
Direct materials purchased	$171,000	

Hosking's payments for wages and salaries:

Direct labour wages	$348,000	[29,000 × $12]
Production supervision salaries	14,000	
Selling and administrative salaries	40,000	
Less increase in salaries and wages payable	(2,400)	
Total payments	$399,600	

MANAGERIAL DECISION CASES

13-41

1. Dr. Jones's monthly cash budget shows that he will have a cash shortage of $2,904 [$21,360 – 24,264. Dr. Jones can use the schedules of cash receipts and disbursements to see where his money is being spent.

    Cash receipts:

Fillings	$ 4,500	[$50 × 90]
Crowns	5,700	[$300 × 19]
Root canals	1,360	[$170 × 8]
Bridges	3,500	[$500 × 7]
Extractions	1,350	[$45 × 30]
Cleaning	2,700	[$25 × 108]
X-rays	2,250	[$15 × 150]
Total receipts	$21,360	

    Cash disbursements:

Salaries	$ 12,700	
Benefits	1,344	
Building lease	1,500	
Dental supplies	1,200	
Janitorial	300	
Utilities	400	
Phone	150	
Office supplies	100	
Lab fees	5,000	
Loan payments	570	
Interest payments	500	
Miscellaneous	500	[includes $200 per month for seminars; $2,400 ÷ 12]
Total disbursements	$24,264	

2. Dr. Jones must increase his cash receipts, decrease his cash payments, or both to solve his financial problems. Some possible actions include:

    *   Although Dr. Jones is reluctant to work additional hours, he may be able to increase his revenue and cash receipts by extending his office hours and taking on more patients. His average revenue is approximately $167 per hour (based on 32 hours per week) [$21,360 ÷ (32 × 4)].

        Many of his costs are fixed and will not change with increased hours. These include the building lease, janitorial, utilities, phone, office supplies, and loan and interest payments.

        The costs of dental supplies and lab fees are likely variable and will increase with the additional activity. These costs may increase an average of $48 per hour [($1,200 + 5,000) ÷ (32 × 4)].

        The other major category of cost is the salaries paid to the dental assistants and receptionist. He is currently not fully utilizing their time and may be able to schedule them to cover any additional hours without spending any more. If he is unable to use their time more efficiently, he may need to pay more to cover the additional office hours. This cost is approximately $27 per hour [($1,900 + 1,500) ÷ (32 × 4)] plus average benefits of $6 per hour [(($1,900 + 1,500) ÷ (12,700 – 6,500)) × $1,344 ÷ (32 × 4)].

        The hygienist may be fully utilized and he will have to pay more if he increases his office hours. The average cost for the hygienist is $14 per hour [$1,800 ÷ (32 × 4)] plus benefits of $3 per hour [($1,800 ÷ (12,700 – 6,500)) × $1,344 ÷ (32 × 4)].

13-41 continued

If Dr. Jones works an additional hour, he will increase his net cash flow by $102 per hour [$167 – ($48 + 14 + 3)] to $69 per hour [$167 – ($48 + 27 + 6 + 14 + 3)]. He would have to work an additional 7 hours per week [($2,904 ÷ 102) ÷ 4] to 10.5 hours per week [($2,904 ÷ 69) ÷ 4] to balance his cash flow.

A new budget based on increased hours is:

	7 more hours	*10.5 more hours*	
Cash receipts	$26,052	$28,390	[$167 × 39 × 4; $167 × 42.5 × 4]
Variable costs	(10,140)	(16,660)	[$65 × 39 × 4; $98 × 42.5 × 4]
Fixed costs	(3,870)	(3,870)	
Other costs	(11,637)	(7,500)	
Net cash flow	$ 405	$ 360	

Fixed costs are the building lease, janitorial, utilities, phone, office supplies, and loan and interest payments [$1,500 + 300 + 400 + 100 + 570 +500 + 500].

Other costs are the salaries of Dr. Jones and his wife [$1,000 + 6,500] plus the salaries and benefits of the dental assistants and receptionist for the first option [$1,900 + 1,500 + (3,400 ÷ 6,200 × 1,344) + 1,000 + 6,500].

The small positive cash flows are due to rounding in calculations of the average effects of working more hours.

Thus it is possible for Dr. Jones to achieve a positive cash flow by working more – assuming that he can attract more patients.

- If Dr. Jones doesn't want to increase his office hours, he should consider reducing the amount of cash that he and his wife receive from the business and to cut back on some personal spending. Dropping the informational seminars would save an average of $200 per month [$2,400 ÷ 12]; the $2,700 difference could be achieved by cutting back Dr. Jones's and his wife's salaries.

Both of these options require a sacrifice by Dr. Jones (either time or money) to bring his cash outflows into line with his cash outflows. He may not be willing to accept this but there are few other realistic choices.

The main behavioural principle that applies to this setting is the need for goal congruence – Dr. Jones must develop personal goals that align with his business goals. In this case Dr. Jones is the owner-manager and his personal goals are the organization's goals – but he needs to recognize the limits on the business to provide his desired cash flow with the time he is willing to devote to the business.

RESEARCH ASSIGNMENTS

13-43

Students' answers will vary depending on their research and sources.

CHAPTER 14

STANDARD COSTING: A MANAGERIAL CONTROL TOOL

ANSWERS TO ODD-NUMBERED QUESTIONS FOR WRITING AND DISCUSSION

1. Standard costs are budgets for one unit of a product. Budgets are developed for the expected level of total activity. Standard costs and flexible budgets are closely related. Flexible budgets are prepared for different levels of activity, both actual and expected. Unit standards are the foundation on which a flexible budget is built.

3. Historical experience is often a poor basis for establishing standards because of process changes and because past performance may include inefficient operations.

5. Ideal standards demand maximum efficiency and can be achieved only if everything operates perfectly – for example, no provision is made for machine breakdowns. Currently attainable standards can be achieved under efficient operating conditions – with provisions made for normal interruptions, fatigue, etc. Currently attainable standards are usually adopted because they provide better control. If standards are too tight and never achievable, workers become frustrated and performance levels may decline. Challenging, but achievable, standards tend to result in higher performance levels.

7. Standard costing is an integral part of many control systems. Standards allow managers to identify variances (the difference between actual costs and standard costs) that provide signals of where performance differs from plans and where corrective or other control action is required.

9. A standard cost sheet provides the details underlying a product's standard unit cost – the standard quantities and prices for direct materials and direct labour and the standard quantities and rates for overhead.

11. A standard cost variance should be investigated if the anticipated benefits are greater than the anticipated cost. Many companies adopt as a general guideline that variances are investigated if they fall outside an acceptable range. This avoids investigating small variances that are more likely caused by normal fluctuations and concentrating on larger variances that are caused by controllable and correctable events.

13. The material price variance is often computed at the time of purchase rather than at the point of issue because the control information is available earlier and control is likely more effective. Another reason is that if price variances are isolated at the time of purchase, materials inventories are carried at standard cost and accounting for materials is simplified.

15. The labour rate variance is often beyond the control of managers (a new contract may lead to higher wage rates) but managers are responsible for using the correct worker for the task. For example, using higher paid, more skilled workers may produce an unfavourable labour rate variance that is controllable.

17. The variable overhead spending variance is not a pure price variance because it is affected by price differences of variable overhead items (the price component) and how efficiently overhead items are used. Waste or inefficiency in the use of variable overhead items will increase the actual cost of variable overhead and cause an unfavourable variable overhead spending variance. The actual and standard variable overhead rates depend on both price and quantity factors.

19. The fixed overhead spending variance is usually small because many fixed overhead items result from long-term commitments and are less likely to change in the short term.

21. The spending variance is more important for control of fixed overhead costs than the denominator variance. The spending variance shows whether actual fixed overhead expenditures were different from budgeted. The denominator variance has no control significance because it is the result of producing more or less units than were used in calculating the fixed overhead rate for product costing purposes.

SOLUTIONS TO ODD-NUMBERED EXERCISES, PROBLEMS, AND CASES

EXERCISES

14-1

1. a. Operating department managers and staff personnel from materials, human resources, and accounting should be involved in setting standards. Operating managers are the primary source of information about the quantity of material and labour required. The materials manager and human resource manager provide input about material prices and wage rates. The accounting department coordinates and develops the standard cost system, provides information about past costs, and develops overhead budgets and rates.

    b. To be effective for planning and control, the standards should be currently attainable – including allowances for normal downtime, scrap, etc. Market prices for materials, wages, and other manufacturing items should be used.

2. Responsibility under a standard costing system should be determined by who is able to influence the cost (controllability) and the cause of the variance. A manager must have the ability to control the cause of the variance (decision responsibility). Typically the materials manager would be responsible for material price variances and the operating department managers responsible for material usage variances, labour and variable overhead efficiency variances, and variable and fixed overhead spending variances. Operating department managers may also be responsible for labour rate variances but the human resource staff may have greater influence for the wages paid. The fixed overhead denominator variance is not controllable in the conventional sense and no one would be held responsible.

14-3

1. The direct materials price variance is $1,092F and the direct materials usage variance is $512U. [Note: assume all materials purchased have been used in production.]

Actual Cost $AP \times AQ$ $1.15 \times 8,400$ $9,660	$SP \times AQ$ $1.28 \times 8,400$ $10,752	Standard Cost $SP \times SQ$ $1.28 \times 8,000 \times 1$ $1.28 \times 8,000$ $10,240
	Price $1,092F	Usage $512U

2. The direct labour rate variance is $125U and the direct labour efficiency variance is $70U.

Actual Cost $AR \times AH$ 7.50×250 $1,875	$SR \times AH$ 7.00×250 $1,750	Standard Cost $SR \times SH$ $7.00 \times 8,000 \times 0.03$ 7.00×240 $1,680
	Price $125U	Usage $70U

14-5

1. The cost of leather for the production of 10,000 leather purses is $480,000 [$48 × 10,000]. The cost of direct labour for 10,000 leather purses is $180,000 [$18 × 10,000].

2. The total budget variance for materials is $5,560U [$480,000 – ($7.96 × 61,000)]. The total budget variance for labour is $15,000U [$180,000 – ($12.50 × 15,600)].

3. The materials price variance is $2,440F. The materials usage variance is $8,000U.

Actual Cost	SP × AQ	Standard Cost
AP × AQ		SP × SQ
$7.96 × 61,000	$8.00 × 61,000	$8.00 × 10,000 × 6
$485,560	$488,000	$8.00 × 60,000
		$480,000

Price $2,440F   Usage $8,000U

4. The labour rate variance is $7,800U. The labour efficiency variance is $7,200U.

Actual Cost	SR × AH	Standard Cost
AR × AH		SR × SH
$12.50 × 15,600	$12.00 × 15,600	$12.00 × 10,000 × 1.5
$195,000	$187,200	$12.00 × 15,000
		$180,000

Price $7,800U   Usage $7,200U

14-7

1. Applied fixed overhead is $1,298,000 [$0.55 × 2,360,000 units].

2. The fixed overhead spending variance is $60,000F. The fixed overhead volume variance is $22,000U.
   [Note: fixed overhead volume variance is another name for the fixed overhead denominator variance.]

Actual Cost	Budgeted	Applied
$1,260,000	$1,320,000	$1,298,000

Spending $60,000F   Denominator $22,000U

Note: budgeted overhead is $1,320,000 [$0.55 × 2,400,000] because the fixed overhead rate is based on 2,400,000 units

14-7 continued

3. Applied variable overhead is $1,357,000 [$0.575 × 2,360,000]. The variable overhead rate is $0.575 per unit [($2,700,000 – $1,320,000) ÷ 2,400,000] and $1.15 per direct labour hour [$0.575 ÷ 0.5].

4. The variable overhead spending variance is $41,500U. The variable overhead efficiency variance is $11,500U.

		Budget/Applied Cost
		SR × SH
	SR × AH	$1.15 × 0.5 × 2,360,000
Actual Cost	$1.15 × 1,190,000	$1.15 × 1,180,000
$1,410,000	$1,368,500	$1,357,000
	Spending $41,500U	Efficiency $11,500U

14-9

1. The standard fixed overhead rate is $3.00 per direct labour hour [$1,440,000 ÷ (120,000 × 4)]. The standard variable overhead rate is $2.00 per direct labour hour [$960,000 ÷ (120,000 × 4)].

2. Applied fixed overhead is $1,428,000 [$3.00 × 4 × 119,000]. Applied variable overhead is $952,000 [$2.00 × 4 × 119,000]. The total fixed overhead variance is $72,000U [$1,500,000 – $1,428,000]. The total variable overhead variance is $2,000F [$950,000 – 952,000].

3. The fixed overhead spending variance is $60,000U. The fixed overhead denominator variance is $12,000U. The fixed overhead spending variance indicates that more was spent on fixed overhead than expected. Each item of fixed overhead should be examined to find where the increased cost occurred. The denominator variance has no significance – the company produced fewer units than expected and there was underapplied overhead.

Actual Cost	Budgeted	Applied
$1,500,000	$1,440,000	$1,428,000
Spending $60,000U		Denominator $12,000U

4. The variable overhead spending variance is $25,800F. The variable overhead efficiency variance is $23,800U. The variable overhead spending variance indicates that less was spent on overhead than expected – each item of variable overhead should be examined to discover where the cost savings occurred. The variable overhead efficiency variance indicates that the company used more labour hours than expected – and incurred more variable overhead costs. The use of direct labour should be analyzed to discover why more time was used.

		Budget/Applied Cost
		SR × SH
	SR × AH	$2.00 × 4 × 119,000
Actual Cost	$2.00 × 487,900	$2.00 × 476,000
$950,000	$975,800	$952,000
	Spending $25,800F	Efficiency $23,800U

14-11

1. Materials price variance is $18,600F. Materials usage variance is $30,400U.

<table>
<tr><th colspan="2" align="center">Purchases</th><th colspan="2" align="center">Production</th></tr>
<tr>
<td align="center">Actual Cost
$1.55 × 372,000
$576,600</td>
<td align="center">SP × AQ
$1.60 × 372,000
$595,200</td>
<td align="center">SP × AQ
$1.60 × 369,000
$590,400</td>
<td align="center">SP × SQ
$1.60 × 5 × 70,000
$1.60 × 350,000
$560,000</td>
</tr>
<tr>
<td colspan="2" align="center">Purchase Price $18,600F</td>
<td colspan="2" align="center">Production Usage $30,400U</td>
</tr>
</table>

2. Labour rate variance is $7,250F. Labour efficiency variance is $45,000U.

<table>
<tr>
<td align="center">Actual Cost
AR × AH
$8.95 × 145,000
$1,297,750</td>
<td align="center">SR × AH
$9.00 × 145,000
$1,305,000</td>
<td align="center">Standard Cost
SR × SH
$9.00 × 2 × 70,000
$9.00 × 140,000
$1,260,000</td>
</tr>
<tr>
<td align="center">Rate $7,250F</td>
<td align="center">Efficiency $45,000U</td>
<td></td>
</tr>
</table>

3. Fixed overhead spending variance is $48,000F. Fixed overhead denominator variance is $8,000U.

<table>
<tr>
<td align="center">Actual Cost
$240,000</td>
<td align="center">Budgeted
$288,000</td>
<td align="center">Applied
$280,000</td>
</tr>
<tr>
<td align="center">Spending $48,000F</td>
<td align="center">Denominator $8,000U</td>
<td></td>
</tr>
</table>

The budgeted fixed cost is $288,000 based on 72,000 units [$4.00 × 72,000].

Applied fixed overhead is $280,000 [$4.00 × 70,000].

4. Variable overhead spending variance is $2,500U. Variable overhead efficiency variance is $7,500U.

<table>
<tr>
<td align="center">Actual Cost
$220,000</td>
<td align="center">SR × AH
$1.50 × 145,000
$217,500</td>
<td align="center">Budget/Applied Cost
SR × SH
$1.50 × 2 × 70,000
$1.50 × 140,000
$210,000</td>
</tr>
<tr>
<td align="center">Spending $2,500U</td>
<td align="center">Efficiency $7,500U</td>
<td></td>
</tr>
</table>

14-13

1. Tom's purchase of a large quantity was made to meet the price standard by obtaining a lower price through quantity discounts. Given the reaction of Nellie Hentel, her objective in setting price standards was not to encourage Tom to make large purchases or to seek quantity discounts. Her objective was likely to have Tom to find sources that can supply the quantity and quality of material desired at the lowest price.

2. If Tom is right, and the only way he could have met the price standards was through large purchases and quantity discounts, Nellie's price standard may be out-of-date. She should revise the price standard to reflect the price attainable at the quantities normally purchased and implement a policy concerning purchase quantities. This would prevent this behaviour from reoccurring.

3. Tom must have known that the quantity discount approach was not the company's objective. Yet, his reward structure suggests that the company places considerable emphasis placed on meeting standard. His behaviour, in part, was induced by the company's reward system. He should be retained with some clear instruction concerning the company's inventory policy and a change in reward policy to help encourage the desired behaviour.

14-15

Summary of answers to required (see below for analysis and calculations):

1. Actual direct labour hours worked is 24,000; the total hours allowed (standard hours) is 20,000.

2. The standard hourly rate for direct labour is $5; the actual hourly rate is $5.25.

3. The actual number of units produced is 5,000.

Note: this is a good question to check whether you understand the cost variance analysis model. Although there is no set way to solve a question of this type, a good starting point is to fit the information given into the general variance analysis format.

Direct labour variances

		Standard Cost
Actual Cost	$SR \times AH$	$SR \times SH$
$AR \times AH$	$\$? \times ?$	$\$? \times 4 \times ?$
$\$?$	$\$?$	$\$?$

Rate $6,000U   Efficiency $20,000U

Variable overhead variances

	Flexible Budget @ AH	Flexible Budget @ SH
Actual Cost	$SR \times AH$	$SR \times SH$
	$\$2.00 \times ?$	$\$2.00 \times 4 \times ?$
$\$?$	$\$?$	$\$?$

Spending $?   Efficiency $8,000U

We are given that 20% more direct labour hours were used than standard or $AH = 1.2 \times SH$. This means that the variable overhead efficiency variance is:

	Flexible Budget @ AH	Flexible Budget @ SH
Actual Cost	$SR \times AH$	$SR \times SH$
	$\$2.00 \times 1.2 \times SH$	$\$2.00 \times SH$
$\$?$	$\$?$	$\$?$

Spending $?   Efficiency $8,000U

We can solve for SH and AH:

$$
\begin{aligned}
\$2.00 \times 1.2 \times SH - \$2.00 \times SH &= \$8,000 \\
0.2 \times SH &= 4,000 \\
SH &= 20,000 \\
AH &= 1.2 \times 20,000 \\
&= 24,000
\end{aligned}
$$

14-15 continued

From the DL efficiency variance we see that:

		Standard Cost
Actual Cost	SR × AH	SR × SH
AR × AH	SR × 24,000	SR × 20,000
$?	$?	$?
	Rate $6,000U	Efficiency $20,000U

or

$$SR \times 24,000 - SR \times 20,000 = \$20,000$$
$$SR \times 4,000 = \$20,000$$
$$SR = \$5$$

From the DL rate variance we can see that:

		Standard Cost
Actual Cost	SR × AH	SR × SH
AR × 24,000	$5 × 24,000	$5 × 20,000
$?	$120,000	$100,000
	Rate $6,000U	Efficiency $20,000U

or

$$AR \times 24,000 - \$5 \times 24,000 = \$6,000$$
$$AR \times 24,000 = \$126,000$$
$$AR = \$5.25$$

Finally, we can find the number of units produced from:

$$\text{units produced} \times 4 = SH = 20,000$$
$$\text{units produced} = 5,000$$

PROBLEMS

14-17

1. a.   The unit-selling price is $53.16.

Raw materials	$13.44	[12 × $1.12]
Direct labour	11.00	[2 × $5.50]
Variable overhead	2.80	[2 × $1.40]
Fixed overhead	8.20	[2 × $4.10]
Unit standard cost	$35.44	
Unit selling price	$53.16	[150% × $35.44]

   b.   Standard cost variances:

   Direct material price variance is $1,400F. Direct material usage variance is $2,240U.

		SP × SQ
	SP × AQ	$1.12 × 12 × 1,000
Actual Cost	$1.12 × 14,000	$1.12 × 12,000
$14,280	$15,680	$13,440

   Price $1,400F   Usage $2,240U

   Direct labour rate variance is $2,250U. Direct labour efficiency variance is $2,750U.

		Standard Cost
		SR × SH
	SR × AH	$5.50 × 2 × 1,000
Actual Cost	$5.50 × 2,500	$5.50 × 2,000
$16,000	$13,750	$11,000

   Rate $2,250U   Efficiency $2,750U

   Fixed overhead spending variance is $160U. Fixed overhead denominator variance is $1,640U.

Actual Cost	Budgeted	Applied
$10,000	$9,840	$8,200

   Spending $160U   Denominator $1,640U

   The budgeted fixed cost is $9,840 based on 1,200 units [$4.10 × 2 × 1,200].

   Applied fixed overhead is $8,200 [$4.10 × 2 × 1,000].

   Variable overhead spending variance is $100U. Variable overhead efficiency variance is $700U.

		Budget/Applied Cost
		SR × SH
	SR × AH	$1.40 × 2 × 1,000
Actual Cost	$1.40 × 2,500	$1.40 × 2,000
$3,600	$3,500	$2,800

   Spending $100U   Efficiency $700U

14-17 continued

2.   The cause of the overhead spending variances is an increase in cost over the budgeted cost of fixed and variable overhead items. This increase may have been caused by higher prices – for example, insurance rates (fixed overhead) and indirect labour rates (variable overhead) may have increased. The increase may also have been caused by using more of the overhead item – for example, more maintenance time was used than expected (variable overhead) or amortization was higher because of the use of an additional machine (fixed overhead).

The cause of the variable overhead efficiency variance is greater use of direct labour (the variable overhead cost driver) than standard. This may be caused by inefficient use of direct labour.

The cause of the fixed overhead denominator variance is lower production than the anticipated production level under normal conditions (used to calculate the fixed overhead rate). This causes underapplied overhead.

3.   It is preferable to compare actual data to standards rather than to historical data because:

   •   standards reflect what is currently attainable while historical figures reflect only what has happened in the past. Historical figures may include past inefficiencies.

   •   historical results are not able to reflect changes occurring in business, economic and operating conditions while standard costs are developed considering business, economic and operating condition changes.

14-19

1.   Direct materials price variance is $4,600U. Direct materials usage variance is $12,000F.

Actual Cost AP × AQ $6.10 × 46,000 $280,600	SP × AQ $6.00 × 46,000 $276,000	SP × SQ $6.00 × 1.2 × 40,000 $6.00 × 48,000 $288,000
Price $4,600U		Usage $12,000F

The new process and the higher quality material affect the material usage variance. The new process produces a savings of $6,000 [$6.00 × 0.025 × 40,000]. If the higher quality material causes the remaining $6,000 of the favourable usage variance, the company has saved $1,400 [$6,000 – 4,600], after considering the higher price. The company should continue to purchase the new material and adjust the standard cost for direct materials.

2.   Direct labour rate variance is $8,000U. Direct labour efficiency variance is $4,000U.

Actual Cost $140,000	SR × AH $10.00 × 13,200 $132,000	Standard Cost SR × SH $10.00 × 0.32 × 40,000 $10.00 × 12,800 $128,000
Rate $8,000U		Efficiency $4,000U

If the direct labour variances are attributable to the new process, the company should not continue it because the cost savings of $6,000 for direct materials is less than the $12,000 of additional direct labour cost [$8,000 + 4,000]. The new process has increased costs by $6,000 [$12,000 – 6,000].

Note that discontinuing the new process will increase direct materials cost by an additional $100 because of the higher cost of the new material [($6.10 – 6.00) × (0.025 × 40,000)]. The cost savings of the new material is still positive.

14-19 continued

3. Direct labour rate variance is $4,000U. Direct labour efficiency variance is $8,000F.

		Standard Cost
	SR × AH	SR × SH
		$10.00 × 0.32 × 40,000
Actual Cost	$10.00 × 12,000	$10.00 × 12,800
$124,000	$120,000	$128,000

Rate $4,000U   Efficiency $8,000F

If the direct labour variances are attributable to the new process, the company should continue it will save costs of $6,000 for direct materials and $4,000 for direct labour [$8,000 – 4,000]. The new process has decreased costs by $10,000 [$6,000 + 4,000] per week for a total savings of $520,000 [$10,000 × 52] annually.

14-21

1. Direct material price variance is $4,000U. Direct material usage variance is $1,500F.

Purchases			Production	
				SP × SQ
Actual Cost	SP × AQ		SP × AQ	$4 × 2.5 × 15,750
$4.10 × 40,000	$4 × 40,000		$4 × 39,000	$4 × 39,375
$164,000	$160,000		$156,000	$157,500

Purchase Price $4,000U   Production Usage $1,500F

Direct labour rate variance is $0. Direct labour efficiency variance is $7,600U.

		Standard Cost
		SR × SH
	SR × AH	$8.00 × 3 × 15,750
Actual Cost	$8.00 × 48,200	$8.00 × 47,250
AR × AH	$385,600	$378,000
$385,600		

Rate $0   Efficiency $7,600U

14-21 continued

Fixed overhead spending variance is $1,600U. Fixed overhead denominator variance is $1,875U.

Actual Cost	Budgeted	Applied
$121,600	$120,000	$118,125

Spending $1,600U   Denominator $1,875U

The budgeted fixed cost is $120,000 based on 16,000 units [$7.50 × 16,000].

Applied fixed overhead is $118,125 [$7.50 × 15,750].

Variable overhead spending variance is $1,200U. Variable overhead efficiency variance is $1,425U.

		Budget/Applied Cost
		SR × SH
	SR × AH	$1.50 × 3 × 15,750
Actual Cost	$1.50 × 48,200	$1.50 × 47,250
$73,500	$72,300	$70,875

Spending $1,200U   Efficiency $1,425U

2. The unfavourable variable spending variance may result from paying higher prices for variable overhead items or using more variable overhead resources (such as indirect materials or indirect labour) than expected for the production of 15,750 units.

   There is an unfavourable fixed overhead denominator variance because Cupar produced fewer units (15,750) than the denominator activity (16,000) it used to calculate the fixed overhead rate.

14-23

1. The standard labour per unit is 4 hours. This can be determined from the variable overhead (direct labour hours is the cost driver for overhead) as follows:

   Variable overhead per unit   =   Change in overhead cost ÷ Change in units
                   =   ($19,000 – 17,000) ÷ (1,200 – 1,000)
                   = $10

   Budgeted production is 1,100 units [$11,000 ÷ $10].

   Standard labour hours per unit is 4 [4,400 ÷ 1,100].

2. Standard absorption cost per unit is $98.00.

Material - sheet metal	$12.00	[8 × $1.50]
Material - copper wire	5.00	[2 × $2.50]
Direct labour	64.00	[4 × $16.00]
Variable overhead	10.00	[calculated above]
Fixed overhead	7.00	[4 × $4.25 – 10.00]
Total standard cost	$98.00	

14-23 continued

3. The sheet metal price variance is \$450F. The sheet metal usage variance is \$600F.

Purchases			Production
			SP × SQ
Actual Cost	SP × AQ	SP × AQ	\$1.50 × 8 × 1,050
\$1.45 × 9,000	\$1.50 × 9,000	\$1.50 × 8,000	\$1.50 × 8,400
\$13,050	\$13,500	\$12,000	\$12,600

Purchase price \$450F   Production usage \$600F

The copper wire price variance is \$66U. The copper wire usage variance is \$125U.

Purchases			Production
Actual Cost	SP × AQ	SP × AQ	SP × SQ
\$2.53 × 2,200	\$2.50 × 2,200	\$2.50 × 2,150	\$2.50 × 2 × 1,050
			\$2.50 × 2,100
\$5,566	\$5,500	\$5,375	\$5,250

Purchase price \$66U   Production usage \$125U

The direct labour rate variance is \$410U. The direct labour efficiency variance is \$1,600F.

Actual Cost		SR × SH
AR × AH	SR × AH	\$16.00 × 4 × 1,050
\$14.64 × 4,100	\$16.00 × 4,100	\$16.00 × 4,200
\$66,010	\$65,600	\$67,200

Rate \$410U   Efficiency \$1,600F

The variable overhead spending variance is \$500U. The variable overhead efficiency variance is \$250F.

	Flexible Budget @ AH	Flexible Budget @ SH
		SR × SH
	SR × AH	\$2.50 × 4 × 1,050
Actual Cost	\$2.50 × 4,100	\$2.50 × 4,200
\$10,750	\$10,250	\$10,500

Spending \$500U   Efficiency \$250F

The variable overhead per hour is \$2.50 [\$10 ÷ 4].

The fixed overhead spending variance is \$850U. The fixed overhead denominator variance is \$350F.

Actual Cost	Budgeted	Applied
\$7,850	\$7,000	\$7,350

Budget \$850U   Denominator \$350F

Budgeted fixed overhead is \$7,000 [\$17,000 − \$10 × 1,000].

Applied fixed overhead is \$7,350 [\$7.00 × 1,050].

14-25

1. The fixed overhead rate is $4.00 based on standard direct labour hours.

Total fixed overhead costs	$4,800,000	[$2,400,000 + 2,400,000]
Total activity	1,200,000	[(300,000 + 300,000) × 2]
Fixed overhead rate	$4.00	

2. The Ste-Foy plant's fixed overhead spending variance is $100,000U. Its fixed overhead denominator variance is $480,000U.

Actual Cost	Budgeted	Applied
$2,500,000	$2,400,000	$1,920,000

   Spending $100,000U   Denominator $480,000U

   Applied fixed overhead is $1,920,000 [240,000 × 2 × $4.00].

   The Calgary plant's fixed overhead spending variance is $100,000U. Its fixed overhead denominator variance is $0.

Actual Cost	Budgeted	Applied
$2,500,000	$2,400,000	$2,400,000

   Spending $100,000U   Denominator $0

   Applied fixed overhead is $2,400,000 [300,000 × 2 × $4.00].

   In the above analysis, we are assuming that the same number of units are produced and sold.

   The most likely cause of the spending variance is the cost of supervisors. Perhaps the start up of the new plants required overtime or extra supervisors as production got underway. Another possible reason is higher salaries paid to the supervisors. The building lease and the equipment amortization are committed costs and are unlikely to change. It is possible that the budget for the plants were set before the leases were finalized and the actual building lease costs were higher than expected. Amortization in the first year may have been higher than expected if the investment in equipment was higher than anticipated.

   The fixed overhead denominator variance is higher for the Ste-Foy plant because it produced fewer units than the denominator production used in calculating the fixed overhead rate. This causes underapplied overhead. The Calgary plant's production was the same as the denominator production and it has no denominator variance.

3. If annual production at the Ste-Foy plant will be 240,000 units rather than 300,000, the company should take steps to reduce its fixed overhead costs or find an alternative used for its excess capacity. Its production can be filled with 8 production lines [(240,000 ÷ 300,000) × 10].

   The company can save $100,000 by reducing the supervisors to 8 from 10 [2 × $50,000]. It may be able to sell the equipment from two of the lines and reduce its amortization cost by $220,000 [$1,100,000 ÷ 10 × 2]. It may have a loss on the sale of the capital equipment. It is unlikely to be able to reduce the building lease but may be able to sublet the extra space or to use it for another purpose.

   Topaz may attempt to use its excess capacity to produce other subassemblies or produce parts for other manufacturers (including competitors).

4. If the fixed overhead rate of $4.00 per hour is used, the fixed overhead cost per unit for the Ste-Foy plant is the same as the Calgary plant's – $8.00 per unit [$4.00 × 2]. If the output of each plant is used, the fixed overhead cost per unit is $8.00 for the Calgary plant [$2,400,000 ÷ 300,000] and $10.00 for the Ste-Foy plant [$2,400,000 ÷ 240,000]. Should the subassemblies produced at the Ste-Foy plant be charged for the its unused capacity? Some argue that products should be assigned the costs of the resources they use, including the cost of capacity. The cost of unused capacity should be reported as a separate item to draw it to management's attention and the need to reduce its cost or to more fully utilize it.

14-27

1. The direct materials price variance is $111,000U. The direct materials usage variance is $4,318F [given].

	SP × AQ
Actual cost	$17.00 × 95,000
$1,726,000	$1,615,000

Material price $111,000U

The direct labour rate variance is $47,565U. The direct labour efficiency variance is $20,300F.

Actual Cost			SR × SH
AR × AH		SR × AH	$14.00 × 10 × 16,000
$14.30 × 158,550		$14.00 × 158,550	$14.00 × 160,000
$2,267,265		$2,219,700	$2,240,000

Rate $47,565U   Efficiency $20,300F

The actual direct labour hours is calculated from the variable overhead efficiency variance of $3,625F [given].This variance is calculated as:

$$(\$2.50 \times AH) - (\$2.50 \times 10 \times 160,000) = \$3,625F$$
$$AH - 160,000 = (1,450)$$
$$AH = 158,550$$

The variable overhead spending variance is $7,245U. The variable overhead efficiency variance is $3,625F [given].

	SR × AH
Actual cost	$2.50 × 158,550
$403,620	$396,375

Spending $7,245U

The fixed overhead spending variance is $2,000U. The fixed overhead denominator variance is $95,000 [given].

Actual cost	Budgeted cost
$515,000	$513,000

Spending $2,000U

Budgeted fixed overhead is $513,000, based on applied fixed overhead of $608,000 [$3.80 × 10 × 16,000] and a favourable denominator variance of $95,000.

2. Henderson's denominator activity was 135,000 hours and 13,500 units [$513,000 ÷ $3.80; $513,000 ÷ $38.00].

14-29

1. The standard direct labour cost per hour is $5.00.

    Analysis:

    The variable overhead rate is $0.80 per direct labour hour [$40,000 ÷ 50,000], which is 16% of the direct labour cost. Thus, direct labour per hour is $5.00 [$0.80 ÷ 16%].

2. The total number of kilograms of materials purchased is 150,000.

    Analysis:

    The direct materials purchase price variance of $12,000 F was $0.08 per kilogram – thus 150,000 kilograms were purchased [$12,000 ÷ $0.08].

3. The total number of kilograms of excess material usage is 20,000.

    Analysis:

    The direct materials efficiency variance is $19,000U. The standard price per kilogram is $0.95. Thus the excess material usage is 20,000 kilograms [$19,000 ÷ $0.95].

4. The price paid per kilogram of direct materials purchased in March is $0.87.

    Analysis:

    The standard price per kilogram is $0.95 with a favourable price variance of $0.08 per kilogram – thus the actual price paid is $0.87 [$0.95 – 0.08].

5. The variable overhead spending variance is $6,600U.

    Analysis:

    The total variable overhead flexible budget variance is $9,000U – made up of a variable overhead efficiency variance of $2,400U and the variable overhead spending variance. Thus the variable overhead spending variance is $6,600U [$9,000 – 2,400].

6. The actual labour rate per hour is $5.50.

    Analysis:

    The standard labour rate is $5.00 per hour [requirement 1]. The actual labour rate exceeded the standard rate by $0.50 per hour. Thus the actual labour rate is $5.50 [$5.00 + 0.50].

7. The actual number of hours worked is 60,000.

    Analysis:

    The actual direct labour cost is $330,000 with an actual labour rate of $5.50 [requirement 1] – the actual hours are 60,000 [$330,000 ÷ $5.50].

8. The total number of standard hours allowed for the units produced is 57,000.

    Analysis:

    The actual hours are 60,000 [requirement 7]. The variable overhead rate is $0.80 per hour [see analysis in requirement 1] with a variable overhead efficiency variance of $2,400U or 3,000 excess hours [$2,400 ÷ $0.80]. Thus the standard allowed is 57,000 hours [60,000 – 3,000].

14-29 continued

9. The actual variable overhead costs are $54,600.

    Analysis:

    Variable overhead is budgeted at $0.80 per labour hour [see analysis in requirement 1] and is $48,000 for the 60,000 actual hours [60,000 × $0.80]. The variable overhead spending variance is $6,600U [requirement 5]. Thus actual variable overhead costs are $54,600 [$48,000 + 6,600].

14-31

1. The variable overhead spending variance is $200F. The variable overhead efficiency variance is $1,500U.

    Analysis:

    The variable overhead cost is $5.00 per direct labour hour [from the flexible overhead budget: ($45,000 – 30,000) ÷ (6,000 – 3,000)]. Actual variable overhead was $25,300 [$40,400 – 15,100].

	SR × AH	SR × SH $5.00 × 4 × 1,200
Actual Cost	$5.00 × 5,100	$5.00 × 4,800
$25,300	$25,500	$24,000
	Spending $200F	Efficiency $1,500U

The fixed overhead spending variance is $100U. The fixed overhead denominator variance is $600U.

Analysis:

The budgeted fixed overhead is $15,000 [from the overhead flexible budget: $45,000 – 6,000 × $5.00]. The fixed overhead applied per unit is $12.00 [$32.00 – (4 × $5.00)]. Total applied fixed overhead is $14,400 [$12.00 × 1,200].

Actual Cost	Budget	Applied
$15,100	$15,000	$14,400
	Spending $100U	Denominator $600U

2. The memo from the controller to the president should cover the following points:

    • the production manager is usually responsible for variable and fixed overhead spending variances. These variances are small and not significant

    • the production manager is usually responsible for direct labour use – the factor underlying the relatively large variable overhead efficiency variance. The company should investigate to determine why 300 extra labour hours were used in May.

    • May's production was less than the denominator activity and this caused the denominator variance. In general, denominator variances are not useful for evaluating control over overhead costs – responsibility is not assigned to anyone.

14-33

1. The upper and lower control limits for materials and labour are:

    April

    Materials: Price standard: $0.25 × 723,000 = $180,750
    Variance control limit: ± 0.08 × $180,750 = ±$14,460

    Quantity standard: 8 × 90,000 × $0.25 = $180,000
    Variance control limit: ± 0.08 × $180,000 = ±$14,400

    Labour: Price standard: $7.50 × 36,000 = $270,000
    Variance control limit: ± 0.08 × $270,000 = ±$21,600

    Quantity: 0.4 × 90,000 × $7.50 = $270,000
    Variance control limit: ± 0.08 × $270,000 = ±$21,600

    May

    Materials: Price standard: $0.25 × 870,000 = $217,500
    Variance control limit: ± 0.08 × $217,500 = ±$17,400

    Quantity standard: 8 × 100,000 × $0.25 = $200,000
    Variance control limit: ± 0.08 × $200,000 = ±$16,000

    Labour: Price standard: $7.50 × 44,000 = $330,000
    Variance control limit: ± 0.08 × $330,000 = ±$26,400

    Quantity standard: 0.4 × 100,000 × $7.50 = $300,000
    Variance control limit: ± 0.08 × $300,000 = ±$24,000

    June

    Materials: Price standard: $0.25 × 885,000 = $221,250
    Variance control limit: ± 0.08 × $221,250 = ±$17,700

    Quantity standard: 8 × 110,000 × $0.25 = $220,000
    Variance control limit: ± 0.08 × $220,000 = ±$17,600

    Labour: Price standard: $7.50 × 46,000 = $345,000
    Variance control limit: ± 0.08 × $345,000 = ±$27,600

    Quantity standard: 0.4 × 110,000 × $7.50 = $330,000
    Variance control limit: ± 0.08 × $330,000 = ±$26,400

14-33 continued

2. The April materials price variance is $8,250U or 4.6% [$8,250 ÷ $180,750. This variance falls within the 8% control limit and would not be investigated. The April materials usage variance is $750U or 0.4% [$750 ÷ $180,000]. This variance falls within the 8% control limit and would not be investigated.

Actual Cost	SP × AQ	SP × SQ
AP × AQ	$0.25 × 723,000	$0.25 × 8 × 90,000
		$0.25 × 720,000
$189,000	$180,750	$180,000
	Price $8,250U	Usage $750U

The April labour rate variance is $0 or 0.0%. This variance falls within the 8% control limit and would not be investigated. The April labour efficiency variance is $0 or 0.0%. This variance falls within the 8% control limit and would not be investigated.

Actual Cost	SR × AH	SR × SH
AR × AH	$7.50 × 36,000	$7.50 × 0.4 × 90,000
		$7.50 × 36,000
$270,000	$270,000	$270,000
	Rate $0	Efficiency $0

The May materials price variance is $500U or 0.2% [$500 ÷ $217,500]. This variance falls within the 8% control limit and would not be investigated. The May materials usage variance is $17,500U or 8.8% [$17,500 ÷ $200,000]. This variance falls outside the 8% control limit and would be investigated.

Actual Cost	SP × AQ	SP × SQ
AP × AQ	$0.25 × 870,000	$0.25 × 8 × 100,000
		$0.25 × 800,000
$218,000	$217,500	$200,000
	Price $500U	Usage $17,500U

The May labour rate variance is $7,000F or 2.1% [$7,000 ÷ $330,000]. This variance falls within the 8% control limit and would not be investigated. The May labour efficiency variance is $30,000U or 10.0% [$30,000 ÷ $300,000]. This variance falls outside the 8% control limit and would be investigated.

Actual Cost	SR × AH	SR × SH
AR × AH	$7.50 × 44,000	$7.50 × 0.4 × 100,000
		$7.50 × 40,000
$323,000	$330,000	$300,000
	Rate $7,000F	Efficiency $30,000U

The June materials price variance is $8,750U or 4.0% [$8,750 ÷ $221,250]. This variance falls within the 8% control limit and would not be investigated. The June materials usage variance is $1,250U or 0.6% [$1,250 ÷ $220,000]. This variance falls within the 8% control limit and would not be investigated.

Actual Cost	SP × AQ	SP × SQ
AP × AQ	$0.25 × 885,000	$0.25 × 8 × 110,000
		$0.25 × 880,000
$230,000	$221,250	$220,000
	Price $8,750U	Usage $1,250U

14-33 continued

The June labour rate variance is $15,000U or 4.3% [$15,000 ÷ $345,000]. This variance falls within the 8% control limit and would not be investigated. The June labour efficiency variance is $15,000U or 4.5% [$30,000 ÷ $330,000] This variance falls within the 8% control limit and would not be investigated.

		SR × SH
Actual Cost	SR × AH	$7.50 × 0.4 × 110,000
AR × AH	$7.50 × 46,000	$7.50 × 44,000
$360,000	$345,000	$330,000

Rate $15,000U   Efficiency $15,000U

3. The control charts are as follows:

Material Price Variance:

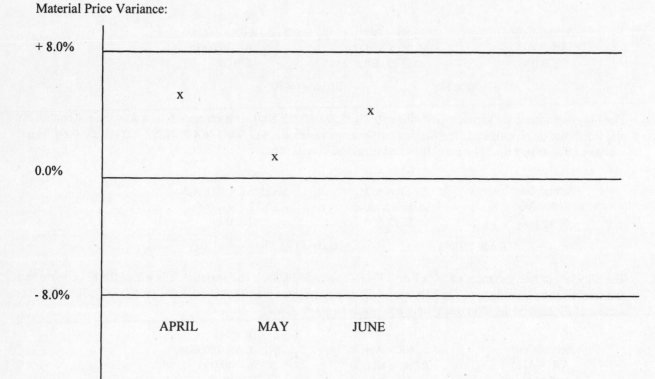

14-33 continued

Materials Usage Variance:

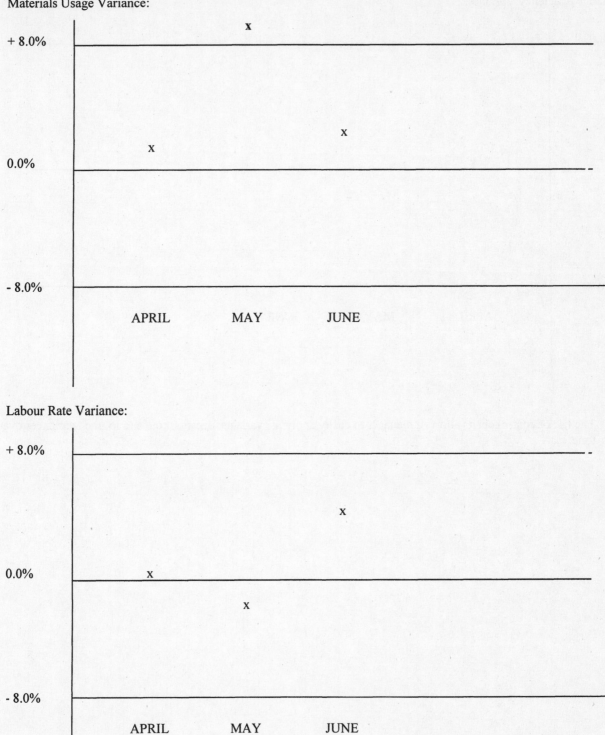

Labour Rate Variance:

14-33 continued

Labour Efficiency Variance:

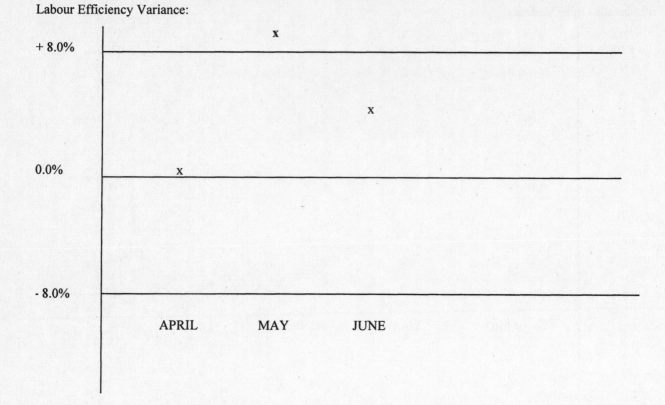

The use of control charts allows a manager to easily apply the variance decision rule and to track variances over time.

14-35

1. 60,000 units of the lower-quality material are required to produce 54,000 good units.

    Analysis:

    The lower-quality material will cause a rejection rate of 10%; 111.11 units will have to be produced for each 100 good units [100 ÷ (100% – 10%)]. 60,000 units will be required to produce 54,000 good units [54,000 ÷ 100 × 111.11].

2. The time required by the new team to produce 54,000 good units is 6,000 hours by Assembler A's, 750 hours by Assembler B, and 750 hours by the machinist.

    Analysis:

    To produce 54,000 good units, the new team will have to produce 60,000 units (to allow for the 10% rejection rate because of the lower-quality material). The old team configuration required 10 hours to produce 100 units [5 + 3 +2] but the new team can produce only 80 units in the same time period. The total time required for 60,000 units is 7,500 hours [60,000 ÷ 80 × 10]. Assembler A's time will be 80% or 6,000 hours, Assembler B will be 10% or 750 hours, and the machinist will be 10% or 750 hours.

3. A total labour variance of $18,480U should be planned for January because of the reorganization of its teams and its use of the lower-quality material. Its labour rate variance is expected to be $5,250F and its labour efficiency variance is expected to be $23,730U.

    Analysis:

    The average labour cost with the old team is $11.30 per hour [$113 ÷ 10]. The average labour cost with the new team is $10.60 per hour [(8 × $10 + 1 × $11 + 1 × $15) ÷ 10]. The expected labour rate variance is $5,250F [($10.60 × 7,500) – ($11.30 × 7,500)].

    The production of 54,000 units should require 5,400 hours [54,000 ÷ 100 × 10]. The expected labour efficiency variance is $23,730U [(7,500 – 5,400) × $11.30].

14-37

1. a. The predetermined overhead rate is $3.40 per direct labour hour or $8.50 per unit [$3.40 × 2.5].

   Analysis:

   The applied total overhead for December is $28,050 [$27,500 – 400 – 100 + 1,050] for 8,250 direct labour hours. Thus the rate is $3.40 per direct labour hour [$28,050 ÷ 8,250]. This can also be calculated from November's applied total overhead of $23,800 [$25,100 + 200 – 800 – 700] for 7,000 direct labour hours, or $3.40 per direct labour hour [$23,800 ÷ 7,000].

   b. The flexible budget formula is $10,500 + $2 × direct labour hours.

   Analysis:

   December's budgeted total overhead is $27,000 [$27,500 – 400 – 100] for 8,250 direct labour hours. November's budgeted total overhead is $24,500 [$25,100 + 200 – 800] for 7,000 direct labour hours. Variable overhead is $2.00 per direct labour hour [($27,000 – 24,500) ÷ (8,250 – 7,000)] and fixed overhead is $10,500 [$27,000 – $2 × 8,250].

   c. The denominator volume is 7,500 direct labour hours or 3,000 units [7,500 ÷ 2.5].

   Analysis:

   The fixed overhead rate is $1.40 per direct labour hour [$3.40 – 2.00] and $10,500 per month. The denominator volume is 7,500 direct labour hours [$10,500 ÷ $1.40].

2. January's overhead flexible variance is $150F and its denominator variance is $350F. [Separate spending and efficiency variances cannot be calculated because we are not given the actual direct labour hours used.

Actual overhead	Budgeted overhead	Applied overhead
	$10,500 + $2.00 × 2.5 × 3,100	$8.50 × 3,100
$25,850	$26,000	$26,350

   Flexible budget $150F   Denominator $350F

14-39

1. The actual price per litre of the direct materials purchased is $0.7625.

   Analysis:

   The standard price of direct materials is $0.75 per litre [$300,000 ÷ 100,000 ÷ 4]. The standard cost of the 440,000 litres purchased is $330,000 [440,000 × 0.75], and the actual cost is $335,500 [$330,000 + 5,500] or $0.7625 per litre [$335,500 ÷ 440,000].

2. The actual prime cost of a case of Magic-Glue during 2005 is $29.98.

   Analysis:

Direct materials	$ 300,425	[394,000 × 0.7625]
Direct labour	2,607,700	[293,000 × ($2,700,000 ÷ 300,000) – $29,300
Actual prime cost	$2,908,125	
Per case	$29.98	[$2,908,125 ÷ 97,000]

3. The variable overhead spending variance is $23,000U. The variable overhead efficiency variance is $2,000U.

Actual cost	Budget @ AH SR × AH	Budget @ SH SR × SH
$316,000	$1.00 × 293,000 $293,000	$1.00 × 3 × 97,000 $291,000

   Spending $23,000U   Efficiency $2,000U

   The standard variable overhead rate is $1.00 per direct labour hour [$300,000 ÷ 300,000].

   The standard direct labour quantity is 3 hours per unit [300,000 ÷ 100,000].

   The fixed overhead spending variance is $21,600U. The fixed overhead denominator variance is $18,000U.

Actual cost	Budget	Applied
$621,600	$600,000	$582,000

   Spending $21,600U   Denominator $18,000U

   The actual fixed overhead cost is $621,600 [$937,600 – 316,000].

   Applied fixed overhead is $6.00 per unit [$600,000 ÷ 100,000] or $582,000 for 97,000 units [$6.00 × 97,000]

14-41

1. The actual quantity of materials purchased is 30,000 litres.

    Analysis:

    The material price variance is $600F – based on the difference between the actual price of $3.98 and the standard price of $4.00. The quantity purchased is 30,000 litres [$600 ÷ ($4.00 – 3.98)].

2. The quantity of materials used is 25,400 litres.

    Analysis:

    The material quantity variance is $1,600U – based on the difference between the actual quantity used and the standard quantity allowed of 25,000 litres [5,000 × 5]. The standard cost of materials is $100,000 [25,000 × $4.00] and the standard cost of materials used is $101,600 [$100,000 + 1,600] – thus 25,400 litres were used [$101,600 ÷ $4.00].

3. The actual direct labour worked is 14,800 hours.

    Analysis:

    The direct labour rate variance is $7,400U – based on the difference between the actual rate of $10.50 and the standard rate of $10.00. The direct labour used is 14,800 hours [$7,400 ÷ ($10.50 – 10.00)].

4. The labour efficiency variance is $2,000F.

    Analysis:

    The standard cost of the direct labour used is $148,000 [14,800 × $10.00]. The standard direct labour cost for the 5,000 units produced is $150,000 [5,000 × 3 × $10.00] for a direct labour efficiency variance of $2,000F [$150,000 – 148,000].

5. The variable overhead efficiency variance is $1,000F.

    Analysis:

    The standard variable overhead rate is $5.00 per direct labour hour [$750,000 ÷ (50,000 × 3)]. The variable overhead flexible budget for the direct labour hours used is $74,000 [14,800 × $5.00]. The variable overhead flexible budget for the standard direct labour hours for the 5,000 units produced is $75,000 [5,000 × 3 × $5.00] for a variable overhead efficiency variance of $1,000F [$75,000 – 74,000].

6. The actual variable overhead is $75,800 [$74,000 + 1,800].

7. The fixed overhead spending variance is $500U.

    Analysis:

    Budgeted fixed overhead per month is $87,500 [$1,050,000 ÷ 12]. Actual fixed overhead is $88,000 – with a fixed overhead spending variance of $500U [$88,000 – 87,500].

8. The fixed overhead denominator variance is $17,500F.

    Analysis:

    Budgeted fixed overhead per month is $87,500 [see requirement 7]. The standard fixed overhead rate is $21.00 per unit [$1,050,000 ÷ 50,000]. Applied fixed overhead is $105,000 [$21.00 × 5,000] – with a fixed overhead denominator variance of $17,500F [$105,000 – 87,500].

14-43

1. Sennen's budgeted and actual income statements are:

	Budget	Actual	
Sales of A	$2,400,000	$2,730,000	[12,000 × $200; 13,000 × $210]
Sales of B	800,000	675,000	[8,000 × $100; 7,500 × $90]
Total sales	$3,200,000	$3,405,000	
Variable cost of A	$1,680,000	$1,690,000	[12,000 × $140; 13,000 × $130]
Variable cost of B	400,000	300,000	[8,000 × $50; 7,500 × $40]
Total Variable cost	$2,080,000	$1,990,000	
Contribution margin	$1,120,000	$1,415,000	
Fixed cost	600,000	620,000	
Operating income	$ 520,000	$ 795,000	

2. The sales price variance is $55,000F. The variable cost variance is $205,000F. The fixed cost variance is $20,000U [$620,000 – 600,000].

    Analysis:

    A's sales price variance is $130,000F [($210 – 200) × 13,000]; B's sales price variance is $75,000U [($90 – 100) × 7,500]. The total sales price variance is $55,000F [$130,000 – 75,000].

    A's variable cost variance is $130,000F [($140 – 130) × 13,000]; B's variable cost variance is $75,000F [($50 – 40) × 7,500]. The total variable cost variance is $205,000F [$130,000 + 75,000].

    The profit volume (gross) variance is $35,000F.

    Analysis:

    The budgeted contribution margin (budgeted selling price – budgeted variable cost) is $60 for A [$200 – 140] and $50 for B [$100 – 50]. A's profit volume variance is $60,000F [(13,000 – 12,000) × $60]; B's profit volume variance is $25,000U [(7,500 – 8,000) × $50]. The total profit volume (gross) variance is 35,000F [$60,000 – 25,000].

    The profit volume (gross) variance of $35,000F can be separated into a sales mix variance of $7,000F and a profit volume (net) variance of $28,000F.

    Analysis:

    The budgeted contribution margin (budgeted mix) is $1,148,000 [(13,000 + 7,500) × ($1,120,000 ÷ (12,000 + 8,000)]. The budgeted contribution margin (actual mix) is $1,155,000 [(13,000 × $60) + (7,500 × $50)]. The sales mix variance is $7,000F [$1,148,000 – 1,155,000]. The profit volume (net) variance is $28,000F [$1,148,000 – 1,120,000].

    The profit volume (net) variance of $28,000F can be separated into an industry volume variance of $104,000F and a market share variance is $76,000U.

    Analysis:

    Based on the budgeted market share of 12% for A [12,000 ÷ 100,000] and 16% for B, the change in industry volume results in an industry volume variance of $144,000F for A [(12% × 120,000 – 12,000) × $60] and $40,000U for B [(16% × 45,000 – 8,000) × $50]. The total industry volume variance is $104,000F [$144,000 – 40,000]. The budgeted contribution margin for the budgeted market share is $1,224,000 [(12% × 120,000 × $60 + 16% × 45,000 × $50]; the budgeted contribution margin for actual market share (budgeted mix) is $1,148,000 [as above]. The market share variance is $76,000U.

14-43 continued

Summary:

Budgeted operating income	$520,000
Sales price variance	55,000F
Variable cost variance	205,000F
Fixed cost variance	20,000U
Sales mix variance	7,000F
Market share variance	76,000U
Industry volume variance	104,000F
Actual operating income	$795,000

3. The company has shown improved performance in both sales prices and variable costs (large favourable variances) with a small increase in fixed costs. The company has benefited from an increase in industry volume but has lost market share. Overall operating income is $275,000 higher than budgeted.

MANAGERIAL DECISION CASES

14-45

1. The major advantages of using a standard cost system include:

    - Standard costs are important for budgeting and planning purposes. Standards are often the starting point in developing budgets and are the basis for flexible budgeting.

    - Variance analysis is important for performance evaluation and control purposes. Managers use cost variance information to identify deviations from expected results, the need to investigate an activity, and the cause of the deviation. This information is fundamental for effective control.

    - Standard costs are used by managers in decision making. Employees are able to clearly understand what is expected of them and what to expect from other parts of the company.

2. The major disadvantages from the use of a standard cost system include:

    - Standards that are too tight can cause dysfunctional behaviour and have poor motivational effects. Standards that are too loose will not provide the benefits identified in requirement 1.

    - Standards may ignore qualitative factors – leading to an overemphasis on cost reduction and a failure to maintain product quality.

    - A standard cost system with detailed analysis of variances may be inconsistent with the emphasis on continuous improvement integral to management in an advanced manufacturing environment.

3. The key individuals who should participate in setting standards include top management, production and operating personnel, and support staff from purchasing, human resources, engineering and operations management, and accounting. Setting effective standards is similar to participative budgeting.

    Top management is an important part of setting standards – without support from top management, a standard costing system is rarely as successful as it could be.

    Operating personnel must be involved because they are responsible for implementing and using the standard costs. Their participation is important both for their knowledge of operations and to secure their commitment to the process.

    Support staff (purchasing, human resources, engineering and operations management, and accounting) have an important role in setting standards. They have information about prices and availability of resources, input-output relationships, and cost-activity relationships.

4. A standard costing system is an effective tool for control if the standards are challenging but achievable and established with the active participation of all key individuals. Participation establishes a sense of legitimacy of the standard cost system. Challenging but achievable standards increases the control information provide by variance analysis.

5. If Mr. Gordon has the consulting firm set McOcean's standards, the benefits of participation and the knowledge of operating and staff personnel may be lost. Employees may react negatively to the standard cost system and view it as illegitimate. Standards may not be achievable and cause dissatisfaction among employees because of the perceived lack of control over their performance.

14-47

1. Pat's decision is not a good decision for the company. Although it will save on the purchase price of the component, it will suffer from higher costs in other areas as well as long-term problems with product quality and customer satisfaction. Pat has made a decision to further his own interests by qualifying for his annual bonus – not a decision in the best interests of his employer. His assessment of his personal risk was important for making the decision – he expects to avoid responsibility for the future problems and consequences of his decision. This should not be a consideration.

2. The company's use of standards has played a substantial role in Pat's decision. He has acted to qualify for a bonus that is part of the company's evaluation/reward system. Often these systems encourage decisions that appear to be good in the short term but which have dysfunctional long-term consequences. A better system will emphasize long-term performance and emphasize ethical conduct over achieving short-term performance objectives.

3. Managers such as purchasing managers are expected to act ethically. Integrity is expected of all managers. Pat should not put his personal interest ahead of the company's interest. Every company should adopt a code of ethical conduct, all employees should be aware of what behaviour is acceptable and unacceptable, performance evaluation and reward systems should be designed to avoid incentives for managers to engage in unethical conduct.

MANAGEMENT ACCOUNTING
CANADIAN SIXTH EDITION
SOLUTIONS MANUAL

CHAPTER 15
QUALITY COSTS AND PRODUCTIVITY:
MEASUREMENT, REPORTING, AND CONTROL

ANSWERS TO ODD-NUMBERED QUESTIONS FOR WRITING AND DISCUSSION

1.   Quality is meeting or exceeding a customer's expectations for a product or service. A customer's expectations may include quality attributes such as performance, aesthetics, serviceability, features, reliability, durability, conformance, and fitness of use.

3.   Quality of conformance is a measure of how a product meets or exceeds its specifications or design requirements.

5.   Quality costs are the costs incurred because poor quality exists (or may exist). If producing good quality goods and services is doing things right, then quality costs are the result of doing things wrong.

7.   External failure costs can be more devastating to a company than internal failure costs because the consequences of loss of market share, lawsuits for product liability, and damage to a company's reputation are far reaching and long lived. Internal failure costs are more localized and limited.

9.   Three methods for estimating hidden quality costs are the multiplier method, the market research method, and the Taguchi loss function method.

11. The AQL (Acceptable Quality Level) model assumes a tradeoff between control costs and failure costs. As control costs increase, failure costs are assumed to decrease. It may be beneficial to produce a certain percentage of defective units – the acceptable quality level where total quality costs are minimized.

     The zero-defects model takes the view that nonconforming units should be reduced to zero. Any defective unit is more costly than preventing its production and quality costs are minimized only when no defective units are produced.

13. Multiple-period trend analysis for quality costs is used to track the change in quality costs through time. This analysis can show the effect of quality improvement efforts over time and opportunities for future improvement.

15. Total measures of productivity consider all inputs at once. Partial measures of productivity consider only one input at a time.

17. A manager can measure productivity improvement through a comparison with a benchmark or standard such as the productivity of a prior period.

19. Profit-linked productivity measurement is important because it allows managers to understand the financial impact of productivity changes. Managers can evaluate the economic effect of input tradeoffs – profit-linked productivity effects can be assigned to individual inputs.

21. Even companies that produce few or zero defective units (that is, are producing high quality products and services) may be using inefficient processes. They may be able to further reduce the inputs they use, and at the same time maintain high quality production.

23. Quality is concerned with producing products and services that meet customer expectations; productivity is concerned with producing output efficiently (at low cost or using minimum inputs). Improving quality often results in improved productivity (reducing waste and rework for example) but productivity can be improved without improving quality (when all output already conforms to product specifications, for example).

SOLUTIONS TO ODD-NUMBERED EXERCISES, PROBLEMS, AND CASES

EXERCISES

15-1

1. c

2. e

3. b

4. a

5. c

15-3

1. Huntington's quality cost report for 2005 and 2006:

	2005 Quality Costs	*Percentage of Sales*	*2006 Quality Costs*	*Percentage of Sales*
Prevention costs:				
Design review	$150,000		$300,000	
Quality training	40,000		100,000	
Total	$190,000	3.17%	$400,000	6.67%
Appraisal costs:				
Materials inspection	$ 60,000		$ 40,000	
Process acceptance	0		50,000	
Product inspection	50,000		30,000	
Total	$110,000	1.83%	$120,000	2.00%
Internal failure costs				
Reinspection	$100,000		$ 50,000	
Scrap	145,000		35,000	
Total	$245,000	4.08%	$ 85,000	1.42%
External failure costs				
Recalls	$200,000		$100,000	
Lost sales	300,000		200,000	
Returned goods	155,000		95,000	
Total	$655,000	10.92%	$395,000	6.58%
Grand total	$1,200,000	20.00%	$1,000,000	16.67%

2. Huntington invested $220,000 in additional control costs [$400,000 + 120,000 – ($190,000 + 110,000)]. This investment reduced failure costs by $420,000 [$245,000 + 655,000 – ($85,000 + 395,000)], for a reduction in quality costs of $200,000 [$420,000 – 220,000] or 3.33 percent of revenue [$200,000 ÷ $6,000,000].

3. The additional profit potential (quality cost reduction) if quality costs are reduced to 2.5% of sales is $850,000 [$1,000,000 – (2.5% × $6,000,000)]. Quality experts believe that optimal quality costs should be between 2 percent and 4 percent of sales – Huntington's goal is within this range and should be a realistic target.

15-5

1. Kumara should add quality training, process control, supplier evaluation, and engineering redesign. Each of these prevention activities reduces failure costs by more than it costs. Product inspection and prototype testing cost more than they reduce failure costs and should not be adopted. The total quality costs will be $1,080,000.

   Analysis:

   Quality training has a cost of $200,000 [$400,000 – 200,000] and reduces failure costs by $500,000 [$1,800,000 – 1,300,000] – reduces quality costs by $300,000 [$500,000 – 200,000].

   Process control has a cost of $250,000 [$650,000 – 400,000] and reduces failure costs by $400,000 [$1,300,000 – 900,000] – reduces quality costs by $150,000 [$400,000 – 250,000].

   Product inspection has a cost of $100,000 [$750,000 – 650,000] and reduces failure costs by $80,000 [$900,000 – 820,000] – increases quality costs by $20,000 [$100,000 – 80,000].

   Supplier evaluation has a cost of $150,000 [$900,000 – 750,000] and reduces failure costs by $570,000 [$820,000 – 250,000] – reduces quality costs by $420,000 [$570,000 – 150,000].

   Prototype testing has a cost of $300,000 [$1,200,000 – 900,000] and reduces failure costs by $100,000 [$250,000 – 150,000] – increases quality costs by $200,000 [$300,000 – 100,000].

   Engineering redesign has a cost of $50,000 [$1,250,000 – 1,200,000] and reduces failure costs by $100,000 [$150,000 – 50,000] – reduces quality costs by $50,000 [$100,000 – 50,000].

   Total quality costs:

Quality training	$ 200,000	
Process control	250,000	
Supplier evaluation	150,000	
Engineering design	50,000	
Appraisal costs	200,000	[current control costs]
Failure costs	230,000	[$1,800,000 – ($500,000 + 400,000 + 570,000 + 100,000)]
Total quality costs	$1,080,000	

2. a. The reduction in total quality costs is $920,000 [$200,000 + 1,800,000 – 1,080,000].

   b. Control costs are 79 percent of Kumara's quality costs [($1,080,000 – 230,000) ÷ $1,080,000]. Failure costs are 21 percent of Kumara's quality costs [$230,000 ÷ $1,080,000].

   c. This year's bonus pool is $92,000 [10% × $920,000].

3. If the quality engineer's approach were adopted, all of the prevention activities would be adopted because each reduces the company's failure costs. This would be the activities added as in requirement 1 plus the prototype testing because the control costs would not be counted in the cost reduction calculation. Product inspection is an appraisal activity and would not be added because its cost is greater than the related reduction in failure costs. Process control is an appraisal activity but it would be added because its cost is less than the decrease in the related failure costs. Appraisal and failure costs will be reduced by $1,420,000 with a bonus pool of $142,000 [$1,420,000 × 10%].

   There is some merit to this approach because it focuses on reducing nonvalue-added activities and encourages investing in prevention activities. It is possible that mangers will over invest in prevention activities (such as prototype testing) that reduce failure costs by less than their added costs.

15-5 continued

Analysis:

New appraisal costs	$ 450,000	[$200,000 + 250,000]
New failure costs	130,000	[$230,000 – 100,000]
New total	$ 580,000	
Current total	2,000,000	[$200,000 + 1,800,000]
Reduction in cost	$1,420,000	

15-7

1. The loss for each unit in the sample (calculated using the Taguchi quality loss function) is shown in the table below. The average loss for the sample is $11.08 [$55.40 ÷ 5].

Unit	Measured weight (Y)	$(Y - T)$	$(Y - T)^2$	$K(Y - T)^2$
1	20.20	0.20	0.04	$ 3.20
2	20.50	0.50	0.25	20.00
3	20.30	0.30	0.09	7.20
4	19.50	–0.50	0.25	20.00
5	19.75	–0.25	0.0625	5.00
Total				$55.40

Target value = T = 20 grams; Constant of proportionality = K = $80.

2. The hidden quality costs for April are $138,500 [$11.08 × 12,500].

15-9

1. The output/input ratio for Combination A is 2 for energy [100 ÷ 50] and 0.5 for labour [100 ÷ 200]. This represents an improvement over the current use of inputs – current productivity is 1.25 for energy [100 ÷ 80] and 0.3125 for labour [100 ÷ 320]. Combination A produces more output from both energy and labour. The total dollar value of the improvement is $2,340. This is a technical efficiency improvement because the same output is produced with proportionately less input (the ratio of energy and labour remains at 1:4).

Analysis:

Cost of current combination	$6,240	[80 × $18 + 320 × 15]
Cost of Combination A	3,900	[50 × $18 + 200 × 15]
Dollar value of improvement	$2,340	

2. The output/input ratio for Combination B is 1.25 for energy [100 ÷ 80] and 0.8 for labour [100 ÷ 125]. This represents an improvement over the current use of inputs – current productivity is 1.25 for energy [100 ÷ 80] and 0.3125 for labour [100 ÷ 320] – for labour. The productivity of energy is unchanged.

Combination B has higher productivity for labour than Combination A (0.8 compared to 0.5) but lower productivity for energy (1.25 compared to 2). There is a trade off between the use of labour and the use of energy when comparing Combinations A and B.

15-9 continued

3. The cost of producing 100 units of output with Combination B is $3,315 [80 × $18 + 125 × $15] – $585 less than the cost with Combination A [$3,900 – 3,315]. Moving from Combination A to Combination B is a productivity improvement (same output at a lower cost). This is an input tradeoff efficiency improvement.

15-11

1. Masterkraft's partial productivity measures are:

	Year Before	Year After	
Materials	4	6	[200,000 ÷ 50,000; 240,000 ÷ 40,000]
Labour	20	60	[200,000 ÷ 10,000; 240,000 ÷ 4,000]
Capital	20	0.4	[200,000 ÷ $10,000; 240,000 ÷ $600,000]

Materials and labour productivity have increased because of the investment in new capital (the automated manufacturing system). Less material and labour is required per unit of output. Productivity of capital has decreased – Masterkraft has made a tradeoff between materials and labour and capital.

2. Productivity changes have caused a decrease in profits of $8,200 (the profit-linked productivity measure). The change in materials productivity increased profits by $40,000, the change in labour productivity increased profits by $40,000, but the change in capital productivity decreased profits by $88,200. If this outcome is expected to continue, the tradeoff is not favourable and automating was a poor decision.

    Analysis:

    The year before is used as the base year. The productivity neutral quantity (PQ) is 60,000 for materials [240,000 ÷ 4], 12,000 for labour [240,000 ÷ 20], and $12,000 for capital [240,000 ÷ 20]. The actual quantity (AQ) is 40,000 for materials, 4,000 for labour, and $600,000 for capital. The profit-linked productivity is summarized in the following table.

	PQ	AQ	Price	(PQ – AQ) × Price
Materials	60,000	40,000	$2.00	$40,000
Labour	12,000	4,000	5.00	40,000
Capital	12,000	600,000	0.15	(88,200)
Total				$ (8,200)

15-13

1. Sohee's partial productivity measures for materials and labour are:

	Current	Automated	
Materials	0.25	0.29	[10,000 ÷ 40,000; 10,000 ÷ 35,000]
Labour	0.50	0.67	[10,000 ÷ 20,000; 10,000 ÷ 15,000]

The automated process results in increased productivity for both materials and labour as the production manager thought.

15-13 continued

2. Sohee's partial productivity measures for all four inputs (materials, labour, capital, and energy) are:

	Current	Automated	
Materials	0.25	0.29	[10,000 ÷ 40,000; 10,000 ÷ 35,000]
Labour	0.50	0.67	[10,000 ÷ 20,000; 10,000 ÷ 15,000]
Capital	0.50	0.10	[10,000 ÷ $20,000; 10,000 ÷ $100,000]
Energy	1.00	0.40	[10,000 ÷ 10,000; 10,000 ÷ 25,000]

The automated process results in increased productivity for both materials and labour but the productivity of capital and energy is lower. We cannot tell whether total productivity has improved without valuing the input tradeoffs.

3. The automated system's profit-linked productivity is $19,500. The profit-linked productivity measure values the tradeoffs between using labour, materials, capital, and energy (the input tradeoff efficiency) – the greater labour and material productivity with the automated system is more valuable than the lower productivity of capital and energy.

Analysis:

The current system is used as the base year. The productivity neutral quantity (PQ) is 40,000 for materials [10,000 ÷ 0.25], 20,000 for labour [10,000 ÷ 0.50], $20,000 for capital [10,000 ÷ 0.50], and 10,000 for energy [10,000 ÷ 1.00]. The actual quantity (AQ) is 35,000 for materials, 15,000 for labour, $100,000 for capital, and 25,000 for energy. The automated system's profit-linked productivity is summarized in the following table.

	PQ	AQ	Price	(PQ – AQ) × Price
Materials	40,000	35,000	$ 4.00	$20,000
Labour	20,000	15,000	9.00	45,000
Capital	20,000	100,000	0.10	(8,000)
Energy	10,000	25,000	2.50	(37,500)
Total				$19,500

PROBLEMS

15-15

	Quality Cost	Type
1.	Prototype inspection and testing.	prevention
2.	Reinspection of reworked product.	internal failure
3.	Packaging and shipping repaired goods.	external failure
4.	Loss of customer goodwill due to inferior-quality products.	external failure
5.	Grinding bumps off a poorly welded steel plate.	internal failure
6.	Maintenance of inspection equipment.	appraisal
7.	Design verification and review to evaluate the quality of new products.	prevention
8.	Design and development of quality equipment.	prevention
9.	Quality training program for new personnel.	prevention
10.	Correcting an improperly filled out purchase order.	internal failure
11.	The cost of purchasing replacement parts to repair a product that breaks down while under warranty.	external failure
12.	Internal audit assessing the effectiveness of the quality system.	appraisal
13.	Replacing a component that was improperly inserted and damaged.	internal failure
14.	Machine jammed and damaged because of an incorrectly sized subassembly.	internal failure
15.	Quality reporting.	prevention
16.	Proofreading.	appraisal
17.	Cost to incinerate scrap.	internal failure
18.	Setup for testing.	appraisal
19.	Lending engineers to help improve processes and products of suppliers.	prevention
20.	Developing a new quality improvement program.	prevention
21.	Extra overhead costs incurred due to returned products.	external failure
22.	Supervision of in-process inspection.	appraisal
23.	Inspection of parts purchased from suppliers.	appraisal
24.	Customer complaint department.	external failure
25.	Outside laboratory evaluation of product quality	appraisal

15-17

1. Ontor's quality cost report is:

	Quality Costs	Percentage of Sales	
Prevention costs:			
Quality training	$160,000		[given]
Total	$160,000	0.80%	
Appraisal costs:			
Product inspection	$300,000		[10 × $30,000]
Test equipment	240,000		[given]
Total	$540,000	2.70%	
Internal failure costs			
Scrap	$ 900,000		[60,000 × $15]
Rework	720,000		[300,000 × 80% × $3]
Total	$1,620,000	8.10%	
External failure costs			
Repair	$ 420,000		[60,000 × $7]
Lost sales	500,000		[given]
Customer complaints	200,000		[8 × $25,000]
Sales allowances	250,000		[given]
Total	$1,370,000	6.85%	
Grand total	$3,690,000	18.45%	

The company's quality cost/sales ratio is 18.45 percent of sales (and quality costs are almost as large as its net income). The company has considerable room for improvement (Linda may see 5 percent as a desirable target). Most of its quality costs are failure costs; control costs are 3.5 percent of sales.

2. Ontor's distribution of quality costs is:

Type of cost	Quality cost	Percentage of total
Internal failure costs	$1,620,000	43.9%
External failure costs	1,370,000	37.1%
Appraisal costs	540,000	14.6%
Prevention costs	160,000	4.3%
Total quality costs	$3,690,000	100.0%

Ontar is spending more on failure activities (81 percent of its quality costs) than on control activities (19 percent of its quality costs). It may be able to reduce its failure costs by increasing its control costs – a shift in emphasis that often results in less total quality costs.

3. The American Society for Quality Control advocates attacking failure costs directly to drive them to zero. Ontor can do this by investing in control costs to discover the cause of failure costs (appraisal) and take steps to eliminate the cause (prevention). Control costs are needed to eliminate failure costs but prevention is believed to be cheaper than failure. Appraisal costs can be reduced as improved quality is achieved and prevention costs should be reviewed to gain further improvement. Ontor needs to pay more attention to control activities and avoid the failure activities that dominate its current distribution.

4. If Ontor can reduce its quality costs to 2.5 percent of sales, and sales remain at $20,000,000, it will save $3,190,000 on quality costs [$20,000,000 × (18.45% – 2.5%] and its net income will increase by $3,190,000 to $7,190,000. If control costs are 80 percent of its quality costs, Ontor will spend $400,000 on control costs [$20,000,000 × 2.5% × 80%] and $100,000 on failure costs [$20,000,000 × 2.5% × 20%].

15-17 continued

5. If the bonus pool is 20 percent of quality cost reductions, $638,000 will be placed in the bonus pool over five years [$3,190,000 × 20%]. Establishing a bonus pool provides an incentive for employees to seek ways to improve quality and decrease quality costs. The manager has suggested basing the bonus pool on only reductions in appraisal and failure costs to encourage investment in prevention activities. A possible downside to this approach is a tendency to over-invest in prevention costs (where prevention may cost more than the reduction in other quality costs).

6. Using a multiplier of 3, the actual external failure costs (including hidden costs) is $4,110,000 [$1,370,000 × 3] Other methods for estimating hidden quality costs include market research and the Taguchi quality-loss function. If hidden costs are considered, the potential profit improvement from a quality improvement strategy increases (hidden costs are almost as great as the observable quality costs). If the hidden costs are included in the bonus pool, employees will have more incentive to seek ways to improve quality and reduce quality costs. Of course, the hidden costs will have to be re-estimated each year. The bonus pool will increase by 20 percent of the reduction in hidden costs.

15-19

1. The division's breakeven point in revenues for 2002 was $120,000,000. The division operating loss was $4,000,000.

    Analysis:

    The division's contribution margin ratio was 0.2 [1 – 0.8] and its fixed cost was $24,000,000. Thus its breakeven point was $120,000,000 [$24,000,000 ÷ 0.2].

    With sales of $100,000,000 in 2002, its operating loss is $4,000,000 [($120,000,000 – 100,000,000) × 0.2].

2. The division's breakeven point in revenues for 2003 was $100,000,000. The quality improvement program increased fixed costs and decreased variable costs. As a result of this shift in costs, the division's breakeven point was lower and the company eliminated the previous period's loss.

    Analysis:

    The division's variable costs decreased by $10,000,000 [$32,000,000 – 22,000,000] or by 10 percent of sales [$10,000,000 ÷ 100,000,000]. As a result of the lower variable costs, the division's new contribution margin ratio contribution margin ratio was 0.3 [1 – (0.8 – 0.1)]. Its fixed cost increased by $6,000,000 [$14,000,000 – 8,000,000] to $30,000,000 [$24,000,000 + 6,000,000]. Thus its 2003 breakeven point was $100,000,000 [$30,000,000 ÷ 0.3].

3. The division's breakeven point in revenues for 2007 is $34,108,527. It often is possible to reduce quality costs to the degree expected. Many companies have been able to achieve the cost targets Westwood has set with accompanying profit improvement (the division's profit will increase to $34,000,000 [$100,000,000 × 0.516 – 17,600,000]).

    Analysis:

    The division's variable costs will decrease by $31,600,000 [$32,000,000 – 400,000]. The division's variable costs (at sales of $100,000,000) are $48,400,000 [$100,000,000 × 0.8 – 31,600,000] or 48.4 percent of sales [$48,400,000 ÷ 100,000,000]. As a result of the lower variable costs, the division's new contribution margin ratio contribution margin ratio is 0.516 [1 – 0.484]. Its fixed cost decreased by $6,400,000 [$8,000,000 – 1,600,000] to $17,600,000 [$24,000,000 – 6,400,000]. Thus its 2003 breakeven point was $34,108,527 [$17,600,000 ÷ 0.516].

15-19 continued

4. Under the 2002 cost structure, the division would have an operating loss of $12,000,000 if it dropped its prices and revenue dropped to $60,000,000 [($120,000,000 – 60,000,000) × 0.2]. Under the 2007 cost structure, the division would have an operating income of $13,360,000 [($60,000,000 – 34,108,527) × 0.516].

   By decreasing its quality costs (and improving its cost-volume-profit relationships), the division is better able to respond to competitive pressure and remain profitable.

15-21

1. The company has exactly achieved its objective of quality costs of no more than 5 percent of sales. The manager's objective of distributing quality costs evenly does not seem to be effective. The best performance is achieved with napkins where more has been spent on control costs (prevention and appraisal) than required for failure costs. He has achieved an equal distribution for towels but towels show poorer performance with higher failure costs (although more has been spent of control costs for towels than napkins or diapers – perhaps this is a more complex or specialized product). The company should consider increasing its spending on prevention costs to further reduce failure costs for diapers and towels.

	Diapers	Napkins	Towels	Total
Prevention	0.9%	1.0%	1.6%	1.1%
Appraisal	0.8%	1.2%	1.6%	1.1%
Internal failure	1.8%	1.1%	1.6%	1.6%
External failure	1.5%	0.8%	1.6%	1.3%
Total	5.0%	4.0%	6.5%	5.0%

   Calculations:

   Prevention: $9,000 ÷ $1,000,000; $6,000 ÷ $600,000; $6,500 ÷ $400,000; $21,500 ÷ $2,000,000

   Appraisal: $8,000 ÷ $1,000,000; $7,000 ÷ $600,000; $6,500 ÷ $400,000; $21,500 ÷ $2,000,000

   Internal failure: $18,000 ÷ $1,000,000; $6,500 ÷ $600,000; $6,500 ÷ $400,000; $31,000 ÷ $2,000,000

   External failure: $15,000 ÷ $1,000,000; $4,500 ÷ $600,000; $6,500 ÷ $400,000; $26,000 ÷ $2,000,000

   Total quality costs: $50,000 ÷ $1,000,000; $24,000 ÷ $600,000; $26,000 ÷ $400,000; $100,000 ÷ $2,000,000

2. The company has not achieved its objective of quality costs of no more than 5 percent of sales. The manager's objective of distributing quality costs evenly does not seem to be effective. The best performance is achieved with napkins where more has been spent on control costs (prevention and appraisal) than required for failure costs. He has achieved an equal distribution for towels but towels show poorer performance with higher failure costs (although more has been spent of control costs for towels than napkins or diapers – perhaps this is a more complex or specialized product). The company should consider increasing its spending on prevention costs to further reduce failure costs for diapers and towels.

	Diapers	Napkins	Towels	Total
Prevention	1.8%	2.0%	3.3%	2.2%
Appraisal	1.6%	2.3%	3.3%	2.2%
Internal failure	3.6%	2.2%	3.3%	3.1%
External failure	3.0%	1.5%	3.3%	2.6%
Total	10.0%	8.0%	13.0%	10.0%

15-21 continued

Calculations:

Prevention: $9,000 ÷ $500,000; $6,000 ÷ $300,000; $6,500 ÷ $200,000; $21,500 ÷ $1,000,000

Appraisal: $8,000 ÷ $500,000; $7,000 ÷ $300,000; $6,500 ÷ $200,000; $21,500 ÷ $1,000,000

Internal failure: $18,000 ÷ $500,000; $6,500 ÷ $300,000; $6,500 ÷ $200,000; $31,000 ÷ $1,000,000

External failure: $15,000 ÷ $500,000; $4,500 ÷ $300,000; $6,500 ÷ $200,000; $26,000 ÷ $1,000,000

Total quality costs: $50,000 ÷ $500,000; $24,000 ÷ $300,000; $26,000 ÷ $200,000; $100,000 ÷ $1,000,000

3. The company has not achieved its objective of quality costs of no more than 5 percent of sales. The manager's objective of distributing quality costs evenly does seem to be effective. The best performance is achieved with towels where control costs (prevention and appraisal) are the same as failure costs. The company should consider increasing its spending on prevention costs to reduce failure costs for diapers but it is already spending more on control costs than failure costs for napkins. Perhaps napkins are more difficult to produce or have more exacting specifications and require more prevention activity to reduce failure costs.

	Diapers	Napkins	Towels	Total
Prevention	1.8%	3.3%	2.0%	2.2%
Appraisal	1.6%	3.9%	2.0%	2.2%
Internal failure	3.6%	3.6%	2.0%	3.1%
External failure	3.0%	2.5%	2.0%	2.6%
Total	10.0%	13.3%	8.1%	10.0%

Calculations:

Prevention: $9,000 ÷ $500,000; $6,000 ÷ $180,000; $6,500 ÷ $320,000; $21,500 ÷ $1,000,000

Appraisal: $8,000 ÷ $500,000; $7,000 ÷ $180,000; $6,500 ÷ $320,000; $21,500 ÷ $1,000,000

Internal failure: $18,000 ÷ $500,000; $6,500 ÷ $180,000; $6,500 ÷ $320,000; $31,000 ÷ $1,000,000

External failure: $15,000 ÷ $500,000; $4,500 ÷ $180,000; $6,500 ÷ $320,000; $26,000 ÷ $1,000,000

Total quality costs: $50,000 ÷ $500,000; $24,000 ÷ $180,000; $26,000 ÷ $320,000; $100,000 ÷ $1,000,000

4. The quality report by segment allows managers to evaluate the effectiveness of their quality improvement efforts. If a manager can identify relationships between control and failure costs he may be able to tell where to devote additional control resources.

15-23

1. Norcan Leather's partial productivity measures are:

	2004	2005	
Materials	0.5	0.6	[100,000 ÷ 200,000; 120,000 ÷ 200,000]
Labour	2.0	2.4	[100,000 ÷ 50,000; 120,000 ÷ 50,000]

Materials and labour productivity have both increased because of the productivity improvement program. Less material and labour is required per unit of output.

15-23 continued

2. Norcan Leather's profit-linked productivity measure is $460,000 – profits increased by $460,000 due to improved productivity. A bonus of 10 percent of productivity gains or $46,000 was paid [$460,000 × 10%] for a net profit improvement of $414,000 [$460,000 – 46,000].

    Analysis:

    2004 is used as the base year. The productivity neutral quantity (PQ) is 240,000 for materials [120,000 ÷ 0.5] and 60,000 for labour [120,000 ÷ 2.0]. The actual quantity (AQ) is 200,000 for materials and 50,000 for labour. The profit-linked productivity is summarized in the following table.

	PQ	AQ	Price	(PQ – AQ) × Price
Materials	240,000	200,000	$ 9.00	$360,000
Labour	60,000	50,000	10.00	100,000
Total				$460,000

3. The price recovery component for 2005 is a decrease of $70,000 [$390,000 – 460,000]. Price recovery is the profit change that Norcan Leather would have realized without any changes in productivity. Without an improvement in productivity, it would have had less profits – the increase in sales would not have recovered the increase in input costs.

    Analysis:

	2005	2004	Difference
Revenue	$3,840,000	$3,200,000	$640,000
Costs	2,300,000	2,050,000	250,000
Profit	$1,540,000	$1,150,000	$390,000

    Revenue (2004): 100,000 × $32.00; Revenue (2005): 120,000 × $32.00

    Costs (2004): 200,000 × $8.00 + 50,000 × $9.00; Costs (2005): 200,000 × $9.00 + 50,000 × $10.00

15-25

1. Cantco's partial productivity measures are:

	2005	2006	
Materials	4.00	5.00	[400,000 ÷ 100,000; 500,000 ÷ 100,000]
Labour	1.00	2.50	[400,000 ÷ 400,000; 500,000 ÷ 200,000]
Capital	0.10	0.05	[400,000 ÷ $4,000,000; 500,000 ÷ $10,000,000]
Energy	4.00	1.67	[400,000 ÷ 100,000; 500,000 ÷ 300,000]

    Materials and labour productivity increased and capital and energy productivity decreased in 2006. Less materials and labour and more capital and energy is required per unit of output. The trade-off would have to be valued to asses whether overall productivity has improved or not.

2. Cantco's profit-linked productivity measure is $2,225,000 – profits increased by $2,225,000 due to the improvement in productivity.

15-25 continued

Analysis:

2005 is used as the base year. The productivity neutral quantity (PQ) is 125,000 for materials [500,000 ÷ 4.0], 500,000 for labour [500,000 ÷ 1.0], $5,000,000 for capital [500,000 ÷ 0.10], and 125,000 for energy [500,000 ÷ 4.00]. The actual quantity (AQ) is 100,000 for materials, 200,000 for labour, $10,000,000 for capital, and 300,000 for energy. The profit-linked productivity is summarized in the following table.

	PQ	AQ	Price	(PQ – AQ) × Price
Materials	125,000	100,000	$ 3.00	$ 75,000
Labour	500,000	200,000	10.00	3,000,000
Capital	$5,000,000	$10,000,000	0.10	(500,000)
Energy	125,000	300,000	2.00	(350,000)
Total				$2,225,000

3. The cost per unit was $10.50 in 2005 and $7.80 in 2006 – a decrease of $2.70 [$10.50 – 7.80]. The division was able to decrease its unit cost by more than $2.50. Its ability to improve its productivity was critical to the division's competitiveness and survival. Lower cost is a result of improved productivity and a key competitive advantage.

Analysis:

2005

Materials	$ 200,000	[100,000 × $2.00]
Labour	3,200,000	[400,000 × $8.00]
Capital	600,000	[$4,000,000 × 15%]
Energy	200,000	[100,000 × $2.00]
Total	$4,200,000	
Units produced	400,000	
Cost per unit	$10.50	

2006

Materials	$ 300,000	[100,000 × $3.00]
Labour	2,000,000	[200,000 × $10.00]
Capital	1,000,000	[$10,000,000 × 10%]
Energy	600,000	[300,000 × $2.00]
Total	$3,900,000	
Units produced	500,000	
Cost per unit	$7.80	

15-27

1. Marco's partial productivity measures are:

	Current	Setting A	Setting B	
Materials	0.40	1.00	0.50	[10,000 ÷ 25,000; 15,000 ÷ 15,000; 15,000 ÷ 30,000]
Equipment	1.67	1.00	2.00	[10,000 ÷ 6,000; 15,000 ÷ 15,000; 15,000 ÷ 7,500]

Setting B indicates a productivity increase for both inputs. Materials productivity increases for Setting A but equipment productivity decreases.

15-27 continued

2. The profits under Setting A are $240,000 and under Setting B are $150,000. Setting A will give the larger increase in profits – by $90,000 [$240,000 – 150,000].

    Analysis:

	Setting A	Setting B	
Revenue	$600,000	$600,000	[15,000 × $20 × 2 for both]
Materials cost	(180,000)	(360,000)	[15,000 × $3 × 4; 30,000 × $3 × 4]
Equipment cost	(180,000)	(90,000)	[15,000 × $12; 7,500 × $12]
Profit	$240,000	$150,000	

3. The profit-linked productivity is $197,784 for Setting A and $107,784 for Setting B. This shows that Setting A is better than Setting B. The profit-linked productivity measure values the tradeoff between using materials and using equipment (the input tradeoff efficiency) – the greater materials productivity with Setting A is more valuable than the greater productivity of equipment with Setting B.

    Analysis:

    The current setting is used as the base. For Setting A, the productivity neutral quantity (PQ) is 37,500 for materials [15,000 ÷ 0.40] and 8,982 for equipment [15,000 ÷ 1.67]. The actual quantity (AQ) is 15,000 for materials and 15,000 for equipment. Setting A's profit-linked productivity is summarized in the following table.

	PQ	AQ	Price	(PQ – AQ) × Price
Materials	37,500	15,000	$12.00	$270,000
Equipment	8,982	15,000	12.00	(72,216)
Total				$197,784

    For Setting B, the productivity neutral quantities (PQ) are also 37,500 for materials and 8,982 for equipment. The actual quantity (AQ) is 30,000 for materials and 7,500 for equipment. Setting B's profit-linked productivity is summarized in the following table.

	PQ	AQ	Price	(PQ – AQ) × Price
Materials	37,500	30,000	$12.00	$90,000
Equipment	8,982	7,500	12.00	17,784
Total				$107,784

MANAGERIAL DECISION CASES

15-29

1. The bonus is intended to reward real productivity improvements and meeting budget targets for quality cost reductions. What Matt is proposing subverts the intent of the program. He is taking steps to manipulate the program – delaying recognition of failure costs and reducing prevention costs. While both of these will increase the chance he and his employees will qualify for a bonus this year, quality costs will increase – although the costs don't show up until next year – and productivity and quality will be reduced.

    What Matt should do is to maintain the productivity and quality programs that he has in place. Appraisal and prevention activities should be continued and both internal failures (rework, for example) and external failures (repairing and replacing defective products for customers, for example) should be handled promptly. His plan will bring about a one-time benefit but cause long-term and possibly permanent damage.

2. The company should take steps to discourage behaviour similar to Matt's plan by designing performance and reward systems that are difficult to manipulate. Its plan concentrates on some inputs and consequences but fails to consider all relationships. Reducing prevention and appraisal costs rarely lead to productivity and quality improvements. A better plan would require that budgeted spending in these areas be maintained – under-spending on some activities may be more costly than over-spending. The plan should also balance long-term and short-term consequences. A manager should not be able to transfer costs into future periods by delaying acting on complaints and problems. Nonfinancial measures could be incorporated to prevent this behaviour. The company could also carefully examine the changes in key variables to be sure that the objectives of the plan have been meet rather than focusing on a single measure.

3. As a CMA, Matt has an obligation to place the legitimate interests of his employer before his own. He is seeking a personal benefit that will have serious negative consequences for his company. This is a clear violation of the standards of ethical conduct expected of CMAs and managers.

MANAGEMENT ACCOUNTING
CANADIAN SIXTH EDITION
SOLUTIONS MANUAL

CHAPTER 16
FINANCIAL PERFORMANCE EVALUATION
AND TRANSFER PRICING IN DECENTRALIZED COMPANIES

ANSWERS TO ODD-NUMBERED QUESTIONS FOR WRITING AND DISCUSSION

1. In centralized decision making, decisions are made at the very top of the organization, and lower-level managers are charged with implementing those decisions. In contrast, decentralized decision making allows managers at lower levels to make and implement key decisions pertaining to their areas of activity. Decentralization involves delegating decision-making authority to lower levels while centralization retains decision making authority at the top level.

3. Companies choose to decentralize for one or more of the following reasons: utilization of local information; reduction of information overload; more timely response; free central management to focus on strategic decisions; training and motivational opportunities and benefits; enhanced competition among divisions.

5. Although we might think that the manager of the division with operating profits of $3 million did the better job, we cannot say without knowing the assets used to earn the profits. Relating operating profits to the assets used to produce them is a more meaningful measure of performance. There may be other factors that should be considered when making relative performance evaluations.

7. Margin is the ratio of operating income to sales – the income earned from each dollar of sales. Turnover is the ratio of sales to average operating assets – the sales generated from each dollar invested. Together margin and turnover determine the ROI of an investment centre. The investment centre's performance can be better evaluated by decomposing its ROI into margin and turnover.

9. Two disadvantages of ROI are that (1) managers may focus on short-term results at the expense of long-term results, and (2) managers may focus on divisional results at the expense of overall company results.

    Decreased profitability may result because managers may make decisions that are profitable in the short-term (reduce prevention quality activities) but are harmful in the long run or because managers may reject investments that increase the company's profitability but earn less than the division's current ROI.

11. Both ROI and EVA may encourage short-term behaviour at the expense of longer-term results. Cutting year-end advertising expenditures may increase this year's ROI or EVA but hurt future years' sales and profitability. Using multiple measures – including nonfinancial measures that reflect longer term consequences – can reduce over-emphasis on short-term financial results.

13. Goal congruence may be difficult to achieve because the interests of managers and owners are often not the same. Managers may not want to work as hard as owners desire or managers may want to use the company's resources for personal purposes. Appropriate reward systems tied to sound performance evaluation are important to promote goal congruence.

15. A transfer price affects the revenues of the selling division and the costs of the buying division and thus each division's profitability and performance measures (for example, its ROI, RI, or EVA).

    Transfer prices affect company wide profits by affecting division behaviour – a transfer price that is too high (or too low) may cause a buyer (or seller) to reject a transaction that would benefit the company overall.

Transfer prices may affect the decision to decentralize decision-making if top management is tempted to intervene and dictate transfers and transfer prices (often to avoid the loss of company wide gains from transfers). This subverts the principle of decentralization and divisional autonomy.

17. The opportunity cost approach to transfer pricing specifies a floor price as the minimum price a selling division would be willing to accept (the selling division's opportunity cost) and a ceiling price as the maximum price the buying division would be willing to pay (the buying division's opportunity cost). The transfer price would fall within this range.

19. The correct transfer price is the market price if a perfectly competitive outside market exists for an intermediate product. The market price is what a seller division would receive if it sold externally (or its opportunity cost of selling internally) and what a buying division would have to pay if it bought externally (or its opportunity cost of buying). If there are internal benefits from the internal sale (for example, lower transaction costs), the company's profits will increase.

21. Negotiated transfer prices can lead to improved profitability for both the selling and buying divisions and for the company overall. Each division is assumed to recognize its own opportunity costs and a transfer will occur when opportunity costs signal that a transfer is desirable for both divisions – when the selling division's opportunity cost is less than the buying division's opportunity cost. A negotiated transfer price in this range will lead to higher revenues for the selling division and lower costs for the buying division. With a balance of negotiating power, negotiated prices will simultaneously satisfy the three objectives of transfer pricing: (1) accurately measure divisional performance, (2) promote goal congruence, and (3) preserve divisional autonomy

23. Three cost-based transfer prices are full cost, full cost plus markup, and variable cost plus fixed fee. Using cost-based transfer prices may result in inaccurate performance measures and loss of divisional autonomy (for example, a selling division forced to sell often receives little benefit and may suffer a loss if it could have sold the product externally at its regular price) or result in decisions that are not goal congruent (at times, a cost-based transfer price may be higher than the maximum or less than the minimum transfer price based on the selling and buying division's opportunity costs and a profitable transfer is rejected). It may be appropriate to use cost-based pricing when transfers are insignificant and a low cost, simple transfer pricing policy is desired.

25. Income tax differences among countries may create behavioural and ethical problems for multinational companies because, although it is not illegal or unethical to reduce taxes, it is illegal and unethical to evade taxes. Unfortunately, the difference between tax evasion and tax avoidance is often not clear. Companies may be tempted to structure their transfer prices to move profits to low tax companies. The Canada Customs and Revenue Agency requires that multinational transfer prices be "at arm's length" and reflect prices that would be agreed to between unrelated parties.

SOLUTIONS TO ODD-NUMBERED EXERCISES, PROBLEMS, AND CASES

EXERCISES

16-1

A. The plant is likely considered a cost centre with manufacturing cost, standard cost and variance analysis used for performance evaluation. It may be a profit centre with operating income and profit variance analysis used to evaluate performance. However the marketing vice-president has responsibility for pricing and sales, therefore treating the plant as a cost centre is more consistent with the plant manager's authority.

B. Joan is the manager of an investment centre with ROI used for performance evaluation.

C. Gil is the manager of a revenue centre with revenue used to evaluate performance.

D. Susan is the manager of a profit centre with operating income used for performance evaluation.

E. The Eastern Division is treated as an investment centre. Performance is likely evaluated using a measure such as ROI, RI or EVA.

16-3

1. Kaminsky's average operating assets are $40,000 [($38,650 + 41,350) ÷ 2].

2. Kaminsky's margin is 6.5 percent [$5,200 ÷ $80,000] and its turnover ratio is 2 [$80,000 ÷ $40,000].

3. Kaminsky's ROI is 13 percent [$5,200 ÷ $40,000 or 6.5% × 2].

16-5

1. For 2004 Theta Division's margin is 8 percent [$4,000,000 ÷ $50,000,000] and its turnover ratio is 2 [$50,000,000 ÷ $25,000,000]. For 2005 Theta Division's margin is 7.4 percent [$3,700,000 ÷ $50,000,000] and its turnover ratio is 2.5 [$50,000,000 ÷ $20,000,000].

2. Theta Division's 2004 ROI is 16 percent [$4,000,000 ÷ $25,000,000 or 8% × 2]. Theta Division's 2005 ROI is 18.5 percent [$3,700,000 ÷ $20,000,000 or 7.4% × 2.5].

3. Theta Division's 2004 RI is $250,000 [$4,000,000 – ($25,000,000 × 15%)]. Theta Division's 2005 RI is $700,000 [$3,700,000 – ($20,000,000 × 15%)].

4. Theta Division has performed better than Delta Division. Theta Division's performance is better in 2005 than it was in 2004. Both its ROI and its RI are higher. Although its margin has decreased, it has improved its turnover ratio. It has earned more than its minimum require rate of return. Delta Division's performance is poorer in 2005 than it was in 2004. Both its ROI and its RI are lower. The RI measure shows that it earned less than its minimum required rate of return (RI is negative in 2005).

16-7

1. Residual income for the Whirlpool Tubs division is $60,000 [$140,000 – ($1,000,000 × 8%)]. Residual income for the Plumbing Supplies division is $90,000 [$330,000 – ($3,000,000 × 8%)]. As an absolute measure of profitability, residual income may not provide a meaningful comparison of the performance of the divisions. The Whirlpool Tubs division is much smaller than the Plumbing Supplies division and is at a disadvantage when dollar level measures of performance such as sales, operating income, or residual income are used.

2. The residual rate of return is 6 percent for the Whirlpool Tubs division [$60,000 ÷ $1,000,000] and 3 percent for the Plumbing Supplies division [$90,000 ÷ $3,000,000]. The Whirlpool Tubs division has exceeded the company's minimum required rate of return by more than the Plumbing Supplies division has. This might indicate better performance.

3. ROI for the Whirlpool Tubs division is 14 percent [$140,000 ÷ $1,000,000]. ROI for the Plumbing Supplies division is 11 percent [$330,000 ÷ $3,000,000]. As a relative measure of profitability, ROI may not provide a meaningful comparison of the performance of the divisions when there is a large difference in their size. The Whirlpool Tubs division is much smaller than the Plumbing Supplies division and has an advantage when relative measures of performance such as ROI are used. Often the available returns decrease as a division grows and its average ROI is lower, even though its investments are profitable. Focusing on ROI may lead divisions to reject new investments that bring lower ROI than the division's current ROI.

4. The residual rate of return from requirement 2 added to the required rate of return is 14 percent for the Whirlpool Tubs division [6% + 8%] and 11 percent for the Plumbing Supplies division [3% + 8%]. These are the same as the ROIs calculated in requirement 3. This will always be the case because RI is the difference between the division's operating income and the operating income earned on the operating assets used with a ROI equal to the minimum required rate of return.

16-9

1. Ernhardt's new weighted cost of capital is 7.7 percent.

    Analysis:

    The after-tax cost of the unsecured bonds is 4.8 percent [8% × (1 – 40%)], the after-tax cost of the mortgage bonds is 3.6 percent [6% × (1 – 40%)], and the after-tax cost of common stock is 11 percent [5% + 6% – based on the assumption in the chapter that overtime returns on shares are 6 percentage points higher than the return on long-term government bonds]. The unsecured bonds are 21.1 percent of the company's capital [$2,000,000 ÷ ($2,000,000 + 2,500,000 + 5,000,000)], mortgage bonds are 26.3 percent of the company's capital [$2,500,000 ÷ ($2,000,000 + 2,500,000 + 5,000,000)] and common stock 52.6 percent of the company's capital [$5,000,000 ÷ ($2,000,000 + 2,500,000 + 5,000,000)]. The company's weighted average cost of capital is 7.7 percent [21.1% × 4.8% + 26.3 % × 3.6% + 52.6% × 11%].

2. Ernhardt's new EVA is $249,600. The new investment is a good idea because it has increased the company's EVA from $210,000 and shows that the company is creating more wealth.

    Analysis:

    Ernhardt's after-tax operating income is $650,000 [$550,000 + 100,000] and its cost of operating capital is $400,400 [7.7% × ($4,000,000 + 1,200,000)] for an EVA of $249,600 [$650,000 – 400,400].

16-11

Note: assume that the company does not pay taxes.

1. The EVA for the answering machine is $100,000 [$1,300,000 – ($10,000,000 × 12%)].

2. The EVA for the video game player is $160,000 [$640,000 – ($4,000,000 × 12%)].

3. The electronics division's EVA if it invests in both the answering machine and the video game player is $4,760,000 [($13,500,000 + 1,300,000 + 640,000) – (($75,000,000 + 10,000,000 + 4,000,000) × 12%)].

4. The electronics division's EVA if it invests in neither the answering machine nor the video game player is $4,500,000 [$13,500,000 – ($75,000,000 × 12%)].

5. Based on the expected EVA for each alternative, the manager will invest in both projects – it will earn a higher EVA than if it continues with its current operations. Both projects have positive EVAs.

16-13

1. The minimum transfer price is $0.65 for the Container Division (its opportunity cost of supplying the can to the Processing Division – the revenue it gives up). The maximum transfer price is also $0.65 for the Processing Division (its opportunity cost of buying the can from an external supplier). It doesn't matter whether the Processing Division buys internally or externally or whether the Container Division sells externally or internally unless there are other cost effects of internal transfers. If the transfer takes place, the transfer price should be $0.65.

2. The minimum transfer price is $0.61 for the Container Division (its opportunity cost of supplying the can to the Processing Division – the revenue of $0.65 it gives up less the avoided selling costs of $0.04 [$0.65 – 0.04]). The maximum transfer price is $0.65 for the Processing Division (its opportunity cost of buying the can from an external supplier). The transfer should take place because both divisions and the company can benefit from an internal sale. The company's benefit is its cost savings of $8,000 [($0.65 – 0.61) × 200,000]. The benefits to the divisions will depend on the transfer price selected – the transfer price should be between $0.61 and $0.65.

3. The manager of the Container Division should accept a transfer price of $0.63. This price is above the division's minimum transfer price identified in Requirement 2. The Container Division will be better off by $4,000 [($0.63 – 0.61) × 200,000] if it accepts the transfer price.

16-15

1. Richmond Furrier's ROI, margin, and turnover are:

	Year 1	Year 2	Year 3	
ROI	8.00%	6.97%	6.30%	[$1,200,000 ÷ 15,000,000; $1,045,000 ÷ 15,000,000; $945,000 ÷ 15,000,000]
Margin	12.00%	11.00%	10.50%	[$1,200,000 ÷ 10,000,000; $1,045,000 ÷ 9,500,000; $945,000 ÷ 9,000,000]
Turnover	0.67	0.63	0.60	[$10,000,000 ÷ 15,000,000; $9,500,000 ÷ 15,000,000; $9,000,000 ÷ 15,000,000]

2. If the sales and operating income are achieved in Year 4 and inventories remain at the same level as year 3, the expected ROI is 8 percent [$1,200,000 ÷ 15,000,000], the expected margin is 12 percent [$1,200,000 ÷ 10,000,000], and the expected turnover is 0.67 [$10,000,000 ÷ 15,000,000]. ROI increased over Year 3 because both its margin and its turnover improved.

16-15 continued

3. If the sales and operating income remain at the same level as year 3 but inventory reductions are achieved in Year 4, the expected ROI is 7.9 percent [$945,000 ÷ (15,000,000 × (1 – 0.2)], the expected margin is 10.5 percent [$945,000 ÷ 9,000,000], and the expected turnover is 0.75 [$9,000,000 ÷ (15,000,000 × (1 – 0.2)]. ROI increased over Year 3 because its turnover improved due to lower inventories.

4. If all expectations for sales, operating income, and inventory reductions are achieved in Year 4, the expected ROI is 10 percent [$1,200,000 ÷ (15,000,000 × (1 – 0.2)], the expected margin is 12 percent [$1,200,000 ÷ 10,000,000], and the expected turnover is 0..83 [$10,000,000 ÷ (15,000,000 × (1 – 0.2)]. ROI increased over Year 3 because both its margin and its turnover improved.

16-17

1. The market price is $48 – the price the Assembly Division is able to purchase the part from an external source. The price is likely lower than the $50 price the Component Division is able to charge because of the large volume the Assembly Division purchases.

2. The full-cost price of the component is $42 – including all product costs both variable and fixed. This is an absorption-costing amount.

3. The price range for short-term intracompany transfers is between $38 and $48. The maximum transfer price is what the Assembly Division can buy at from external suppliers. The minimum transfer price is the Component Division's variable cost [$18 + 14 + 6] because it has enough idle capacity to fill the Assembly Division's requirements.

4. From the company perspective, the Assembly Division should not purchase from external sources. The Component Division has the capacity to supply at a lower cost to the company. The company will save $5,000,000 per year [500,000 × ($48 – 38)] if the transfer takes place.

5. A transfer price based on market price, opportunity costs, or negotiation will benefit both divisions. The divisions should be able to recognize the benefits from transferring at a market price of $48 – the Assembly Division will be at least as well off and the Component Division will be better off by $5,000,000 per year [500,000 × ($48 – 38)] if it can sell the part to the Assembly Division from its idle capacity. Their benefits will be larger if there are any cost savings from internal sales. The opportunity costs suggest that the transfer price should be between $38 and $48 [see Requirement 3]. A price in this range, possibly negotiated, will increase the performance of both divisions with the overall benefit shared depending on the transfer price agreed to.

    Cost-based transfer prices may be useful to establish routine transfer prices – variable costs (plus a lump sum) or full cost often will lead to the correct decisions (goal congruence) but may restrict each division's autonomy and distort its performance measurement.

16-19

A's EVA is $(200) [$2,200 – ($20,000 × 12%)].

B's EVA is $720 [$18,000 – ($144,000 × 12%)].

C's EVA is $0 [$12,000 – ($100,000 × 12%)].

D's EVA is $48 [$1,200 – ($9,600 × 12%)].

16-21

1. d

2. e

3. e

4. c

PROBLEMS

16-23

1. The minimum transfer price for the Central Division is $75 per 100 pots – its opportunity cost of supplying the pots to the Western Division. The pot facility is operating at capacity and can sell all it produces at $75 – the same price the Western Division is paying to outside suppliers. There is no advantage to Green Thumb of internal transfers (unless there are some other cost savings).

2. The minimum transfer price for the Central Division is $53 per 100 pots – its opportunity cost is its variable cost of producing pots. The pot facility is operating below capacity and can supply the 3,500 pots to the Western Division from its idle capacity of 4,000 pots [20,000 – 16,0000] without affecting its outside sales. The maximum transfer price for the Western Division is $75 per 100 pots – its opportunity cost is what it must pay to outside suppliers.

    The manager of the Central Division should be willing to accept the $70 transfer price – the division will earn $59,500 from the transfer [($70 – 53) × 3,500].

3. The transfer price based on the company's cost-plus policy is $75.60 [$63 × 120%]. This price is higher than the maximum transfer price the Western Division will pay (see Requirement 2). Although economically beneficial to the company as a whole, a transfer would not occur.

16-25

1. Lagoma Steel's unit contribution margin is $5.00.

    Analysis:

Sales revenue	$25,000,000	
Cost of goods sold	(16,500,000)	[all variable]
Selling expenses	(1,080,000)	[$2,700,000 × 40%]
Contribution margin	$ 7,420,000	
Units produced and sold	1,484,000	
Unit contribution margin	$5.00	

16-25 continued

2. a. Lagoma Steel's 2005 ROI is 12 percent [$1,845,000 ÷ 15,375,000].

Analysis:

Operating assets, November 30, 2005	$15,750,000	
Operating assets, December 1, 2004	15,000,000	[$15,750,000 ÷ 105%]
Average operating assets	15,375,000	[($15,750,000 + 15,000,000) ÷ 2]

   b. Lagoma Steel's 2005 EVA is $153,750 [$1,845,000 – (15,375,000 × 11%)].

3. The management of Lagoma Steel is more likely to accept the capital investment if EVA is used because the estimated ROI of the investment is 11.5 percent which is higher than its cost of capital of 11 percent. Therefore the capital investment has a positive EVA and the division's EVA is higher with the investment. The management of Lagoma Steel is likely to reject the capital investment if ROI is used because the estimated ROI of 11.5 percent is less than its current ROI of 12 percent [see Requirement 2 a.]. Although the capital investment earns a return greater than the division's cost of capital, its overall ROI is lower with the investment.

4. Lagoma should control the items that are part of the calculation of ROI or EVA – including operating income decisions (revenues and expenses) and investment decisions. Lagoma does not need to control the cost of capital used in the EVA calculation – this represents the target set by Northern Resources for Lagoma Steel's operations.

16-27

1. Newden will earn additional profits of $5,000 if it manufactures the order rather than going to an outside supplier. The Sales Division should not be allowed to purchase Model 403 externally.

Newden should also consider qualitative factors. The company policy of requiring that all products be manufactured internally is likely intended to provide more control over quality, delivery time, and other nonprice factors.

Analysis:

The Manufacturing Division's variable cost of producing the order with overtime is $28,000 [($300 + 200 +200) × 40]. The cost of buying from another supplier is $33,000 [$825 × 40]. Its cost savings is $5,000 [$33,000 – 28,000]. Note that fixed costs don't change and are irrelevant. Manufacturing doesn't have any outside customers and has capacity (using overtime) to fill the order.

2. Newden's decentralization and transfer pricing policies have several problems. Treating the Manufacturing Division as a "profit centre" is not appropriate. Its only customer is the Sales Division and the transfer pricing policy of full cost plus a 10 percent markup often overstates its opportunity cost – in this case its opportunity cost is the variable cost of producing the order. Newden should treat the Manufacturing Division as a cost centre and use standard costing to control its costs. The Sales Division would continue as a profit centre. In addition, using a variable cost transfer price with a lump sum "transfer" of the Manufacturing Division's fixed cost would improve the information the Sales Division uses in marketing the company's products.

Changing the company's policy will improve goal congruence (the Sales Division will make the correct decisions), improve performance evaluation (each division will be evaluated on the factors it controls), and recognize the interdependence between the divisions (neither division is autonomous but depends on the other),

16-29

1. The minimum transfer price is the Auxiliary Components Division's opportunity cost of $26 per unit – its revenue from an external sale less the cost savings from an internal sale or $31 – $5. The maximum transfer price is the Audio Systems Division's opportunity cost of $31 per unit – its cost of buying externally.

2. The transfer price halfway between the minimum and maximum transfer prices is $28.50 [($31 + 26) ÷ 2]. The transfer price would be expressed as full-cost ($20) plus a 42.5 percent markup [($28.50 – 20.00) ÷ $20.00].

3. The new minimum transfer price is the Auxiliary Components Division's opportunity cost of $27 per unit – its revenue from an external sale less the cost savings from an internal sale or $32 – $5. The maximum transfer price is the Audio Systems Division's opportunity cost of $32 per unit – its cost of buying externally.

   If they agree to a price halfway between the minimum and maximum transfer prices, the new transfer price is $29.50 [($32 + 27) ÷ 2]. The transfer price would be expressed as full-cost ($20) plus a 47.5 percent markup [($29.50 – 20.00) ÷ $20.00].

4. The divisions are likely to renegotiate the transfer price. With excess capacity the Auxiliary Components Division's opportunity cost will be lower (essentially its variable costs if it has enough capacity to meet both internal and external demand) – thus the minimum transfer price will be lower. The Audio Systems Division may be able to buy from outside suppliers at lower prices – thus the maximum transfer price is also lower. The new transfer price will be lower than the current agreement.

16-31

1. The minimum transfer price for the Metal Fabricating Division is its opportunity cost of filling the Industrial Machine Division's order. Its opportunity cost is the variable cost of producing the subassembly plus the contribution margin its would have earned on the two displaced jobs or $285.

   Analysis:

Variable cost of subassembly	$1,750,000	[10,000 × ($100 + 25 +50)]
Contribution margin – Job 1	650,000	[$2,600,000 – 1,950,000]
Contribution margin – Job 2	450,000	[$1,500,000 – 1,050,000]
Total opportunity cost	$2,850,000	
Transfer price per unit	$285	[$2,850,000 ÷ 10,000]

2. The minimum transfer price for the Metal Fabricating Division is its opportunity cost of filling the Industrial Machine Division's order. Its opportunity cost is the variable cost of producing the subassembly if it can produce the subassembly without displacing any work from outside customers or $175 [$100 + 25 +50].

3. The transfer price based on full cost plus average markup of 35 percent is $276.75 [$205 × 135%]. The full cost plus markup price may be a good approximation of the market price for the Metal Fabricating Division's products and is a reasonable transfer price (note that it is close to the price determined by its opportunity cost when outside sales are affected). If the division has enough idle capacity to fill the order, this may be an approximation of the maximum transfer price. The divisions can negotiate a price between the minimum transfer price of $175 [see Requirement 2] and $276.75.

4. If the Industrial Machine Division has a firm outside price of $200 for the subassembly, $200 is its opportunity cost and the maximum transfer price it should pay. With excess capacity, the Metal Fabricating Division's minimum transfer price is $175 [see Requirement 2]. The price the manager of the Industrial Machine Division is an average of $187.50 [$175 + ($125,000 ÷ 10,000)] and is within the transfer price range. The benefit from an internal sale is shared equally between the two divisions (cost savings are $25.00 per unit [$200.00 – 175.00] and shared $12.50 each [$25.00 ÷ 2]) and should be acceptable to the manager of the Metal Fabricating Division.

16-33

1. The transfer price based on variable manufacturing costs plus opportunity cost is $1,869.00 [$1,329.00 + 540.00].

    Analysis:

    Variable cost per 100 units:

Direct materials - padding	$ 264.00	[$2.40 × 110% × 100]
Direct materials - vinyl	440.00	[$4.00 × 110% × 100]
Direct labour	375.00	[$7.50 × 0.5 × 100]
Variable overhead	250.00	[$5.00 × 0.5 × 100]
Total variable costs	$1,329.00	

    Variable overhead rate per direct labour hour:

Supplies	$ 420,000	
Indirect labour	375,000	
Power	180,000	
Employee benefits – direct labour	450,000	[20% × 300,000 × $7.50]
Employee benefits – indirect labour	75,000	[20% × $375,000]
Total	$1,500,000	
Variable overhead rate	$5.00	[$1,500,000 ÷ 300,000]

    The opportunity cost comes from the shift from producing deluxe office stools to producing cushioned seats for the Commercial Division and economy office stools. The difference in contribution margin is $540.00 per 100 units [$2,520.00 – 1,980.00].

    The difference in the labour hours required for deluxe office stools and economy office stools allows for 125 economy stools and 100 seat cushions for the Commercial Division to be produced in place of 100 deluxe office stools.

Hours for 100 deluxe office stools	150	[100 × 1.5]
Hours for 100 cushions	50	[100 × 0.5]
Hours for economy office stools	100	
Economy office stools that can be produced	125	[100 ÷ 0.8]

    Contribution from 100 deluxe office stools or 125 economy office stools:

	Deluxe	Economy	
Direct materials	$1,455.00	$1,970.00	[100 × ($8.15 + 2.40 + 4.00); 125 × ($9.76 + 6.00)]
Direct labour	1,125.00	750.00	[100 × 1.5 × $7.50; 125 × 0.8 × $7.50]
Variable overhead	750.00	500.00	[100 × 1.5 × $5.00; 125 × 0.8 × $5.00]
Total variable cost	$3,330.00	$3,220.00	
Sales revenue	$5,850.00	$5,200.00	[100 × $58.50; 125 × $41.60]
Contribution margin	$2,520.00	$1,980.00	[$5,850.00 – 3,330.00; $5,200.00 – 3,220.00]

2. The variable cost plus opportunity cost would be the best basis for an intracompany transfer pricing policy. This approach provides for goal congruence, appropriate performance evaluation, and divisional autonomy. The selling division is as well off as it would be if it sold to an external customer rather than internally. The transfer price reflects the contribution the selling division makes to overall company profits. The buying division makes a decision to purchase internally with the same information as a centralized decision maker would use – assuring goal congruence. Both the buyer and seller retain autonomy in their buying and selling decisions.

MANAGERIAL DECISION CASES

16-35

1. Alfonso turned down the proposal because it would decrease his ROI. Without the investment, his ROI is 16 percent [$2,560,000 ÷ $16,000,000]. With the investment his ROI is 15.8 percent [($2,560,000 + 156,000) ÷ ($16,000,000 + 1,200,000]. The investment's ROI is 13 percent [$156,000 ÷ $1,200,000] – less than Alfonso's current ROI.

2. The new product line will increase the company's profitability. Its ROI of 13 percent is higher than the company's 9 percent cost of capital. The division should produce the new product line.

3. The new product line's EVA is $48,000 [$156,000 – ($1,200,000 × 9%)]. If the company used EVA instead of ROI, Alfonso would have accepted the project because the project's positive EVA would have increased his division's performance.

4. EVA encourages managers to make goal congruent investment decisions – those that increase a company's wealth by earning a return greater than the company's cost of capital. ROI is a good measure of relative performance – as a ratio it allows for comparison of divisions of different sizes.

5. Some may consider Alfonso's decision unethical. He acted in his self-interest and turned down a project that would be profitable for the company to avoid receiving a poorer performance evaluation. His chances for a bonus and promotion are reduced with a poorer performance evaluation. Another view is that Alfonso has done exactly what the company's evaluation system expected him to do. Motivating and rewarding managers with a system based on ROI encourages this behaviour, and at least part of the blame for his decision rests with corporate headquarters.

CHAPTER 17

STRATEGIC PERFORMANCE EVALUATION AND MANAGEMENT

ANSWERS TO ODD-NUMBERED QUESTIONS FOR WRITING AND DISCUSSION

1. Functional-based control systems focus responsibility on functional organization units and the individual in charge. Performance is evaluated in financial terms based on comparisons between actual results and budgets and currently attainable standards. Performance rewards are designed to encourage managers to control costs and meet or exceed budgetary standards.

3. Strategic-based control systems focus on links between strategies and operational objectives considering financial, process, customer, and learning and growth perspectives. Performance measures are balanced and aligned with objectives and liked to strategies. Performance measurement uses both financial and nonfinancial factors. Rewards are multidimensional and tied to strategic perspectives.

   Strategic-based control systems differ from activity-based control systems by adding the customer and learning and growth perspectives to the activity-based financial and process perspectives. More formal linkages are developed between an organization's mission and strategy and its objectives, performance measures and processes. Performance measures are integrated to be mutually consistent and reinforcing, communicate the strategy, and align individual and organizational goals and actions.

5. Activity inputs are the resources an activity consumes in producing outputs. Activity outputs are the results of performing an activity – the product produced for example. Activity output measurement is the number of times an activity is performed.

7. Value-added activities are activities that are necessary to keep the company in business. Some are required activities, necessary to comply with legal requirements. Others are discretionary and value-added if they produce a change of state that is not achievable by preceding activities and enable other (value-added) activities to be performed. Value-added costs are the costs of performing value-added activities with complete efficiency.

9. Four different ways of managing activities to reduce costs are:

   1. activity elimination – activities that fail to add value are eliminated

   2. activity selection – choosing among different sets of activities required by competing strategies. The lowest-cost design strategy is chosen.

   3. activity reduction – decreasing the time and resources required by a value-added activity. The efficiency of value-added activities is improved. Activity reduction may also be used to improve the efficiency of a nonvalue-added activity until it can be eliminated.

   4. activity sharing – increase the efficiency of necessary activities by using economies of scale. The quantity of the cost driver is increased without increasing the cost of the activity. More activity output is produced with the same activity input.

11. Trend reports of nonvalue-added costs reveal cost reductions in nonvalue-added from activity improvements over time.

13. Benchmarking is a process that uses the best practices of other departments or organizations as standards for evaluating performance. The performance of the best performing unit serves as the standard for other units. Information may also be shared on how superior results are achieved.

15. The activity volume variance is the difference between the actual activity level acquired (practical capacity) and the value-added standard quantity of activity that should be used. It is a measure of nonvalue-added cost. The unused capacity variance (the difference between the activity available and the activity used) is important because it allows management to act to reduce the quantity of activity when capacity exceeds demand (and reduce nonvalue-added costs).

17. Target costing is the use of a target cost (the difference between the sales price required to capture a desired market share and the desired profit per unit) to reduce costs using reverse engineering, value analysis, and process improvement. Reverse engineering tears down competitor's products to discover design features that allow cost reductions. Value analysis assesses the value that customers place on different product features – features that cost more than the customer's value are eliminated and lower costs are achieved. Process improvement finds ways of increasing process efficiency and reducing costs.

19. Strategy in the balanced scorecard framework is defined as the process of choosing the business's market and customer segments, identifying its critical internal business processes, and selecting the individual and organizational capabilities needed to meet internal, customer, and financial objectives.

21. A testable strategy is a set of linked objectives aimed at an overall goal that can be restated into a sequence of cause-and-effect hypotheses.

23. The three strategic themes of the financial perspective are revenue growth, cost reduction, and asset utilization.

25. Cycle time is the length of time it takes to produce a unit of activity output. Velocity is the number of units of output that can be produced in a given time period.

27. Three objectives of the learning and growth perspective are increasing employee capabilities; increasing motivation, empowerment, and alignment; and increasing information systems capabilities.

29. Factors in an organization's external environment will affect its management control system and its strategic performance management. Its control systems should be compatible with its environment. A company operating in a dynamic environment requires a system that promotes change and adaptation.

    Environmental factors include competition, economic conditions, regulation and legislation, social values, and political climate.

31. Value chain analysis is a strategic tool designed to provide an understanding of a company's competitive advantages and its relationships with suppliers, customers, and competitors. A value chain is a set of interrelated activities that increase the usefulness or value of products and services to customers. Value chain analysis is concerned with the evaluation of strategic alternatives and their longer-term consequences – important elements of effective performance management.

33. Nonfinancial measures contribute to effective performance measurement because operating employees may better understand nonfinancial measures than financial measures – nonfinancial measures often more directly relate to the employees' activities and processes. Often nonfinancial measures can be collected and analyzed on a timelier basis than financial measures and serve as effective early warning signals. Effective nonfinancial measures are leading indicators of future financial measures.

35. Goal congruence exists when individuals and groups in an organization work towards the achievement of the organization's goals. An organization will find it difficult to be successful without goal congruence.

37. Performance measurement has both potential positive and negative aspects. Appropriately used, performance measures promote positive behaviours and goal congruence. If used to blame or punish employees, performance measures can be perceived as threatening. In response, employees may react by engaging in dysfunctional behaviour and manipulate data, make sub optimal decisions, and take unethical actions.

39. The performance of the divisional manager is not equivalent to the performance of a division. The performance of a manager's division may be affected by factors beyond the manager's control – uncontrollable factors. Managers should be evaluated on those things they can control – controllable factors or the items and events that are affected, although not necessarily determined, by a manger's decisions and actions.

SOLUTIONS TO ODD-NUMBERED EXERCISES, PROBLEMS, AND CASES

EXERCISES

17-1

1. e
2. d
3. b
4. c
5. a
6. b
7. b
8. d
9. e
10. d

17-3

The memo requested by Cameron would cover the following points:

Similarities between activity-based and strategic-based control systems

- emphasis on both financial and process responsibility
- use of both financial and nonfinancial performance measures
- emphasis on continuous improvement
- team orientation
- rewards based on multidimensional performance, team performance, and gain-sharing

Differences between activity-based and strategic-based control systems

- strategic-based approach features four responsibility perspectives – the financial and process perspectives common with the activity-based approach plus customer and learning and growth perspectives
- with a strategic-based approach, performance measures reflect four perspectives rather than two
- with a strategic-based approach, performance measures are more integrated, linked to the mission and strategy of the company, and balanced. A balance is struck between lag and lead measures, objective and subjective measures, financial and nonfinancial measures, and internal and external measures.
- continuous improvement is more directed to a company's strategy with a strategic-based approach
- with a strategic-based approach, performance measures are chosen to be mutually consistent and reinforcing, to communicate the strategy, and to be objective driven.

17-5

Situation A

1. The nonvalue-added cost is $22.00 per unit $[((45 - 15) \div 60) \times \$12 + (6 - 4) \times \$8]$.
2. The root cause of the activity cost is process design.
3. The cost reduction approach is activity selection.

Situation B

1. The nonvalue-added cost is $2,900 per setup $[(15 - (30 \div 60)) \times \$200]$.
2. The root cause of the activity cost is product design.
3. The cost reduction approach is activity reduction.

Situation C

1. The nonvalue-added cost is $80 per unit $[(8 - 0) \times \$10]$.
2. The root cause of the activity cost is plant layout.
3. The cost reduction approach is activity elimination.

Situation D

1. The nonvalue-added cost is $136,000 per year $[\$120,000 + (8,000 \times \$2)]$.

2. There are multiple root causes of the activity cost including product design, process design, and approach to quality management.

3. The cost reduction approach includes activity selection, activity elimination, and activity reduction.

Situation E

1. The nonvalue-added cost is $180 per unit [(5.3 – 5) × $600]

2. The root causes of the activity cost are supplier selection and quality management.

3. The cost reduction approach is activity elimination.

Situation F

1. The nonvalue-added cost is $900,000 per year [given].

2. The root cause of the activity cost is product design.

3. The cost reduction approach is activity sharing.

17-7

1. Value-added and nonvalue-added cost report:

Activity	Value-added cost	Nonvalue-added cost	Actual cost
Purchasing parts	$ 150,000	$ 60,000	$ 210,000
Assembling parts	720,000	78,000	798,000
Administering parts	660,000	286,000	946,000
Inspecting parts	0	375,000	375,000
Total	$1,530,000	$799,000	$2,329,000

Analysis and calculations:

Purchasing parts:
Value-added cost	$150,000	[500 × $300]
Nonvalue-added cost	60,000	[(700 – 500) × $300]

Assembling parts:
Value-added cost	$720,000	[60,000 × $12]
Nonvalue-added cost	78,000	[(66,500 – 60,000) × $12]

Administrating parts:
Value-added cost	$660,000	[6,000 × $110]
Nonvalue-added cost	286,000	[(8,600 – 6,000) × $110]

Inspecting parts:
Value-added cost	$ 0	[0 × $15]
Nonvalue-added cost	375,000	[(25,000 – 0) × $15]

Note: value-added cost is SQ × SP; nonvalue-added cost is (AQ – SQ) × SP.

2. Inspecting parts is a nonvalue-added activity – its SQ is zero which indicates that the activity is nonvalue-added and should be reduced or eliminated. Inspecting parts is nonvalue-added because it doesn't produce a change in state (only detecting an existing state) and isn't required to enable other activities to be performed.

    A value-added activity may have nonvalue-added costs if the activity is not performed efficiently.

17-9

1. Activity analysis:

   Setting up equipment:

   Value content: this is a value-added activity because it produces a change of state (equipment is set up to new specifications), the state change could not have caused by a prior activity, and it is necessary for other activities to be performed. Often setting up equipment takes more time than necessary and may include a nonvalue-added component. Setup time should be minimized – the ideal would be zero. The activity may be performed inefficiently and ways to reduce the activity should be found.

   Root causes: setup activity is affected by product design, process design, and equipment choice. If managers know and understand the root causes of the setup activity they will be able to make changes in product design, process design, and equipment to reduce or eliminate the activity. For example, using similar product designs may reduce the time required to change for one product to another. Different equipment may be more capable of being quickly reconfigured. Changing from a departmental process to a cellular process may eliminate (or significantly reduce) the need for setups – a work cell is dedicated to the production of each product and setups are not required.

   Creating scrap:

   Value content: this is a nonvalue-added activity because it produces an undesirable change of state (defective output or wasted material). Managers should look for ways to reduce and ideally eliminate scrap.

   Root causes: scrap is affected by supplier choice, product design, process design, and quality management approach. If managers know and understand the root causes of scrap they will be able to act to reduce or eliminate the activity. For example, evaluating suppliers on the basis of their ability to deliver zero-defect parts may reduce the number of defect units produced. Changing product and process designs may reduce the amount of wasted material. Different equipment may cut down on material waste. A total quality management program may reduce waste and the rate of defect (to zero) by preventing internal failures.

   Welding subassemblies:

   Value content: this is a value-added activity because it produces a change of state (subassemblies welded as required), the state change could not have caused by a prior activity, and it is necessary for other activities to be performed. If the welding activity is performed inefficiently, managers should look for ways to improve efficiency and reduce the activity costs.

   Root causes: the welding activity is affected by product design, process design, and equipment and technology choice. If managers know and understand the root causes of the welding activity they will be able to act to improve the efficiency of the activity. For example, the need for the welding activity may be reduced by changing the product design – for example, subassemblies may be designed to require fewer welds. Efficiency may be improved by changing technology – for example, better welding equipment may reduce the time to complete a subassembly. The welding process may be automated – using robotic welding equipment with greater efficiency and less variation in output.

   Handling materials:

   Value content: this is a nonvalue-added activity because it doesn't produces a change of state (results in a change of location of material, parts, and subassemblies but not state). Handling materials does allow other activities to be performed but this may be accomplished with less or no material handling – that is, a nonvalue-added activity can be performed more efficiently. Managers should look for ways to reduce and ideally eliminate material handling.

   Root causes: material handling is affected by primarily by process design, plant layout, and relationships with suppliers. If managers know and understand the root causes of material handling they will be able to act to reduce or eliminate the activity or improve its efficiency. For example, arrangements can be made with suppliers to have them deliver parts as needed to reduce the amount of material handling activity – materials don't have to go through the company's storeroom before being issued but are delivered directly to the shop

17-9 continued

floor. Changing the plant layout may cut down on the number of moves – a cellular layout may eliminate the need for material moves during the production process.

Inspecting parts:

Value content: this is a nonvalue-added activity because it is a state detection activity (no change in existing state) and is not necessary for other activities to be performed. Managers should look for ways to reduce and ideally eliminate the inspection activity.

Root causes: inspecting parts is affected by the quality of parts and processes. If managers know and understand the root causes of the inspection activity they will be able to act to reduce or eliminate the activity. For example, the company may search for suppliers that are able to deliver parts with zero defects – eliminating (or at least reducing) the need to inspect incoming shipments.

2. Behavioural activity analysis:

Setting up equipment:

If *setup time* is used as the activity driver, managers will have an incentive to reduce setup time and setup activity costs. If the *number of setups* is used as the activity driver, managers may reduce the number of setups (and setup activity cost) by using longer production runs, producing in larger lots, and maintaining large inventories to meet demand. Although setup costs are lower, other costs such as inventory carrying costs are increased. A nonvalue-added activity is substituted to achieve lower nonvalue-added costs for the setup activity. Reducing setup time will improve the company's competitive advantage; longer product runs and increased inventories will likely impair the company's competitive position.

Creating scrap:

If *kilograms of scrap* are used as the activity driver, managers will have an incentive to reduce the amount of scrap and waste and scrap activity costs. If defective units are the source of scrap, managers will have an incentive to reduce the number of defective units. If the *number of defective units* is used as the activity driver, managers will have an incentive to reduce the number of defective units and amount of scrap (and scrap activity cost). Both activity drivers have a similar effect and will cause similar behaviour. If managers improve the quality of production (aim for zero defects) and process efficiency (reduce waste) to reduce the kilograms of scrap produced and the number of defective units, the company will have lower costs and a competitive advantage. On the other hand, if managers respond by allowing defective units to "go out the door" to customers, they will reduce the number of defective units and scrap discovered (but not produced) but will also transfer the costs to customers. Customer value will decrease with unfavourable consequences for the company. Returns will be higher; some customers will stop buying the company's products; etc. The company's competitive advantage will decline.

Welding subassemblies:

If *welding hours* are used as the activity driver, managers will have an incentive to reduce the amount of welding time and welding activity costs. Managers will look at the root causes of the welding activity for ways to reduce the activity required. They will also look for ways to improve the efficiency of the welding activity. If the *subassemblies welded* are used as the activity driver, managers will have an incentive to reduce the number of subassemblies welded – perhaps by product redesign. Both activity drivers will cause similar behaviour. The company will have lower costs and a competitive advantage. Of course, managers may also respond by reducing welding hours or subassemblies welded by doing a poorer job – for example, by rushing the activity or skipping some welds. If they act in this way, the quality of the product will decrease and the company's competitive advantage will suffer.

Handling materials:

If *number of moves* is used as the activity driver, managers will have an incentive to reduce the amount of material handling activity costs. Managers will look at the root causes of the handling materials activity for ways to reduce the activity required. They will also look for ways to improve the efficiency of the activity. They may consider reorganizing the plant layout or adopt a cellular structure to minimize the need to handle materials

17-9 continued

during the production process. They may arrange with suppliers to have materials delivered to the shop floor to eliminate some material handling activity. If *distance moved* is used as the activity driver, managers will have similar incentives to reduce the handling materials activity. Both activity drivers will cause similar behaviour and the company will have lower costs and a competitive advantage.

Inspecting parts:

If *hours of inspection* are used as the activity driver, managers will have an incentive to reduce the amount of inspection activity. Managers will look at the root causes of the inspection activity for ways to reduce the activity required. They will also look for ways to improve the efficiency of the activity. They may consider working with suppliers to ensure the correct quality of parts is supplied (aim for zero defects). If good relationships are created, the need for inspection can be reduced. If *number of defective parts* is used as the activity driver, managers will have similar incentives to reduce the inspection activity. Both activity drivers will cause similar behaviour and the company will have lower costs and a competitive advantage.

On the other hand, managers may respond to these activity drivers by simply reducing the amount of inspection activity – without changing any processes. Less inspection will reduce the hours of inspection and the number of defective parts discovered but will not reduce the company's nonvalue-added cost. In fact, its nonvalue-added costs will likely increase because it will have more scrap and defective production, decrease in customer value, more returns and claims, etc. The company's competitive advantage will suffer.

17-11

1. The desired total life cycle profit for the new model is $8,000,000 [$40 × 200,000].

2. The projected life cycle profit for the new model is $6,000,000 [($90 × 200,000) – $12,000,000].

3. The target cost is $50 per unit [$90 – 40] or $10,000,000 in total [$50 × 200,000]. Costs must be reduced $10 per unit [($12,000,000 ÷ 200,000) – $50] or $2,000,000 in total [$12,000,000 – 10,000,000].

   Three ways to reduce costs to the target cost are: *reverse engineering* – find more efficient product designs by assessing competitors' products; *value analysis* – assess the value customers place on different features and retain only those than add value; and *process improvement* – redesign production processes to be more efficient. The first two methods look to reduce costs by improving product design. Process improvement is concerned with selecting only activities that add value and reducing or eliminating those that don't.

4. The company should include postpurchase costs in its design decisions and whole-product costs. Reducing customer sacrifice increases customer value and gives the company a competitive advantage. Including postpurchase costs in target costing is not required – target costing focuses on the company's cost of delivering a product; postpurchase cost is a determinant of the product purchase decision and its value to the customer.

17-13

	Perspective	Financial/Nonfinancial	Subjective/Objective	External/Internal	Lead/Lag
(a)	customer	nonfinancial	objective	external	lag
(b)	process	nonfinancial	objective	external	lag
(c)	financial	financial	objective	internal	lag
(d)	financial	financial	objective	external	lag
(e)	learning and growth	nonfinancial	subjective	internal	lead
(f)	process	financial	objective	internal	lag
(g)	customer	nonfinancial	subjective	external	lag
(h)	process	nonfinancial	objective	external	lag
(i)	learning and growth	nonfinancial	subjective	internal	lead
(j)	customer	nonfinancial	objective	external	lag
(k)	financial	financial	objective	external	lag

PROBLEMS

17-15

1. Measures for 2005 and 2006:

		2005	2006	
a.	theoretical velocity	2.4	2.4	[96,000 ÷ 40,000; 96,000 ÷ 40,000]
	theoretical cycle time	25.0	25.0	[60 ÷ 2.4; 60 ÷ 2.4]
b.	actual velocity	1.9	2.2	[76,000 ÷ 40,000; 88,000 ÷ 40,000]
	actual cycle time	31.6	27.3	[60 ÷ 1.9; 60 ÷ 2.2]
c.	percentage change in postpurchase costs	n/a	50%	[($20 – 10) ÷ 20]
d.	labour productivity	1.9	2.2	[76,000 ÷ 40,000; 88,000 ÷ 40,000]
e.	scrap as a percentage of total material	10%	8%	[10,000 ÷ 100,000; 8,000 ÷ 100,000]
f.	percentage change in actual product cost	n/a	20%	[($125 – 100) ÷ 125]
g.	percentage change in days of inventory	n/a	50%	[(6 – 3) ÷ 6]
h.	defective units as a percentage of total units produced	5.9%	2.3%	[4,500 ÷ 76,000; 2,000 ÷ 88,000]
i.	new customers	2,000	8,000	[given]
j.	hours of training	100	400	[given]
k.	selling price per unit	$150	$140	[given]
l.	total employee suggestions	40	120	[2 × 20; 6 × 20]

2. Strategic objectives and measures:

Strategic objective	Measure	Lead/Lag
Financial perspective:		
reduce unit cost	unit cost	lag
Customer perspective:		
reduce customer sacrifice	selling price per unit	lag
	postpurchase costs	lag
increase customer base	number of new customers	lag
Process perspective:		
decrease process time	cycle time and velocity	lead
decrease defect rate	number of defective units	lag
	scrap as a percentage of material	lag
decrease inventory	days of inventory	lag

17-15 continued

Learning and growth perspective:

increase employee capabilities	output per hour	lag
	training hours	lead
	suggestions	lead

All the measures have shown improvement over the period 2005/2006. This indicates that the strategy is successful, as long as the measures are tied to the strategy and the strategy is valid. The company has been able to reduce unit cost, reduce customer sacrifice and increase its customer base, improve cycle time and velocity, decrease the defect rate, decrease inventory, and increase its employees' capabilities. To provide a complete evaluation, we would like to know the targets for the lead and lag measures. Comparing targets with actual results allows a manager to assess the success of implementation and the viability of the strategy (double-loop feedback).

3. The company's strategy as if-then statements:

If hours of training are increased, *then* employee productivity and participation will increase; *if* employee productivity and participation increases; *then* process time and product quality will improve; *if* process time improves, *then* inventory will decrease; and *if* inventory decreases and product quality improves, *then* cost (including postpurchase costs) will decrease; *if* costs decrease, *then* customer sacrifice decreases – lower selling price and lower postpurchase costs; *if* selling price and postpurchase costs are lower, *then* the number of customers will increase.

The if-then statements relate the balanced scorecard measures to the company's strategy – properly specified measures will reveal the company's strategy. In this case, the strategy may not be completely specified – how does reduced costs increase the number of customers? Why increase the number of customers? A more complete strategy would include market share and profit objectives.

17-17

1. The nonvalue-added usage and costs for 2005 are:

Material usage:		
Actual usage	600,000	[125% × 80,000 × 6]
Value-added standard quantity	480,000	[80,000 × 6]
Nonvalue-added usage	120,000	
Nonvalue-added cost	$600,000	[120,000 × $5]
Engineering activity:		
Actual usage	48,000	[24 × 2,000; capacity acquired]
Value-added standard quantity	27,840	[(4 × 6,000 + 10 × 2,400) × 58%]
Nonvalue-added usage	20,160	
Nonvalue-added cost	$604,800	[20,160 × ($60,000 ÷ 2,000)]
Total nonvalue-added cost	$1,204,800	[$600,000 + 604,800]

The cost of unused engineering capacity for 2005 is $60,000 [(48,000 – 46,000) × ($60,000 ÷ 2,000)] or one engineer.

2. With the targeted reduction the kaizen standards for 2006 are 552,000 kilograms of materials [(80,000 × 6) + (60% × 120,000)] and 39,936 hours for engineering [27,840 + (60% × 20,160)].

17-17 continued

3. The kaizen standard usage variances for 2006 are:

Material usage:
Actual usage	584,800
Kaizen standard quantity	552,000
Kaizen usage variance (kilograms)	32,800U

Kaizen usage variance (cost) $164,000U [32,800 × $5]

Engineering activity:
Actual usage	35,400
Kaizen standard quantity	39,936
Kaizen usage variance (hours)	4,536F

Kaizen usage variance (cost) $136,080F [4,536 × ($60,000 ÷ 2,000)]

The company has been able to meet (and exceed) its targeted reductions for the engineering activity but not for material usage. For the engineering activity the company has unused engineering capacity of 12,600 hours [48,000 – 35,400] or more than 6 engineers [12,600 ÷ 2,000 = 6.3]. To realize these cost savings, the company must either reassign the engineers to value-added activities or lay them off. The potential cost savings are $360,000 but these will only be realized if the company reduces its resource spending or uses the freed-up resources for value-added activities.

17-19

1. To improve its life cycle management and life cycle costing, Manley Manufacturing should take more of an activity management approach to its development costs. It should use activity analysis to discover the root causes of its activities and use this information to better manage its activities – improving the efficiency of its value-added activities and reducing and eliminating its nonvalue-added activities. Its will also be able to trace development costs to individual product projects. Treating research and development as period costs is limiting its ability to make good decisions about product features and their value to customers. It is important that they make these decisions early because once a product goes to market, it has a short time to produce profit.

2. Revised income statement:

	Product A	Product B	Total	
Sales	$4,000,000	$5,000,000	$9,000,000	
Cost of goods sold	2,000,000	2,500,000	4,500,000	
Gross margin	$2,000,000	$2,500,000	$4,500,000	
Research and development	1,200,000	800,000	2,000,000	[$2,000,000 × 60%; × 40%
Marketing	575,000	575,000	1,150,000	[$1,150,000 × 50%; × 50%]
Life cycle income	$ 225,000	$1,125,000	$1,350,000	
Return on sales	5.6%	22.5%	15.0%	

If the company requires a 20 percent return on sales for an acceptable return on investment, it will accept Product B but reject Product A.

3. There is no need to reduce the costs of Product B – it is already acceptable. Of course reducing its costs will increase its profitability and the company may choose to use activity analysis to discover and eliminate any nonvalue-added costs.

Product A is currently not acceptable. The target cost for Product A is $3,200,000 [$4,000,000 × 80%]; its projected cost is $3,775,000 [$4,000,000 – 225,000]. A cost reduction of $575,000 is required to make the product acceptable [$3,775,000 – 3,200,000].

17-19 continued

The company can use activity analysis to identify the activities associated with Product A, the activity drivers for each activity, and assess whether the activity is value-added or not. This information can be used to redesign Product A – find more efficient ways to perform value-added activities, and reduce and eliminate nonvalue-added activities.

Activity analysis is needed during the product development and design phase – this is the time when a product's life cycle costs are most likely to be influenced. Once the product enters production there is little time to make changes that will significantly affect its performance. Value and efficiency should be designed into the product.

4. A customer's postpurchase costs may play a significant role in her purchase decision. Offering customers lower postpurchase costs will give a company a competitive advantage – and may even support premium pricing. Postpurchase costs are an important part of the product's whole-life cost – excess postpurchase costs wi!l reduce the customer's willingness to pay for the product and reduce the revenue a company will receive from the product over its life cycle.

17-21

1. The MCE ratio for this product is 0.3.

    Analysis:

Processing time	30 hours	
Total time	100 hours	[30 + 2 + 5 + 8 + 24 + 31]
MCE ratio	0.3	[30 ÷ 100]

2. Process value analysis can help improve the MCE measure by finding ways to reduce nonvalue-added time – search for changes to the way the process is done. Process improvement requires a good understanding of the process activities – identifying activities and assessing their value content (activity analysis) and identifying the root cause of each activity (driver analysis) are important tools for managers engaged in process improvement. Managers will be more likely to seek improvements in process efficiency when measures such as MCE are used. MCE is a measure of the value-added activity as a percentage of total activity. As nonvalue-added activity is eliminated and value-added activity increases, MCE increases.

3. MCE is a lag measure – a measure of outcomes and results. Some lead measures that will affect MCE are performance drivers such as hours of process redesign (to find ways of improving process activities), hours of quality training (to reduce inspection activity and rework time through improved quality), and the number of employee suggestions (ideas about reducing nonvalue-added activities and process improvement).

17-23

1. The theoretical velocity is of the paint gun cell is 7.5 paint guns per hour [30,000 ÷ 4,000]. Its theoretical cycle time is 8 minutes per paint gun [60 ÷ 7.5].

2. The actual velocity is of the paint gun cell is 6.25 paint guns per hour [25,000 ÷ 4,000]. Its actual cycle time is 9.6 minutes per paint gun [60 ÷ 6.25].

3. The paint gun cell's MCE is 0.83 [8 ÷ 9.6]. The paint gun cell's operations are very efficient – most of its activity is value-added and it is approaching its theoretical cycle time.

4. The budgeted conversion cost per minute is $10.417 [$2,500,000 ÷ (4,000 × 60)]. The conversion cost per paint gun if the theoretical output is achieved is $83.34 [$10.417 × 8]. The conversion cost per paint gun for the actual output is $100.00 [$10.417 × 9.6].

17-23 continued

This product costing approach provides the cell manager with an incentive to reduce cycle time if she is responsible for production costs. She can reduce the cost per paint gun by reducing its cycle time. The potential gain is $16.66 per paint gun [$100.00 – 83.34] by reducing cycle time from 9.6 minutes to 8 minutes.

17-25

1. Strategic Objectives and Performance Measures:

    Financial Perspective:

Strategic Objective	Performance Measure
Increase profitability	Operating income (lag)
Increase revenue	Percentage of revenue from new customers (lag)
Reduce costs	Unit cost (lag)

    Process Perspective:

Strategic Objective	Performance Measure
Improve production quality	Quality cost (lag)
	Percentage of defective units (lag)
	Redesign time (lead)
Increase quality of purchased components	Percentage of defective units (lag)
	Engineering hours to assess suppliers (lead)

    Customer Perspective:

Strategic Objective	Performance Measure
Increase new customers	Number of new customers (lag)
Increase customer satisfaction	Survey ratings (lag)
Increase market share	Market share (lag)
Increase product quality	Percentage of returns (lag)
Improve product image and reputation	Survey ratings (lag)

    Learning and Growth Perspective:

Strategic Objective	Performance Measure
Increase employee abilities	Training hours (lead)
	Job coverage ratio (lead)
Increase motivation and alignment	Number of suggestions implemented (lag)
	Suggestions per employee (lead)
Increase information system capabilities	On-time reporting percentage (lead)

17-25 continued

2. Sequence of *if-then* strategy statements:

If training and strategic job coverage are improved and *if* information systems capability are improved, *then* employees will increase the number of suggested improvements; *if* the number of suggested improvements increases, *then* the number of suggestions implemented will increase; *if* the number of suggestions implemented increases, *then* process quality will increase; *if* supplier selection is improved, *then* the number of defective components will decrease; *if* process quality increases and *if* the percentage of defective components decreases, *then* the number of defective units will decrease; *if* the number of defective units decrease, *then* product quality will increase; *if* product quality increases, *then* product image and reputation will improve and *then* the costs of quality will decrease; *if* product image and reputation will improve, *then* customer satisfaction will increase; *if* customer satisfaction increases, *then* the number of new customers will increase; *if* the number of new customers increases, *then* market share will increase; *if* the market share increases, *then* revenues will increase; *if* revenues increases and *if* costs of quality are decreased, *then* profitability will increase.

17-25 continued

If-then Strategy Diagram:

Financial Perspective

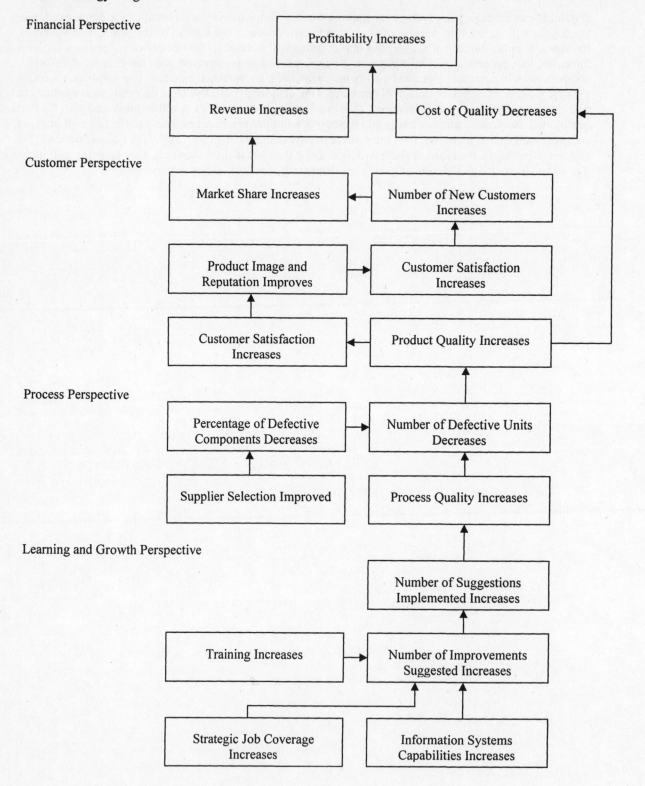

17-16

17-25 continued

3. The success of the quality-driven turnaround strategy would be evaluated using double-loop feedback. Double-loop feedback requires information about both the implementation of the strategy (if part) and the viability of the strategy (then part). Implementation effectiveness is evaluated by comparing the actual values of the measures with their targeted values. If the actual values meet or exceed the targeted values for both performance drivers (lead measures) and outcomes (lag measures), then effective implementation has occurred. If the actual performance driver measures are equal to or greater than their targeted values and the outcome measures are less than their targeted value, then the viability of the strategy is questioned. Information about actual and target values would be needed to evaluate the strategy.

4. The balanced scorecard is a means for directed continuous improvement. Performance measures are linked to the strategy. The strategy is articulated and communicated to employees, increasing the likelihood of aligning employee and organizational goals.

5. The kaizen standard for rework costs of six percent of sales for 2006 is a cost of $1,560,000 [$26,000,000 × 6%]. The actual costs were $1,500,000 – the standard was surpassed in 2006. The maintenance standard at the end of 2006 is $1,500,000 (assuming the same level of sales) or 5.8 percent of sales.

    Kaizen costing is a means to provide specific improvement goals – kaizen standards would be established for each performance measure.

6. All but the supplier evaluation and training are nonvalue-added activities. These activities each produce a change of state (fewer defective components and more capable employees) that cannot be achieved by a prior activity and are required for other activities to be performed. The other activities (inspecting incoming components and finished products, rework, scrap, warranty, sales returns, and customer complaints) don't produce a change of state but either detect the existing state, correct a failure, or represent waste or a loss. By eliminating all nonvalue-added activities, the company could reduce costs by $3,410,000 over 2007's costs [$4,140,000 – ($500,000 + 230,000)].

17-27

1. a. The 2005 bonus pool for the management team at Meyers Service is $41,700 [$417,000 × 10%].

    b. The 2005 bonus pool for the management team at Wellington Products is $50,500 [($10,000,000 – 4,950,000) × 1%].

2. a. One advantage of the bonus incentive plan at Meyers Service is that managers have an incentive to increase revenues by promoting maintenance service. Another advantage is that managers have an incentive to control costs and find more efficient ways to deliver the maintenance service. One disadvantage of the bonus incentive plan is that managers may concentrate on short-term results – and make decisions that improve current operating income but have undesirable long-term effects. Another disadvantage is that the plan does not direct managers to the company's strategic objective of providing the best service in the industry but concentrates only on the financial perspective.

    b. One advantage of the bonus incentive plan at Wellington Products is that managers have an incentive to increase revenues by promoting the company's products. Another advantage is that managers have an incentive to focus on selling the most profitable mix of products. One disadvantage of the bonus incentive plan is that managers have no incentive to control operating costs. Another disadvantage is that the plan does not direct managers to the company's strategic objective of providing high quality products (zero defects and low scrap) but concentrates only on the financial perspective.

17-27 continued

3.   a.   The Meyers Service managers may believe that they are not being treated equitably because they are responsible for all operating costs. Their dissatisfaction may reduce the incentive value of the bonus plan. The Wellington Products managers may believe that they are not being rewarded for their efforts to operate efficiently and achieve the company's strategic quality objective. They may not be as motivated to pay attention to these areas.

   b.   The differences in the bonus plans may be justified by the differences in the activity of the divisions – Meyers Service is a service business and Wellington products is a manufacturing business. A well-designed performance measurement and reward system should be designed for the particular division's activities and strategic objectives. "One-size fits all" is usually not a good choice. It should also be noted that the current systems could be substantially improved and different optimal systems may be appropriate.

MANAGERIAL DECISION CASE

17-29

1.   Tim faces pressure to comply with Jimmy's request because of their long time friendship. Jimmy has asked him for a favour that is a "one-time thing" but will have a significant effect on Jimmy's career. Tim should see that incorporating the falsified test results in his report is wrong. He should tell Jimmy that he can't do what he is asked to do and that the only solution is to redesign or reject the product. If he wants to do Jimmy a favour, he could try to get an extension for the redesign and convince the divisional manager that Jimmy is willing to do the right thing rather than take unethical action.

2.   If Tim cooperates with Jimmy and covers up the design deficiency he is clearly in violation of the standards of ethical behaviour expected of management accountants and managers. Although Tim has not personally directly benefited, he has knowingly provided false information and subverted the best interests of his employer.

3.   Tim should try to convince Jimmy not to send the false results to the divisional manager. Failing that, he should determine what company policies are in place to handle these issues and take the necessary steps to bring the deception to the attention of the proper manager. Perhaps Jimmy is not as good a friend as Tim thought – Jimmy has put Tim in a difficult position where Tim's choice will cause trouble for Jimmy and Linda. If the company doesn't have policies to resolve the problem, he should take the problem to the division manager to have it resolved. If the division manager is unwilling to resolve the problem, Tim may have to take his case higher up the organization. In the end, his only choice may to be to seek employment elsewhere.